JAYAPRAKASH NARAYAN

SELECTED WORKS

Volume One (1929 – 1935)

Jayaprakash Narayan

SELECTED WORKS

Volume One (1929-1935)

Edited by

BIMAL PRASAD

Issued under the auspices of

Nehru Memorial Museum & Library

MANOHAR
2024

First published 2000
Reprinted 2021, 2022, 2023, 2024

ISBN 978-81-7304-353-6 (Series)

ISBN 978-81-7304-354-3 (Vol. I)

Published by
Ajay Kumar Jain *for*
Manohar Publishers & Distributors
4753/23 Ansari Road, Daryaganj
New Delhi 110 002

Printed at
Replika Press Pvt. Ltd.

CONTENTS

Appendices

ILLUSTRATIONS

FOREWORD

It gives me great pleasure to present the first volume of *Jayaprakash Narayan: Selected Works* which is being published under the auspices of the Nehru Memorial Museum & Library. Prof. Bimal Prasad who has authored as well as edited several books on Jayaprakash Narayan has undertaken the arduous task of editing the volume, which is the first in a series of volumes to be published.

The present volume covers the period 1929-35. During this period, J.P. played an important role in the formation of the Congress Socialist Party and was its first General Secretary. The volume consists of hitherto unpublished letters written by J.P. to prominent personalities, speeches given at important political meetings and conferences, and other writings. These are of historical importance and throw light on the evolution of the political thought of J.P. during the formative years of his chequered political career.

The book will be of interest to scholars as well as members of the general public interested in the history of the socialist movement in India.

Nehru Memorial Museum & Library
New Delhi
8 June 2000

O.P. Kejariwal

ACKNOWLEDGEMENTS

It is a pleasure to thank all those who have helped in making it possible to begin the publication of this series. First of all my thanks are due to the trustees of the Jayaprakash *Amrit Kosh*—a fund collected on the occasion of J.P.'s seventy-fifth birthday celebrations in October 1977—in particular Sri Siddhraj Dhadda, the late Sri Radhakrishna, and Sri Narayan Desai for encouraging me in 1986 to launch the project of preparing J.P.'s selected works and agreeing to pay the salary of a research assistant and the cost of photocopying selected material. This help continued for about seven years and was later handled—after the sad demise of Sri Radhakrishna—by Sri Kanakmal Gandhi, who succeeded the former as Managing Trustee of the *Kosh*. I am also thankful to Dr. C.D. Amar, Ms. Madhu Mehndiratta and Dr. (Kumari) Amrit Varsha Gandhi who worked by turns for short periods, and to Smt. Sangita Mallik, who worked for about five years in all.

As the files of J.P. Papers were arranged by subject and not chronologically and that arrangement was not changed after they were transferred to the Nehru Memorial Museum & Library, one was required to wade through a very large number of files before arranging the papers for publication.That apart, all of J.P.'s works were not available in his files and the papers of several other leaders, besides the A.I.C.C. Papers, and a large number of newspapers and periodicals had to be looked into. At the same time, I had my teaching as well as other research commitments at J.N.U. and could not devote all my time to the project. My posting to Nepal as Ambassador in January 1991 made my task even more difficult. As a result, work on the project had to be suspended in 1993.

I am extremely beholden to the then Prime Minister of India, Sri P.V. Narasimha Rao, Chairman of the Jayaprakash Narayan Memorial Committee and its other members, particularly Sri Chandra Shekhar, former Prime Minister of India, the late Sri Madhu Limaye, eminent socialist leader; and Sri Bhuwanesh Chaturvedi, then Minister of State in the Prime Minister's office, for their kind interest in the matter. They accepted my suggestion in 1994 to sponsor the project on the selected works of Jayaprakash Narayan and, on their own initiative decided to ask the Nehru Memorial Museum & Library, with its vast repository of J.P.'s and many other leaders' papers as well as rich experience and expertise in handling such projects, to undertake this task. I am also thankful to the then Chairman of the Executive Council of the NMML, Sri Narayan Datt Tiwari, its Vice-Chairman, the late Sri B.K. Nehru and its other members, particularly the late Sri G. Parthasarathi, Sri Abid Hussain (who later succeeded the late Sri B.K. Nehru as Vice-Chairman), Sri H.Y. Sharada Prasad, and Sri A.K. Damodaran, for accepting the suggestion made by the J.P. Memorial Committee and inviting me to shoulder responsibility for it as editor. Shortly after this the Prime Minister agreed to my request to relieve me from my responsibilities as Ambassador to Nepal. I returned to New Delhi at the end of January 1995 and immediately communicated to the late Sri B.K. Nehru my willingness to aceept the kind invitation extended to me by him on behalf of the Executive Council of NMML. He was most encouraging and did his best to get the project started as soon as possible.

In this Sri Nehru had the ardent support of the then Director of the NMML, Professor Ravinder Kumar, who handled all necessary correspondence regarding the project with the Department of Culture, Ministry of Human Resource Development, and extended to me all necessary courtesy and cooperation. With his efforts the project was formally launched in December 1995, and he remained fully supportive till his retirement from Directorship at the end of November 1997. The new Director, Dr. O.P. Kejariwal, who joined in June 1999 has been taking an equally keen interest in the project and has been more than willing to offer any help required. Thanks to this, he for the first time made available to the project the services of the serving, experienced research staff of NMML. I am most thankful to both Professor Ravinder Kumar and Dr. O.P. Kejariwal for their support.

I must also thank Dr. Hari Dev Sharma, Deputy Director of NMML for a long time and Director-in-charge during the period of interregnum between the two Directors. He had been taking interest in the J.P. Project right from the days when it was financed by the *Amrit Kosh*. His association became closer after the project was restarted as part of the programme of activities of NMML and continued in that form till he retired from NMML in August 1999. In this phase he contributed some important material from his private collection and also helped me in more ways than one in carrying out my task as editor.

My thanks are also due to the supporting research staff, who have worked on the J.P. Project for varying periods. For about two years (1996-8) Smt. Sangita Mallik was the only person in this capacity. She collected most of the materials—some from the earlier stock and some new ones—included in this volume and also prepared the first drafts of many of the biographical notes. After she left, the strength of the Project's research staff was expanded and it had the services of Sri A.K. Avasthi and Sri S.L. Manchanda. Though they worked only for about an year, they were able to contribute valuable inputs into the volume. The same is true of Sri S.S.A. Abidi who has been associated with the project since February 1999.

After Dr. Kejariwal assumed charge as Director, the services of Kumari Deepa Bhatnagar, Dr. (Kumari) Amrit Varsha Gandhi and Smt. Usha Gururaj of the Research and Publications Division became available to the Project. They have contributed significantly to this volume, helping to finalise the manuscript and seeing it through the press.

From the administrative side, Sri Desh Raj, Administrative Officer, has been helpful to the Project in various ways. Sri Anand Bhushan Sharma ungrudgingly helped me with typing and other work whenever required. The late Sri Mukesh Jain worked as a typist for the project for a short period. Since his untimely passing away, Kumari Deepa Sharma has been working as typist for the project for the last three years and has prepared the typescript. I am thankful to all of them.

BIMAL PRASAD

INTRODUCTION

Jayaprakash Narayan (1902-79), popularly known as J.P., occupies a unique position among the galaxy of political leaders produced by India in modern times. He played a major role not merely in the struggle for independence, but also in the foundation and growth of the socialist movement, acquiring a stature in public life next only to that of Jawaharlal Nehru, who had become the nation's helmsman as Prime Minister in 1947. Even though the Socialist Party which J.P. led had not become very large or strong, in view of J.P.'s growing popularity among the masses as well as the elite many, both in India and abroad, began to look upon him as the person most likely to succeed Nehru as Prime Minister. J.P., however, cherished no such ambition. In 1953, he did not accept Nehru's invitation to join his cabinet, thus abandoning an opportunity which would have put him in a position of vantage from the point of view of succession. On the other hand, he identified himself more and more with the non-party Bhoodan (land-gift) movement led by Vinoba Bhave. Seeing in it the seeds of a non-violent social revolution, he publicly dedicated his whole life to it in 1954. Finally in 1957, he announced not merely his resignation from the Praja Socialist Party (the new name of the Socialist Party since its merger with the Kisan Majdoor Praja Party in 1953), but also his complete withdrawal from all party and power politics—admittedly an act of renunciation in view of his position in the public life of the country at that time. Although thus opting out of party and power politics, J.P. remained as active in public life as ever before in support of the causes he believed in—publishing tracts, addressing meetings and seminars all over the country and organising workers at various levels engaged in public activities under his supervision and guidance. For the next fifteen years or so most of his time and energy was spent on the Bhoodan and Gramdan (gift of village) movements, the latter emerging as an offshoot of the former. However he also occupied himself with several other causes like the restoration of freedom in Tibet, and harmony and peace in Nagaland and Kashmir. Sometimes his stand on certain issues like Kashmir, made him somewhat unpopular among the Indian elite, but that did not bother him and he persevered on his closen path as long as that appeared right to him. Towards the end of his life (1974-7), sensing a serious threat to democracy in India because of rampant corruption in government and growing authoritarianism on the part of those in power, he mobilised the people in Bihar as also outside for what became famous as the J.P. movement and even founded a new political party (Janata Party) and ardently campaigned for it in the national election held in 1977. While the Janata Party succeeded in overthrowing Indira Gandhi and forming its own government, thereby ensuring the end of authoritarianism, J.P. was far from satisfied. He had set a much higher goal—Total Revolution—for his movement and that seemed nowhere around. Most of the persons who had come to power through the Janata Party, with J.P.'s blessings and support, had no longer any use for him or his ideas. Dogged by severe ill-health, he could do little to remedy the situation except to give occasional expression to his disillusionment with the performance of the Janata regime and his hope that the Indian people would not abandon the vision of a social revolution based on freedom, social justice and peace. Although there was little sign of it in 1979, when he passed away, he drew solace from the thought that some of his ideas might be found useful by those who were interested in working for the realisation of that vision. This series of volumes has been planned with a view to giving the reader an idea of the varied activities which occupied J.P. during his public life, extending over more than half a century, as well as of the evolution of his political and social thought. In many ways he was a mirror of his times and his selected works, it is hoped, will not merely give the reader an idea of his own activities and thinking, but also of the times in which he lived and worked—a useful supplement in this respect to similar works of Gandhi and Nehru.

II

J.P.'s debut into public life took place in 1921, as a fighter for Indian freedom under the leadership of Mahatma Gandhi. Born in a lower rural midle class family in Bihar[1] on 11 October 1902, he had shown promise early in his student career and won a merit scholarship on the basis of his performance at the Matriculation examination in 1919. Entering Patna College, then the premier educational institution of higher learning in that province, he was in the second year science class when the wave of the non-cooperaton movement reached its portals. Tall (5 feet, 9 inches), fair and handsome as well as bright and studious and noted for his simplicity and elegance, he was among the most promising students of the college. The university intermediate examination was only a few weeks away and the fee for it had already been deposited. But Gandhi's call of non-cooperation with all educational institutions maintained or aided by the Government, conveyed to the students at Patna through the eloquence of Maulana Abul Kalam Azad, proved irresistible and J.P. walked out of his college with a select band of students. He never turned back. "That brief experience of soaring up with the winds of a great idea," he recalled much later, "left imprints on the inner being that time and much familiarity with the ugliness of reality have not removed". It was then that freedom became one of the beacon lights of his life and always remained so as long as he was alive. With the passing of the years, it transcended the mere freedom of India and embraced the "freedom of man everywhere and from every sort of trammel—above all, it meant freedom of the human personality, freedom of the mind, freedom of the spirit."[2]

[1] The village, Sitabdiara, where J.P. was born, lies at the confluence of two rivers—Ganga and Ghaghra. Its location has been changing with changes in the course of the rivers. When J.P. was born, it lay in the Saran district of Bihar. Now, for many years, it has been in the Ballia district of U.P.

[2] Jayaprakash Narayan, 'From Socialism to Sarvodaya', in Bimal Prasad, ed., *A Revolutionary's Quest: Selected Writings of Jayaprakash Narayan* (New Delhi, 1980), p. 183.

While J.P. received the beacon light of freedom from Gandhi it was from Marx that he derived the ideals of equality and brotherhood. After leaving Patna College he enrolled himself as a student in the Bihar Vidyapith, founded by the Congress leaders for the benefit of non-cooperating students and not recognised by the Government, but that institution did not have any provision for teaching science beyond the second year stage. On the other hand, unlike many other students in similar circumstances, J.P. could not persuade himself to return to Patna College or to any other educational institution maintained or aided by the Government. But the desire for higher education remained strong. At that time J.P. came to know that it was possible for a student in the United States to pay for his education through part-time work. So in 1922 he proceeded to the United States, without adequate resources and leaving behind his beautiful wife, Prabhavati (then sixteen) to whom he had been married two years earlier, as per the custom in those days. He lived in that country for seven years, studying by turns at the universities of California (Berkeley), Iowa, Wisconsin and Ohio (from where he graduated, with a scholarship and took the Master's degree in Sociology) and working during vacations and other holidays in fields, factories and hotels to meet his expenses. While studying at the Wisconsin University (Madison) he came into close contact with some communist students, and avidly read the writings of Marx, Engels, Lenin and their followers, including M.N. Roy, and became converted to Marxism. Freedom still remained his goal, but the Marxian science of revolution seemed to offer a surer and quicker way to it than the technique followed by Gandhi. Besides, Marxism provided him with another goal, namely equality. He now became convinced that political freedom was not enough and that it must be accompanied by freedom from exploitation and poverty. At that time he was not aware of the fact that Gandhi too was concerned with the problem of poverty and had his own concept of a social revolution.

J.P. was keen to work for his Ph.D. degree in Sociology, but the news of the serious illness of his mother forced him to return home towards the end of 1929. India was again in ferment, reminiscent of the days of 1919-22. J.P., with all his Marxism, was first and foremost a votary of Indian nationalism and found himself inevitably drawn into the struggle then unfolding. The bond with Gandhi had also now become much stronger than before. While in 1920-1, he was only a great leader for J.P. at whose call the latter had left Patna College, now he was also a revered elder in the family. That bond had been established by Prabhavati. While J.P. was in the United States she had lived for more than a year with Gandhi and Kasturba at the Sabarmati Ashram and been lovingly treated by them as their own daughter. One of the first things that J.P. did after his return home was to pay a visit to Gandhi at Wardha and was overwhelmed by the love and affection showered on him. J.P. also met Nehru there and the two were instantly drawn towards each other. Gandhi, Nehru, J.P. and Prabha travelled together to Lahore where Nehru presided over the annual Congress session in the last week of December 1929. With Nehru's encouragement J.P. gave up the idea of joining Banaras Hindu University with a view to starting the teaching of Sociology and began to work as secretary of the recently created Labour Research Department in the office of the All India Congress Committee. This further cemented the bond between J.P. and

Nehru and the former always respected the latter as an elder brother. A parallel relationship of friendship and affection developed between their wives, Prabha and Kamala. The close personal bonds with Gandhi and Nehru, particularly with the former, played an important role in the evolution of J.P.'s political life and thought.

Because of the passing away of his mother and the ill health and financial difficulties of his father J.P. could not play an active role in the first civil disobedience campaign (1930-1), but he more than compensated for it by his role in the second (1932-3), which soon followed. After the arrest of the top leaders of the Congress he became the acting General Secretary of the Congress in 1932, and in that capacity, built up an underground organisation in order to continue the civil disobedience campaign in various parts of the country. When he was arrested in September 1932, the *Free Press Journal* of Bombay splashed the news with a headline "Congress Brain Arrested".

J.P. did not notice the communists anywhere in the nationalist struggle at that time (1930-3). Many of them were in prison, facing trial at Meerut, but even those who were out of prison had, under the instructions of the Comintern, stayed out of that struggle and even denounced it as being waged in the interest of the bourgeoisie. To an ardent nationalist like J.P. this came as a rude shock and led him to conclude that the socialist movement in India could not be carried on under the leadership of the Communist Party of India or under the guidance of the Comintern. He was convinced that, although preparations for ushering in socialism must begin instantly, the achievement of freedom must have top priority in the national agenda so long as the country remained under foreign rule. This pointed to the need of organising a socialist party, which would function within the broad framework of the nationalist movement and help keep it on the path of struggle and away from that of constitutionalism, towards which it seemed to be drifting in 1933-4. Besides, it would broaden the base as well as the social outlook of that movement by drawing a much larger number of workers and peasants to its ranks than was otherwise possible. Such thoughts on J.P.'s part, shared by some of his fellow-inmates in Nasik Central Prison, notably Achyut Patwardhan, M.R. Masani, Asoka Mehta, N.G. Goray, and M.L. Dantwala, as also by several other leaders then lying in other prisons, notably Narendra Deva, Yusuf Meherally, Purshottam Trikamdas and Rammanohar Lohia, led to the foundation of the Congress Socialist Party in 1934, with J.P. first as its Organising Secretary and then General Secretary. Yusuf Meherally aptly observes: "Jayaprakash came out of prison with an idea, a purpose and a vision. And out of that was born the Congress Socialist Party."[3] During 1934-5, J.P. was mainly preoccupied with carrying the message of the C.S.P. to the youth, intelligentsia, workers and peasants all over the country, organising as many branches of the new party as possible, elucidating its ideology and programme and defending it against its critics.

[3] Jayaprakash Narayan, *Towards Struggle*, ed. Yusuf Meherally (Bombay 1946), Editor's Introduction, p. 7

III

The items included in this volume reflect J.P.'s preoccupations and activities as well as the evolution of his political and social outlook between 1929 and 1935, sketched above. While there is no need to refer to them here, item by item, and stand between them and the reader, it may be in order to mention a few words about the first item—J.P.'s thesis on Cultural Variation submitted to the Ohio State University (U.S.A.) in partial fulfilment of the requirements of the Master's degree in Sociology. Being a Master's thesis it is naturally quite a preliminary study and can not be called profound in any way. However, it does indicate the early beginnings of J.P.'s talent as a social analysist—sifting all kinds of views on a particular theme and coming to a well-reasoned conclusion—as well as his ability in marshalling arguments, on the basis of varied data, in support of the view being upheld by him. At the same time, it contains the earliest expression of his innate yearning for a new and a better world. This should be clear from the following paragraph of his Introduction:

> The aim of science is often said to be the discovery of Truth (which is always written in this case with a capital T). This perhaps is a noble ideal. But to a more mundane nature the chief purpose of science appears to be to make human life fuller and richer, to rid it of its inner and outer limitations, to endow it with comfort, health, beauty, to render it more creative, more rational. Perhaps the discovery of truth is the first step towards all this. But it is a deceitful term—this truth. There may be 'true' ways of destroying life and happiness. And alas! Science has discovered enough of such 'truths' already![4]

Certain pieces which were not published exclusively in the name of J.P., but carried other names also have been placed as appendices. Also included therein are a few items to which J.P. reacted at some length in the form of an article or a statement. This should give the reader an idea of the context of some of his writings and statements. The (partially incomplete) report on the first civil disobedience movement (1930-1) prepared in 1931 in the office of the A.I.C.C. and included as Appendix 1 falls in a different category. The Foreword written by the three general secretaries of the Congress—Syed Mahmud, Jairamdas Doulatram and Jawaharlal Nehru—records their thanks to J.P. and Raghubir Sahai (also working in the A.I.C.C.) for having 'collected the material for this report . . . and helped in drafting it'.[5] That might have been formally the position, but there is some basis for assuming that J.P. had been largely responsible for drafting it. This is proved by what Ramvriksh Benipuri, an eminent Hindi writer as well as a close friend and colleague of J.P. in the socialist movement, recorded in his biography of J.P., first published in 1947 and written on the basis of information made available by the latter. Benipuri writes that while working at the office of the A.I.C.C. at Allahabad, J.P. had written a history of the civil disobedience movement and that unless ants managed to eat it up, some day someone might discover the manuscript among the A.I.C.C. Papers.[6]

[4] See item no. 1 in the present volume.

[5] See Appendix 1 in the present selection.

[6] Ramvriksh Benipuri, *Jayaprakash* (in Hindi) (Patna, 1947), p. 77.

Indeed it is Benipuri's lead which made me search for this manuscript among the papers suggested by him and I consider it my good luck that I was able to lay my hands on it, even though it is far from complete. The remaining portion could not be traced. As J.P. was a stickler for truth and not used to making boastful statements, it is safe to assume that he had done most of the drafting. It will surely be of use to historians of our freedom movement. At the same time, it will afford some insight into J.P.'s way of looking at an important event of history as a sympathetic contemporary observer.

1. Cultural Variation: A Thesis Presented for the Degree of Master of Arts, Ohio State University, 1929[1]

I

INTRODUCTION

"Whence, and oh Heavens! whither?"—once exclaimed the bewildered Carlyle. And a recent volume of essays, written by leading scholars of West and East, has been significantly named "Whither Mankind". Thus the question remains—though somewhat simplified. We now pretend not to be interested in the problem of "whence". Upon such questionings we merely fasten the stigma of theology, or perhaps of metaphysics.

But though we have simplified Carlyle's problem, we have done little to solve it, even in its humbler form. This ponderous, aimless, ubiquitous movement of society still remains largely unintelligible to us. And as for taking control of this movement, that is, as for self-direction, we have achieved a scandalously negative result. Thomas Hardy was not too bitter when he wrote these lines:

> Peace upon earth, was said. We sing it,
> And pay a million priests to bring it.
> But, after two thousand years of mass,
> We've got as far as poison gas![2]

Evidently, the notorious "blind forces" still preside over our destiny.

It is the faith of contemporary scientists that the universe is in constant flux—it is a "movement continuum". Particles of matter, or of energy,—they believe—are constantly jumping about, building and unbuilding atoms, molecules, rocks, animals, societies, planets. The various sciences merely take particular sections of this continuum, and study the nature of the changes occurring there. This is not to say that all science is merely a study of change. However, we think that all scientific problems are at least subsidiary to this main problem. Why?

The aim of science is often said to be the discovery of Truth (which is always written in this case with a capital T). This perhaps is a noble ideal. But to a more mundane nature the chief purpose of science appears to be to make human life fuller and richer, to rid it of its inner and outer limitations, to endow it with comfort, health, beauty, to render it more creative, more rational. Perhaps the discovery of

[1] *Brahmanand Papers* (Nehru Memorial Museum & Library, hereinafter referred to as NMML). Prof. Nageshwar Prasad had obtained a copy of this thesis from Ohio in 1966. The footnotes in this item form part of the thesis. We have not altered or added any footnote to this item.

[2] Written on Christmas Eve, 1924, published in *Winter Words*.

truth is the first step towards all this. But it is a deceitful term—this truth. There may be "true" ways of destroying life and happiness. And alas! science has discovered enough of such "truths" already!

What should be the aim of sociology? Discovery of Truth? Perhaps. But ultimately it should be to make it possible for man to control his social environment, to direct his social destiny intelligently and rationally. But, how can this be made possible? It is a commonplace that man's control over the physical world has increased in the proportion in which his knowledge of physical laws has grown. By physical laws I merely mean statements of relationships which seem to us to hold between the movements of physical objects. In other words, they are laws of change, involving in most cases statements which indicate certain results that will follow certain conditions. As I said above, without knowing such laws we would have been unable to control the physical world, even in the small way that we have.

Now in the social world a similar condition obtains. There also certain given cultural conditions, all other things remaining the same, are followed by certain definite social results. Therefore, anyone aspiring to control social[3] phenomena must acquaint himself with laws of cultural change, that is, if these can be known. Without such knowledge he will only succeed in making matters worse. Herbert Spencer somewhere shows that of about thirty-two parliamentary measures thirty or some produced results which were contrary to those desired. We all know how society abounds with quacks and their panaceas. And it does so because no one knows what is best to do. This, I hope, justifies me in laying emphasis upon the study of change and in considering this study as the core of all scientific work.

I am glad to be able to quote a statement of Professors [W.G.] Sumner and [A.G.] Keller in support of my general argument:

> Whereas no one would think of engaging in chemical experimentation without knowing about chemical laws or without direction from one who knows, in matters having to do with the destiny of human society the idea is to pitch in forthwith and do something. This means, in the case of collisions of national interests, to fall back on the old expedient of belligerency and begin to growl and brandish fists. It is easier to do that than to think the thing out and act rationally. And yet any candid man is forced to admit that there must be laws covering the evolution and life of society which can be discovered and taken into account, as the laws in the physical world have been,—to the race's immense advantage. To strive to learn these laws and operate in the light of them is the only course that deserves the name of rational. The laws and the forces go on, despite futile attempts to ignore them or to act in opposition to them, and it is they that determine, in their highly efficient, automatic manner, the destiny of society. It would be better for man if he fell in with these powers and forces, for they go forward unperturbed, in serene indifference to what he thinks or does not think.[4]

[3] The term "social" as used in sociological writings, in spite of several attempts at definition, has remained more or less vague. However, in deference to popular and traditional usage, and in order to avoid irksome repetition, I have retained this term in the present paper. But I should like to make it clear that I use it only in the sense of "cultural". Whether one may agree with [A.L.] Kroeber's view or not, that the subject matter of sociology is *culture*, this much seems to be incontestable, that the study of social change really resolves itself into the study of cultural change.

[4] Sumner and Keller, *The Science of Society*, pp. 412-13.

In conclusion I may record my opinion that the primary function of the sociologist is the study of social or cultural change.[5] Otherwise he may become what Sumner called a "social quack"[6] but never a social scientist. Furthermore, all quests for social guidance are foredoomed until real knowledge of social change is forthcoming.

[5] "Just as in biology the central problem is organic evolution, so in sociology the central problem is social evolution", Ellwood, C.A., *Society in Its Psychological Aspects*, p. 20.

[6] Sumner, *What Social Classes Owe to Each Other*, passim.

II

THE PROBLEM

In the previous chapter I have shown the importance of the study of cultural change. My immediate concern is with cultural variation, however, as is apparent from the title. In this chapter I wish to show the relation between these two topics and point out specifically what the problem of cultural variation is.

I shall take the problem first. Perhaps the problem of cultural variation will be better defined if I begin by pointing out a similar problem which biologists are facing at present. For this purpose I shall start with Darwin's theory of evolution. The propositions that underlie the Darwinian theory are the following:[1]

1. All organisms produce more young than can survive to maturity.
2. This involves competition among the offspring for a share in the limited means of subsistence.
3. No two individuals are exactly alike in structure and capability.
4. Given the struggle for existence and the inequality of individuals, it follows that on the average the ones to survive will be those which happen to have the better adaptational qualities.
5. Through heredity these better qualities will be transmitted to a majority of the next generation.

Overlooking the apparent inadequacies and tautologies involved in this theory, even if we accept it as an essentially correct description of organic evolution, a basic question yet remains unanswered, to wit, what causes variations? The third proposition (above) merely takes variation as a fact.

This much is clear that if there were no variations in nature there could be no "selection" and thus no "evolution".

> Variation is the first and most fundamental evolutionary factor; in fact, the causes of variation are among the prime causes of evolution itself. . . . It is the progressive factor in evolution, for without variation no change could occur and evolution would be impossible.[2]

If all this is true then one would be justified in claiming that organic evolution is not explained by the fact that unfit variations are destroyed "naturally", and those fitted to survive live and propagate their kind. This is mere tautology. The real problem is to discover the causes of these variations. Biologists have made little progress in this field, however.[3]

The problem of social variation is similar to that of organic variation. Professor Keller, in his *Societal Evolution*, has attempted to describe the process of social

[1] Parshley, in [H.E.] Barnes (ed.), *History and Prospects of the Social Sciences*. Article on biology, p. 119.

[2] [Richard Swam] Lull, *Organic Evolution*, p. 99.

[3] Professor Lull says in this connection: "Although the fact is not open to argument, the means

evolution, or, as he prefers to call it, of societal evolution, using the same concepts as those applied by Darwin to organic evolution. He begins by noting that there is variation in social life. "Variation in the folkways is practically self-evident",[4] he avers. Then, taking the *fact* of variation as a starting point, he proceeds to show how societal evolution also is a result of the operation of the principles of selection, transmission, and adaptation upon a given set of variations.

Here again we have the same difficulty, to wit, how do social variations arise? Keller has left this question almost wholly unanswered. But is it not obvious that the process of social evolution cannot be comprehended unless we are able to understand the origin of social or cultural variations?

In recent years sociologists have insisted upon using the term "social change" instead of "social evolution". And some have claimed that the new usage is not merely a matter of terminology, but that it reflects a shift in point of view.[5] Whether this claim is justified or not, at least, this much is clear that no matter what method is followed and what terminology is used, the problem of the origin of variation retains its paramount and fundamental importance.

Let us follow this new concept of social change a little further. What is social change? To answer this question let us take an ideal social group—a primitive community of, say, a hundred members, all acting alike. Now we shall suppose that one member of this group, for some reason or other, begins to perform a certain act in a way different from the traditional way. Will this be an example of social change? Suppose this individual acted in that eccentric way till his death but no one paid any attention to his innovation; he would have had no influence upon his group. In such a case it seems but proper to answer the above question in the negative. Dixon seems to be in agreement with this judgement: "Now a discovery or invention, once it is made, is without result and sterile unless it is adopted. Without its diffusion beyond the discoverer or inventor the new trait remains merely a personal eccentricity, interesting or amusing perhaps, but not significant."[6]

To continue the illustration. Suppose another member of the group copies the innovation. Would that be social change? If not, what portion of the group must adopt the new behaviour before we may speak of a social change having occurred in that group? No answer, as far as the writer is aware, has been given to these questions. Nor are these questions of trifling worth to the practical student of social change. At this point we are not interested in these questions, however. Here I

---

whereby variation has been brought about, the character of the variations, whether regular or irregular, determinate or fortuitous, and the amount and the part of the organism affected are subjects for debate" (op. cit., p. 100). Messrs Sinnott and Dunn have expressed the same idea as follows: "It must be admitted at the outset that very little is definitely known about the origin of most of the variations which have been discussed in this book. Such familiar characters as the colour of rodents or fowls or the simple qualitative variation in corn have arisen by processes which remain mysterious even after the details of inheritance have become well known" (*Principles of Genetics*, pp. 272-3). To quote one more biologist. Professor Parshley says: "Let it be said at once that this question (what causes variation) remains unanswered; it is perhaps the major problem of modern theoretical biology" (Article on Biology in Barnes (ed.), *History and Prospects of the Social Sciences*, p. 120).

[4] Keller, A.G., *Societal Evolution*, p. 44.

[5] Ross, E.A., *Foundations of Sociology*, 1919, p. 189. Also Chapin, F., *Stuart in Cultural Change*.

[6] Dixon, R.B., *The Building of Cultures*, p. 59.

simply wish to emphasize the idea that social change is a process, made up of various subsidiary processes. Two of these we have noted above: (1) origin of a variation, (2) the spread of this variation in the group. Need it be emphasized that the basic problem is the first of these processes?

Thus, no matter how we study the dynamics of society, whether we call it social evolution or social change, the most important problem that faces us is that of the origin of social variations.

III

SOME PRELIMINARY CONSIDERATIONS: METAPHYSICAL AND PRACTICAL

Necessary Assumptions

Part of the current and past confusion in sociology is and has been due to the slovenly habit of not clearly defining or stating the primary assumptions on which the various sociological theories must ultimately rest. And part of the disagreement among sociologists can be traced back to divergent starting points, rather than to any difference in method or data.

Some sociologists may perhaps deny that there is any need of defining the assumptions of social science. They may stubbornly resist any attempt to introduce "metaphysics" into the "science" of society. Some, perhaps those who occupy themselves too insistently with data-collecting, may even have the hardihood to maintain that "arbitrary assumptions" are useless. Yet, the fact remains that no one can, nor does any one interpret any observation or data without the use of presuppositions.

In the opinion of the writer, therefore, it is necessary for the healthy development of sociological theory that those who engage themselves in this department of knowledge trace out painstakingly their presuppositions, carefully examine them and state them explicitly. The mistrust of all philosophizing that has grown up in this age of statistical methods and other tabulating and formularizing techniques, though having rendered certain salutary services, is beginning to be actually injurious by its dogmatism. I am glad to be able to quote a recent protest against the same tendency in psychology by Professor Weiss, "It seems to me that the reprimand implied in the frequently used expression, *a purely metaphysical conception*, has restrained scientific speculation and development unnecessarily".[1]

The following assumptions have been adopted in this paper:

1. Human behaviour is a part of the electron-proton changes that constitute the "movement continuum", and is ultimately reducible to the same laws that describe these changes.
2. All social phenomena are part of these electron-proton changes, and are thus inevitably determined.

It seems unnecessary to justify the use of these assumptions. However, I wish to add that the popular notion that assumptions are made quite arbitrarily is far from the truth. No philosophical or scientific assumptions, not even those of geometry, are arbitrary. They are all based on certain well-advised judgements. If this were not the case, then, instead of finding only three or four types of basic assumptions in metaphysics, we should have found as many as are the whims of "idle speculators".

[1] Weiss, A.P., *A Theoretical Basis of Human Behaviour*, p. 40.

The Concept of Cause

Already I have used such phrases as "the causes of variations" and in the following pages the term "cause" will occur quite often. Therefore, it seems reasonable to make explicit the sense in which I am using this term. It is especially advisable to do so because several interpretations have been given to it in the past.

I shall make no attempt to go into philosophical complexities inherent in the problem of causation. I shall simply state the significance that I attach to it. The significance is the same as Professor S. Alexander gives to the term.[2]

> Space-Time or the system of motion is a continuous system, and any motion within it is continuous with some other motion. This relation of continuity between two different motions is causality, the motion which precedes that into which it is continued in the order of time being the cause and the other the effect.[3]

Further on Alexander adds:

> Finally, the causal relation is a relation of existents. One substance is the agent and the other is patient which suffers its effect. Agent and patient together form a relatively closed system and, as we have seen, within that system the causality is immanent. There is no causal relation between the infinite whole and any one of its parts. There is only such relation between one part and another. The whole system of things does not descend into the arena and contend with one of its creatures. The business of science in its search for causes (and it is not asserted that this constitutes the whole business of science) is to discover what precise events are connected as causes with what other precise events as effects. . . . The rules of the logic of discovery are rules of procedure in this quest. Where the causal connection can be established, it is done by an elaborate machinery of negative instances, by which the cause is narrowed down so as to contain only so much as is relevant to the effect. . . . This procedure is not open to the objection that the only satisfactory statement of a cause is the whole universe. If this were true the idea of cause would indeed retain a certain usefulness in practice, but as a theoretical basis of procedure in science it would be useless. But the objection rests on a misconception. It assumes that the operation of the stars is a motion which interferes with the causal act by which a man knocks another down; and does so because there is direct or indirect connection between all parts of the universe, throughout Space-Time. The question rather is whether the intimate causal relation mentioned is interfered with by the universe which undoubtedly sustains it. The question is the same as when we ask whether the properties of a triangle which undoubtedly imply the Space from which the triangle is delimited are affected by the sustaining and surrounding space. What science has to do is just to discover these limited, intimate, relations of existents which are called causal ones.[4]

Even Mr. Bertrand Russell, who holds that in the more advanced realms of science there is no such thing as cause, but only formulae,[5] permits the use of such a concept of cause as the one given above. He says,

[2] See his admirable chapter on Causality in his *Space-Time and Deity* (Gifford Lectures at Glasgow, 1916-8), Vol. 1, pp. 279-99.

[3] Op. cit., p. 279.

[4] Op. cit., pp. 288-9.

[5] See criticism of Russell in Alexander, op. cit., p. 293. Alexander also gives a criticism of Mr. [K.] Pearson's view in the same chapter.

There is, however, a somewhat rough and loose use of the word 'cause' which may be preserved. The approximate uniformities which lead to its pre-scientific employment may turn out to be true in all but very rare and exceptional circumstances, perhaps in all circumstances that actually occur. In such cases it is convenient to be able to speak of the antecedent event as the 'cause' and the subsequent event as the 'effect'. In this sense, provided it is realized that the sequence is not necessary and may have exceptions, it is still possible to employ the words 'cause' and 'effect'.[6]

Such being the concept of cause used here, what is meant by the causes of social variations? Simply the occurrences and conditions which are followed by these variations. Here again the task is to narrow down the antecedent occurrences to what Alexander calls the "relevant" ones or what Lumley calls the "adequate" ones.

In our search for relevant antecedents we may employ the logical, as well as the empirical, method. Since the empirical method is unique in each instance, no general remarks can be made about it. About the logical method, however, it is possible to lay down certain rules that may prove useful. The occurrences and conditions antecedent to a certain social variation may be numerous. It is required to isolate the relevant ones. A safe guide to this search is to disregard those occurrences and conditions which remain unaltered at the time the variation appears. This line of reasoning leads to the conclusion that a variation is to be explained in terms of other previous variations. It is not implied here that those conditions and occurrences that remain unaltered have no relation with the variation that takes place. To use the language of Alexander, they undoubtedly "sustain" it. But by definition they are not its cause, so we are not interested in them. A somewhat similar idea has been expressed by Ross in his characteristic style:

> The appearance of a new situation is considered to be the effect of the *precipitating* factor. The ferment, the igniting spark, the touching of the electric button, the knocking away of the stay block, the turning of the lever, is looked upon as the cause of what ensued. The factors already present are termed the *conditions*, not the *causes*, of the change. Suppose, for example, a given phenomenon cannot occur without the conjuncture of factors *a*, *b*, and *c*. If *a* and *b* are present and the phenomenon occurs on the addition of *c*, then *c* is regarded as the cause, *a* and *b* as the conditions. But it is possible that either of these may be the precipitating factor working within the framework constituted by the other two factors.[7]

All this discussion may appear to be mere verbosity. But I have dealt with the concept of cause at this length because some very interesting results follow from our conclusions. Ellwood[8] and De Laguna,[9] in their summaries of the theories of social evolution, have mentioned the geographical interpretation as one of these theories. Let us take this interpretation and apply to it the concepts I have developed above. Suppose we grant the position of the extreme geographical determinists. Accordingly, let us grant that the culture of the Periclean Greeks was wholly

[6] Russell, B., *Our Knowledge of the External World*, p. 220.

[7] Ross, E.A., "Moot points in Sociology" (chapter on the Factors of Social Change), *Am. Jour. of Soc.*, Vol. 9, May 1904, p. 786.

[8] *Cultural Evolution.*

[9] *The Factors of Social Evolution.*

"determined" by their physical environment. Since that period this environment has remained practically the same. But Greek culture has gone through very striking and fundamental changes. How could the same environment have produced such different cultural situations? Or, to put it another way, how could conditions and occurrences that have remained unaltered be the cause of such radically varying changes? Thus geographic determinism falls to the ground as a theory of social evolution. Only in one case can the geographical environment be held responsible for social change—when it changes itself. The same argument can be applied to the theories of racial determinism, the so-called "psychological interpretations" of social change, the genius-theories, and many other theories which endeavour the impossible task of explaining change in terms of constant factors.

In the course of his criticism of Kroeber's "superorganic" theory, as expounded by him in his two brilliant essays—"Superorganic"[10] and "The Possibility of a Social Psychology"[11]—[F.H.] Allport makes the following remarks, which I am quoting at length to illustrate my point:

> A rich field, but little explored, lies ahead for the elucidation of cultural development in psychological terms. Though ethnologists may well lose patience with the poverty of attempts thus far made, the fact that there are great possibilities still remains. A few illustrations may here be in place.
>
> First, as to the origin and programs of culture. Invention, a term lightly used by ethnologists, must be explained in psychological rather than cultural terms. The need or prepotent drive behind inventive behaviour exists only in individuals. In manner of procedure invention is but a variation of trial and error learning, shortened by the implicit random movements of thinking. The culture base short-cuts individual inventive behaviour. . . .
>
> As another example we may cite the universal culture pattern described by Dr. Wissler. The origin of this universal pattern is inscrutable until we conceive its various parts as means for the adaptation of the prepotent, or instinctive, needs of man. Thus the innate responses of struggle and defense are behind the development of such culture products as government and warfare. The hunger drive gives rise to property, scientific knowledge and material culture in tools, though these, of course, serve other needs as well. Family and social systems are evolved largely as satisfactions of sexual interests.
>
> A third phase of culture explanation lies in the problem of continuity. In its most essential nature culture is not a group of superorganic products. It is distinctly organic and lies within the individual. Social causation lies not in the tool but in the socially inculcated habits of constructing and using the tool. . . . Culture upon a descriptive plane may be studied at large. This is the task of the anthropologists. In an explanatory sense, however, it must be sought within the individual. Explanation of this sort is part of the program of the sociologist. The theory of the superorganic is a well meant but futile attempt to transplant the historical and descriptive method of ethnology into the field of social causation.
>
> At every turn we are thus led back to the behavior of the individual as the source of explanation of social facts. Does this prove that the social as such is to be banished from consideration? By no means. The fact that we decline to use the group, its products, or its changes as principles of explanation does not lessen our interest in these phenomena.[12]

[10] *American Anthropologist*, N.S., Vol. 19, No. 2.

[11] *Am. Jour. of Sociology*, Vol. 23, No. 5.

[12] Allport, F.H., "The Group Fallacy", p. 11 (A reprint from *Journal of Abnormal Psychology*, Vol. 19, No. 1, published by the Sociological Press, Hanover).

It is a pity that there is still room for such reasoning in sociology. The "instinct" of hunger *explains* the development of property, knowledge and material culture in general! A very illuminating explanation indeed! And what is yet more confounded is, how such instincts explain not only the origin of these things but also their development. That is, if we take property to illustrate our point, how does the hunger instinct account for the various phases through which property has developed in any given area? Social evolution certainly becomes a plain and simple process upon Allport's hypothesis: Social change is the result of the working of the "pre-potent reflexes" of man. Whoever can make anything out of such explanations is, to say the least, not aware of the more serious problems which confront the student of social change.

The drive behind inventive behaviour exists only in individuals. Therefore, invention is to be explained in psychological rather than cultural in terms. So argues Professor Allport. But does this explanation answer the question, why, of two groups of people, one is immeasurably less inventive than the other? Or, if the dogma of race be made to account for this, how can it explain the circumstance that the same 'race' is sometimes highly inventive and at other times woefully sterile? The inventive drive, if it is a natural endowment of the human race, should not vary at different times in the history of a race. And yet no one will question that the amount of inventions made by any people does vary with the times. Certainly, Dr. Allport will not go so far in his zeal for psychology as to insist that the "psychological" explanation of invention really explains the problem we have raised. Furthermore, it is not only the variation in the amount of invention that the individualistic explanation of Allport fails to explain, but it also leaves another important problem unsolved, namely, why a certain invention was made at a certain time? After all what we want to understand is not why man invents at all, but why he invents what he invents when he invents. And only a cultural explanation can be given, as Professor Kroeber has eloquently argued,[13] of these problems.

That inventing is a psychological process is not denied by the present writer. But it is a process which is directed and controlled by the social environment of the inventor. The instincts of man together with his physical structure are in the ultimate analysis the source of culture. Surely no other animals have developed anything approaching man's civilization. But that is the most we can say about them. The same instincts are responsible for monogamy and polyandry, monarchy and democracy, horse-chariots and aeroplanes, Christianity and Mohammedanism. When man passes through various cultural states his instincts do not change, at least not in the course of a century. Yet a century works immense changes in culture when conditions (which are cultural conditions) are ripe enough. It is the writer's opinion that sociologists must give up the search that [F.H.] Giddings, [L.F.] Ward, [Albion W.] Small and the rest of the pioneers in sociology had begun for "social forces" which were fundamental, for the "springs" of social causation which were hidden and deep-seated. All the theories of "wishes", "desires", "interests" that

[13] In his articles entitled "Superorganic" (in the *American Anthropologist*, N.S., Vol. 19, No. 2) and "The Possibility of a Social Psychology" (in the *Am. Jour. of Sociology*, Vol. 23, No. 5).

have grown up as a result of this search are as useless as they are speculative.[14] Whatever the social forces, whatever the springs of human action, whatever the original nature of man, they have remained practically constant during the historical period. Or at least, they may be supposed to have remained constant by the student of social change, without any prejudice to his results. It is not to imply by this that as constant factors they have had no influence on the stream of culture. Perhaps it may never be possible to ascertain the weight of this influence. But are we interested in knowing about these constants? Can we do anything about them? What we really need to know is, what are those cultural or other environmental conditions which, working upon a group of human beings, will produce a certain cultural effect. Wherever or whenever we study social change what we shall always have will be a group of people, residing in a given locality, with a given culture, whose ancestors had a slightly different culture and whose descendents again probably will have a somewhat varying culture. Now if we wish to find an explanation for the differences between the preceding, the present and the succeeding cultures, it will be little consolation to know that man has a hunger instinct and a sex instinct. These, or other instincts, were always there, and statistically speaking, the succeeding generations of people were structurally the same. But to these samenesses were added environmental conditions which were not identical. Thus we get a formula something like the following: Given a certain organic structure and instincts *plus* certain environmental conditions, certain cultural changes arise. Again these changes *plus* all the previous conditions produce another set of changes and so on. Now if we are after the cause of cultural change it is needless to consider prepotent reflexes, etc. Behind every cultural phenomenon is the same human nature. What we are after is the knowledge of those conditions which warp this nature and make out of it now a savage and now a civilized being. To explain war in terms of a pugnacious instinct is worse than useless. If this nature is original with man it is with him always, yet he fights only in certain circumstances. It is these circumstances which we should try to know. A theory somewhat similar to the psychological theory which we have just discussed is the much debated genius-theory of historic fame. It is not my purpose here to join in the tiresome controversy that has raged round this topic for so long. I wish only to raise the question, how can the student of social change use the data of geniuses?

No matter which side of the said controversy one belongs to, this much should be clear to him, that if the work of a genius is entirely independent of his social milieu, he is outside the ken of the scientist. He is an unpredictable, unclassifiable, unknown quantity, capable of originating all kinds of unexpected innovations. There can be, in that case, no available clue as to future social changes, for geniuses may be born, and will be born, who may change the face of the earth. Not only the future would baffle scientific divination, but even the past, so largely influenced by geniuses, and therefore, on this hypothesis, so full of eccentricities and irregularities and so marked with sudden and unexpected turns, would be futile for scientific purposes. That is, the past would be as unaccountable, due to the unique

[14] A severe criticism of this type of sociology is to be found in Sorokin, *Contemporary Sociological Theories*, pp. 646-59.

achievements of geniuses, as the future would be unpredictable. No logic of social change would be discerned because, as we have supposed, geniuses would not act according to the logic of exterior circumstances. In other words, it would be impossible to create a science of social change.

If, on the other hand, geniuses were mere executors of what social situations demand and determine, our social scientist would have fine sailing indeed. Past history would seem to follow logically from previous situations. The future would be less of an enigma, and we could, with greater certainty predict it. The student of social change would have merely to accept geniuses as constant data together with the brain of man, his free hands, his erect position, his natural "drives" and everything else that has been held accountable for man's progress on this unfriendly earth. Of a given population a certain proportion is always constituted of geniuses.[15] They, together with the rest of the human beings, make up the uniform substratum on which the superorganic drama is enacted.

To sum up, it is not necessary for a student of social change to decide the question whether the achievements of geniuses are determined by the social environment or are merely the unfoldment of their latent power. He has simply to realize that it is only that part of genius' achievements which *has* been so determined that can be made the subject of his studies. (This, of course, is another limitation which the sociologist has to recognize, that is, if there *is* any portion of a work of genius which cannot be socially interpreted.)

A rather significant conclusion follows from the above discussion: It is possible to study social change without considering either individuals or groups. From a methodological standpoint it may even be essential and most helpful.[16] The human element may be left out entirely, unless it is to be specifically considered in a particular case or unless changes have occurred in the biological constitution of the population (immigration of another racial stock, differential birth rates and death rates resulting in the disproportional increase of lower mentalities or vice versa, etc.). We are interested in changes in culture. And since we have taken the elements to be constant, we may leave out both individuals and groups and explain these changes in terms of environmental factors. And where the physical environment is taken as constant, as in short time studies it can be so considered in most cases, only cultural factors can be held responsible for cultural changes. The formulas that we would get then would simply state that given such and such cultural conditions, such and such changes would occur.

I have discussed this topic at some length because I am not aware of an adequate treatment of it anywhere else, and the topic itself seemed important to me. Another

[15] ". . . the march of history, or as it is current custom to name it, the progress of civilization, is independent of the birth of particular personalities; *since these apparently averaging substantially alike, both as records genius and normality, at all times and places, furnish the name substratum* for the social" (emphasis ours). Kroeber, A.L., "Superorganic", p. 31, reprinted from the *American Anthropologist* by the Sociological Press, Hanover, N.J.

[16] "In short, social science, if we may take that word as equivalent to history, does not deny individuality any more than it denies the individual. It does refuse to deal with either individuality or individual as such. And it bases this refusal solely on denial of the validity of either factor for the achievement of its proper aims." Kroeber, A.L., op. cit., p. 33.

justification that I have is the fact that so considerable space is still given to "biological" and "geographical" factors of social change. Neither are such arguments as I have given even alluded to in some most recent works as [F. Stuart] Chapin's *Cultural Change* and Ellwood's *Cultural Evolution*. However, the thought is not a new one, though the writer arrived at them independently. Professor Kroeber presents a similar viewpoint in his "Superorganic". But the clearest statement of it that I have come across is that of Ross.

In fact, a fixed trait, whether of race or of locality cannot figure as cause of a social transformation. Geography, to be sure, acquaints us with the framework within which social changes occur, and by which they are moulded and limited. But the physical environment, while it may inhibit variative tendencies, cannot initiate them. Natural waterways and an indented coast may favour progress, but they cannot produce it. Soil and climate account for the enduring lineaments, but not for the metamorphoses of peoples. Unlikeness of surroundings may cause differences between societies, ***but it cannot bring about differences between successive epochs in the same society***, unless in the meantime the people has migrated [emphasis ours]. Still, to the eye of the geologist, the environment is not quite stable. Elevation, subsidence, desiccation, the silting up of streams or ports, the shifting of river beds, the formation of pestilential marshes, or changes in flora and fauna, may cause disturbance in the social equilibrium, and should, therefore, find a place in the theory of social dynamics.[17]

The Area and Unit of Study

There is no such entity as the "social" which changes at once and as a whole. When we speak of "social evolution", what we mean is the evolution of man's institutions, his arts and industries, his customs and knowledge. Nor is there any such thing as "society" which "evolves". Here again when we speak of the evolution of *society* we really mean the evolution of *culture*. The terms "social" and "society" are extremely vague and their use is quite confusing.[18] Society is a group of people residing in a given area and living through all phases of life together. What may the evolution of these people mean except the evolution of their folkways, their government, their industry, the forms of their relationships, in short, their culture?

But culture itself does not change at once and as a whole. This is a trite statement, it is true, but its significance has been missed. If the full meaning of this statement were grasped we would cease looking for the "factors of social change". For even if there were such generalized factors which explained the change of culture as a whole, they would in all probability be so general as to be practically useless. And such indeed is the case. Take, for example, Thomas's crisis-attention-control theory of inventions, which has been considered as "epoch-making" by Professor Ellwood.[19] What light does it throw upon such questions as "Why are sex mores changing in America?", "Why are the Chinese going through such bewildering

[17] Op. cit., p. 79.

[18] Professor [W.F.] Ogburn tries to distinguish between "social" and "cultural". See his *Social Change*, pp. 53-60. While agreeing in the main with the distinction he makes, I fail to see why "mechanisms of association", or even forms of interaction, cannot be considered as cultural facts.

[19] Ellwood, C.A., *Cultural Evolution*, p. 45.

social crisis at present?", "Why is the Indian caste system disintegrating?", or such questions as "What will be the future of the American family?, what will be the future of the Soviet state?" etc. The theory is too general to be of any use.

It has been generally recognized that invention is the most important factor of social change. But unless inventions are explained the process of change still remains obscure. Of course, attempts have been made to solve the mystery of inventions. As a result we have a theory like that of Thomas', which was mentioned above. Professor Ronald Dixon, summarizing H.S. Harrison's articles[20] on inventions states that inventions rest on the triad of opportunity, need, and necessity.[21] According to Chapin two things are necessary for an invention to come to light: A requisite cultural threshold, and a precipitating factor. "Cultural threshold" he says "is merely a term to describe a stage of development of several independent but related culture traits which may be combined into a new pattern, given a precipitating or initiating factor".[22] The precipitating factor may be a felt need or a crisis. Of course, Chapin would consider genius to be an essential factor, too.

All these theories are perhaps all right. But of what use are they? It is obvious that quite different conditions may be responsible for an invention in physics, industrial chemistry, public finance, religious practice, costume, educational system, government, etc. We are interested in controlling our social destiny. We wish to understand how and why the various aspects of our social life change and alter, so that we may be able to do something about them. For this we need concrete, specific knowledge. We do not wish to know the conditions under which inventions, in general, occur. Rather, we want to know what conditions are necessary for inventions, or in other words, changes in specific institutions, fields of knowledge and other culture traits and complexes. Both prediction and control depend upon this type of knowledge. But this knowledge will not be forthcoming until we stop looking for "factors of social change". To secure it we should begin searching for formulas which will simply state that such and such conditions will produce such and such cultural results. These formulas, obviously, will not be universal social laws, but statements of very limited applicability. How this detailed knowledge is to be obtained is the question. We shall attempt to answer it below.

The culture of a people is made up of units which have been called traits. As a rule a number of these traits go together to form a larger unit of culture known as a "culture complex". It is a matter of common observation that these traits and complexes change at different rates and perhaps according to their own laws of evolution. The starting point of Professor Chapin's theory of "synchronous culture cycles"[23] is the idea that culture traits grow and decline at different rates, and in accordance with laws which are peculiar to each. In view of this fact it would seem that the logical way to study cultural change is to study in detail the history of each trait. Such a study should reveal how this trait has been changing in the past, how

[20] Dr. Dixon mentions three articles: "Inventions: Obtrusive, Directional, and Independent", published in *Man*, Vol. 26, No. 74. "Variations and Mutations in Invention", ibid., No. 101; "Analysis and Factors of Invention", ibid., Vol. 27, No. 28.

[21] Dixon, Ronald B., *The Building of Cultures*, Ch. 2.

[22] Chapin, F. Stuart, *Cultural Change*, pp. 345-54, ibid., p. 352.

[23] See his *Cultural Change*, Ch. 7.

these changes have been related to other cultural facts, what have been the causes of these changes and so forth. With such knowledge at hand it may be possible, by analysing present conditions, to foretell what trend a certain cultural trait may follow in the near future. Such information will be many times more valuable than the knowledge that inter-communication, or increase in population, or crises, are the cause of "cultural" change. It will be more concrete, more immediately applicable, though more bound up with special cultural groups and less ambitious in its sweep—or, perhaps it will have no sweep at all. It will tell us under what given conditions a given trait will vary, or did vary in the past, thus avoiding the use of general terms such as diffusion, contact, crises, at the same time refraining from applying the term change to culture as a whole.

It seems to me that sociologists, for the present at least, must give up all ambitious attempts to arrive at uniform and universal laws. These laws, even when arrived at, will be either too general to be useful or too trite to have any significance. I have already given some examples of the first type of laws, such as the theories which set forth "fundamental drive" as causes of cultural change. Many pages have been filled with lively discussions of these "drives", as a result of all of which we learn that motives, desires, prepotent reflexes, organic urges, such as hunger and sex, are the real propellers of social life. It is futile to prove or disprove these contentions; they remain condemned because of their sheer worthlessness.

So far I have tried to show that cultural traits should be taken as units of study by students of social change. For the practical student, however, this merely serves as the starting point, it merely orients him, enables him to get down to the bottom of his problem without much circum-locomotion. There are other initial problems which he must solve for himself. For example, what traits should be chosen for study? Even the rudest cultures are made up of thousands of these traits. To study any one of these will, perhaps, be valueless. While no definite rule can be laid down about this problem the following passage from Mr. Willey is quite pertinent and suggestive:

> It should be understood that the trait and all of the concepts that follow are methodological concepts, and cannot be defined in any hard and fast way. For example, one can say that an automobile is a trait of our culture. Is the tyre of the automobile also a trait? If we answer in the affirmative this is seemingly inconsistent, since the part is thereby made a trait, as well as the whole. But whether one considers the tyre as a trait or not depends largely upon his purpose. In many analyses the unit might be the automobile and where the analysis calls only for such units, there would be no difficulty in disregarding the tyre. In other cases it might be necessary to analyze so as to include the tyre as a trait. Then it should be done. But one might ask if the inner tube of the tyre is not also a trait. Or the valve. Which merely indicates again that the concept is not rigid, but simply useful in analysis, and will vary according to the needs of the analysis.[24]

Not all students of cultural change have treated a whole culture as a unit. Some of them have, in fact, traced the evolution of different parts of culture. Thus, we have studies of the evolution of religion, of morals, of the state, of the industrial organization, and so on. These studies generally begin with primitive societies and

[24] Malcolm Willey in [H.E.] Barnes and [K.] Davis (ed.), *Introduction to Sociology*, p. 517.

include Egypt, ancient Asia Minor, Greece, Rome, Medieval Europe—triumphantly ending with modern and contemporary Europe. They are, in addition, mostly descriptive in nature, i.e., they merely detail the forms taken by these institutions in various places and at various times. In most cases too coarse data are used to yield any theory of evolution. Besides, it does not seem justifiable to me to skip over the whole world in following the evolution of a cultural trait. The modern European state has not "evolved" from the Greek state, nor has the present morality of the English people descended from the primitives of the South Seas. It is the present Greek State that has evolved from the ancient one, and it is the present morality of the South Sea Islanders that has evolved from the morals of their ancestors. There is no such thing as the evolution of *the* State: rather, we have the evolution of the states of various peoples. There is no such thing as the evolution of morality, but the evolution of the morality of this or that group. The study of the evolution of these institutions, or of any other culture traits, should, therefore, be confined to the cultural setting in which they occur.

Perhaps I have not made myself clear. A culture area is something like a species. A species is a group of animals or plants which differ among themselves only in minor details which are capable of interbreeding. The biologist in studying organic evolution studies the evolution of species. He selects species for his study because of the likenesses which their members bear to each other. If he began with a group of animals in which all sort of diversities were to be found his study of evolution would not make any progress. Evolution of species means the change from one type to another. But, if he did not have a *type* to begin with, how could he ascertain the *type* of changes that might occur or the *type* of animals that may result from these changes? The same sort of reasoning may be applied to the study of social change.

A culture area is a territory the people whereof possess a common culture. It seems to be the nature of culture to become differentiated territorially. The culture of each such area is unique and distinguishable from others. Each is a neatly balanced whole, the elements of which are all dovetailed together. When one of these elements changes, the rest are forced to adapt themselves to the new situation. A culture area represents a "species" of culture, so to speak. And just as the study of organic evolution is the study of the evolution of species, so the study of cultural evolution should be the study of the species of culture. And just as in the case of an organic species, any given variation can be explained only in terms of specific conditions peculiar to that group, so in the case of cultural species.

These considerations induce the writer to lay down the proposition that a student of cultural change should carefully isolate a homogeneous culture group and confine his study to it. For the development of our knowledge of cultural evolution it is essential that a complete study of all the significant traits of a given culture be made and their evolution correlated and interlinked. It has been held by many writers on social evolution that only changes in certain traits of culture are primary; the remaining changes are mere adaptations to this primary change. Such for instance is Professor [Eduard] Zeller's theory. He claims that changes in maintenance-mores are fundamental and primary, all other changes are secondary. Ogburn and Chapin also contend that in modern society, at least, changes in the material culture are the primary causes of all other social changes. If those contentions are true then we undeniably are in possession of a great and useful secret. But whether or not this is true is to be shown by the type of correlation which we have just now said is necessary to establish. That is, the study of social change in a large measure becomes the study of social adaptation. It becomes a question of finding out what changes follow previous changes. After such complete studies have been made of a number of cultures, it may become possible to formulate universal laws of cultural change which may not be too general or too trite.

The Possibility of a Science of Social Change

Some historians, a few philosophers of history, and a number of miscellaneous writers have maintained that in the history of society each event is unique, that social phenomena are not repetitious. From this, in a way not unsound observation, they draw a conclusion which, when pressed to an extreme position, becomes not only untenable, but also threatens to strike at the very root of sociology. Stated briefly, it is that a *science* of history is impossible, because "it is impossible to establish a 'law' of the unique, or to construct a schematic science of the unrepeatable".[25] The most famous and influential philosopher of history who adheres to this view is Benedetto Croce.[26] Among miscellaneous writers of considerable influence is Mr. H.G. Wells[27] who subscribes to this view, and the same idea is, one way or another, held by pluralists in general. Among historians it is becoming less and less popular. Earlier historians such as [Leopold Van] Ranke, [Max] Lenz and [E.A.] Freeman were entirely suspicious of any generalizing in history. Even later historians such as [G.L.] Burr, [F.M.] Fling, G.B. Adams, while not supporting the view that *nothing* is repetitious in society, nevertheless, maintained that the *unique* was the subject matter of history.[28] Professor Larsen of the Ohio State University accepts the Crocean point of view.

Croce's ideas on this topic are well summarized by Professor Catlin:

> For Croce, the endless and objectless world-process, as known, is History, and being known by thought, its knowledge in all its tissue of variety is also philosophy. History is the very intellectual vision of the
>
> Murmer of living.
> Stir of existence,
> Soul of the World.
>
> This process, every moment of which issues from all previous moments and is related in its entire contemporary extent, is something at every point unique, and is incapable of repetition

[25] Catlin, G.E.C., *The Science and Method of Politics*, p. 41.

[26] This is not the opinion of Mr. Catlin: he is merely presenting Croce's viewpoint. Philosopher of history is perhaps an unique title for Croce for whom history *is* philosophy. For Croce's view on the subject of history, see his *On History, History, Its Theory and Practice*.

[27] See his "The So-called Science of Sociology"—a paper read before the Sociological Society of England, Feb. 1905, published in *Sociological Papers*.

[28] "When our attention is directed towards *uniqueness*, the *individuality* of past social facts, when they interest because of their importance for the *unique evolution of man in his activities as a social being*, in selecting the facts and in grouping them into a complex, evolving whole, we employ the

without difference. Hence a conclusion of the first importance: *There can be, from the nature of the case, no science of History.* For science is concerned not with the 'content' but with the 'form', and 'form' which can ultimately be reduced to a formula. And History, like Nature for the Nature-lover, like the rainbow of Keats, is essentially 'content', full of the unique joy of things not recurrent.[29]

This is an argument to which we must give some thought. Science is built on regularities, i.e., on regular and uniform occurrences. Of course, this is not to assert that uniformity is *universal* or *eternal.* There may be more irregular movements than regular ones in the continuum as a whole. But it is only these movements in which we discover uniformities that furnish the basis of science, or at least that part of science which is interested in making generalizations, in developing principles, in prediction and so forth. Now if in social life changes occur without uniformity, without regularity, how can we deduce any laws of social change? If every change is different from every other, if every situation is unique, then surely it would be difficult to do anything with them scientifically. And this is exactly what Mr. H.G. Wells maintains. The individuality of atoms and molecules may perhaps be covered by formulas, but the individuality of human beings, of social situations? No, it is the artist alone who can interpret these, not the scientist. And that is why Mr. Wells argues that the task of sociologists is to write Utopias.

Now, no one will doubt that in our gross world there are no exact duplicates of anything. An electron *may* be exactly like another electron, but certainly not the leaves on a flower-tree. Every human being is likewise quite individual. This much will be granted by every one. It is a limitation which science has to struggle against. But those people who insist so adamantly upon the individuality of every substance and event overlook the similarity that is pervasive in the universe. The generalization that is implied in the statement "hundred sheep", is based on just such likeness. Though it does not for a moment question the uniqueness of each sheep, it indicates that all the hundred of them have some common qualities of sheepishness, which make it possible for us to class them together. Likewise, though no two events are exactly similar, they always share in common certain features which enable us to make partial generalizations about them. We can, with some certainty, predict what will happen tomorrow in the office, in the shop or in the home. We can predict quite a number of things about the next Christmas, the next labour strike in Passaic, the next business depression. Every war is individual, no doubt, but at the same time all wars of a given period, and even all wars of all periods have some common

---

historical method; the result of our work is history." Fling, "The Writing of History", pp. 16-17, quoted in Barnes, *The New History and the Social Studies*, p. 320. Later on Professor Fling adds, "If this be history, then history cannot repeat itself, there cannot be 'historical laws' for law is a generalization and a generalization assumes repetition." Ibid., p. 320. However, Fling admits that there *are* repetitions in social life. (He only contends, which is not a fair contention, that the repetitions are not the subject matter of history and therefore not history.) He says: "If, on the contrary, we are interested in *what past social facts have in common*, in the way in which social facts repeat themselves, if our purpose is to form generalizations, or *laws* concerning social activities, we employ another logical method, the method of the natural sciences. . . . The result of our work is sociology, not history." Ibid., p. 320. Thus Professor Fling not only admits repetitions, but even grants to sociology the privilege of studying them and even of evolving "laws" out of them.

[29] Catlin, op. cit., pp. 39-41.

features. And we build on this commonness. What we build may not exactly be science, and Signor Croce and Mr. Wells may well deny to it this title. But whatever it will be, it will, at least, be better than a philosophy of history or a utopia—more useful and more positive. The sociologist may not be able to go about the world "with the authority of a sanitary engineer",[30] but he certainly is able to render a more useful service to society, even at present, than a utopist or a philosopher of history.

I might stop to criticize Croce's distinction between form and content of history and examine his notion that science concerns itself with form rather than with content, but that would carry us far afield. The above remarks, I believe, are sufficient, as far as the topic of this paper is concerned. I may only add that the viewpoint which I have developed in previous sections of this chapter, fully recognizes such limitations as those pointed out by Croce and Wells. Especially, when I deny the possibility of universal laws of social change, when I insist that the study of such change be limited to specific culture areas and traits, and when I admit that the principles deduced from such studies will naturally be limited by the nature of the particular culture and the particular trait, the criticism of Croce, Wells, and others hardly applies to the point of view presented in this paper.

[30] In the same paper which I mentioned above, Mr. Wells avers "that all this talk of the organization of sociology, as though presently the sociologist would be going about the world with the authority of a sanitary engineer, is and will remain nonsense".

IV

CONCLUSIONS

What Is Cultural Change?

I raised this question once before without supplying an answer. Culture has been defined as the complex whole that includes material goods, knowledge, belief, art, morals, law, custom, and any other capabilities and habits acquired by man as a member of society.[1] This definition does not express, but perhaps implies, the significant fact that people who belong to the same culture have similar habits, customs, beliefs, etc. It is not denied that these people do not have individual habitudinal differences at all. But, unfortunately, it is exceedingly difficult for the sociologist to make any scientific use of those individual eccentricities. He deals in large numbers and averages. A common fallacy is to say that sociology is the study of "group behaviour". Rather, it is the study of those individual behaviours which are *coenotropic*. He studies them, in fact he is *able* to study them, precisely because they are common in the group. Furthermore, if there were no individual habits, beliefs, etc., which were shared by several individuals at the same time, there could be no sociology. Therefore, for practical purposes we may say that the culture of a group is that complex whole of practices, beliefs, material goods, etc., which are fairly widespread in that group. And a change in this culture would occur when a new folkway or belief, etc., has been adopted by a fairly large number of people who belonged to this culture, or when a widely held belief or a common practice has disappeared or nearly disappeared. It is impossible to fix categorically the amount of widespreadness, or the lack of widespreadness, which may be said to constitute cultural change. The important point to note is that there must be a change in the *commonly* shared habits, beliefs, etc., before a cultural change may be said to have happened. Those habits, etc., which are absolutely individual may change and alter, but from practical considerations they have to be left out. This is unfortunate, because such practices and beliefs have no insignificant effect on the trend of social movement. But who can make anything out of thousands of eccentricities which cannot be classified at all?

Having made the concept of cultural change somewhat clearer we may turn to inquire how it is brought about. It seems to me that there are three types of processes which together constitute the larger process of cultural change. First, a variation is originated in some of the cultural traits. Second, this variation is diffused in the group. Third, some previously established culture trait is gradually eliminated from group practice. If the first occurs and the second does not, we have no cultural change; and, of course, the second cannot occur without the first. The third, while it appears independent of the other two, may in fact be closely related to them. It is

[1] [E.B.] Tylor's definition as modified by Malcolm Willey. See Barnes and Davis (eds.) *Introduction to Sociology*, p. 513.

true, however, that if only the first two occurred, there would be cultural change, or again, if only the last one occurred there still would be this change. In reality, however, these go together and have almost a functional relationship.

In this paper we are concerned chiefly with the first problem, which we will simply call the "problem of the origin of cultural variation". But before entering into it we shall briefly touch upon the other two.

It appears to the writer that as far as the immediate destiny of culture is concerned it does not depend on the origin of new variations or inventions. It depends upon which of the variations already originated will be accepted by the group. This seems to have been almost overlooked by students of social change. Here is a variation—municipal ownership. Will it be accepted or not? Here is another variation—companionate marriage. Will it be accepted? Here is another—internationalism. How about that? Numerous other examples may be cited, but these will do.

It is a commonplace observation that out of numerous variations, or to use the more popular term, inventions, only a very few are actually adopted. Here is a major problem for the students of social change. What are the principles of primary diffusion?[2] Here again our results will be only empirical and limited in their applicability—limited by the peculiar character of each specific culture. An advance in the direction of such a study has been made by Dr. Dixon in his *Building of Cultures*[3] even though his discussion is general rather than specific.

Much the same thing can be said about the third process, though with less emphasis. We generally are not much concerned about the disappearance of existing culture traits. But wherever social values are concerned this statement is far from being true. We *are*, or some people are, most terribly concerned about the decline of democracy or of religion, or of established family mores and so on. Here again there is the enticing question, why do some cultural traits begin to lose hold of the people till they finally disappear?

It may be presumptuous for me to think so, but I believe that, had the problem of cultural change been approached in a manner similar to that which I have outlined instead of being explained in terms of crisis, invention, intercommunication, etc., we would have had by this time a fairly coherent mass of facts and principles so as to be able to lift the stigma of infecundity[4] that has attached to sociology for so long.

It seems necessary to point out again that these processes are not to be studied in general terms. That is, we should not concern ourselves with diffusion and decline as general processes and with formulating "laws" of diffusion and decline. What needs be done is to study them in relation with particular traits, so as to yield such information as, such and such traits under such and such conditions decline and

[2] The diffusion of an indigenous invention in the group in which it was invented has been called by Dixon "primary diffusion". See his *The Building of Cultures*, Ch. 3.

[3] Dixon, R.B., *The Building of Cultures*, Ch. 3.

[4] "Modern sociologists are rather to be blamed not so much for the illusion in which they are involved when they talk of an impossible science of sociology, as for the infecundity which almost always accompanies their illusion." Croce, B., *Aesthetic*, p. 40.

such and such variations under such and such conditions are adopted or diffused. It is this type of knowledge that will throw light upon the future destiny of society.

Now, to come to our main problem—the origin of variations. What can be said about it? From the tenor of my argument it must be clear that I believe that the next step in the solution of our problem lies in the direction of fieldwork. We must take social changes that are occurring at present and explain them not in terms of genius or original nature, the brain of man or his free hands, but in terms of previous social situations. What is needed is detailed, minute, work and interpretation rather than mere description. The work that is being done in America under the leadership of Professor Ogburn is almost wholly descriptive. This is not enough. We must interpret these changes. If we commit mistakes, later workers in the field will, at least, profit by them. The immediate value of such work will not lie in the results obtained but in the method of study that will slowly emerge. At present there is hardly any method that is adequate. The anthropologists have made some advances in this line. [Leslie] Spier in his study of ghost dances, [Robert Harry] Lowie in his study of the sib and the family. [Clark] Wissler in his *Influence of the horse upon Plains Indians.* [V.G.] Bogoraz in his *Chukehee* (the influence of reindeer culture) have shown the anthropological approach to the study of change. Professor Chapin has made valuable suggestions about the quantitative approach to the problem. *Middletown* by R.S. Lynd and H.M. Lynd which is said to represent the first attempt to apply the method of anthropology to civilization,[5] makes a comparative study of the *Middletown* of 1890 and 1924. But all this is a mere beginning and a lot of it will have to be cast aside as we progress.

I said above that the student of social change must take to fieldwork. This is not quite true. Another valuable field for him is the mass of anthropological data that has collected. These should be studied and recorded changes interpreted as closely as possible. In his preface to *Primitive Art* Professor [F.] Boas writes that the popular belief that primitive cultures are static is wholly unfounded. Primitive culture does change and sometimes very rapidly. If this is so, and if the changes have been carefully recorded it may be possible to gain something from the anthropological data.

A third field, of course, is written history. And had historians been wiser, history might have been a much more valuable source of study than it is at present.

By way of conclusion, I may add that there are two complementary approaches to the study of cultural evolution, as I have shown above. First, the reduction of the process into minor processes. This has been done to sufficient satisfaction. Almost every writer recognizes some such classification of these processes as that I gave above, namely, variation, diffusion, elimination. For instance, Keller thinks the process as of societal evolution is made of the processes of variation, selection (automatic, rational and counter), transmission and adaptation; Chapin thinks it is made up of invention, accumulation, selection, and diffusion; and so on. These are sufficiently alike to indicate that this aspect of the problem—the easiest aspect—is near solution. The other part of the problem is to classify culture traits and study each class in relation with variation, diffusion and elimination, thus getting, perhaps,

[5] See Clark Wissler's foreword to *Middletown.*

an empirical law of the evolution of each. Of course, attention should be concentrated upon the study of the more vital aspects of social life. The study of the evolution of housing or of the evolution of a tin can does not promise much social good. Those who want truth for its own sake may perhaps be impatient with my repeated emphasis on utility. I think, however, that science should be made subject to social values and considerations of social welfare, even at the cost of some interesting but useless truth.

V

SOME RECENT WORKS ON SOCIAL EVOLUTION

The writer does not know of any worthwhile history, that has been written of the theories of social change. A number of works have summarized theories of social progress. The more outstanding of these are [A.J.] Todd's *Theories of Social Progress*, [L.M.] Bristol's *Social Adaptation*, [V.] Weatherly's *Social Progress* and [J.B.] Bury's *The Idea of Progress*. All of these books also present as is unavoidable, some theories of social change. Professor Ellwood has written a short history of the theories of social evolution which appeared in the *American Journal of Sociology*, Vol. 23, pp. 779-800. An enlarged version of the article appears as Chapter IV of his *Cultural Evolution.* Floyd N. House in his recent book *The Range of Social Theory* devotes a chapter to the theories of social evolution. And, of course, almost every elementary textbook in sociology at least mentions a few of these theories. But no complete and satisfactory history has been published yet. This I believe, is a serious impediment to the development of social theory in this department. An authentic and exhaustive history of these theories would save much of the time and labour of the student who intends to do further work in this field. So much by way of preface.

In the present chapter I do intend, of course, to remove the impediment which I pointed out above. Here I shall merely summarize some recent writings on this topic. I shall do so not with the pretence of writing a history of the recent theories, but merely to indicate, by selecting a few of the more outstanding works, the status that sociological research has reached in this department. Also I wish, by doing so, to illustrate concretely the general criticism that I made in the previous chapters.

One of the most interesting and stimulating books in social theory is Ross' *Foundations of Sociology,* which is made up of reprints of articles published in periodicals towards the close of the last century and at the beginning of the present. Most of these appeared in the *American Journal of Sociology.* Chapter VIII of this book is entitled "The Factors of Social Change" and is made of three articles which appeared in the May, July and September numbers of the *Am. Jour. Soc.* Though written exactly a quarter of a century ago, these articles represent, in my opinion, the best treatment of this subject.

To begin with, Ross distinguishes between the cause of a social phenomenon and the cause of a *change* in this phenomenon. And he says that:

> The former is *human desire*. Desire is the steam which drives the machinery of society. It is behind all social activities, beneath all groupings and relationships. Its action is essentially statical. (This is similar to my own position). . . . The causes of social transformation are to be sought, not among desires, but in something of a different nature which changes their direction or modifies the framework within which they operate. The causes are the innovating example, the foreign influence, or the new knowledge, which engenders now wants, etc.[1]

[1] Ross, E.A., *Foundations of Sociology*, p. 193.

The former Ross calls "social forces" and the latter "factors of social change".

While considering Ross's factors of social change, or the causes of social transformation, one should keep in mind his definition of cause, which I quoted at the beginning of the third chapter. It is the "precipitating" factor which he calls the "cause" of what follows.

Ross divides the causes of social change into three classes: 1. statico-dynamic processes, 2. transmutations, and 3. stimuli. I shall consider them in the order given.

Changes due to *statico-dynamic processes* are those that result *incidentally* from the *normal* course of social activities.

Most of the 'functions' of society have no tendency to disturb the *status quo*. The round of love, marriage, and reproduction, so long as births and deaths balance: production, so far as it is balanced by consumption; exchange, so long as the argosies of commerce carry goods, but not ideas; education, so far as it passes on the traditional culture—these, together with recreation, social intercourse, worship, social control, government and the administration of justice, are essentially statical. They might conceivably go on forever without producing change.[2]

But certain of these "regular processes" "leave behind them as by-product a permanent effect, and in time these effects must accumulate until they strain and warp social structure".[3] This point is convincingly backed by illustrations:

Hunting, by selective elimination of the loss cautious creatures, eventually makes the game scarcer and shyer, and so renders the chase a more precarious mode of livelihood. In the pastoral stage the continual escape of wilder animals from the herd, and the consequent breeding from the more tractable tends to complete domestication, and so paves the way to agriculture... Dykes, levees, canals, drains, causeways, and roads alter the economic plane on which society rests. In China and about the Mediterranean deforestation has produced momentous changes... The destruction of the middle class, the *curiales*, in later Roman society was brought about by the prolonged operation of an iniquitous tax system which ground them slowly to powder. In the Dark Ages the short-sighted practice of rewarding military services with estates, which, at first granted for life, later becoming inheritable, eventually dissipated the resources of the crown and led to the decentralization seen in the feudal system. In the course of centuries the death-bed gifts of the rich to religious corporations accumulated a fifth of the soil of Europe in the 'dead hand' and thus profoundly modified the position of the Church.[4]

Changes due to *transmutations* are those that result from "the difficulty one generation has in accurately reproducing the copy set by its predecessor".[5]

The speech of parents being imperfectly imitated by their children, there results that accumulation of minute unnoticed changes which is described by the Law of Transmutation of vowels and consonants. Refracted through successive scribes, pictographs drift into

[2] Ross, op. cit., p. 200.
[3] Ibid., p. 200.
[4] Ross, op. cit., pp. 200-3.
[5] Ibid., p. 204.

conventional ideographic characters. . . . Coins cast at first as miniature spades or knives drift into unrecognizable shapes. An epithet of a deity comes finally to designate a new deity distinct from the old.[6]

Changes due to *stimuli* are those that are brought about by extra-social or sub-social forces. These are: (1) Growth of population, (2) Accumulation of wealth, (3) Migration to a new environment, (4) The innovating individual, (5) The contact and cross-fertilization of cultures, (6) The interaction of societies, (7) The conjugation of societies, (8) Alteration of the environment. It is needless to go into a detailed discussion of each of these. They are treated as Ross would treat a theoretical problem—with a large mixture of bold generalizations, based upon a slender foundation of haphazardly selected data.

It may be well at this point to make a few remarks about the "factor" theories of social change. First, if we take Ross' theory as an example, I fail to see why only eight extra-social factors *plus* "transmutations" and "statico-dynamic processes" should be responsible for social change. *Any* social event may be such a factor, *any* previous change may be the cause of a later change. Of course, Ross does say that "in social dynamics the sociologist may not content himself with accounting for one social change by another social change, but must follow up the causal chain link by link until he reaches either a regular social process or an extra-social factor".[7] First of all, we are not told why the sociologist must do so, secondly, no hint is given as to how this tracing backwards of causal antecedents is to be accomplished (certainly Ross has not done so himself), thirdly, I am not sure if the factors considered by Ross are the only "regular" social processes and extra-social factors to which all social changes may be traced.

Another objection that I have to these theories is that they are not usable. It is true that social interaction results in social change, but this knowledge scarcely helps us in any given case.

A third objection is that these theories are concerned only with (what their authors consider) "primary" causes of social change. Granting that there are these primary causes, it is still a mistake to think that only their knowledge alone can explain all the numerous changes in culture that we constantly witness. What we need to know is, not a few primary causes, which supposedly explain a myriad of social phenomena, but *all* the links by which these phenomena are causally related. And this leads back to such formulas as: given such and such conditions, such and such results follow.

Another criticism of these theories is that they do not analyze the process of cultural change into its component parts. Are these "factors of change" responsible for the origin of variations, their diffusion, or the elimination of already existing traits? The concept of factors is quite unclear in this respect.

A later work than Ross' *Foundations,* etc., is A.G. Keller's *Societal Evolution*. Keller's theory of social change, if he has one, is rather simple. The main purpose of his work seems not to be the exposition of such a theory, but the demonstration of the proposition that the Darwinian factors (?) of evolution "are active in the life

[6] Ross, op. cit., p. 205.

[7] Ibid., p. 192.

of societies as in that of organisms".[8] Thus he shows that there *is* variation in the folkways. (For Keller societal evolution practically means the evolution of the folkways.) Likewise he shows that the processes of selection, transmission and adaptation are also operative in society. But he does not go very far beyond this demonstration. His theory is weakest at the most vital point. The origin of variations, as we pointed out, is the basic problem. And Keller has treated it rather lightly.

> The case of societal variation reduces ultimately, then, to the mental reaction of individuals. These, unconsciously, and later to some extent consciously, throw out a series of tentatives under the stimulus of need. Certain of these tentatives cancel out at once or otherwise disappear, while others are concurred in (or, are diffused, as we would put it) and become characteristic of a group.[9]

There is no doubt that all cultural variations originate from men's minds and, therefore, are the "mental reaction of individuals".[10] But this is not saying very much. Just what determines the nature of these reactions is still unanswered, and this is *the* question before us. Aside from this inadequacy in Keller's theory there is another questionable feature of it. He assumes that changes in social phenomena are to be traced back to changes in "racial character". It must not be forgotten that they (social changes) probably go back to physical change in the individual brain, and so root in organic processes and organic evolution, and in the resultant "race-character" or temperament.[11] This is hardly tenable.

Keller, perhaps, succeeds better in his treatment of the other processes—selection, adaptation, etc. Though, here also his treatment does not rise above broad generalities. For instance, he asserts that automatic societal selection is brought about by a struggle between the exponents of the folkways that have newly sprung. Similar treatment is accorded the rest of the processes, which are, according to him, rational selection, counter-selection, transmission, and adaptation. We should keep in mind, however, that Keller is interested in merely showing that these processes are at work in human society also, as they are in the organic world. Only incidentally does he stop to ask the why and the how of these processes.

However, in his chapter on "rational selection", Keller develops an argument which is something more than a demonstration of the operation of the Darwinian "factors" in society. It is really a *theory* of societal evolution. It is based on the idea that the whole superstructure of folkways and mores is founded on those mores which have to do with the maintenance of life—the "maintenance-mores".

> The ultimate activity of society is to preserve (food, clothe, shelter, and protect—Keller) itself, and so the mores and institutions that contribute to this end are in a very real sense, fundamental. It is upon these forms as a basis that the rest of the societal structure is erected;

[8] Keller, A.G., *Societal Evolution*, p. vi (Preface).

[9] Keller, op. cit., p. 51.

[10] It should not be assumed that Keller in any way holds the individual responsible for any social change. "For the explanation of this rise and fall (of institutions) we do not look to the individual or to the limited group of individuals, except as he or they stand forth as the leading agency or exponent of the societal change. This is the only way in which the sociologist can view the 'great man in history'; he may sign an Emancipation Proclamation, but he does it only as a delegate or representative", Keller, A.G., *Societal Evolution*, pp. 54-5.

[11] Ibid., p. 51.

and the form of the superstructure *cannot vary* (our emphasis) except in detail from the type conditioned by the character of the foundation.[12]

If this is true we can at once see how societal changes must be brought about: The foundation undergoes changes, which cause the whole superstructure to be modified. That is, maintenance mores are the independent variables, and therefore, the prime initiators of all other social changes. Now, the question remains to answer, why do the maintenance-mores themselves change? Keller holds that the very nature of these mores is such that, in the first place, they do not resist change, as many other mores do, and in the second place, man seeks to change them deliberately. This is so, because the maintenance-mores can be put to objective test and rejected or modified accordingly; whereas, in the case of the other mores testing is not possible at all—at least not in a very tangible fashion.

It is conceivable that society could live on for a long time under almost any religious form or marriage-system, without seeing it subjected to some visible and conclusive test. But this is not so when we have to do with the institutions crystallized out of the mores of societal self-maintenance. If the mores lead to such ill success in the struggle for existence that the group in question is weakened in number or vitality, annihilation or subjugation is at hand.[13]

Therefore, "invention has never been widely effective except in the range of the primary societal forms. In fact it has been confined largely, and has become recognizedly successful and cumulative only in the development of the mechanical aids to the prosecution of the struggle for existence."[14]

Here is a theory of social evolution, the only criticism of which is that more factual evidence is needed to support it. If the theory is correct, it should prove to be immensely helpful. But in that case it would need to be more developed and carried farther than its general statement. It should be noted that upon the acceptance of this theory our study of social change will automatically turn into a study of social adaptation. For, if changes in subsistence mores are primary, and if all the other changes in society are dependent upon these, then it follows that these latter changes are adaptational in nature. And we will have to study this adaptation in detail, if the theory is to be made more concrete, or if it is to offer us a programme for social guidance. Both these ends will be served by only that method which studies culture traits specifically—that is, a method for which we have argued above.

Of the works which we have selected for this review, the one which comes next in chronological order is Ogburn's *Social Change.* This is a semi-popular work, conveniently summarizing sociological thought relevant to the problem of cultural change. Perhaps the original section of the book is that which contains Ogburn's concept of cultural lag—a term now quite popular with sociologists. This principle supplements Sumner's theory of "strain toward consistency", which is exhibited by the mores, by pointing out the opposite side of the situation—the situation in which the mores fail to adjust themselves.

[12] Ibid., p. 142.

[13] Keller, op. cit., p. 135.

[14] Ibid., p. 137.

Ogburn's theory of social change—if it can be called *his*—is simple. There are three main topics which he takes up in the course of his development of this theory: (1) The biological factor and the cultural factor in social change and their correlation, (2) The cumulative nature of material culture and its diversification, (3) Inventions, mental ability and culture.[15]

He gives considerable space to the first topic. His justification is that the biological factor in cultural change has been overemphasized. His conclusion with regard to this factor is that it has probably played an insignificant role since the last ice age. He argues that the presumption is in the favour of the supposition that there have not been important biological changes in man since this age. Accordingly, the cultural development that has taken place since then cannot be explained as a result of biological improvements in man.[16]

As to the second topic he shows, by presenting a brief review of the early records of culture, that material culture is cumulative, though he admits that there are many material traits which have been lost.[17]

In his treatment of the third topic he restates the well recognized principle that culture grows by invention, and he also restates the theory that Kroeber so brilliantly developed in his "Superorganic", namely, that there is an inevitability in inventions which depends on cultural conditions. Geniuses are necessary, but since they are always present in a population, in a given proportion, the nature of the various inventions that appear in the course of time can be accounted for in cultural terms only. Here again Ogburn follows Kroeber rather closely.

Perhaps we should take note before concluding the section on Ogburn, of his emphasis on material culture as a source of the larger part of social changes—a view quite similar to that of Keller, though less extreme. Especially, the modern social changes, he thinks, are initiated by inventions in material culture. He thinks that the very nature of material culture is such that it makes it more susceptible to change. His reasons are the following: In the first place, material culture is accumulative, while non-material culture does not seem to be.

> The non-material culture is so diverse that it is difficult even to make a general guess. But religion does not appear to be particularly accumulative, neither is the family organization. Art, literature, government, seem to be somewhat accumulative but probably not so much so as material culture. Science seems to be rather highly accumulative. The cumulative aspect of customs, mores, and 'ways of doing things' would appear to rest in part on the cumulative nature of material culture. It may, therefore, be that the increasing cultural base as an immediate factor in producing inventions or change may be more characteristic of material culture.[18]

Another argument in favour of this supposition is the fact that material traits are diffused and borrowed quicker and more readily than non-material traits. This is based upon the study of anthropologists, particularly, Clark Wissler.[19] In fairness

[15] Ogburn, W.F., *Social Change*, Part II.

[16] Ibid., pp. 61-6.

[17] Ibid., pp. 66-79.

[18] Ogburn, op. cit., p. 273.

[19] Ibid., pp. 273-4.

to Ogburn it should be noted that he admits that sometimes changes in the spiritual aspects of culture may, and do occur independently of material culture and even influence it.

Two years after the publication of Ogburn's book appeared *Society and Its Surplus* (sub-title: *A study in social evolution*) by N.L. Sims. This book represents quite a different approach to the problem we are considering. It can almost be called retroactive. The study of cultural change has been gradually passing from the stage of generalities to that of detailed work. Professor Sims raises a voice for a return to Spencerian theorizing. And this is the reason we include Sims' book in this review; it represents a unique type.

Sims claims that the *why* of evolution has not been given sufficient attention by sociologists; they have been busy only with its *how* and *what* (what has evolved):

> Herbert Spencer, of course, grappled with this fundamental question. The formula which he propounded in explanation of cosmic evolution . . . was a truly notable attempt to describe the operation of the primary factor in the process. . . . If it proved to be more or less inapplicable, inaccurate and inadequate, particularly when applied to things social, it does not follow that the endeavour to find an answer to the question *why* was ill-advised, and should, in consequence, be henceforth and forever avoided. However, since Spencer's attempt there has been but little interest shown in the question as to what constitutes the dynamic of social change.[20]

(This is hardly a justifiable claim. The *why* of social change is today as paramount a question with sociologists as it was in the time of Spencer. Only the interest in the search for the "fundamental" cause of change has waned; and very naturally, for the conviction has grown that such a search is fruitless.)

How can we know the *why* of evolution then? Dr. Sims has an answer.

> If, then, any fundamental explanation is to be reached, we must go back of and outside of ourselves; for the 'drives' from within taken by themselves are not enough. We need to return again to Spencer's and Comte's starting point, and from thence take our departure in quest of the motive-power and the laws governing social evolution, for possibly a more valid account than has been rendered can be given.[21]
>
> Quite certain it is that social change like change in other realms of the universe must have its driving force in energy. It is commonplace enough that every transformation is to be accounted for in terms of energy redistribution—its concentration and dissipation. The only question, then, is what constitutes effective social energy and how does it act? Our contention, already stated, is that distinctively social change derives its impulse from the presence of surplus. It is not so much the sum total of energy that a group may inventory; that is the determining factor as the amount of surplus possessed. The marginal power is the essential thing.[22]

Mr. Sims recognizes that quite an opposite theory of social change has been advanced by some—the deficit theory. And he grants that

> rightly understood, there is some validity in the deficit theory. A hungry, impoverished, and suffering social aggregate is, of course, not absolutely powerless. For so long as there is

[20] Sims, N.L., *Society and Its Surplus*, pp. 170-1.

[21] Sims, op. cit., p. 173.

[22] Ibid., p. 174.

life, some degree of action is possible; but activity without surplus is erratic and negligible. Under such conditions the normal state is essentially a static one, while surplus alone confers dynamic qualities. No doubt, from situations in which a sharp curtailment of surplus threatening exhaustion has taken place a quick rebound sometimes occurs that makes the source of change appear to lie in untoward conditions. But these conditions only act as a stimulus to the remaining surplus, while it is the presence of the latter that makes possible the response. The normal conditions of social change are always those where surplus abound.[23]

A few words about social surplus.

All living things, when possessed of more energy than the struggle for existence requires, may be said to have a surplus. Living things include, of course, aggregates of human beings or societies. In the animal and social worlds surplus becomes highly kinetic, that is, it is manifested as power in motion. In human society such is its distinguishing characteristic. All that this moans is that abundant energy will expend itself in activities. If vital surplus, activity will appear in such phenomena as multiplication of numbers, creative endeavours, a general strenuosity and push, enterprise and aggressiveness. If fullness of tradition, activity will be seen in such things as expansion of knowledge, invention, elaboration of thought systems, broadcasting of culture, propagation of faiths, and proselytizing. If an overplus of wealth, activity will take such form as quest for markets, widening of trade, concession-hunting, investment placing, philanthropic adventure, conquest. If accumulation of organization, activity will show itself in rivalry, competitive struggle, movements for union and disunion, agglomeration of forms.[24]

It is needless to follow this theory through its elaborations. Its kernel we have presented already. A good deal can be said in criticism of it, but it will suffice to say that it is factual evidence alone that can support it. We are not at all satisfied with the evidence, both as to its range and interpretation, that Dr. Sims has given. It would seem that groups that decay and decline must do so because of lack of social surplus, yet decline *is* social change and all social change is made to depend upon this surplus. The theory has found little recognition at the hands of sociologists. Also we may remark in conclusion that all that we have said with regard to *general* theories is also applicable to the present one.

A very recent work on social change in Ellwood's, *Cultural Evolution*. If I were to express myself frankly and honestly I would say that, from a theoretical point of view, this is the most worthless book written on the subject in recent years. The only excuse for including a discussion of this book in this chapter is the author's current reputation and the consequent respect with which his work is looked upon.

There are 262 pages in the book, of which some 38 cover the theoretical portion. The rest deal with stages of cultural evolution (eolithic, paleolithic, etc.), and *descriptive* accounts of the evolution of certain cultural traits and complexes, such as housing, family, religion. No attempt is made to give a *theory* of the evolution of any of these. Sometimes the *origin*[25] of some of these is discussed, followed by

[23] Sims, op. cit., p. 177.

[24] Sims, op. cit., pp. 178-9.

[25] I believe that altogether too much time is wasted on the first beginnings of social phenomena. We continue to ask such questions as, how did the family originate? and text books continue to answer them. But, in the first place, we all know that it is impossible to answer such questions, and, in the second place, outside of being interesting, the answer, even if we had it, would be worthless. It would

accounts of the various forms assumed by them in the course of cultural evolution. The value of such accounts for a theory of social change is obvious. It is not the description of the types of housing that will bring us to the knowledge of the causal factors in the evolution of housing. Studies should be made of the concrete changes in the dwellings of peoples and the explanation of these changes in terms of cultural and environmental factors should be attempted.

After many such studies have been made, it may be possible to formulate a law of the evolution of housing. Etienne B. Renaud contributed an article to *Social Forces* in which he summarized what archaeologists and anthropologists know of the evolution of south-west Indian dwellings.[26] It is a very interesting article. There seems to be a close relationship between the increase in population, invasions from without, type of industry and housing in the case of the pueblos. If more studies of this kind were made we might have been nearer to knowing the "laws" of the evolution of housing.

Before we take up Ellwood's theory we should remark that the more important portion of it is taken from W.I. Thomas. Thus in presenting Ellwood's theory I shall also be presenting Thomas'. That which constitutes Ellwood's original (sic) contribution to the theory seems to me to be mere verbosity.

Cultural evolution is a process of "collective learning",[27] that is, a "process of learning new patterns of action".[28] The method in which these patterns of behaviour are learned by the group is the following (1) the creation, under the spur of some crisis, of new patterns of action, by means of imagination and reasoning, utilizing the materials of the physical and social environment and to some extent also instinctive impulses and psychic accidents. These new patterns of action are usually formed by some individual in the group of exceptional attainments—a leader. (2) The diffusion of these new patterns of action throughout the group by means of imitation and communication. (3) The incorporation of these patterns into the traditions of the group. (4) The inculcation of this tradition in the young.[29]

The first of these steps—invention—is the keynote to the whole process. In fact, "the (very) essence of culture is invention".[30] How are inventions brought about? They appear in time of a crisis, i.e., when "something in the situation calls for a readjustment of habits".[31] When this occurs "there is focusing of consciousness upon the situation", i.e., attention is drawn towards it. Attention "calls into action all the powers of the mind" which discover the cause of the disturbance and evolve a new pattern of action to control the situation.[32] Thus crises, by focusing attention,

---

not throw any light upon any sociological problem of the present. When the family came into being man was perhaps a very different animal from what he is now, especially in his most human feature—the brain.

[26] Renaud, Etienne B., "Evolution of population and dwelling in the Indian southwest", *Social Forces*, Vol. 7, No. 2, pp. 263-70.

[27] Ellwood, *Cultural Evolution*, Chs. 3 and 4. He repeats this idea again and again in these chapters.

[28] Ibid., p. 45.

[29] Ibid., pp. 48-9.

[30] Ibid., p. 44.

[31] Ibid., p. 44.

[32] Ellwood, op. cit., pp. 44-5.

are the cause of invention, the purpose of which is control over the environment. Three other conditions which influence the character of inventions are also named by Ellwood: "As Thomas points out, three very important factors come into this process of collective learning which we call cultural evolution: (1) the presence of extraordinary individuals in the group, (2) the level of the culture of the group, and (3) the character of the ideas which are in circulation in the group."[33]

So far Thomas. Now Professor Ellwood comes with his contribution:

> What we have described in terms of crisis, attention, and control is simply the process of learning new patterns of action. This process is not confined to human beings, but is also found among many of the animals below man. Why, then, does it result in culture in the case of man, but not in the case of the brutes? There can be only one answer, which we shall have to return to later, and that is that the human mind is different from the brute mind.[34]

Further on he says:

> It would be foolish to deny the existence and the influence of those other factors, such as geographic conditions, technological environment, instincts, habits, and even 'psychic accidents'. But they give us no clear insight into the origin and development (?) of culture, because they fail to point out the *differential* factor or factors which produced this new evolutional series.

These differential factors are: (1) the superior human brain, (2) articulate speech, (3) capacity for indefinite habit formation, (4) erect posture, (5) free hands, (6) certain peculiar human instincts, such as constructiveness and curiosity.[35]

Now, one wonders who denies the fact that for the *origin* of human culture the biological endowments of man are ultimately responsible. But that is only our starting point. We *are* discussing the works of man and not of animals. We accept all that man physically is. And then we ask, why man, physically the same, does at one time and in one place have one type of culture and at another time[36] and in another place another type of culture? That culture is at all possible is, no doubt, due to what man physically is. But why cultures differ and change cannot be explained on that basis. There are other extraneous factors and these are what we are after. The sciences of social evolution and comparative ethnology are concerned with the latter conditions and not with the free hands of man or his un-opposable toes!

We shall conclude this chapter with a review of Chapin's recent work, *Cultural Change*. We cannot say that Chapin has an original theory of cultural change. The chief merit of his work is not its originality as far as a theory of change is concerned. Rather, its main contribution, and it is a very valuable one, is the attempt that it makes to introduce quantitative methods in measurement and prediction of social change.

In the concluding chapter of his book he writes: "To summarize the findings of our study we may say that the fundamental processes of cultural change are:

[33] Ibid., p. 47.

[34] Ibid., p. 45.

[35] Ellwood, op. cit., p. 68; ibid., p. 70.

[36] If too long a period has not elapsed between the two points of time.

(1) invention, (2) accumulation, (3) selection, (4) diffusion." And he adds that in the said volume he has discussed only the first two of these processes. We shall try to summarize this discussion.

The first six chapters of Chapin's book discuss "The Perspective of Man's Past", "The Accumulation of Culture", "Culture and Recorded History", "The Civilization of Greece", "The Civilization of Rome", "Medieval England". These are merely descriptive chapters, and in my opinion, may well have been left out. Chapin, however, thinks that a survey such as he has given, of civilizations was necessary for the development of his "cycle" theory. This he does in the seventh chapter. This theory is not opposed to Wissler's idea that "tribes may come and tribes may go, but culture goes on forever". Chapin, in fact, admits that "the main stream of human culture . . . is continuous", but he insists that "culture traits and complexes" go through a life-cycle of birth, growth and decay. (This undoubtedly is a sound observation, though an obvious one. Curiously enough, Chapin labours this point so much as to give the impression that he is bringing to light something which is of immense import.) To continue with the summary, however, upon this culture-trait-cycle concept Chapin bases his theory of "synchronous culture cycles". In simple words, this theory is that culture traits grow and decline at different rates, in accordance with laws which are peculiar to each, and that the said growth and decay may be cyclical or simply periodic. Also that when the growth cycles or periods of a number (perhaps a majority) of material and non-material traits are synchronous we have an era of maturity of a given cultural group.[37]

We do not find much unity between the chapters of Chapin's book. Our presentation, therefore, will be necessarily unconnected and topical. We shall take up only some of the more important topics discussed.

In Chapter 8 Chapin develops a theory of "the societal reaction pattern". This is the pattern in which groups react in changed situations. This pattern has three phases. Phase one is that in which the group tries to enforce its mores, but, owing to the requirements of a changing order, the mechanism does not work. Then the second phase starts in which various expedients are tried out. This leads to the third phase in which the group integrates its trial and error efforts into a stable plan. These conclusions are based upon a study conducted under the guidance of Chapin, of the changes in the curriculum of the State University of Iowa.

Chapters 9 and 10 are devoted to "Power Machinery and Cultural Changes", and "The Cultural Lag in the Family" respectively. The burden of these chapters is that changes have been more considerable and more frequent in material culture than in non-material culture. The reason that he has given for this opinion is the following: first, inventions and discoveries have been applied to manufacturing production (this is only a tautology, however), second, the test of an experiment with a new method in material culture is decisive and impersonal.[38] Taking up the family, Chapin says "Changes in material culture have revolutionized the family as a home environment, as a place of work, as a place of recreation and as a center of protection." Then he goes on to illustrate these changes and the problems

[37] Chapin, F.S., *Cultural Change*, pp. 210-11.

[38] Keller gives the same argument, see above p. 28.

originating from them—the problems of cultural lag in the family. He interprets the disintegration of the family in terms of these lags. The whole discussion is a valuable interpretation of a vital social change. The conclusions may be inaccurate[39] but the attempt itself is a praiseworthy one.

Chapter 11 deals with "Invention of cultural traits". Here Chapin rejects the psychological and individualistic approaches to the problem of invention. Instead of these he proposes another technique of study which "consists in utilizing: (1) an historico-statistical analysis guided by certain concepts such as (2) cultural threshold, (3) the accumulation of culture, (4) the diffusion of culture". We have already described his theory of invention in terms of cultural threshold and a precipitating factor. There is nothing new in this technique. Ogburn, Kroeber and others have insisted upon the same method.

Chapter 12—the last chapter excepting the "conclusion" chapter—is devoted to "The growth of social institutions by the accumulation of culture". It is here that Chapin makes measurable advance over previous studies. In this chapter his main problem is to *measure* the growth of institutions. This leads him to a discussion of quantitative units of growth. He does not succeed in solving the problem, but is able to demonstrate its complexity. The interest in the measurement of institutional growth is due to the fact that, if it becomes possible to represent mathematically the growth of an institution, a curve can be made to fit the data of its growth. This curve then may be used in predicting the future course of institutional growth. Chapin does not think that we can predict forthcoming discoveries. If prediction is at all possible it is to be made from the curve of cumulative growth of institutions and culture traits and complexes.

A few words may be added in criticism of Chapin. We commend his attempt to introduce mathematical technique in the prediction of cultural change. He has made a distinct contribution in this. But as far as causal analysis of social change is concerned we doubt if he has made any advances. Even the methodological problems that arise in connection with the problem have not been formulated. We should keep in mind that after all, we are not interested in prediction for its own sake. If Chapin's growth curve predicts that next year there may be a revolution in America, of what use will the prediction be unless we know the cause of revolutions? Or if the prediction is that next year there will be a great business depression, can we do anything about it unless we know what causes these depressions?[40] In other words, we must know the *cause* of social changes, that is, we must know the antecedent cultural and environmental conditions which produce a given cultural

[39] Sorokin has questioned the validity of Chapin's conclusion. See his *Contemporary Sociological Theories*, pp. 745-6.

[40] It may be urged that the mere knowledge of an imminent business depression may enable us to do something about it. That is, such a knowledge may force business men to modify their activities so that the depression would not occur or would incur in a mild form. But even in that case, would not the business man be working upon some *theory* of depression? Moreover, people in business are at present not so much interested in forestalling a depression as in saving themselves. And in so doing they indirectly may succeed in staving off. This, however, can hardly be said to be conscious control of depression. For that, we must know the causes of depressions. And this is one of the chief problems before all our economic institutes and foundations. The Pollach Foundation was expressly organized for the study of business cycles and their causes.

result. Now Chapin's curve cannot throw any light upon that. Nor does Chapin's discussion of cultural "thresholds" and "horizons" throw any light upon it. We have already shown that general discussion of the factors or the conditions of invention is almost worthless. We should add further that inventions are not the only source of social change. We have shown that the first step in social change is the origin of a social variation. Now, all social variations are not inventions. The caste system in India is disintegrating. This is a social change. But it did not begin with an invention. It grew as an unconscious adaptation to other social changes. When the Hindu villager leaves his caste-ridden countryside to find employment in a Bombay mill he finds himself in a situation which makes it difficult for him to observe his caste restrictions. When the Hindu high case travels by railroad, next to him may be sitting a pariah and he may not even know it! Even if he does there is nothing that he can do except to squeeze himself as much as possible so as to leave enough physical space between himself and the "untouchable"! Such are some of the causes of one of the most significant social changes that are taking place in India. Its origin does not lie in invention. The over-emphasis on invention in current discussions of social change disregards adaptation as a source of change, and much the more important one.

In conclusion I may add that if such knowledge about social change is available, as I have been insisting upon, we would not need a growth curve even for prediction purposes. That is, if we knew the typical antecedents of, say, a business depression, we could form a knowledge of present conditions, predict whether or not we might expect a depression in the next twelve months. Thus such knowledge makes prediction and control both possible.

BIBLIOGRAPHY

Books

Alexander, S., *Space, Time and Deity*, London, McMillan, 1920, 2 Vols.
Bagehot, W., *Physics and Politics*, New York, D. Appleton, edition of 1906.
Barnes, H.E., *History and Prospects of the Social Sciences*, New York, A. Knopf, 1926.
Barnes, H.E., *The New History and the Social Studies*, New York, Century & Co., 1925.
Bell, C., *Civilization: An Essay*, London, Chatto & Windus, 1928.
Boas, F., *The Mind of Primitive Man*, New York, W.W. Norton & Co., 1928.
Boas, F., *Primitive Art*, Oslo, H. Aschehong & Co., 1927.
Bowley, A.L., *The Nature and the Purpose of the Measurement of Social Phenomena*, London, P.S. King, 1915.
Bristol, L.M., *Social Adaptation*, Harvard University Press, 1915.
Burgess, E.W., *Functions of Socialization in Social Evolution*, Chicago, University of Chicago Press, 1916.
Bury, J.B., *The Idea of Progress*, London, McMillan, 1920.
Catlin, G.E.C., *The Science and Method of Politics*, London, K. Paul, Trench, Trubner & Co., 1927.
Chapin, F.S., *Introduction to the Study of Social Evolution: The Prehistoric Period*, New York, Century & Co., 1927.
Chapin, F.S., *Cultural Change*, New York, Century Co., 1928.
Conn, H.W., *Social Heredity and Social Evolution*, New York, Abingdon Press, 1914.
Cooley, C.H., *Social Process*, New York, Scribner's Sons, 1918.
Croce, B., *Aesthetics* (translated by D. Ainslie), London, McMillan, 1922.
Croce, B., *History: Its Theory and Practice* (translated by D. Ainslie) New York, Harcourt, Brace, 1921.
Dixon, R.B., *The Building of Cultures*, New York, Scribner's Sons, 1928.
Ellwood, C.A., *Sociology in its Psychological Aspects*, New York, Appleton, 1912.
Ellwood, C.A., *Cultural Evolution*, New York, Century Co., 1927.
Flint, Robert, *The Philosophy of History*, Vol. I, New York, 1875.
Giddings, F.H., *Principles of Sociology*, New York, McMillan Co., 1899.
Giddings, F.H., *Studies in the Theories of Human Society*, New York, McMillan , 1922.
Gineberg, Morris, *The Psychology of Society*, London, Methuen & Co., 1921.
Granger, F.S., *Historical Sociology*, London, Methuen & Co., 1911.
Hankins, E.H., *The Racial Basis of Civilization*, New York, Knopf, 1926.
Hobhouse, L.T., *Social Development*, New York, H. Holt, 1924.
Hobhouse, L.T., *Social Evolution and Political Theory*, New York, Columbia University Press, 1911.
Hobhouse, L.T., *Morals in Evolution*, London, Chapman and Hall, 1923.
House, F.N., *The Range of Social Theory*, New York, H. Holt, 1929.
Huntington, E. & Cushing, S.W., *Principles of Human Geography*, New York, John Wiley & Sons, 1921.
Huntington, E., *The Pulse of Progress*, New York, Scribner's Sons, 1926.
Keller, A.G., *Societal Evolution*, New York, McMillan, 1915.
Keller, A.G. & Sumner, W. G., *The Science of Society*, 4 Vols., Yale University Press, 1927.
Kidd, B., *Social Evolution*, New York, McMillan, 1894.
Kroeber, A.L., *Anthropology*, New York, Harcourt, Brace and Company.

Laguna, De, *The Factors of Social Evolution*, New York, F.S. Crafts, 1926.
Lichtenberger, J.P., *Development of Social Theory*, New York, Century Co., 1923.
Lynd, R.S. & Lynd, H.M., *Middletown*, New York, Harcourt, Brace and Company, 1929.
McCabe, J., *Evolution of Civilization*, London, Watts & Co., 1921.
McCabe, J., *The Evolution of Mind*, London, A.C. Black, 1910.
Marx, K., *The Critique of Political Economy*, Chicago, C.H. Kerr, 1913.
Marx, K., *The Communist Manifesto* (Numerous editions).
Marx, K., *Capital*, 3 Vols., Chicago, Charles H. Kerr (Numerous editions).
Muller-Lyer, F.C., *History of Social Development*, London, Allen & Unwin, 1920.
North, C.C., *Social Differentiation*, Chapel Hill, University of North Carolina Press, 1926.
Ogburn, W.F., *Social Change*, New York, Huebsch, 1922.
Ogburn, W.F., *Recent Social Changes*, Chicago, University of Chicago Press, 1928.
Pollard, A.F., *Factors in Modern History*, London, Constable & Co., 1926.
Rivers, A.H.L. Fox–Pitt-, *Evolution of Culture and Other Essays* (ed. by J.L. Myers), 1926.
Ross, E.A., *Foundations of Sociology*, New York, McMillan, 1908.
Rowe, H.K., *Society: Its Origin and Development*, New York, Scribner's Sons, 1916.
Russell, B., *Our Knowledge of the External World*, Chicago, The Open Court Publishing Co., 1914.
Sims, N.L., *Society and its Surplus: A Study in Social Evolution*, New York, Appleton, 1924.
Small, Albion W., *General Sociology*, Ch. 26, Chicago, University of Chicago Press, 1905.
Sorokin, P., *Contemporary Sociological Theories*, New York, Harper's, 1928.
Sorokin, P., *The Sociology of Revolution*, Philadelphia, Lippincott, 1925.
Sprague, F.H., *Laws of Social Evolution* (A Critique of Kidd), Boston, Lee and Shepard, 1895.
Sumner, W.G., *What Social Classes Owe to Each Other*, New York, Harper & Bros., 1883.
Sumner, W.G., *Folkways*, Boston, Ginn & Co., 1907.
Teggart, F.J., *The Process of History*, Yale University Press, 1918.
Teggart, F.J., *The Theory of History*, Yale University Press, 1925.
Thomas, F., *The Environmental Basis of Society*, New York, Century Co., 1925.
Thomas, W.I., *Source Book for Social Origins*, Chicago, University of Chicago Press, 1909.
Todd, A.J., *Theories of Social Progress*, New York, McMillan, 1918.
Tozzer, A.M., *Social Origins and Social Continuities*, New York, McMillan, 1925.
Ward, L.F., *Pure Sociology*, Ch. 5, New York, McMillan, 1911.
Weatherly, V., *Social Progress*, Philadelphia, Lippincott, 1926.
Williams, M., *The Social Interpretation of History*, New York, Jos. Ellner Co.
Wissler, C., *Man and Culture*, New York, Thomas Y. Crowell Company, 1923.

Articles

Allport, F.H., The Group Fallacy, Sociological Press, Hanover, N.J., 1927.
Barrows, H.H., Geography as Human Ecology, *The Annals of the Association of American Geographers*, Vol. XIII, 1923, pp. 1-14.
Bernard, L.L., Neuro-Psychic Technique in Social Evolution, *Psychological Review*, 1923.
Brigham, A.P., Problems of Geographic Influence, *The Annals of the Association of the American Geographers*, Vol. V, 1915, pp. 3-25.
Chapin, F.S., A Theory of Synchronous Culture Cycles, *Social Forces*, Vol. III, No. 4, May 1925, pp. 1-9.
Ellwood, C.A., Theories of Cultural Evolution, *American Journal of Sociology*, Vol. XXIII, No. 6.

Giddings, F.H., A Theory of Social Causation, *American Economic Association Publications*, 3rd Series, Vol. 5, No. 1, Part II. Reprinted in *Studies in Theories of Human Studies.*

Hayes, E.C., Classification of Social Phenomena, *American Journal of Sociology*, Vol. XVII, pp. 90-118, 188-205, 375-99.

Hayes, E.C., Darwinism in the Theory of Social Evolution, *American Journal of Sociology*, Vol. XXV, pp. 75-89.

Herskovitz, M.J. & Willey, M.M., The Cultural Approach to Sociology, *American Journal of Sociology*, Vol. 29, pp. 183-99.

Herskovitz, M.J., Fortuitous Present, *Survey*, Vol. 53, pp. 535-8.

Huxley, J.S., Biology and Sociology, *The Honist*, Vol. XXXIII, pp. 369-89.

Kent, C.B.R., Evolution in Human Society, *Fortnightly Review*, Vol. 99, pp. 1165-74.

Kroeber, A.L., On the Principle of Order in Civilization as Exemplified by Changes in Fashion, *The American Anthropologist*, Vol. 21, p. 3.

Kroeber, A.L., Superorganic, *The American Anthropologist*, Vol. 19, No. 2.

Kroeber, A.L., The Possibility of a Social Psychology, *American Journal of Sociology*, Vol. 23, No. 5.

Lederer, E., Social Evolution during War and Revolution, *Political Science Quarterly*, Vol. 36, pp. 9-29.

McKenzie, R.D., The Ecological Approach to the Study of the Human Community, *American Journal of Sociology*, Vol. 30, pp. 287-301.

Sorokin, Pitrim, A Survey of the Cyclical Conceptions of Social and Historical Process, *Social Forces*, Vol. 6, pp. 28-40.

Ward, L.F., Social Darwinism, *American Journal of Sociology*, Vol. 12, pp. 675-718.

Ward, L.F., Tendencies in Social Evolution, *Westminster Review*, Vol. 169, pp. 28ff.

Wells, H.G., The So-Called Science of Sociology, *Sociological Paper*, London, McMillan, 1985.

2. Letter to Mahatma Gandhi, 11 January 1930[1]

Arrah
11 January 1930

Dear Bapuji,[2]
Loving Salutations,

After leaving Lahore that day, we stayed at Bindhyabasini Babu's[3] place at Gorakhpur for two days. From there we went to Shrinagar.[4] Prabhavati[5] is still there. I came here to meet Babuji.[6] I wish to go to Allahabad or Varanasi and have a frank talk with Pandit Malaviyaji[7]. He was too busy on that day at Lahore. I want to meet him because he had said that whenever he was free, I should meet him. Secondly, since I am very keen to be at Hindu University,[8] I want that I should talk to Panditji at least once.

I also want to meet Pandit Jawaharlal[9] at Allahabad. I have great respect for him and my ideas are to a great extent similar to his. I shall, therefore, derive great satisfaction if somehow I can be with him. At Lahore I had spoken to him about the Labour Research Department[10] and he had asked me to come to Allahabad. I hope I will be going to Allahabad in a day or two from here; I am waiting for Prabhavati's letter.

Rest is fine. My health is all right though I have some cough. Hope you are fine. I am eagerly looking forward to your civil disobedience programme.[11] If at all I

[1] *Gandhi Papers* (Gandhi National Museum, New Delhi). Original in Hindi.

[2] M.K. Gandhi (1869-1948); India's greatest national leader, popularly called Mahatma Gandhi; also Bapu and Father of the Nation.

[3] Bindhyabasini Prasad Verma (1891-1943); lawyer and prominent Congress worker, Gorakhpur (U.P.); also worked in the office of the A.I.C.C. for some time.

[4] Shrinagar; village home of J.P.'s father-in-law, Braj Kishore Prasad, located in Saran (now in Siwan) district of Bihar.

[5] Prabhavati Devi (1906-73); born at Darbhanga, Bihar; daughter of Braj Kishore Prasad; married J.P., 1920; stayed at Gandhi's Ashram at Sabarmati, 1928-9, while J.P. was in the United States for higher studies; she took the vow of *brahmacharya* (celibacy) at the Ashram; jailed several times; called from Bhagalpur Jail (Bihar) in 1944 to serve Kasturba Gandhi in the Aga Khan Palace at Poona; founded Mahila Charkha Samiti, 1940, and Kamala Nehru Shishu Vihar, 1954, Patna.

[6] Harsoo Dayal (1865-1937); born at Sitabdiara, then placed in Saran district, Bihar, now in Ballia district, U.P.; father of Jayaprakash Narayan; educated at Patna; revenue assistant in the canal department in Shahabad district in Bihar.

[7] Madan Mohan Malaviya (1861-1946); born and educated at Allahabad; President, Indian National Congress, 1909, 1918, 1933, and Hindu Mahasabha, 1916, 1917, 1923, 1924, and 1926; Founder, Banaras Hindu University, 1916, and its Vice-Chancellor, 1919-39.

[8] Banaras Hindu University was founded in 1916 by Madan Mohan Malaviya.

[9] Jawaharlal Nehru (1889-1964); one of the prominent leaders of the freedom movement in India and its first Prime Minister after the achievement of independence, 1947-64.

[10] Labour Research Department was set up at the office of the A.I.C.C. (Allahabad) by Jawaharlal Nehru after he became Congress President in 1929. J.P. was appointed its Secretary in 1930.

[11] The Indian National Congress at its Lahore Session in December 1929, adopted Complete Independence as its goal and in February 1930 authorised Gandhi to launch a civil disobedience programme including non-payment of taxes. The campaign started with the Dandi March from Sabarmati Ashram on 12 March 1930.

could gather enough strength, I hope to make my humble contribution to the movement.

Seeking your blessings,
Jayaprakash

3. Letter to Mahatma Gandhi, 24 February 1930[1]

A.I.C.C. Office
52 Hewett Road
Allahabad
24 February 1930

Dear Bapuji,
Loving Salutations,

It has been long since I wrote to you and I apologize for it. I am fine and hope the same at your end, too.

I am here nearly for last one week and will start the work of the Labour Research Department from 1st March. I will be going back to Patna for a few days after arranging a house and going through my office papers, etc. After returning from there I will somehow start my work systematically.

I am starting this work but not too enthusiastically. At times I doubt whether it is right for me to devote my time to research in the present state of my country. Well, let us see how long I can repress myself.

Seeking your blessings,
Jayaprakash

Dear Bapu,
I forgot to mention something important. One of my American Professors, Dr. Herbert Adolphus Miller[2] (Professor of Sociology, Ohio State University, U.S.A.) is on tour to India. He is a gentleman and has a great sympathy for the oppressed people. He is a great friend of Masaryk,[3] the President of Czechoslovakia, and it is he who had drafted the Declaration of Independence for Czechoslovakia. He is going to Beirut, Syria, to teach after teaching in China for $4^{1}/_{2}$ months. He will be going to Ahmedabad to meet you and might stay at the Ashram[4] for a day or

[1] *Gandhi Papers* (Gandhi National Museum, New Delhi). Original in Hindi.

[2] Herbert Adolphus Miller (1875-1951); an eminent sociologist; one of J.P.'s teachers at the Ohio State University during 1927-9.

[3] Tomas Garrigue Masaryk (1850-1937); Czechoslovak statesman and philosopher; first President of Czechoslovakia, 1918-35.

[4] Satyagraha Ashram at Sabarmati established in 1915 by Gandhi. It served as his headquarters from 1915 to 1930 and as a centre for various types of constructive and educational activities in which he was interested.

two. Mrs. Miller is also accompanying him. He will write to you before leaving for Ahmedabad. If possible, kindly send someone to receive them at the station and make some arrangement for their stay at the Ashram. I shall be most grateful.

Jayaprakash

4. Circular to Secretaries of Trade Unions, 16 March 1930[1]

16 March 1930

To
The Secretaries, all 52 affiliated Trade Unions
as per Report of the A.I.T.U.C.,[2]
Ninth Session, Jharia, 1928

Dear Sir,
Our department, as you will notice, is engaged in labour research and is accordingly desirous of being in direct and close touch with labour and trade union organizations. We request you, therefore, to cooperate with us in our work by supplying us with past copies, if possible, of your publications, including reports, bulletins etc., as well as by regularly sending to us your current publications. We shall be particularly obliged if you could send us your publications for the last year, for we are now working on a Labour Year Book for 1929.

Thanking you,

Yours truly,
(J.P. Narayan)

[1] *AICC Papers* (NMML).

[2] The All India Trade Union Congress was established in 1920. Its chief objective was to cooperate with and coordinate the activities of all labour organizations in the country and to give a lead for extension of trade unionism in localities where it had not penetrated.

5. Letter to S.V. Deshpande [some date in March 1930][1]

[Some date in March 1930]

Mr. S.V. Deshpande
Secretary, All India T.U.C.
Khandke Bldg., Dadar
Bombay

Dear Mr. Deshpande,
Our department is desirous of being in direct and close touch with labour and trade

[1] *AICC Papers* (NMML).

union organizations of the country. Accordingly, as yours is the central organization, we are approaching you for cooperation in this matter. We shall feel very much obliged if you can supply us with a list of labour periodicals, bulletins, gazettes, newspapers, etc., that are published in this country in English as well as in the vernaculars by trade union or labour organizations or by public, private or government institutions. Also we wonder if you could send us the annual reports of the All India Trade Union Congresses for the years 1926, -24, -23, -22, and -21.

We also wish to draw your attention to our previous letters requesting you to supply us with the back numbers of the All India T.U.C. Bulletin. I may mention that this letter was addressed to the Secretary, All-India T.U.C., Servants of India Society Home, Sandhurst Rd., Bombay.

Thanking you,

Yours truly,
J.P. Narayan

[2] S.V. Deshpande (1900-53); left studies to join the non-cooperation movement, 1920; joined Communist Party of India, 1929; General Secretary, Bombay Girni Kamgar Union, 1929, and A.I.T.U.C., 1929; Secretary, C.P.I., 1930, and Red Trade Union Congress, 1931; arrested at Singapore while on his way to Moscow to attend the Seventh World Congress of the Communist International, 1934; later detained at Bhingar and Shevagao in Ahmadnagar district in Maharashtra till 1937; arrested during workers' strike in Bombay, 1940, and released, July 1942; member, Central Committee, C.P.I., 1951; translated into Marathi Stalin's *Foundations of Leninism* and *Economic Problems of Socialism in the USSR*.

6. Letter to R.R. Bakhale [some date in March 1930][1]

[Some date in March 1930]

Dear Mr. Bakhale,[2]
I am writing to you upon the suggestion of Pandit Jawaharlalji. No doubt Panditji has already talked to you about the labour research department of the National Congress. This department is planning to bring out annually an 'Indian Labour Year Book'. At the present time I am engaged in collecting material for such a book for 1929. At this moment I have not made sufficient progress so as to be able to ask you for definite help. I am writing this letter merely to invite your cooperation which I shall need and also to ask you for any general suggestions that you may care to make. Also, I shall feel obliged if you can point out to me relevent materials, in the shape of special reports, publications, etc., which may be of use to me.

Thanking you,

Yours truly,
J.P. Narayan

[1] *AICC Papers* (NMML).

[2] Raghunath Ramchandra Bakhale (1895-1952); became life member of the Servants of India Society, 1923; Editor, *All India Trade Union Bulletin*, 1924-9; Assistant Secretary, A.I.T.U.C., 1925-9, and its Secretary, 1929; one of the founders of Bombay Textile Labour Union, 1926, and its General Secretary for many years; member, Bombay Legislative Council, 1930-7.

7. Letter to Secretary, The League for Cultural Relations with Foreigners [some date in March 1930][1]

[Some date in March 1930]

To
The Secretary
The League for Cultural Relations with Foreigners
Moscow
U.S.S.R.

Dear Sir,
We in India, as you are well aware, are facing a big 'minorities' problem. We are therefore, naturally interested in the minority problems of other countries and in the manner these countries are solving them. Our department would be greatly indebted to you if you could send us material (in English, French & German) on your national minorities, the nature of these minorities—the problems arising from them and the way in which the Union is solving these problems.

I remain yours fraternally,
Jayaprakash

[1] *AICC Papers* (NMML).

8. Letter to Motilal Nehru, 22 May 1930[1]

22 May 1930

My dear Panditji,[2]
I am enclosing a letter of Rev. Holmes[3] of New York, addressed to Jawaharlalji,[4] which will speak for itself. Mr. Holmes is an American of great distinction and is very well regarded in all progressive circles both in Europe and America. He is a true friend of India and a seasoned crusader in the cause of peace. His

[1] *AICC Papers* (NMML).

[2] Motilal Nehru (1861-1931); prominent leader of the Congress and twice its President (1919 and 1928); father of Jawaharlal Nehru.

[3] John Haynes Holmes (1879-1964); Minister of the Community Church of New York for about half a century; declared Gandhi 'the greatest man in the world today' in a famous sermon, 1921; drew parallel between the lives of Jesus and Gandhi; went to London to meet Gandhi, 1931; conferred Community Church Medal on Gandhi for distinguished religious service, 1932; staged his play *If This be Treason*, a passionate plea for a Gandhian solution to problems of war and peace, 1935; visited India, 1947; Gandhi regarded him as his 'conscience keeper'; publications include: *My Gandhi* and *I Speak for Myself.*

[4] The letter of John H. Holmes dated 14 April 1930 addressed to Jawaharlal Nehru was sent to Motilal Nehru who was the Acting President of the Congress in the absence of Jawaharlal Nehru imprisoned in Naini Central Prison in connection with the civil disobedience movement.

suggestion,[5] which is an excellent one, should therefore receive your serious attention. Of course a man of Lalaji's[6] calibre cannot be spared at this juncture, but even so the question of sending an able and honest representative of the Congress to the States should be seriously considered.

With regards,

Yours sincerely,
Jayaprakash

[5] In his letter John H. Holmes had suggested that Sailendra Nath Ghose be replaced by some Indian leader of the stature of Lajpat Rai as the spokesman of Indian independence in the United States. A copy of this letter was also sent to Gandhi.

[6] Lajpat Rai (1865-1928); prominent leader of the Congress and its President, 1920; Founder, Servants of the People Society, 1920; President, Hindu Mahasabha, 1925.

9. Letter to John Haynes Holmes, 22 May 1930[1]

22 May 1930

Dear Rev. Holmes,

Your letter of 14th April to Mr. Nehru to hand. You surely have learned already of the arrest of Mr. Nehru and his imprisonment for a term of six months. It is a queer coincidence, you will notice, that the President was arrested on the very day on which you were writing to him!

The savage feuds which rage incessantly among the Hindus of New York, especially—and unfortunately—in that very section of them from which one expects a more decent, a more intelligent behaviour, are well known to me for I have lived in the States for seven years and have even spent a few months in New York. It is deplorable, but I am afraid irremediable. The suggestion which you make in your letter is an excellent one and I personally am in complete sympathy with it. However, I doubt if at this juncture there is in India any one of the calibre of Lala Lajpat Rai, or even approaching his greatness whose services can be spared. Even if there were such a man available I doubt if the Indian Government would issue a passport to him in these turbulent days. However I am putting this matter before Pandit Motilal Nehru, the father of Pandit Jawaharlal Nehru and the Acting President of the Indian National Congress. I myself am hoping that some one may be found who may go to the United States as our representative and in whom we may have complete faith. But if that is not possible, I am afraid, we will have solely to rely upon the support of our American friends. The efforts that these friends have already made, under your leadership, in the behalf of India, have placed the Indian people under the deepest obligations to them and to you. I take this opportunity here to express this sense of obligation. And I wish to thank you particularly for the fresh

[1] *AICC Papers* (NMML).

assurance you have given us to continue the valued support which you have unremittingly lent to our cause.

I do not know in what form and in what proportion you are getting news from India these days. I am sure you are receiving neither full nor accurate reports of current developments. We, who are right here in India and are working at the very centre of the Congress organization, are almost isolated. Press reports are not reliable. Our mail and telegrams are not delivered to us nor to those to whom we send them, or they are hopelessly censored. However, we are managing somehow to get as full and accurate news as possible. The war—if one may use such a barbarous term to represent the present struggle—goes on with unabated vigour. The government have apparently lost their balance which had so surprised us in the beginning. The Viceroy has promulgated three Ordinances,[2] of which the Press Ordinance is the most dreadful. Nationalist papers have been forced to suspend publication. Police terrorism has not relaxed. Even women have been assaulted, at some places in the most indecent manner. Martial Law has been declared in Sholapur (in the Bombay Presidency). In the course of the operation of this so-called law, an editor, to give only one instance, has been sentenced to seven years rigorous imprisonment and a fine of Rs. 10,000. At Peshawar and Calcutta any gathering of more than five has been declared unlawful assembly (except religious gatherings). Crowds have been fired upon without sufficient cause. Terrible things have happened at Peshawar. A peaceful crowd was fired upon for several hours, it seems, causing several deaths. A remarkable thing is that of the 65 dead bodies found by the Congress people not one had a wound in the back. Rows upon rows of men marched forward quietly to receive bullets in their chests. Much of the Peshawar happenings are yet a mystery. The Congress has appointed a Committee of enquiry,[3] but the committee have been disallowed to enter the North West Frontier. The Government also have appointed an enquiry committee but the report of this committee will hardly command the confidence of the people. Mahatmaji, as you know, has been imprisoned without trial for an indefinite term. From today's report it appears that Mrs. Sarojini Naidu[4] has also been arrested. Previously two other ladies of distinction were arrested, viz., Ms. Kamala Devi Chattopadhyaya,[5] one of the Indian

[2] To curb the civil disobedience movement the Viceroy Lord Irwin promulgated three ordinances in 1930: *Bengal Ordinance* on 19 April to suppress terrorist outrages and *Press Ordinance* on 27 April to provide better control of the press. It was applied with great rigour, specially in the Punjab and Bengal; and *Sholapur Martial Law Ordinance* on 15 May to regulate the military administration.

[3] The Indian National Congress appointed the Peshawar Enquiry Committee in May 1930 with V.J. Patel as Chairman to enquire into and report on the events preceding and following the happenings at Peshawar on 23 April 1930. The committee submitted its report on 25 June 1930. It reported that the most barbarous atrocities were committed on unarmed people who had taken out a non-violent procession in Peshawar on 23 April 1930 to protest against the arrest of many Congress leaders. The report was proscribed by the Government.

[4] Sarojini Naidu (1879-1949); eminent poetess and political leader; Congress President, 1925; Governor, U.P., 1947-9.

[5] Kamaladevi Chattopadhyay (1903-88); one of the founders of the Congress Socialist Party, and member of its National Executive, 1934-9; Chairperson, Congress Socialist Party Conference, Meerut, 1936; member, A.I.C.C. and Congress Working Committee, 1946; Organising Secretary and President of All India Women's Conference; Founder-President, Indian Co-operative Union; awarded Ramon Magsaysay Award for community leadership, 1966.

representatives at the Frankfurt Congress of the Anti-Imperialist League,[6] and Mrs. Rukmini Lakshmipathi,[7] a very prominent Indian lady and member of the All India Congress Committee. On the people's side the peaceful disobedience of government laws continues with great energy. In Gujarat several talukas have refused to pay the land revenue till the release of Gandhiji. Other taxes such as 'chowkidari' tax in Behar will soon be refused payment. In the meanwhile picketing of foreign cloth and liquor shops is going on with great vigour. In short the movement is progressing with unflagging energy. Despite some reported incidents of mob violence, such as pelting stones, the people have remained absolutely peaceful. It was given out that at Sholapur several policemen have been killed, but even the government communique says: "Nearly all rumours of hideous brutalities by the mobs which have been freely circulated are without foundation. It is not true that the policemen were tied together and burned alive, nor that one had his eyes gouged out, nor is there any suspicion whatever that two were thrown into a well. It is hoped that all the eight missing policemen will yet be found."

One of my American Professors, Dr. Herbert Adolphus Miller of Ohio State, who left India just before Gandhiji's march began, wrote to me from Bombay that nothing could stop the movement. And, so it seems. The spirit of the people is undaunted and gives promise to remain so for some time. Nothing will stop the movement.

I am sending this letter to a friend in America who will forward it to you. I am afraid that if I address it directly to you it will be held up somewhere between here and London.

With respectful regards,

Yours sincerely,
Jayaprakash Narayan

[6] Kamaladevi Chattopadhyay attended the session of the League Against Imperialism held at Frankfurt in 1929.

[7] Rukmani Ammal Lakshmipathi (1891-1951); President, Youth League, Madras; Secretary, Bharat Stri Mandal, Madras; attended 10th International Women's Suffrage Alliance Congress, Paris, 1926; participated in the national movement and imprisoned, 1930, 1932, and 1940; member, Madras Legislative Assembly, 1937-9, and 1946-51.

10. Letter to Profulla C. Mukherji, 2 June 1930[1]

2 June 1930

Dear Mr. Mukherji,[2]

Thank you for your letter of April 9. With reference to the points raised in your letter I wish to advise you that for the present there is no question whatsoever of the Congress accepting Dominion Status. The Lahore Congress took the pledge of

[1] *AICC Papers* (NMML).

[2] Profulla C. Mukherji (1884-1982); joined the swadeshi movement against the partition of Bengal,

complete independence in no unambiguous terms, and there has been no change in its policy since. Of course, the opinions of individual Congressmen, you will realize, are another matter entirely.

As to Mr. Sailen Ghosh,[3] you perhaps know that the American branch of the Indian National Congress has been disaffiliated. There can be no question of giving any official help to Mr. Ghosh under the circumstances.

The fight in India is going with unabated vigour; in fact, the fight is growing intenser (*sic*) day by day. About 3000 are in jail already, about a thousand have been wounded by lathis or bullets, a dozen ladies have been put behind prison bars, six ordinances—the Bengal Ordinance, the Press Ordinance, the Lahore Conspiracy Case Ordinance, the Martial Law Ordinance—Sholapur, the Prevention of Intimidation Ordinance (to checkmate picketing and boycott of officials etc.), the unlawful Instigation Ordinance (to forestall a no-tax campaign)—have been promulgated, several Congress Committees have been declared unlawful bodies. But in spite of these the movement is going as strong as ever. The Viceroy's announcement of the date of the Round Table Conference has left even the moderates cold and unresponsive. Some of the latter such eminent ones as Pt. Hirday Nath Kunzru,[4] and Sir Purshottamdas Thakurdas[5] have even resigned their seats in the Assembly. It would be a miracle if the movement failed.

The question of the A.I.C.C. passing a resolution regarding Mr. Blaine's efforts[6] in the behalf of India will be placed before the next sitting of the Committee.

Yours sincerely,
JPN

1905; left for the U.S., 1906; helped organize Hindustan Students' Association, 1912, and Friends of Freedom for India, 1915; became an American citizen, 1920; associated with India League of America; founded Tagore Society of New York, 1959; participated in anti-Vietnam war movements and save Bangladesh activities.

[3] Sailendra Nath Ghose (1892-1949); went to the U.S. in 1916 and worked for India's freedom for 20 years; Secretary, India Freedom Foundation, New York, 1928; President of New York branch of the Indian National Congress, 1929; returned to India in 1936 and served in various capacities in the field of education.

[4] Hirday Nath Kunzru (1887-1978); joined Servants of India Society, 1909; member, Liberal Party delegation to England, 1919, U.P. Legislative Council, 1921-3, Indian Legislative Assembly, 1927-30, and Council of States, 1937-46; President, National Liberal Federation, 1934; elected Life President, Servants of India Society, 1936; member, Constituent Assembly, 1946-9, Provisional Parliament, 1950-2, Council of States, 1952-62, States Reorganisation Commission, 1953-5, and U.G.C., 1953-66; President, Indian Council of World Affairs, 1948-78, and Indian School of International Studies, 1955-70.

[5] Purshotamdas Thakurdas (1879-1961); industrialist; member, Indian Retrenchment Committee, 1922-3, Council of State, 1922-3, Indian Legislative Assembly, 1923-30, and Royal Commission on Indian Currency and Finance, 1926; delegate to Indian Round Table Conference, 1930-2.

[6] Senator John J. Blaine introduced a resolution in the Senate of the United States on 6 January 1930 recommending early recognition of the sovereignty and independence of India by the President of the United States. The resolution was referred to the Committee on Foreign Relations.

11. Letter to Roger N. Baldwin, 11 June 1930[1]

11 June 1930

Dear Mr. Baldwin,[2]
I have opened your letter to Jawaharlal as he is in jail[3] and not permitted to receive letters in the usual course. He is allowed to write and receive letters only once every fortnight and naturally the privilege is availed of by the family.

He is also allowed to be interviewed every fortnight by not more than three members of the family, which means father, mother and wife. I shall communicate the contents of your letter to him at our next meeting.

You will be glad to hear that he is fairly well treated in the jail and is allowed to have six books at a time, and all kinds of food and clothing that he may wish to have from outside. Except as regards the books, however, he does not take advantage of the latitude shown to him. He is keeping good health and is writing another book for children.

With good wishes,

Yours sincerely,
Jayaprakash Narayan

[1] *AICC Papers* (NMML).

[2] Roger N. Baldwin (1884-1981); American reformer; Secretary, Civic League of St. Louis, 1910-17; Founder-Director, American Civil Liberties Union, 1920-50.

[3] Jawaharlal Nehru was jailed in Naini Central Prison, Allahabad, 14 April-11 October 1930.

12. Letter to Govind Malaviya, 28 September 1930[1]

P.O. Sitabdiara
Dist. Saran
28 September 1930

Dear Govindji,[2]
My mother[3] expired on the 25th at Patna. Her death has completely unnerved me; it is impossible for me to do any kind of work at present. Therefore, much as I regret it, I beg to tender my resignation[4] to you. You may perhaps know that I owe nearly Rs. 250 to the office. I shall straighten up this matter as soon as I am physically able to go to Allahabad.

With kindest regards,

Yours sincerely,
Jayaprakash

[1] *AICC Papers* (NMML).

[2] Govind Malaviya (1902-61); youngest son of Madan Mohan Malaviya; one of the prominent Congress leaders in U.P.; Acting General Secretary, A.I.C.C., 1930-1; member, U.P. Legislative Assembly, 1937-45, Indian Legislative Assembly, 1945-6, Constituent Assembly, 1946-50, and Provisional Parliament, 1950-2; Pro. Vice-Chancellor, Banaras Hindu University, 1948, and its Vice-Chancellor, 1949-51.

[3] Phul Rani Devi, who died on 25 September 1930.

[4] J.P. tendered his resignation as secretary of the Labour Research Department of the Indian National Congress.

13. Circular to Presidents of all Provincial Congress Committees, 29 April 1932[1]

Circular No. 9

Bombay
29 April 1932

To
The Presidents of all Provincial Congress Committees

Dear Friend,
It has been decided to publish a full report of the 46th Session at Delhi. Among other things it will contain photographs of the session taken on the occasion and it being a momentous session we mean to publish the names of the delegates who braving all odds undertook to venture up to Delhi. You are hereby requested to supply information on the following points:

1. Number of delegates nominated by you to represent your province with full names;
2. Number of persons arrested
   (a) at starting station
   (b) on the way
   (c) at Delhi while attending the session.
3. Names of persons who succeeded in attending the session in spite of notices restraining their movements;
4. Names of persons arrested while defying such restraint notices in order to be present in Delhi;
5. Names of lady delegates, if any.

Any other information re.: activity in your province in connection with the Delhi session.

It is requested that the above information be sent as soon as possible.

Yours sincerely,
Jayaprakash Narayan
Ag. General Secretary

P.S.
Some provinces have not sent the report of their activity during the National Week.[2] You are requested to send the report early if not already sent.

[1] *AICC Papers* (NMML).

[2] National Week was celebrated from 6 April to 13 April during the national movement in remembrance of the first nationwide protest against the Rowlatt Bills on 6 April 1919 and in memory of those who lost their lives in Jallianwala Bagh on 13 April 1919. Constructive programme of the Congress was strictly followed during the week with prayers and fasting and complete hartal on 13 April.

14. Circular to Presidents of all Provincial Congress Committees, 9 May 1932[1]

Circular No. 10

Bombay
9 May 1932

To
The Presidents of all Provincial Congress Committees

Dear Friend,
The Acting President[2] has decided that the 24th of May 1932 should be observed as the "Congress Day" all over the country. Meetings should be organised in every town and village at which the resolution of the last Delhi Congress should be read and confirmed. We have sent you copies of the resolutions which have to be translated into your vernacular and distributed as widely as possible. Along with the resolutions other literature relating to the session, e.g., the address of the Chairman of the Reception Committee,[3] the Report of the Indian National Congress for the year 1931-32 and the reply of the present Acting President to Sir Samuel Hoare,[4] should also be distributed wherever possible. This office shall try to supply as many copies as it can possibly do. But owing to the difficulties in arranging the delivery of packages, we may not be able to send you adequate number of copies. You will therefore have to depend mostly on your own resources to multiply the copies that we are able to send.

The holding of a meeting is the essential part of the day's programme and therefore no efforts should be spared to hold a successful meeting in spite of the Government ban wherever it exists.

Some provinces have decided to hold their conferences during the last week of this month. In such cases the dates of the conferences should be so fixed as to coincide with the Congress Day.

[1] *AICC Papers* (NMML).

[2] Sarojini Naidu.

[3] Pyare Lal Sharma (1873-1941); leading criminal lawyer of Meerut district; joined the Congress, 1905; gave up practice to join the non-cooperation movement and was imprisoned; Secretary, U.P.P.C.C. for a number of years; provided legal assistance to those involved in Meerut Conspiracy Case; President, Delhi P.C.C. for some time; Chairman, Reception Committee of Delhi Congress Session, 1932; member, U.P. Legislative Assembly, 1937-8, and Minister of Education, U.P., 28 August 1937-2 March 1938; elected to Indian Legislative Assembly, July 1939; arrested for participating in the individual satyagraha, December 1940, and sentenced to imprisonment for a year; released on 4 January 1941 on grounds of ill health.

[4] Sir Samuel Hoare (1880-1959); statesman; member, British Parliament, 1910-44; Secretary of State for Air, 1922-9, 1940, for India, 1931-5, for Foreign Affairs, 1935, and for Home Office, 1937-9; member, Joint Select Committee on Indian Constitution, 1933; First Lord of Admiralty, 1936-7; Lord Privy Seal and a member of War Cabinet, 1939-40.

It is needless for me to emphasise the importance of this day; the President is confident that every effort would be made to make it a success.

Yours sincerely,
Jayaprakash Narayan
Ag. General Secretary

15. Circular to Acting Presidents of all Provincial Congress Committees, 14 May 1932[1]

Circular No. 11

Bombay
14 May 1932

To
The Acting Presidents of all Provincial Congress Committees

Dear Comrade,
The Executive of the All India Trade Union Congress has fixed May 26 for holding labour demonstrations as a protest against the repressive measures adopted by Government for suppressing the Congress and the national movement. It is possible that labour organisations may stand in need of the cooperation of the Congress in order to make the demonstrations successful. It is therefore desired that wherever such cooperation is required the Congress Committees should freely render it without at the same time doing anything which may be inconsistent with the creed and policy of the Congress.

Yours sincerely,
Jayaprakash Narayan
Ag. General Secretary

[1] *AICC Papers* (NMML).

16. Letter to Waman P. Kabadi, 19 May 1932[1]

Bombay
19 May 1932

My dear Waman,[2]
Friends here feel that if the railways can't be stopped from running there would not be much use in wasting money and time over the strike day programme. We

[1] *AICC Papers* (NMML).
[2] Waman P. Kabadi; a journalist from Bombay.

have therefore dropped the idea altogether. We shall try to do whatever is possible to bring about the railway general strike. I expect we shall be able to send some money to Mr. Ruikar[3] for propaganda work in this connection. I am also writing to Govind to see Brijesh[4] about the E.I.R. We shall also try to tackle the N.W.R. people.

Since the plan has been dropped you may return to Bombay. There may be something for you here to do. I am sending money for your travelling expenses.

Yours sincerely,
J.P.

[3] R.S. Ruikar (1895-1954); joined the Bar, 1921; participated in the civil disobedience movement and imprisoned, 1930 and 1932; President, A.I.T.U.C., 1932 and 1935; joined Forward Bloc, 1939, its General Secretary, 1948-54; participated in the Quit India movement and detained, 1942-5; member, C.P. and Berar Legislative Assembly, 1946-51; President, Hind Mazdoor Sabha, 1948.

[4] Kunwar Brajesh Singh (1908-66); associated with the trade union movement and the Congress Socialist Party in the U.P. in the thirties; worked with the Socialist Party in the forties and fifties; later joined the Communist Party.

17. Letter to R.S. Ruikar, 24 May 1932[1]

Bombay
24 May 1932

Dear Mr. Ruikar,

I wonder if you or Kabadi received my previous letter. I wrote to you to say that the one-day strike idea has been dropped but that we would do whatever little we could to precipitate the railway strike. I also said that I would be sending some money for propaganda in connection with the strike. I find that you have already begun this work. The first number of your Bulletin is really very good. I am sure that it will prove very useful. I am sending you tomorrow Rs. 250 with a messenger to be used for publicity work. What is Kabadi doing? He has not written to me since I left. I have been expecting him here every day. Please tell him to write.

I have written to a friend in U.P. to tackle Kunwar Brajesh and to a friend in Lahore to tackle the N.W.R. Let us see what happens.

I have received a copy of your letter to Panditji. I doubt very much if he would make the statement you want. He may be willing to help otherwise.

I shall be obliged if you keep me in touch with you. My address would be: (Outer cover) H.R. Pradhan Esq., Western Engineering Co., 43 Apollo Street, Fort, Bombay; (Inner cover) J.P. Narayan.

Sincerely yours,
Jayaprakash Narayan

[1] *AICC Papers* (NMML).

18. Letter to Waman P. Kabadi, 27 May 1932[1]

Bombay
27 May 1932

My dear Kabadi,

I was very much surprised to get your letter of 22nd May from Nagpur saying that you were completely in the dark about our decision and also that you were leaving for Lahore on the 22nd. The fact is that as soon as I came back to Bombay I discussed with my friends here and it was decided to drop the one-day strike idea entirely in view of the fact that it was not possible to affect the running of the railways. People here did not feel that there would be any justification for incurring such a considerable expense as Rs. 4000 if we could not stop the railways from running. I wrote accordingly to Mr. Ruikar and also to you. The letter was sent to the 'safe' address given to us by the Nagpur Congress people. It seems that that letter was intercepted. And that is how you were kept in the dark all this time. It is really a great pity that this has happened. I am afraid your trip to Lahore has been more or less needless. However, I hope that you would be able to do something with regard to the general strike. I have sent Rs. 250/- to Mr. Ruikar for publicity work in connection with the general strike. That is the most that we can do. I have also written to a friend in U.P. to do whatever he can with regard to the E.I.R.

I do not know what is your programme now but I think you had better come back unless the T.U.C. is willing to utilise you and also to bear your travelling expenses. I have paid your brother the Rs. 30 that you had borrowed from him and have also given him the thread rolls which you gave me in Nagpur. I also sent you Rs. 25/- to Ruikar's address for your travelling expenses from Nagpur to Bombay. I shall be eagerly expecting your reply.

Yours sincerely,
J.P.

[1] *AICC Papers* (NMML).

19. Circular to all Provincial Congress Committees, 11 June 1932[1]

Circular No. 14

Bombay
11 June 1932

To all Provincial Congress Committees

The following programme is suggested for the First All-India Prisoners' Day on July 4th, 1932:

[1] *AICC Papers* (NMML).

Programme for Congress Committees

The Congress Committees should call an all-day hartal in the cities and towns. In the afternoon they should organise processions. The processions should be accompanied with placards giving facts about jail atrocities, particularly about the ill-treatment of women and boys and displaying protests against them. If possible, it is desirable that some sort of demonstration should be made in front of local jails. This may be done by leading the afternoon's procession to the jail gates. The day's programme should end with a public meeting.

General Instructions

To make the day a success the Congress Committees should do a good amount of propaganda beforehand. The President's appeal should be distributed in thousands. Appeals by provincial and local dictators should also be prepared and distributed several days in advance. The Committees should also prepare small pamphlets or leaflets giving facts about conditions in their local jails and have them printed and distributed. Posters, *bhoi-patrikas* (writing on the streets) should be fully made use of.

The Committees should place the following programme before the general public:

(1) To fast on the Day.
(2) (If fasting be not possible) to take simple food as nearly approaching jail diet as possible.
(3) Not to make any purchases.
(4) Not to attend cinemas, theatres and other pleasure resorts or parties.
(5) To make the least possible use of the Post and Telegraph.
(6) To postpone travelling on the day unless absolutely necessary.
(7) To take a vow not to buy foreign cloth or goods of British manufacture.

Jayaprakash Narayan
Ag. General Secretary

SUGGESTIONS FOR POSTERS AND PLACARDS

(1)
NO
CINEMAS OR THEATRES
ON
THE PRISONERS' DAY
4TH JULY, 1932

(2)
DO YOU NOT WANT TO RELEASE
GANDHIJI
FROM PRISON?

THEN TAKE A VOW TODAY THAT YOU
WILL NOT BUY TILL HIS RELEASE A
YARD OF FOREIGN CLOTH OR A SINGLE
ARTICLE OF BRITISH MAKE.

(3) PRISONERS' DAY
JULY 4TH, 1932

PRISONERS' DAY
JULY 4TH AND THE 4TH OF EVERY MONTH

How?

(1) Can you express your loyalty to your great leader, Mahatma Gandhi, the greatest man of modern times?
(2) Can you express your sympathy with the 80 thousand of your countrymen and countrywomen suffering imprisonment?
(3) Can you help them and your Motherland in their hour of trial?

By doing the following things at least once a month and taking a vow today not to use or purchase any foreign cloth or any article of British make:

By

(1) Fasting for a day on the Prisoners' Day, July 4th and the 4th of every month.
(2) (If fasting not be possible) eating the simplest diet as nearly approaching jail ration as possible.
(3) Stopping all purchases for a day on the Prisoners' Day.
(4) Not making any use of the post and telegraphs on that Day.
(5) Not attending cinemas, theatres and other pleasure resorts and parties.
(6) Not travelling on that day unless absolutely necessary.

20. Letter to R.S. Ruikar, 12 June 1932[1]

Bombay
12 June 1932

My dear Mr. Ruikar,

I have been regularly getting your bulletins for which please accept many thanks. I have sent the last copy to the *Chronicle*.[2] Kabadi has come back but has no encouraging news about Lahore. From press interview which Jamnadas Mehta[3]

[1] *AICC Papers* (NMML).

[2] *Bombay Chronicle*, a nationalist daily of western India, founded by Pherozeshah Mehta and others in March 1913. Its publication was stopped from April 1959.

[3] Jamnadas Madhavji Mehta (1884-1955); member, A.I.C.C., 1921-31; President, Maharashtra P.C.C., 1921-3, and Bombay P.C.C., 1929-30; participated in the salt satyagraha and imprisoned, 1930; President, All India Railwaymen's Federation, 1931-44, and Indian Federation of Labour, 1941-4.

has given to the press it seems that only two more Unions need to vote for the general strike in order that the Federation may definitely resolve to declare the strike. If that is true then I think there should be no trouble at all in getting two more unions out of the six which have not balloted yet. I hope you will be able to do something about it.

I am wondering if you will be free for a couple of days. I should very much like to see you and discuss certain things with you. Then the friends who are here may also want to meet you. I have not met Dr. Gonde yet. I am anxious to sound him on the programme we had discussed in Nagpur. Please let me know immediately when I may expect you here.

My address is: (Outer cover) Mr. H.R. Pradhan, P.O. 75, Bombay. (Inner cover) For J.P. Narayan.

Yours sincerely,
J.P.

21. Letter to R.S. Ruikar, 19 June 1932[1]

Bombay
19 June 1932

Dear Mr. Ruikar,

Your letter of 15th May. I see from the papers that Jamnadas is trying his best to avert the strike. However, I feel that you have done your best and am confident that you will continue to do whatever is possible even now to force the hands of these reactionary leaders. As for your coming to Bombay I am sorry to say that I have to go out of Bombay on the 20th and don't expect to be back before a fortnight. I shall therefore suggest that you don't come here in the meantime because I doubt if any purpose would be served thereby. I should very much have liked to meet Dr. Gonde. But now I must wait for at least a fortnight before I could see him. Kabadi is still here. I am trying to find some work for him outside of Bombay so that he may be out of reach of his anxious Bombay friends. As for the local press supporting our propaganda, the *Chronicle* has already written a rather decent leader about the strike. Sadanand,[2] of course, does not understand the situation as is expected from him and is therefore very chary of writing anything about the strike. Have you received any letter from Panditji[3]?

Yours sincerely,
J.P.

[1] *AICC Papers* (NMML).

[2] Swaminathan Sadanand (1900-53); eminent journalist, noted for his ardent championship of India's freedom; founded Free Press of India News Agency, 1927; started *Free Press Journal*, 1930, *Nawabharat* (Gujarati), and *Free Press Bulletin*, Bombay, 1932.

[3] Refers perhaps to Jawaharlal Nehru.

22. Circular to Secretaries of all Provincial Congress Committees, 21 June 1932[1]

Bombay
21 June 1932

Dear Comrade,

I wish to draw your attention to two important communications from the Acting President. One is in connection with the All India Prisoners' Day on July 4th and the other in connection with a new programme for the month of July. With regard to the first I should like to stress that every attempt should be made to make the Day's celebrations as impressive as possible. Recently, there have been too many "days" celebrated and it has often been noticed that some of the celebrations have been a poor show. The Prisoners' Day especially since it coincides with the lapsing of the Ordinances, should be made the occasion for as large and impressive demonstration as possible. With adequate previous propaganda and with a bold and catching enough programme it is quite possible to achieve this result. The President's appeal should be translated into the vernaculars and widely distributed. Posters and placards have been found to be very useful means of propaganda. It is hoped that the suggestions which we have made in this regard will be found to be useful.

With regard to the new programme—the programme calling for the enrolment of thirty thousand volunteers and the 'raiding' of confiscated Congress buildings—there is little to say beyond what has already been written in the President's circular and the detailed instructions. To many of you the programme may appear to be too ambitious. Perhaps it is ambitious, but certainly not too ambitious for the Congress to take up. If we throw ourselves heart and soul into it we shall find that the programme is not at all difficult to carry out. And you can easily see what stirring effect it will have on the people and what embarrassment it will mean to the Government. The present comparative lull calls for just such an exciting and stimulating programme. Its success would mean added strength to the boycott and every other item of our programme. So let us buckle up and put our shoulders to the task!

I also wish to tell you a few things about the provincial reports. From time to time we have been making suggestions about these reports. However, we find that even yet the reports have not (barring a few exceptions) improved very much. Our general criticisms are that most of the reports are too wordy and indefinite and often appear to have been written for the press. The latter leads to exaggerations and general statements which as far as we are concerned are not only useless but also misleading. We are at war with an enemy. We ought to have, therefore, military despatches—short, precise, tersely evaluating gains and losses, so that we may be enabled to think out details of plans of attack and of means of defence. Such a statement, for instance, as "boycott movement is going very strong" helps us in no manner whatever. If instead of this ambiguous statement we were told that out of

[1] *AICC Papers* (NMML).

so many towns, in such and such of them merchants have got their foreign cloth sealed, in such and such picketing is still going on and in such and such nothing has yet been done, we would at once know where we stand and what we ought to do. In certain parts of the country there are no-rent or no-tax movements in progress. We have very little definite information about these, there being one exception perhaps, Karnatak. Precision and definiteness should be the essence of the reports. Again, it is not necessary for the P.C.Cs. to make political comments in their reports to us. Some provincial reports received as late as the end of May have devoted pages to the circumstances under which Gandhiji was arrested and the movement was revived. This is obviously irrelevant and unnecessary in a report sent to the A.I.C.C. Office. The whole purpose of the reports should be to apprise the headquarters of the true situation in the provinces so that (1) the Acting President may give effective aid and guidance to the P.C.Cs. and may take whatever other steps he may deem necessary; (2) the A.I.C.C. office could prepare on the basis of the provincial reports an all-India report for private circulation among the Congress Committees with a view to keep each committee informed of what is being done by the others; (3) the A.I.C.C. office might make use of the reports in its propaganda work by publishing accounts of the success achieved and of cases of unusual and striking atrocities. The provincial reports have not been adequately helpful in fulfilling any of these objects. Take the case of atrocities, descriptions of which find great favour with the reports. Many times it has happened that there would be a gruesome tale of some beating or something but no mention of names, dates, the place and no mention of any responsible witnesses who might have seen the affair and might be prepared to vouch for its accuracy. Obviously, we are reluctantly forced to just file away such reports without making any use of them. There are no doubt difficulties in collecting information. But we should all realise that unless we have information and facts before us our work will suffer whether that be local or central work.

Recently, the reports have shown a tendency to further deterioration. I hope you will not allow it to proceed further. The method of tabular reporting should be encouraged—information should be represented in forms of tables and charts rather than in form of essays. I am certain that it will prove helpful. Possibly we shall ourselves prepare charts and send them to you for filling out. But you should not wait for this. And please keep in mind that the reports are to be periodical, i.e., they are to review the gains and losses of a certain period and not to give each time an account from the beginning. Only figures such as those of arrests, convictions, lathi charges, firings, deaths, attachments of property, fines, etc. should be given *also* as from January. Please also try to send duplicate copies of your reports.

Perhaps you will welcome the appearance of a Boycott Supplement to the A.I.C.C. Bulletin. No. I is being sent with other papers. It only reviews India's import trade in recent years and recent months and makes a few remarks about them. I hope it will be useful in giving you a general idea of the situation. The later issues will deal with specific commodities.

Yours sincerely,
J.P. Narayan
Ag. General Secretary

23. Letter to Sri Prakasa, 18 December 1933[1]

Patna
18 December 1933

Dear Sri Prakasaji,[2]
Namaskar,

Narendra Devaji[3] had discussed with you about Socialist Research Institute and you had agreed to be on its Board. I wish we could hold a meeting of the Board so that the work of the Institute could be done systematically. The programme also has to be decided. I feel, the meeting could be called some time in January. Kindly intimate dates that suit you. Also, do you think it should be held at Patna or Benares? I am sending a copy each of the Draft Constitution of the Board and Resolutions proposed to be placed before the forthcoming meeting. There are five members on the Board as of now.

1. Yourself
2. Acharya Narendra Deva
3. Ramvriksha Benipuri[4]
4. Bisheswar Prasad Sinha[5]
5. Jayaprakash Narayan

[1] *Sri Prakasa Papers* (NMML). Original in Hindi.

[2] Sri Prakasa (1890-1971); member, A.I.C.C., 1918-45; General Secretary, U.P.P.C.C., 1928-34, and its President, 1934-5; member, Indian Legislative Assembly, 1934-45; Governor, Assam, 1949-50; member, Provisional Parliament, 1950-2; Minister of Commerce, 1950-1, and of Natural Resources and Scientific Research, 1951-2, Government of India; Governor, Madras, 1952-6, Bombay, 1956-60, and Maharashtra, 1960-2; Chancellor, Kashi Vidyapith, 1969-71.

[3] Acharya Narendra Deva (1889-1956); a close colleague of J.P.; gave up legal practice to join the non-cooperation movement, 1920; taught Indian History at Kashi Vidyapith, 1921-6, and its Principal, 1926-36; participated in the civil disobedience movement and imprisoned, 1930, and 1932-3; presided over Congress Socialist Conference, Patna, 1934; President, U.P.P.C.C., 1936-8; member, Congress Working Committee, 1936-8; associated with *Congress Socialist*, an English weekly, and *Sangharsh*, a Hindi weekly; member, U.P. Legislative Assembly, 1937-48; took part in the individual satyagraha, arrested, January 1941, and released, September 1941; participated in the Quit India movement, 1942, and detained, 1942-5; Founder-Editor, *Janavani*, 1946; Vice-Chancellor, Lucknow University, 1947-51, and Banaras Hindu University, 1951-4; Chairman, Socialist Party, 1949, and Praja Socialist Party, 1954-6; member, Rajya Sabha, 1952-6.

[4] Ramvriksh Benipuri (1902-68); gave up studies to participate in the non-cooperation movement, 1921; one of the prominent socialist leaders of Bihar; acquired national eminence as a journalist and author; edited several papers; participated in the freedom struggle and imprisoned; Founder-member, Bihar Socialist Party, 1931; substitute member, National Executive, C.S.P., 1934; President, Bihar Socialist Party Parliamentary Board, and Bihar Kisan Sabha; Vice-President, All India Kisan Sabha; member, Bihar Legislative Assembly, 1957-62.

[5] Bisheshwar Prasad Sinha (1903-94); participated in the civil disobedience movement and imprisoned, 1932; one of the founding members of the Congress Socialist Party and member of its National Executive, 1936; Secretary, Bihar C.S.P., 1935-6, U.P.C.S.P., 1937-8, and 1946; taught at Kashi Vidyapith, 1936, and 1939-42; Editor, *Sangharsh*, 1937; participated in the Quit India movement and detained, 1942-5; member, National Executive, Socialist Party, 1948; member, P.S.P.; later left politics and resumed teaching.

In my opinion Phulan Prasad Verma[6] (Advocate High Court) from Bihar and Raghukul Tilak[7] or Harihar Nath Shastri[8] from U.P. may be taken.

Rest is fine. I trust you are alright.

Yours,
Jayaprakash

Please reply at this address:
Jayaprakash Narayan
C/o Babu Brajbehari Sahay[9]
High Court Quarters
Adalatgunj, Patna

THE SOCIALIST RESEARCH INSTITUTE

Constitution

1. This Institute is founded on the conviction that the interests of the people of India—particularly of the masses—and of the Nation as a whole would be best served by the establishment of a socialist society in the country.
2. The object of the Institute is to help in the establishment of a socialist society in India by (i) propagating socialism among the people through books, pamphlets, lectures, classes, etc., (ii) studying Indian problems and disseminating the information so gathered.
3. The management and control of the Institute shall vest in a Board of . . . members.
4. The Board shall have powers to co-opt new members as well as to remove members from its rolls with the concurrence of the majority of its members.
5. The Board shall have powers to amend the constitution, frame, amend and repeal bye-laws of the Institute with the concurrence of the majority of its members.
6. The majority of the members of the Board shall form a quorum.
7. One member of the Board shall act as Executive Secretary who shall be in

[6] Phulan Prasad Verma (1900-57); participated in the national movement and suffered imprisonment, 1930, and 1942; one of the founders of Bihar Marriage League in the 1930s; Founder-member, Congress Socialist Party, 1934; was on the editorial board of *Searchlight*, Patna; President, Patna Youth League, 1937; member, Bihar Legislative Assembly and Constituent Assembly, 1946-50, Bihar University Syndicate and Senate for many years, and Damodar Valley Corporation, 1948-57.

[7] Raghukul Tilak (1900-89); lecturer, Kashi Vidyapith, 1935-8; member, U.P. Legislative Assembly, 1939-48; resigned from the Congress and U.P. Legislative Assembly, 1948; Vice-Chancellor, Kashi Vidyapith, 1971-4; Governor, Rajasthan, 1977-80.

[8] Hariharnath Shastri (1904-53); Life-member, Servants of the People Society; started, *Mazdoor*, a Hindi weekly from Kanpur, 1928; Secretary, Kanpur Mazdoor Sabha, 1929; participated in the civil disobedience movement, and jailed, 1930-1; President, A.I.T.U.C., 1933-5, and I.N.T.U.C., 1947-9; member, U.P. Legislative Council, 1937-44, U.P. Legislative Assembly and Constituent Assembly, 1946-50, Provisional Parliament, 1950-2, and Lok Sabha, 1952-3.

[9] Brajbehari Sahay; brother-in-law of J.P.; married to his elder sister Chandravati.

charge of the work of the Institute subject to the control and guidance of the Board.

Resolutions to be placed before the next meeting of the Board:

1. Resolved that the members named below shall form the Board of the Socialist Research Institute.
2. Resolved that the "Constitution" of the Socialist Research Institute be accepted.
3. Resolved that in view of the fact that the members of the Board are scattered all over the country the Executive Secretary may, by circulating among the members, gain their assent to any proposal or measure regarding the work of the Institute. Such assent gained from the majority of the members of the Board shall have the force of a regular resolution of the Board passed by the majority of its members.
4. Resolved that the Institute shall maintain a Circulating Library to be worked under the following Rules:
   (1) Books shall be lent only to the members of the Library.
   (2) Members shall be enrolled on the payment of Rs. 2/- as caution money (which shall be kept in deposit in the name of the members) and of a membership fee of Re. 1/- per year.
   (3) Members shall have to bear any expenses which may be incurred in sending them books according to their instructions.
   (4) Members shall have to pay the price of any book or books that they may lose, the price being deducted from their caution money. In case the price exceeds the amount of the caution money members shall have to pay the difference.
   (5) No books shall be issued to members who have forfeited their caution money till they make a fresh deposit of Rs. 2/-.
   (6) Books shall be issued only for a period of one month after which a fine of half-an-anna per day per book shall be charged.
   (7) Owing to the small number of books in the Library not more than one book shall be issued to one member at a time.
   (8) Valuable and rare books shall not be issued and can be consulted only at places specified in the case of each book.
   (9) A catalogue of books in the Library shall be sent to members on request.
   (10) The Head Office of the Library shall be at ______________. The address shall be ______________________________.
5. Resolved that for the time being one of the members of the Board shall act as Librarian of the Library of the Institute.
6. Resolved that Shri ______________________ be appointed Executive Secretary of the Institute.
7. Resolved that Shri ______________________ be appointed Librarian of the Institute Library.

24. Circular to Congress Socialists, 5 May 1934[1]

Patna
5 May 1934

Dear Comrade,

I have great pleasure in inviting you on behalf of the Bihar Socialist Party and in pursuance of its resolution given below,[2] to a conference of Congress socialists from all over the country to be held at Patna on 17th May. Our Party has drawn up an agenda for this conference, which is being herewith attached for your consideration, along with the Party's suggestions regarding the different items on the agenda.[3] I hope you will favour us with your presence and will intimate to the undersigned the date and time of your arrival.

Allow me to extend our invitation through you to other comrades whom you may know. We are adopting this procedure because we are not in touch with all those of our Congress friends who are interested in socialism.

Please note that we are extending our invitation to individuals only. Where a socialist party or group exists it is open to the group or party to decide whether it will send delegates or its members will attend the conference in their individual capacity. We advise the latter course for the sake of uniformity.

Yours fraternally,
Jayaprakash Narayan
Secretary
(Bihar Socialist Party)

[1] *Kamalashanker Pandya Papers* (NMML).

[2] See Appendix 3 for the resolution of the Bihar Socialist Party.

[3] See Appendix 4 for Agenda suggested by the Bihar Socialist Party for the Congress Socialist Conference, Patna, 17 May 1934.

25. Statement on Congress Working Committee Resolution, 22 June 1934[1]

The resolution of the Working Committee[2] regarding the Congress Socialist movement is shocking beyond words. It shows how reactionary the present

[1] *Bombay Chronicle*, 23 June 1934. Statement issued at Patna.

[2] The resolution passed by the Congress Working Committee at Bombay on 17-18 June 1934 declared: "Whilst the Working Committee welcomes the formation of groups representing different schools of thought, it is necessary, in view of loose talk about confiscation of private property and necessity of class war, to remind Congressmen that the Karachi resolution as finally settled by the A.I.C.C. at Bombay in August 1931, which lays down certain principles, neither contemplates confiscation of private property without just cause or compensation, nor advocacy of class war. The Working Committee is further of opinion that confiscation and class war are contrary to the Congress creed of non-violence. . . ."

J.P.'S ANCESTRAL HOME AT SITABDIARA

J.P.'S FATHER, HARSOO DAYAL

J.P.'S MOTHER, PHUL RANI DEVI

J.P.'S FATHER-IN-LAW, BRAJ KISHORE PRASAD

J.P.'S WIFE, PRABHAVATI DEVI

J.P.'S WITH WIFE, PRABHAVATI DEVI

leadership of the Congress has become. For us Socialists it can mean only one thing—the redoubling of our efforts to overthrow the leadership.

Loose talk indeed. If there has been loose talk, it is the Working Committee, which has indulged in it. It has spoken of the Socialist talking of the "necessity" of class war. It is only its colossal ignorance which could have induced it to use this language. Surely, there is no necessity of creating a thing which is ever present. It is not of class war that our programme as adopted by the Patna Conference[3] speaks but of the necessity of organising the masses on the basis of their economic interests and fighting for the removal of their immediate demands lead them to their final goal—independence and socialism.

The Working Committee talks again of "confiscation of private property". Nowhere in our Patna programme has this phrase occurred. What that programme advocates is the socialisation of the means of production, distribution and exchange. In view of this what is it if not loose talk on the part of the Working Committee to use the phrase "confiscation of private property"? Socialisation does mean abolition of private property in the means of production, distribution and exchange but certainly not the confiscation of all private property, such as a house, a table and a chair.

The Working Committee further says that confiscation of private property and class war are contrary to the Congress creed of non-violence. I do not know anything about non-violence. The creed of the Congress is the attainment of Purna Swaraj through legitimate and peaceful means. I hold that the programme of the Congress Socialists as framed by the Patna Conference in no way goes against this creed. We want definitely to ally ourselves with the oppressed classes and take part in their struggles. As for the question of confiscation of property, I have pointed out that we stand only for the abolition of private property in the means of production, distribution and exchange. This question would, however, arise only after independence has been won. Even then, the Socialists would attempt to enforce this programme through legislation.

Here it may be well to remind the Working Committee that Karachi resolution[4] also advocates State ownership of mineral resources. How this confiscation, to use the committee's own language, of the property of the mine-owners has been reconciled with their high conception of non-violence.

The Working Committee reminds Congressmen of the Karachi resolution. Is it because we may not advance beyond it? Just as Karachi passed a set of resolutions on the politico-economic policy of the Indian State so another set of resolutions can again be passed at Bombay. Why flaunt Karachi in our face?

The Working Committee says that it is contemplating a wiser and more just use of private property. We should be obliged if it would publish the result of its contemplation. I warn the people, however, that there can be no equitable, lasting and just solution of the problems of the present capitalistic society without the

[3] The first Conference of the Socialists was held at Patna on 17 May 1934 under the chairmanship of Acharya Narendra Deva.

[4] Refers to the Resolution on Fundamental Rights and Economic Programme passed at Karachi Congress, 1931.

abolition of private ownership of the means of production, distribution and exchange.

A word to my comrades. The Working Committee has thrown us a challenge. Let us accept this challenge and put forth our utmost energy to have this reactionary resolution rescinded and our programme adopted by the Bombay Congress.[5]

[5] Bombay Congress was held on 21-2 October 1934 under the presidentship of Rajendra Prasad.

26. Letter to Nabakrushna Chaudhuri, 5 July 1934[1]

5 July 1934

Dear Comrade Chaudhuri,[2]

I learnt from Masani[3] that you are taking keen interest in organisation of a Congress Socialist group in Orissa. I have also seen reports in the papers of your activities. I congratulate you for your energetic efforts.

I had asked the office at Benares to send you some copies of the draft constitution & programme of the All India Party. I hope you have received them. I wonder if you have already formed a provincial group in Orissa. If not I should like to request you to act as organising secretary for Orissa on behalf of the All India Conference. The accompanying letter[4] will be your letter of authority. I am also announcing in the papers that you have been appointed organising secretary for Utkal.

Please let me hear from you soon. I shall be glad to give you any information

[1] *Nabakrushna Chaudhuri Papers (*NMML).

[2] Nabakrushna Chaudhuri (1901-84); left studies to join the non-cooperation movement, 1921; participated in the civil disobedience movement, 1930-1 and 1932, and imprisoned; founded the Congress Socialist Party in Orissa, 1934; member, National Executive, Congress Socialist Party, 1934-7; elected to Orissa Legislative Assembly in 1937; resigned from the Assembly to lead an agitation against the repression in Talcher and Dhenkanal States, 1938; offered individual satyagraha and joined the first batch of satyagrahis in Orissa and courted arrest, December 1940; arrested for participating in the Quit India movement, 1942, and released, 1945; elected to Orissa Legislative Assembly, 1946, and became Minister of Revenue, Supply and Transport, Orissa Government, 1946-7; resigned from the Ministry and Legislature, 1948; Chief Minister, Orissa, 1950-6; later joined Sarvodaya movement; Chairman, Akhil Bharat Sarva Seva Sangh, and Institute of Gandhian Studies, Varanasi; joined movement for total revolution launched by J.P., 1974; imprisoned during Emergency, 1975.

[3] M.R. Masani (1905-98); Founder-member, Congress Socialist Party, and its Joint Secretary, 1934-9; Mayor of Bombay, 1943-4; member, Indian Legislative Assembly, 1945-7, and Constituent Assembly, 1946-8, and 1949-50; Ambassador of India in Brazil, 1948-9; member, Provisional Parliament, 1950-2, and Lok Sabha, 1957-70; General Secretary, Swatantra Party, 1960-7, and its President, 1970-1; publications include: *Our India, Socialism Reconsidered, The Communist Party of India: A Short History, The Constitution: Twentyfive Years Later, Bliss was it in that Dawn . . . , Against the Tide*, and co-author with C.Y. Chintamani of *India's Constitution at Work.*

[4] Not available.

you require in this connection. My address for the next week will be C/o Seth Jamnalal Bajaj,[5] Wardha, C.P.

Yours fraternally,
Jayaprakash Narayan

P.S.
The procedure for organisation of provincial parties is the following:

1. The enrolment of members on the basis of the programme of the All India Party.
2. Formation of district committees after a certain number of members have been enrolled.
3. Holding of a provincial conference at which the provincial party should be formed—its committee & office-bearers elected, there.

JP

[5] Jamnalal Bajaj (1889-1942); Chairman, Reception Committee, Nagpur Congress, 1920; elected Treasurer, Indian National Congress, 1920; joined the non-cooperation movement, and surrendered the title of Rai Bahadur, 1921; founded Wardha Satyagraha Ashram, 1921; led Nagpur National Flag Satyagraha, 1923, and sentenced to 18 months' imprisonment; founded Gandhi Seva Sangh, 1923; elected President, Nagpur Pradesh Congress Committee, 1924; helped found Sasta Sahitya Mandal, 1925; elected Treasurer of Charkha Sangh (All India Spinners' Association), 1925, and its President, 1927; President, All India Hindi Sahitya Sammelan, Madras, 1937, and Jaipur Rajya Praja Mandal, 1938; interned in Jaipur, 1939; imprisoned, 1941; founded Goseva Sangh at Wardha, 1942.

27. Comment on Mahatma Gandhi's Statement on Congress Working Committee Resolution, 10 July 1934[1]

The statement of Mahatma Gandhi[2] made recently at the meeting of the Gujarat Socialists discloses a much friendlier attitude than before and must be welcome to all Socialists. There is one remark in his statement about which I should like to say a few words.

Explaining the Working Committee's resolutions regarding the Congress Socialists, Mahatma Gandhi has said that the resolution applied only to those who talked of violently overthrowing the present capitalist order. The Working

[1] *Bombay Chronicle*, 13 July 1934. Statement issued at Jabalpur.

[2] Refers to the speech of Gandhi at a meeting with some Congress Socialists at Ahmedabad on 30 June 1934. Gandhi welcomed the formation of the Socialist Party within the Congress, but felt that certain items of the programme could be modified. He said that the Bombay resolution of the Congress Working Committee did not refer to *bona-fide*, non-violent Socialists, but to those who talked about violently overthrowing the present capitalist order and confiscation of property.

Committee can point out if any Socialist Congressman has advocated violent overthrowing of the present order. The entire movement throughout the country is being organised on a common and well thought out programme. That programme was drafted by the Patna Conference of the Congress Socialists and a copy of it was duly placed before the Working Committee at Patna.[3] Any criticism, therefore, of the programme of the Congress Socialists made by a responsible body like the Working Committee, should have been made, keeping in view the Patna programme.

I am quite clear that in view of Mahatma Gandhi's explanation the Working Committee must, in fairness to itself and the Congress Socialist movement, withdraw its Bombay resolution.

[3] Refers to Congress Working Committee meeting held at Patna, 18-20 May 1934.

28. Comment on Vallabhbhai Patel's Speech at Bombay, 18 July 1934[1]

I don't know the exact words used by the Sardar,[2] but if the reported version of his speech[3] is correct, then I am constrained to say that the Sardar is labouring under certain misapprehensions. Firstly, it is wrong to believe that the Socialists desire to split the Congress. In fact, to cause a split or not is in the hands of the leaders themselves. If the Working Committee persists in its attitude that the Socialist programme is against the creed of the Congress, it would mean only one thing, so far as the Working Committee is concerned, namely, that the Socialists must either give up their programme or leave the Congress. I think such an attitude would be wholly unfair and whatever the consequences it may have, it would not be Socialists who would be to blame for them. Our position is not that the Congress must accept our programme or we shall leave it. We merely place our views before the Congress and the country and, through the most proper and legitimate methods, expect to bring the Congress to our point of view. This can in no way be construed to mean causing or contemplating a split. As for creating differences, we believe that differences of opinion are vital to the growth of a body like the Congress. And I respectfully beg to differ from the Sardar when he says that it is no occasion for a

[1] *Searchlight*, 25 July 1934. Statement issued at Wardha.

[2] Vallabhbhai Patel (1875-1950); one of the most prominent leaders of the Congress during the Gandhian era; popularly called Sardar Patel since 1928 when he led the Bardoli satyagraha; President, Karachi Congress, 1931; Deputy Prime Minister of India, and Minister of Home Affairs and States, 1947-50.

[3] Vallabhbhai Patel in his speech at Bombay (published in *Bombay Chronicle*, 16 July 1934) appealed to the Congress Socialist Party not to create a split within the Congress, to go to the rural areas and work among the peasants and concentrate their energies on the struggle which was being carried on by the Congress. See also P.N. Chopra (ed.), *The Collected Works of Sardar Vallabhbhai Patel*, Vol. IV.

new programme. We believe on the contrary that if there was ever a time when a new programme, both of immediate day to day work and of an ideological nature, was required, it is the present. It is so because we must prepare for the future. We have finished one stage of our battle and now we must be ready for the next. The present constitutionalist programme of the Congress is the last programme which can prepare us for our next and final struggle. Nor can the present constructive programme of the Congress do it. Then shall our current of national effort lie stagnant? The answer of the Socialists is an emphatic "No". Their programme which includes a programme of action is the only one that can add fresh strength to our movement by rallying all anti-imperialist elements under a common banner and march them to the destined goal. The Sardar has asked us to go to the peasants. Our programme has already raised the slogan and it has added another one to it, "go to the workers". The Congress shall further ignore the immense latent force of the working class at its peril. The Congress, however, cannot, let me impress it on everyone, ask anyone to go to the workers except with a socialist programme. Finally, my answer to the Sardar's call is a "Yes". We shall go to the peasants, but we shall go to them not with a spinning wheel but with the militant force of economic programme. And I hope we shall be able to do it under the Sardar's leadership.

29. Letter to Syed Mahmud, 20 July 1934[1]

Nagpur
20 July 1934

My dear Doctor Saheb,[2]

I am enclosing an official letter which I request you to place before the Working Committee. The letter speaks for itself.

Since the resolution of the Working Committee I have been looking for your resignation. Really, I am not joking. I cannot understand how you could put [up] with such reactionary high-handed *tactics*. It would not have mattered if the Committee had said that it strongly disapproved of the socialist programme. But to say that it was against the creed of the Congress—well, that was too much for me. Already they want to drive us out—well, I hope you will fight our case in the Committee. You must get that resolution withdrawn. Has Jawaharlalji sent you any word in this connection? He must have.

I am leaving in a couple of hours for Bezwada.

With kindest regards,

Yours sincerely,
Jayaprakash

[1] *AICC Papers* (NMML).

[2] Syed Mahmud (1889-1971); joined the non-cooperation movement, 1921; member, Bihar Legislative Assembly, 1937-9, 1946-52, and Lok Sabha, 1952-62; Minister of Education and Development, 1937-9, and Development and Transport, 1946-52, Bihar Government; Minister of External Affairs, Government of India, 1954-7.

Nagpur
20 July 1934

To
The General Secretary
A.I.C.C.
Swaraj Bhawan
Allahabad

Dear Sir,
I wish to place before you, and through you before the Working Committee of the Congress, the following points with regard to the resolution of the Committee passed recently at Bombay regarding the Congress socialist movement.

1. *It was not proper, to my mind, for the Working Committee to refer to the socialist agitation as loose talk. I am not aware of any instance in which a Congress socialist has indulged in loose talk about class war or confiscation of private property or anything else.* But, even if there have been such instances, the Working Committee should not have judged the whole movement on the strength of stray instances. The proper course for the Working Committee was to take for criticism only such programmes of the socialists as have been published in their manifestos. Furthermore, the Committee could not be unaware of the fact that at the time of the Patna meeting of the A.I.C.C. an All-India conference of socialist Congressmen was held at which a unified programme was drafted to serve as a common basis for the socialist movement throughout the country. *Any criticism that the Working Committee wanted to make of the movement should have been made on a careful examination of this authoritative programme*, or, as I have already said, if the Committee so desired, of the programmes published by the various provincial groups that existed before the all India Conference.
2. I do not know what the Working Committee means by "*loose talk*". If, by it is meant such talk as is really loose in the sense of being unrelated to the principles of scientific socialism, I have nothing to say about it. I have, however, a suspicion that, in the opinion of the Committee, to talk of the established principles of socialism, such as the theory of class struggles, is itself loose talk. If, I am right in my suspicion, then I should like most respectfully to ask the Working Committee to appreciate the fact that the ideas which socialists preach are, far from being loose or irresponsible, based on a scientific analysis and understanding of the social process; they are based, in short, on a science of society—a science which has withstood the criticism of at least half a century & has steadily gained in prestige and influence, till it has come to be looked upon by millions of people the world over as their only guide and saviour. *The Working Committee may not agree with this science, but, in my humble opinion, it would be hardly dignified for it to speak of the ideas contained in this science as loose talk.*
3. The Working Committee refers to the Congress creed of "*non-violence*". I should like to point out in this connection that the Congress creed speaks of "peaceful and legitimate means" and not of non-violence. *I am drawing this distinction because I feel that non-violence as preached by Gandhiji means*

a good deal more than "peaceful & legitimate". Neither the Congress nor the overwhelming majority of Congressmen has accepted non-violence as its creed in the sense which Gandhiji attaches to it. It is likely, I say likely because I do not fully understand non-violence, that some items of our programme may not be in keeping with the spiritual & religious meaning of non-violence. Yet, it cannot be doubted by anyone who has read our programme that every single item on it is fully consistent with the present creed of the Congress.

4. It is not clear if the Working Committee meant to say that "*class war*" and "*confiscation of private property*" *are in themselves opposed to the creed of the Congress or the loose talk about them*. If the latter, nothing more need be said about it except this that in that case the resolution would have no force as far as the Congress socialist movement is concerned. If, however, class war and confiscation of property are themselves meant to be opposed to the Congress creed, I should like to make our position clear.
5. Let me take class war first. The Working Committee seems to think that socialists in their wickedness are planning to set class against class & bring unnecessary disunion and discord in the country. With all the respect that I have for the Working Committee, I am constrained to say that the Committee has completely failed to appreciate the true nature of human society. Classes or class struggles are not created by political parties. If anything political parties are the result of classes & the conflict of classes. A class, in the sense the term is used in socialist literature, comes into being independently of individual wills and desires. In every known form of social organisation, excepting the most primitive forms, men have been marked off into classes, depending upon the part they played in the process of production and the relationship they bore to the instruments & materials thereof. The formation of classes carried with it the corollary of definition of rights, privileges and duties. In every known form of society there have been classes of privilege & power & others of toil and subjection. It is here that the source of class war has lain & not in the theories of socialists. Class war existed before man discovered it and raised it into a first class sociological doctrine. Therefore, it is meaningless to speak of socialists preaching class war. Class war is there. What the socialists preach is that we must fight on the side of the oppressed. In fact, if there is any one who desires to end class war it is the socialist. He says, however, that it is possible to do so only after classes have been abolished. A classless society, i.e., a society of producers alone can be a society which is free from class war.
6. As for class war being opposed to the creed of the Congress. It can be opposed to it only if it is accompanied by violence (i.e., in the common sense of the term & not its esoteric sense). Nowhere in the programme of the Congress socialists has the use of violence been advocated. Therefore, the question of class war being opposed to the Congress creed does not arise.
7. As for "confiscation of private property", I cannot say whence the Committee has borrowed this phrase. It does not appear anywhere on our programmes. What we advocate is the socialisation of the means of production, distribution, etc. This means abolition of private property in these spheres. In other spheres

private property may exist. *The principle of socialization has already been accepted by the Congress in as much as it advocates state ownership of key industries and railways.*[3] *We merely want this principle to be extended & applied to the entire economic organization.* If this means confiscation of private property then I can only say that the Congress too has accepted the idea of consficating the property of the railroad masters & the owners of the key industries. Neither the Congress has talked of compensation nor have we, therefore no argument on that score can be introduced into the discussion. Socialization of industry, commerce, banking, agriculture through the legitimate agencies of the State can never be opposed to the present creed of the Congress.

8. Gandhiji said in the course of a statement at a Conference of Gujarat socialists *that the Working Committee's resolution referred only to those who talked of violently overthrowing the present capitalist order & of confiscation of property. The resolution of the Working Committee clearly referred to the Congress socialists, who have never talked of violence.*

In view of the above points *I appeal to the Working Committee to reconsider its previous resolution & either to withdraw it or so to modify it as to represent our case with fairness & allow us to remain within the Congress. I hope the Working Committee realises the seriousness of its resolution.* It means that if the Congress socialists do not modify their programme they must leave the Congress, for no group can remain within the Congress & have a programme opposed to its creed.

If the Working Committee desires to have any further information regarding our movement, you may invite Principal Narendra Deva, who presided over our Conference in Patna and Babu Sampurnanand[4] who is in charge of the office of the Organising Secretary of the All India Congress Socialist Party to give the desired information.

Yours faithfully,
Jayaprakash Narayan

[3] Resolution on Fundamental Rights and Economic Programme passed by the Indian National Congress at Karachi in March 1931 stated that the Swaraj Government would provide for control by the state of key industries and ownership of resources.

[4] Sampurnanand (1891-1969); Founder-member, Congress Socialist Party, 1934, Chairman of its first Conference, Bombay, 1934, member of its National Executive, 1934-6, and Joint Secretary, 1937; Minister, U.P. Government, 1938-9, and 1946-54; President, Hindi Sahitya Sammelan, Poona, 1940; Chief Minister, U.P., 1955-60; Governor, Rajasthan, 1962-7.

30. Statement on Participation in Elections, 27 July 1934[1]

The All India Conference of Congress Socialists held at Patna has not decided either for or against participation by Congress Socialists in the ensuing elections.[2]

[1] *Bombay Chronicle*, 30 July 1934. Statement issued at Ellore (Madras).

[2] Refers to Indian Legislative Assembly elections, 1934.

Therefore, it is open to individual Socialists to participate in elections in their individual capacity if they desire, but not in the name of the Socialist Party.

In principle, there is no inconsistency between Socialism and Legislative work. The question is one of tactics, so far as Socialists were concerned.

31. Genesis of Congress Socialist Group: Reply to S.K. Patil, 11 August 1934[1]

It seems to me that Mr. S.K. Patil[2] in his article[3] on the Congress Socialist Movement has attempted to do some clever election propaganda. For in no other way can I explain the deliberate confusion of issues which have been clear from the very beginning and the most unfair insinuations that he has made. Apparently the Congress Socialists have caused some serious offence to this lover of indigenous socialism, who went "mad with joy" when Jawaharlal made "an open declaration of the future economic policy of the country". When the Congress Socialists take up Jawaharlal's cry and make a similar declaration, Mr. Patil instead of rejoicing pours his wrath on them. Were not politics a proverbial field for the practice of somersaults one would have really wondered at this strange phenomenon.

Let us analyse Mr. Patil's criticism. In substance, his main point seems to be that the Congress under its present leadership is slowly moving towards socialism, therefore, there, is no need of forming a Socialist Party within the Congress, unless that party has fundamental differences with the Congress in which case again it would be futile for the party to remain within the Congress.

It is strange that Mr. Patil should display such a naive understanding of the growth of ideas and social movements. He imagines that some people at the top—two to be fair to Mr. Patil—have from time to time injected small doses of socialism into the Congress and that they would naturally continue to do it in the future, thus making it absolutely unnecessary to develop any Socialist Movement in the Congress.

I am afraid I am unable to accept this version of the radicalisation of the national movement. Its causes have been far deeper and beyond the wills of individuals. This is not the place to discuss this process, but, in short, it can be said that the entire post-war history of the world, the Russian Revolution, the Chinese movement, the labour movement in India, the Meerut case, the gradual broadening of the basis

[1] *Bombay Chronicle*, 11 August 1934.

[2] S.K. Patil (1900-81); participated in the national movement and imprisoned several times; General Secretary, Bombay P.C.C., 1929-46, and its President, 1946-56; member, Constituent Assembly, 1946-50, Provisional Parliament, 1950-2, and Lok Sabha, 1952-67, and 1969-70; Mayor of Bombay, 1949-52; member of A.I.C.C. and Congress Working Committee for several years; Minister, Government of India, 1957-67; Treasurer, A.I.C.C., 1960-4, and 1969-71.

[3] S.K. Patil in his article entitled "Where do they differ? Socialist claim analysed", published in the *Bombay Chronicle*, 10 August 1934, had questioned the need for the formation of the Congress Socialist Party. Here J.P. rebuts the main points made by Patil. See Appendix 6 for text of the article.

of the Congress, the economic depression—all these have reacted upon the Congress; and the radicalization seen in its resolutions has been the reflection of the radicalization of its ranks—more the lower ranks than the upper. It was the pressure of these ranks—the Socialist elements within the Congress—that was responsible for the Karachi resolution and not a few leaders at the top.

The time has come when these elements think that they would be more effective if they joined together and made a united effort. This, in short, is the genesis of the Congress Socialist movement. Mr. Patil is surely mistaken if he thinks that the Congress can come to accept socialism in any other way.

When complete Independence had to be made its goal, a concerted effort was needed and it bore fruit. If socialism has to be made the goal of the Congress, another concerted effort must be made. Mr. Patil, who undoubtedly calls himself some sort of socialist, wants to sit down with folded hands and watch Jawaharlal and Gandhiji bring the Congress to socialism. It is undoubtedly a more comfortable policy to adopt without any risks and losses.

A word about Pandit Jawaharlal's relation to our movement. It is being repeated "ad nauseum" by people who had no occasion to discuss the matter with Jawaharlal and have taken no trouble to find out the facts, that the Congress Socialists are exploiting Pandit Jawaharlal's name. It is said that though Jawaharlal would never have agreed to the formation of socialist groups within the Congress, these groups are taking shelter behind his name. Since the charge is often repeated, let us see what the facts are.

The facts are that Panditji fully approved of the idea of forming Socialist groups within the Congress. I can personally vouch for this because I had on several occasions discussed the matter with him.

There is then the documentary evidence of Pandit Jawaharlal's letter to Mr. M.R. Masani,[4] which has been published in the Bombay Group's Manifesto and in the Press. Here is what Jawaharlal wrote:

> I would welcome the formation of socialist groups in the Congress to influence the ideology of the Congress and the country. As you are aware, I have been laying stress on the socialist idea very much in my recent speeches and writings. I feel that the time has come when the country should face this issue and come to grips with the real economic problems which ultimately matter.

In view of all this, let the reader judge for himself who is exploiting Jawaharlal's name. Mr. Patil has made another use of Pandit Jawaharlal for creating prejudice against us. He says that our movement is responsible for Jawaharlal not being released. I do not know what manner of access Mr. Patil has to the Government's secrets, but I am constrained to say that it is most unfair for him to indulge in such tactics. The public, I am sure, would know what value to attach to them. In any case, I do not think Pandit Jawaharlal would very much appreciate the solicitude shown by Mr. Patil in the matter of his release.

Mr. Patil talks a good deal about split, re-union, "strain" on "loyalty". Let me hasten to assure Mr. Patil that all these are more imagined than real. There is no split, no re-union.

[4] For full text of the letter see *Selected Works of Jawaharlal Nehru*, Vol. 6.

The Congress Socialist groups are within the Congress and they do not desire to cause any split. There is no question of strain on loyalty because we are all loyal to the Congress and subject to its discipline—unless the question of discipline arises on the fundamental question of socialism. All we claim for ourselves is the right of criticism and propaganda. Our work, which is within the masses, can in no way conflict with the Congress programme.

Mr. Patil finally ends up by calling upon us to elucidate the issues involved. It seems too late in the day for Mr. Patil to pretend that the issues have not been clarified. In a separate article[5] I shall avail myself of this opportunity to state the issues as clearly as possible.

The Bombay Socialists are appealing to the Congress electorate this Sunday.[6] Socialists all over the country would wish to see them successful and I hope that Bombay citizens who lead India in other matters will not fail to give the lead to the country by returning every one of the candidates put up by the Bombay Party.

[5] See next item.

[6] Refers to Bombay Provincial Congress Committee elections.

32. Basic Ideas of the Congress Socialist Party: Reply to S.K. Patil, 13 August 1934[1]

There are two main ideas on which the Congress Socialist Movement is based. First, that the goal of the Congress must naturally be a free socialist state, and second, that in order to achieve even its present objects the Congress must accept a socialist programme.

Let me take up the first of these ideas first. The Congress claims to represent the masses of India, i.e., the workers and peasants. It has been the fashion recently to speak of the Congress as representing all groups and classes of people. Such talk is in keeping with the general backward swing of the Congress pendulum, but is it justified? Is it possible that an organisation can represent groups whose interests conflicts? Or shall we deny the existence of this conflict itself?

That would be an ideal solution of the problem, no doubt, but hardly consistent with reality.

No, the Congress cannot represent and fight for the rights and freedom of all classes and satisfy their respective demands. In the event of a conflict of group interests, the existence of which cannot be questioned, the Congress must, if it is true to its own professions, side with the vast millions—the masses, the peasants and workers. They are its strength and it is for their freedom that it fights or at least should fight.

And what is the freedom of the masses? Is it merely complete independence? No, along with political freedom they must also have economic freedom, i.e., an economic system in which there is no exploitation and the producers are the owners

[1] *Bombay Chronicle*, 13 August 1934.

of wealth and the instruments of its production. In other words, if we want a Swaraj for the masses that Swaraj must be based on socialism. There is no other alternative.

There is a lot of mystifying talk these days of the vagueness of socialism and the peculiar conditions of India. Indigenous socialism seems to be a favourite topic in certain quarters. I should like to emphasize that while in details a socialist system must differ from country to country, its basic principles remain the same everywhere.

Socialism is not bounded by national frontiers. It is a system of social organization which becomes applicable wherever society has reached a certain stage of development. Wherever there is large scale capitalist production socialism is bound to grow there—whether it is Japan or China or India or England.

Socialism is a remedy to cure the evils of capitalist society and wherever capitalism exists socialism is bound to grow. If in a free India we are to keep to machinery and to make full use of the modern means of production, as we must, unless we establish a dictatorship to thwart the ordinary working out of economic laws, we must have a socialist economy if we mean to do justice by the masses. And this socialist economy while undoubtedly differing from similar systems that may be found in other parts of the world must share with them their basic nature. And the basis of socialism in spite of the much talked of differences in socialist camps is the social ownership of the means of production, distribution and exchange. There can be no indigenous brand of socialism that is not based on this principle.

We are often told that while socialism may be all right, the occasion to talk about it would arise only after we have achieved independence.

We firmly believe that we will not have socialism after independence unless we make it our goal beforehand. Those who are afraid of talking about socialism now cannot be reasonably expected to apply it when they have captured power. Their class affiliation and the basis of their power will be such as will prevent them from doing it, i.e., even if they wanted to do it, which would not be likely.

It is said that the masses after achieving their independence would not fail to achieve their economic independence. Quite so. But why should masses be afraid to talk of socialism before they have achieved independence?

The present opposition of the Congress to socialism is due to the fact that it is not an organisation of the masses, but is dominated by middle class elements. The more the Congress becomes a mass organisation, the nearer will it move towards socialism.

This brings me to our second basic idea. The Congress socialist movement aims at converting the Congress into a real, mass organization. We believe that unless we build a real mass organization and a real mass movement we cannot even achieve complete independence.

And how can we bring the masses into the freedom movement. By putting some content into that freedom; raising the slogan of socialism.

So far the Congress has established no political contacts with the working class and its influence over the peasantry is none too deep. In order that a strong working class and the peasant movement may be developed we feel that we must take up a socialist programme to-day.

In this connection we hold that the present constructive programme of the Congress is wholly inadequate for the purpose of developing such a movement. Khadi, Harijan, prohibition work while all right as far as they go, cannot create a powerful mass movement in India. For this we believe that we must take up the work of organising the workers and peasants in their class organisations on the basis of their economic interests. The political consciousness and the organisational strength requisite for this can only be developed in the course of their economic struggle. They must learn from experience what their political task is.

Our purpose in organising ourselves into a party is merely to make a concerted effort, and, by spreading our ideology, to convert the Congress to our views. In the meanwhile we shall, of course, carry on our programme of work according to our strength and resources and I have no doubt in my mind that it is on the quality of our work that our success depends.

Before concluding this very brief statement of the basic ideas I must say a few words about our position with regard to the present position and programme of the Congress.

We object strongly to the manner in which reactionary elements, from the point of view even of the present ideals of the Congress, are being given prominence in the Congress and the manner in which the Congress is almost being handed over to them.

Further, while we do not object to legislative work in principle, we do not approve of the humiliating manner in which the Congress is being driven into the present Assembly. We do not think that the objects for which the Congress is to contest elections for the Assembly are consistent with the dignity and the ideals of the Congress.

Finally, we object to the manner in which the idea of a Constituent Assembly has been degraded by making it dependent on the consent of the British Government.

33. Resolution on the Constructive Programme of the Congress, 16 September 1934[1]

While not disapproving of the constructive programme as outlined by the All India Working Committee, this committee feels that it is totally inadequate as a programme intended for the achievement of independence. This committee is of the opinion that such a revolutionary mass movement can only be developed by the Congress taking up the economic problems of the masses and fighting courageously for their solution. It therefore considers it necessary that the chief constructive programme of the Congress should be the creation of or participation in workers' and peasants' organizations based on the demands of these classes.

[1] *Searchlight*, 19 September 1934. Resolution moved at a meeting of Bihar Provincial Congress Committee held at Patna, 16 September 1934.

34. Speech in support of the Resolution on Constructive Programme of the Congress, 16 September 1934[1]

I would like to make it clear at the very outset that I am not opposing the constructive programme of the Congress, but only wish to emphasise that the programme is inadequate and incomplete. I want you to seriously consider if the Congress constructive programme is not inadequate to secure political independence. I want you to look at the matter not from the point of view of whether one or other item of the programme is good or bad, but whether as a whole the programme is such as to prepare the country for freedom. I am not opposed to Khadi or untouchability, which are good enough in their way—Khadi as a means of unemployment—relief and untouchability as social service. These items do help in establishing contact with the people and create in them a sort of awakening. But a Congressman is a soldier of freedom and a revolutionary and the question is whether he should concentrate on these items to the extent it was being done. Hindu-Muslim unity is a laudable objective, but I feel that if ever it came, it would be as a result of an economic programme. If we develop a mass movement, the problem would be solved of itself. Temperance and prohibition are similarly alright as far as they go, but I for one cannot agree that political freedom is dependent on moral reform. These items may help us to swell the number of those going to jail but there they will end. A revolutionary situation is already there in the condition obtaining in the country. What I plead for is a new approach. Up till now the approach has been of social service and it is obvious that a new approach is necessary. Reconstruction can only follow from political power and we have to see if our present programme is calculated to secure that power. I do not understand what Gandhiji implies when he criticises the political exploitation of labour. The truth is that mere trade unionism is not enough; workers must also be made politically conscious. The basis of the new approach which I am advocating must be economic. That is to say, if we could organise the Kisans on the basis of their grievances and encourage them to fight for their rights, they would create a force that would know how to assert itself. The Kisans, who submitted to the Zamindars, could not be relied upon to fight the mightier force of Government. Only those would fight, who knew how to stand up for their rights. It is absurd to talk of Khadi to the Kisans of Gaya where the agrarian problems are well nigh appalling. In fighting for their rights the Kisans are bound to realise that it is the Government which stands in the way of the realisation of their rights and that these can never be achieved unless the system of present Government is brought to an end. Thus will be created real political awakening among the masses, who will soon learn how to organise themselves effectively in the course of the struggle.

[1] Adapted from the report of the speech at a meeting of Bihar Provincial Congress Committee at Patna, published in the *Searchlight*, 19 September 1934.

35. Letter to the Editor of the *Searchlight* clarifying his stand on the Resolution moved at Bihar P.C.C., 22 September 1934[1]

Sir, I was not a little pained to read your remarks made in a recent editorial note on the resolution[2] I moved in the last meeting of the P.C.C. You write:

> The resolution was in the nature of a demonstration. Not many agreed with the speaker that hitherto they had been traversing a blind alley that had led nowhere. Some people are apt to forget that the conditions which obtain today are the creation of yesterday and the resultant of a programme they deride. There is something unseemly in the derision poured on Khadi and the characterization of untouchability as something fit for old women and betrays both lack of practical sense and inability to appreciate their deeper significance.

I do not wish to dispute your opinion regarding my parctical sense and the ability to appreciate the deeper significance of the Khadi and Harijan movements, though I wonder if the fortyfive gentlemen who voted for my resolution would fully agree with you. However that is beside the point. What I am surprised at is how could it be possible for anyone who heard my speech to make the criticism which you have made. Allow me, first of all, to say that the resolution was not at all meant to be in the nature of a demonstration. The resolution was moved in all seriousness and, as I said again and again, its purpose was to place certain ideas and a certain programme before the members of the P.C.C. for their earnest and serious consideration. I did most emphatically feel, as I do now, that the future of the freedom movement depended very much on the programme adopted today by Congressmen. It was this belief that prompted me to ask the chosen representatives of the Provincial Congress organization to examine the programme that was already before them and decide if they were to remain content with it. In doing so I analysed, as dispassionately as was possible for me, each item of the constructive programme of the Congress. In course of my analysis I fully and frankly admitted the results gained from it but also attempted to show its serious limitations. I cannot understand how in view of my analysis you have thought it proper to remind me of the truism that today is the product of yesterday. Then you accuse me of pouring forth derision on certain items of the constructive programme and you say there was something unseemly about it. I find it difficult to believe that a cold dispassionate criticism should have merited such language. While not questioning your privilege as a journalist to say what you please, I should like to express my resentment at the language used. I should also like to assure you and those who may be interested that it was as far from my purpose as anything could be to deride the present programme. All I wished to do was to lay bare its shortcomings, its limitations by challenging its fundamental assumptions and analysing its detailed working. And

[1] *Searchlight*, 26 September 1934.

[2] See item no. 33.

it was enough for me that I was able to express my views and carry a considerable portion of the House with me as was evident from the voting: 45 for, 63 against.

In view of the importance of the matter, I should like you to publish this letter.

Patna
22 September 1934

Yours faithfully,
Jayaprakash Narayan

36. Circular to Provincial Secretaries, Congress Socialist Party, 14 October 1934[1]

Dadabhai Manzil
Congress House, Bombay
14 October (1934)

Comrade,

The office has already sent you particulars regarding the forthcoming session of the All India Congress Socialist Party. I should like, however, to draw your attention once again to the following points:

1. *Delegation*: Only Provincial Parties can send delegates to the Conference. Provinces where no Party has been organised can send one fraternal delegate each to the Conference who may participate in its proceedings but who will not have the power to vote. Provincial parties will send one delegate for every ten members or fraction thereof.

   For this particular year owing to lack of uniformity in membership and lack of proper control over enrolment of members every party will have equal number of votes, namely, three, which will be cast in a manner as to allow for proportionate representation of different views, if such exist in any party on any issue.

2. *Subjects Committee*:
   Every provincial party will nominate three members for the Subjects Committee. Members of the Drafting Committee will be ex-officio members of the Subjects Committee.

3. *Chairman*: The chairman of the Conference will be elected at the Conference.

4. *Dates*: The Subjects Committee will meet on Oct. 20th & 21st; the sittings beginning at 1 P.M. on Oct. 20th. The Conference opens at 3 P.M. on Oct. 21st; its session continuing till the night of the 22nd. Another session of the Conference may be held if necessary after the sessions of the Congress are over. The Conference will be held at Ready Money Hall, Warly.

[1] *Kamalashanker Pandya Papers* (NMML).

5. *Boarding & Lodging of Delegates*:

The Reception Committee of the Conference has made the following arrangements for the lodging and boarding of delegates:

Delegates will be put up in the Khan Abdul Ghaffar Khan Nagar. The reception of the Congress shall be Rs. 3/- for a Congress delegate and Rs. 5/- for a visitor to the Congress Session for accommodation for the entire period of 9 days, i.e. from 20th to 28th Oct. Thus our delegates who are also delegates to the Congress shall have to pay Rs. 3/- and those of our delegates who come as visitors to the Congress shall have to pay Rs. 5/- except that the Reception Committee of our Conference shall take responsibility for one-third of these amounts. Thus our delegates shall have to pay either Rs. 2/- or Rs. 3/8 for accommodation for 9 days in the Nagar beginning from 20th Oct.

As for boarding charges, twelve annas per day for the meals will be charged.

6. *Intimation to the Reception Committee*:

I should particularly like to impress on you the urgent necessity of intimating the Reception Committee, All India Congress Socialist Party, Dadabhoy Manzil, Congress House, Bombay, the names of the delegates from your province and of the members of the Subjects Committee and the time and the date of their arrival in Bombay.

If you find that there is not sufficient time to send the intimation by post please wire the same.

7. *Correction of the mistake*:

In the Draft Constitution which has been sent to you, you will please read "excluding" instead of "including" in section 6 under the head of 'Plan of Action' on page 4.

Yours fraternally,
Jayaprakash Narayan
Org. Secretary AICSP

37. Report to the First Conference of the Congress Socialist Party, Bombay, 21 October 1934[1]

Comrades,

As you all know a Conference was held at Patna six months ago, on May 17th, to

[1] *All India Congress Socialist Party. Constitution, Programme and Resolutions of the First Conference of the Party and Report of the Organising Secretary, 1934.*

consider, among other things, the advisability of uniting the socialist and other radical elements within the Indian National Congress into an organisaton in order to accelerate the growth of the latter into an anti-imperialist body having the requisite ideological and organisational basis. That Conference entrusted to me the duty of organising Provincial Socialist Parties and also this Conference which is meeting here today and to which you all have come as delegates representing your respective parties.

I do not know how well I have discharged my duties. That is for you to judge. I shall briefly summarise for your information the work that has been done, the policy that I have followed and the problems which I have had to face. Today the All India Party will be formally formed and henceforth it will be the task of the All India Executive to guide, direct and build up this movement. While feeling a great relief at this heavy burden being lifted off me, I hope I am not leaving things in a shape that will hinder the work of the Executive but in a condition that will facilitate and further it.

At the time the Patna Conference met there were only two Provincial Congress Socialist Parties or groups existing in the country, namely, the Bombay Presidency Group and the Behar Socialist Party. There was a District Group in Benares which was organised just before the Conference. We were told that there were some other groups also in other provinces, but these, as I found out later, did not exist. Even of the organisations that existed before May 17th, only the Bombay Presidency Group had any record of work. Having been formed in February, 1934, it had time to function for nearly three months during which period it showed considerable political activity. Some of its members had participated in the Bombay and Sholapur Textile strikes.[2] As for the Behar Party, it had really been formed in 1931, but on account of the Civil Disobedience movement that was started soon afterwards, the party had little time to do any work. It was revived only a few weeks before the Patna Conference.

Immediately after the Conference I took up the work of organising Provincial Parties. A central office was opened at Benares and was placed in charge of Babu Sampurnanand. Acharya Narendra Deva visited Delhi where he helped in the formation of the Delhi Provincial Party. The Bombay Presidency Group was reorganised on the basis of Congress Provinces. Thus the Maharashtra, the Bombay City and the Gujarat Parties came into existence. This work was carried out entirely by the Bombay Presidency Comrades. I visited the following provinces: Bengal, U.P., C.P. (Hindi), C.P. (Marathi), Berar, Andhra, Tamil Nadu and Kerala. In two of these, namely, Andhra and Kerala, Provincial Parties were already in existence when I visited them. In the others, I formed organising committees. Up to the date of writing I have intimation of the formation of the following provincial parties: Andhra, Assam, Bengal, Berar, Behar, Bombay, C.P. (Hindi), Delhi, Gujerat, Kerala, Maharashtra, U.P. and Utkal. Apart from organisational work most of these parties have had little time for any other activity. They have been in existence for too short a period to take up any programme of work. Some of them, however, have been

[2] Refers to the strike of textile workers of Bombay and Sholapur, 23 April-20 June 1934.

active in the peasant and Trade Union movement. The Bengal Party has been able to bring out a fine weekly, the *Congress Socialist*[3] which, we hope, we shall be adopting as the official organ of the All India Party.

A few remarks regarding problems of organisation. I feel that there is a good deal of looseness of organisation and discipline in most of the parties that exist. Many of them I feel have to be reconstituted with a better appreciation of the fundamentals of our movement and its tasks. I have found that in enrolling members some of our parties have been anxious merely to increase their numbers. I say this not to censure or accuse. It is natural that there should be confusion at the beginning. Most of this will no doubt disappear in coarse of time. Much depends, however, on the kind of lead this Conference gives in this matter. My idea of our party is that of a working, well-disciplined organisation. This means that our membership must be selective and restrictive, and the guidance and control of the organisation, central as well as local, must be in the hands of those who are active in the movement. Furthermore, the party while not being a mass party must have organic contact with the masses through the participation of its members in the organisations of the masses.

A few words about the problems facing us.

The first and for me the biggest problem is that of finding sufficient resources to carry out our programme of work. Those of you who have attempted to execute any part of that programme know how heavy are the demands which you are called upon to meet. However, this is a topic which cannot be discussed in an open Conference. Every party has to face this problem and solve it in some manner if it has to work at all. I have brought up this matter here only so that, while discussing theoretical issues, we may not lose sight of this great practical problem.

The second problem before us is to hammer out in detail our immediate programme of work. Different provinces have different problems and while the principles underlying our work may be the same everywhere, immediate issues are bound to vary from province to province. It may not be possible for the Conference to draft an All-India programme in any great detail. This is a task which I feel the Executive Committee should be entrusted with.

Another problem which faces us is the question of our relation with the Congress. The problem is a simple one and can be easily solved. First of all, our organisation is within the Congress. That itself defines our relationship to a great extent. Being part of it, there is no question of any opposition or hostility towards it. On the other hand, we as a party must participate in the activities of the Congress and consider them our own, except where we disagree with a particular policy of the Congress. At the same time, we must exercise our right as a minority to propagate our views within the Congress, to work along our own lines, to criticise and even oppose such policies of the Congress which may appear to us to be not in the interests of the masses.

[3] *Congress Socialist*, an English weekly, was started from Calcutta under the editorship of Rammanohar Lohia as a mouthpiece of the Congress Socialist Party in September 1934; from December 1935 it was published from Bombay with Asoka Mehta as Editor. It stopped publication towards the end of 1939.

Yet another problem is to define our attitude towards the various Labour groups and come to some working agreement with them. This also, I feel, is a task which only the All India Executive, in consultation with the bodies concerned, can tackle. The Conference can, however, indicate the lines on which such agreement should be negotiated.

Finally, I wish to touch upon certain criticisms that have been levelled against us. Criticisms have come both from the right and the left. Most of these have been due to misunderstanding and lack of appreciation of the real nature of our movement. The criticisms from the right have been chiefly that we are disrupting the Congress, weakening the national struggle and that we are mere talkers. As for disruption, it must be understood that every organization goes through crises, evolves and changes its character. This is not the first time that the cry of disruption has been raised. If on account of the socialist movement, "moderates" and other "seasonal patriots" leave the Congress, the latter instead of losing would really gain thereby. As for weakening the national struggle we feel that far from weakening it, our movement, by creating the proper basis for the rise of a real mass movement in the country, would considerably strengthen and further it. As for the criticism that we are mere talkers, I do not consider it worth replying to. We have been as much in the thick of the national struggle as any other group of people. The least I can say in this regard is that it is highly ungracious for responsible Congressmen to indulge in such remarks.

The critics from the left have been singularly lacking in appreciation of the real issues involved. The main criticism from this quarter has been that it is a mistake to form our party within the Congress. Socialism and Congress are said to be a contradiction in terms. Far from contradicting each other they are interdependent in the peculiar conditions of India. Socialism without the overthrow of Imperialism is an absurdity. The National Congress is the only political organization which has led major struggles against British Imperialism in this country and there is no reason to expect that it will abandon its anti-imperialist task at this stage. I do not imply that the Congress, as it is, is competent to overthrow Imperialism. That exactly is our task. We must so develop the Congress that it does become such a body. The alternative of forming such a body outside the Congress means sheer and foolish waste of energy even if it were possible to do so. I have not the slightest doubt, nor have any of you I am sure, that it is possible for us to so influence and change the Congress as to make it a real anti-imperialist body. Those who do not entertain this belief have clearly no place in this movement.

The Congress Socialist Party is not the party of any one class. It is not the party of the working class alone. It is a political party uniting on its platform all anti-imperialist elements and its task is to lead such elements to the overthrow of British Imperialism and the establishment in India of a real Swaraj for the masses.

With these remarks I wish to take your leave.

Jayaprakash Narayan

38. Statement on Misleading Reports, 24 October 1934[1]

My attention has been drawn to a report[2] in this morning's papers that there is a split in the Congress Socialist Party as a result of the adoption by the Conference[3] yesterday for the non-acceptance of Congress offices except under certain conditions and that about eighteen and twenty members of the U.P. Executive of the Party have resigned.

On enquiry from the Secretary of the U.P. Party, I find that only three members[4] of the U.P. Executive have written to him yesterday tendering their resignations. In view of this all talk of split is alarmist and misleading.

[1] *Bombay Chronicle*, 24 October 1934.

[2] Refers to the report regarding the resignation of some Socialist members from the Executive of the U.P. Congress Socialist Party, published in the *Bombay Chronicle*, 23 October 1934.

[3] Refers to the Congress Socialist Party Conference at Bombay, 21-2 October 1934. For resolution on conditions for acceptance of Congress offices see Appendix 7.

[4] (i) Govind Sahai (1897-1967); joined the Congress in 1930 and participated in the civil disobedience, individual satyagraha and Quit India movements; jailed several times; member, U.P. Legislative Assembly, 1946-52, and 1957-67; Parliamentary Secretary, 1946-9, Minister of State, 1961-3, and Minister, 1967, U.P. Government.

(ii) Damodar Swarup Seth (1896-1960); imprisoned in connection with Banaras and Kakori Conspiracy Cases, 1915-20, and 1925-8; jailed several times for participating in the freedom struggle; General Secretary, U.P.P.C.C., 1936, and its President, 1946; member, National Executive of C.S.P., 1938; President, U.P. Kisan Conference, Jaunpur, 1942; member, Constituent Assembly, 1946-50, and Provisional Parliament, 1950-2.

(iii) C.B. Kantak; a prominent member of the U.P. Congress Socialist Party.

39. Statement on Resignations from the U.P. Congress Socialist Party, 27 October 1934[1]

I have read with pain the statement[2] published in yesterday's papers of some of my valued U.P. comrades who have decided to resign from the U.P. Congress Socialist Party. I assure them that I have not attempted to avoid issues. I can only remind them of the compromise resolution regarding the Parliamentary Board, which was passed in the form only to accommodate our U.P. comrades, who have special difficulties in the matter.

However, I feel it is too late now to open the discussion. Much as I regret the

[1] *Bombay Chronicle*, 27 October 1934.

[2] Refers to the statement issued by C.B. Kantak, Damodar Swarup Seth, Govind Sahai and Balkrishna Sharma stating reasons for their resignations from the U.P. Congress Socialist Party. See Appendix 9 for the text of the statement.

decision of my friends, I am still as strongly of the opinion as ever that the decision taken by the Conference in this matter was the only correct one possible. And, if I may remind my friends that the presidents of both the First and Second All-India Congress Socialist Conference, Acharya Narendra Deva and Babu Sampurnanand, both members of the U.P. Party are one with us on this point.

There is another point to which I should like to draw the attention of our dissident comrades. In the statement issued by them they speak of "conditions in respect of holding offices and being members of the Congress Executive". If my friends read the resolution again they would find that it laid down no conditions at all regarding membership of Congress Executives. It speaks of conditions only regarding holding offices in Congress Committees, i.e. the offices of President, Vice-President, Secretary and Treasurer. A Congress Socialist is entirely free to contest elections to any Congress Executive. It is regrettable that these comrades have taken such a far-reaching decision without even understanding the resolution against which they are protesting so strongly.

40. Circular to Secretary, Utkal Congress Socialist Party, 4 November 1934[1]

Circular Letter No. 1

Dadabhai Manzil
Congress House, Bombay
4 November 1934

To
The Secretary
Utkal Congress Socialist Party

Dear Comrade,
You know that this year's Armistice Day will be celebrated on November 11. I think that would be a good opportunity for us to raise the anti-war issue and do some propaganda for our views on the matter. I therefore suggest that you should arrange meetings in the important centres of your province under the auspices of the Party, where the resolution, adopted by our last Conference, should be passed and speeches made in support of it. The speeches should of course be within the bounds of the existing law. It should be remembered in this connection that advocacy of a general strike for such a purpose is illegal. The speeches should also critcise the Congress leaders for not paying any heed to the question of war and not considering the resolution that our Party had given notice of.

The following is the text of the anti-war resolution passed by the Bombay Conference recast so as to be placed before your public meeting:

[1] *Nabakrushna Chaudhuri Papers* (NMML). The same circular was sent to all the provincial secretaries of the Congress Socialist Party.

"In view of the international situation and the danger of the sudden outbreak of a war in which the British Government may be involved, this public meeting held under the auspices of the Congress Socialist Party declares its opposition to the participation by India in any such war and calls upon the Indian National Congress to undertake forthwith the preparation of the entire Indian Nation to resist actively the utilisation of Indian men, money and resources for the purposes of such a war and to utilise such a crisis for securing Swaraj."

Yours fraternally,
Jayaprakash Narayan
(General Secretary)

P.S.
I have also sent you a wire in this connection.

J.P.

41. Circular to Secretary, Utkal Congress Socialist Party, 13 November 1934[1]

Circular Letter No. 2

Bombay
13 November 1934

To
Secretary
Utkal Provincial Congress Socialist Party

Dear Comrade,
I am enclosing herewith a copy of the Constitution and Programme[2] of the All India Party as finally adopted by the last Party Conference as well as a copy of Resolutions[3] passed by the Conference and Rules and Recommendations[4] framed by the Executive Committee regarding membership and other matters of organisation. I am also sending you a copy of an agreement[5] we have arrived at

[1] *Nabakrushna Chaudhuri Papers* (NMML). The same circular was sent to all the provincial secretaries of the Congress Socialist Party.

[2] See Appendix 7 for Constitution and Programme of the Congress Socialist Party, 1934.

[3] See Appendix 7 for Resolutions passed by the Congress Socialist Party Conference, Bombay, 1934.

[4] See Appendix 8 for Rules and Recommendations framed by the Executive Committee of the Congress Socialist Party, 1934.

[5] See Appendix 10 for Agreement of the Congress Socialist Party with the All India Trade Union Congress, 1 November 1934.

with the All-India Trade Union Congress and the names of the members of various Sub-Committees appointed by the Executive Committee.[6]

I desire you to go carefully through the material that is being sent and carry out the instructions contained therein. In this connection I wish to draw your attention particularly to the following:

(i) You will have to amend the Constitution of your Party so as to bring it in line with the Constitution of the All India Party and the Rules framed by the Executive Committee. Likewise, you will have to adopt the Programme of the Party, with such modifications in the Immediate Demands as may be necessitated by conditions in your Province. Please send final draft of your Constitution and Programme as soon as possible.

(ii) Decisions of the Conference regarding the Congress Parliamentary Board and holding of offices in Congress Committees should soon be carried out.

As regards your Party's work in the peasant and labour fields, I suggest that you write to Comrades Gautam[7] and Purshottam[8] respectively for necessary advice and guidance. In the meanwhile I wish to suggest a few things. As far as labour work is concerned, you will note that the Executive Committee has come to a working agreement with A.I.T.U.C. Accordingly, if there is scope for labour work in your province, please get in touch with the branch secretaries of the A.I.T.U.C. in your place or its affiliated unions and draw up a plan of work. Wherever possible, our members should take up those industries particularly which are politically strategic.

If there is no T.U.C. branch in your province you may negotiate with other Trade Union groups and arrive at some working agreement with them. You must, however, consult the secretary of the Labour Sub-Committee before entering into any such agreement. I expect the Secretary will soon send you detailed suggestions regarding this whole matter.

As for peasant work, the problem is rather difficult on account of the great variety of agrarian conditions and our relative inexperience in this type of work. However, it is clear that if our Party and, in truth, the independence movement itself is to make any progress, we must concentrate our efforts on the vast peasant population of the country.

Our manner of approach to the peasants is quite different from that of the Congress. It is an economic approach and its purpose is to link up the political

[6] Not printed.

[7] Mohanlal Gautam (1902-77); participated in the non-cooperation and Khilafat movements; joined Servants of the People Society, 1924; General Secretary, U.P.P.C.C., 1930-1, its Secretary, 1936, 1963-4, and President, 1969; Joint Secretary, Congress Socialist Party, 1934, and member of its National Executive, 1936; member, U.P. Legislative Assembly, 1937-46, 1952-62, and 1967-9, Constituent Assembly, 1946-50, Provisional Parliament, 1950-2, and Rajya Sabha, 1969-72; Minister, U.P. Government, 1952-4, and 1956-60.

[8] Purshottam Trikamdas (1897-1969); Founder-member, Congress Socialist Party, and member of its National Executive for several years; Chairman, Socialist Party, 1948, and Legal Inquiry Committee on Tibet appointed by the International Commission of Jurists, 1959-60.

struggle with the present economic struggles of the peasants and vice-versa. The grievances of the peasants and the wrongs from which they suffer are numerous. It is our task to organise those grievances and develop on their basis a militant agrarian movement. A difficult task undoubtedly, requiring skill, courage and patience. Just now with our resources in men and money we can only make a modest beginning. But even that beginning has to be properly planned. At present, I do not believe that most of us are clear in our minds as how best to tackle the problem. Each locality has its own peculiar condition. One thing, however, is plain. No time should be lost in putting ourselves in touch with the peasants. If there are no local issues at hand with which we can link up our activities, I would suggest that some of the most competent members of your party should undertake a tour of investigation and incidentally of propaganda. Through some or all parts of the province, with a view to acquaint themselves with conditions obtaining there and, more than that, to explore avenues of work. I also suggest that full use should be made of Bills that may be pending in the Legislature regarding tenancy, indebtedness or any other agricultural question for the purpose of establishing contact with the peasants. An agitation, involving holding of peasant meetings, to oppose or demand amendments in such "Bills" will give us at this stage a foothold in the countryside. In any case I wish to emphasise that in some manner or other we must establish contact with the peasants, even though we may not be able to do anything more than that for some time to come.

I should advise your Executive Committee to prepare in the next month a tentative scheme of work among the peasantry of your province. In a month or so the Central Executive will be meeting in Nagpur and the various Sub-Committees will also meet at the same time. I should like then to have scheme from each Provincial Party regarding its activities in the various fields, particularly in the peasant and labour fields. Probably each province would be requested to send its representatives to discuss these schemes in detail with the Executive.

Now, a few words about publicity and propaganda. The All India Party has taken over the *Congress Socialist* (hitherto published by the Bengal Party) as its official organ. The Party will also soon bring out a Hindi weekly as its organ. In addition to this the Party shall publish tracts and pamphlets. Most of this will be in English and Hindustani. The Provincial Parties will therefore have to arrange for publicity in their own provincial languages.

Party news should be regularly sent to the Editor, *Congress Socialist* as well as contributions from Party members particularly regarding peasants and labour problems of the province.

Kindly send a report of anti-war demonstrations held under the auspices of your Party.

After you have reorganised your Party on the basis of the new All India Constitution and Rules, kindly send me a list of your active members and the number of ordinary members.

Fraternally yours,
Jayaprakash Narayan
General Secretary

42. Circular to Secretary, Gujarat Congress Socialist Party, 30 November 1934[1]

Circular No. 3

c/o Bombay Congress Socialist Party
Dadabhai Manzil, Congress House
Girgaum, Bombay
30 November 1934

Re.: Congress Socialist

To
The Secretary
Gujarat Provincial Congress Socialist Party

Dear Comrade,
You know that the All India Party is issuing an official organ in English, the *Congress Socialist*, from Calcutta. In view of the numerous handicaps with which a socialist publication must start in a country like India it would be impossible for the Party to continue the *Congress Socialist* without the help of every provincial Party. So far the Editor of the *Socialist* has received no cooperation from you. It is not necessary for me to impress upon you the importance of a Party organ or the responsibilities of every Party member in the matter. I wish to make, however, the following suggestions:-

(1) Request every member of your Party to get as many subscribers as possible.
(2) Arrange for the sale of as many copies as possible every week and write to Dr. Lohia to send you the number of copies required.
(3) Send to the editor regularly news of your Party's activities.
(4) Send regular notes regarding the Labour and Peasant movements in your Province.
(5) For (3) and (4) I suggest that you appoint some Party member Correspondent, Publicity Officer or Local Editor and entrust the work to him.
(6) Have suitable members of your Party write articles for the *Congress Socialist.*
(7) Arrange to advertise the *Congress Socialist* in the local press.

I hope this matter will receive your urgent attention.

Fraternally yours,
Jayaprakash Narayan

[1] *Kamalashanker Pandya Papers* (NMML). The same circular was sent to all the provincial secretaries of the Congress Socialist Party.

P.S.

The address of the *Congress Socialist* is as below:

Dr. Ram Manohar Lohia[2], Editor, *Congress Socialist*, Albert Hall, 15, College Square, Calcutta.

[2] Rammanohar Lohia (1910-67); Founder-member, Congress Socialist Party, 1934, its Joint Secretary, 1936, and member of its National Executive for many years; tendered resignation in protest against the Party's policy towards the Communists, 1939; Editor, *Congress Socialist*, 1934-5; Secretary, Foreign Department of A.I.C.C., 1936-8; led underground movement in 1942, and detained, 1944-6; initiated Goa and Nepal struggles, 1946; Chairman, C.S.P. Conference, Kanpur, 1947; arrested several times after independence for leading civil disobedience against the policies of the Government; General Secretary, P.S.P., 1954; formed Socialist Party, 1955, and its Chairman, 1956; elected to Lok Sabha in a bye-election from Farrukhabad, May 1963; re-elected in 1967; wrote *Fragments of a World Mind, Aspects of Socialist Policy, Wheel of History, Marx, Gandhi and Socialism, Interval during Politics,* and *Guilty Men of India's Partition.*

43. Statement to Press on the New Constitution, 3 December 1934[1]

I welcome the clear and outspoken verdict of Sardar Vallabhbhai Patel[2] on the Joint Parliamentary Committee Report. *Wreck It* is a realistic slogan. The Congress programme of rejection had little more than educative value. The new slogan raised by the Sardar defines concretely the policy that the Congress should adopt with regard to the new Constitutional shackles that are being forged in Westminster for India. It is hoped that the Working Committee at Patna will unequivocally decide that the Congress shall not only reject the coming Constitution by a resolution in the Assembly, but shall also follow a fighting and constructionist policy in the legislatures in order to tear it up into shreds and make its working impossible.

It would be a national calamity if the Congress succumbed to the sweet and reasonable "Statesmen" of India and decided to work the Constitution for what it was worth. There is no doubt in my mind that, if the Congress ever decided to follow the latter policy, it would be liquidating the struggle for Independence and dissolving itself as an organisation destined to lead that struggle.

It should also be made clear from now that Congressmen shall not accept ministerial offices. That would be incompatible with the scheme of wrecking the Constitution. Acceptance of such offices would mean one step forward towards the working of the Constitution and it would create unnecessary difficulties and weaknesses in the position of the Congress. Nor is it possible to argue that the Constitution can be wrecked more effectively by accepting offices. I, therefore, hope that the Working Committee particularly in view of the rather disquieting

[1] *Bombay Chronicle*, 3 December 1934.

[2] This refers to Vallabhbhai Patel's speech at Nagpur on 30 November 1934 where he had asked Congressmen to wreck the New Constitution.

talks in certain circles, will make a clear declaration of its policy that Congressmen shall not accept ministerial offices under the New Constitution.

I should also like most respectfully to suggest to the Working Committee that, as a part of its campaign for wrecking the Constitution, it should organize meetings throughout the country, where the new Imperialist move should be exposed and the right of the Indian people to formulate their own Constitution through a Constituent Assembly, should be reiterated. In this connection I support the recommendation of the Sind Congress Executive that effigies of the J.P.C. Report should be burnt at public meetings all over the country.

With regard to the Constituent Assembly, I should like to draw the attention of the Working Committee to the misleading statement[3] of Mr. Satyamurti.[4] The kind of Assembly that Mr. Satyamurti has suggested has been rightly characterised as a "travesty" of the Constituent Assembly. His suggestion, it will be remembered, was that the elected members of the Legislatures together with members of the A.I.C.C. would constitute the Constituent Assembly. It is a grotesque misconception of the entire nature of the Constituent Assembly to think that people elected on such a narrow franchise—the A.I.C.C. franchise is narrower, if anything than that of the Legislatures—should take the place of the members of the Constituent Assembly, which must represent the entire people.

It should also be borne in mind that a real Constituent Assembly can only be called when there is popular sanction behind it and when it has the strength to enforce its decisions. These conditions do not exist today. Therefore, our task is first to bring about such conditions and not proceed to call a sham Constituent Assembly.

There is also talk in some quarters of the Congress forming an alliance with other parties against the J.P.C. Report. I should like to suggest to the Working Committee that it should associate with itself only such parties as agree with its policy of wrecking the Constitution and with no others. No possible gain can come out of an All-Parties Conference unless all the Parties concerned do not accept this fundamental policy.

[3] S. Satyamurti in a statement from Madras on 23 November 1934 criticised the Joint Select Committee's Report and said that the Government should be pressurised to summon the Constituent Assembly. He further stated that the Constituent Assembly should consist of members of the Indian Legislative Assembly and Provincial Councils, and the newly-organised A.I.C.C.

[4] S. Satyamurti (1887-1943); member, Madras Legislative Council, 1923-30, and Indian Legislative Assembly, 1934-43; President, Tamil Nadu P.C.C., 1935-6; Mayor of Madras, 1939-40; arrested in December 1940 for participating in the individual satyagraha; released in August 1941; arrested again in 1942.

44. Letter to Nabakrushna Chaudhuri, 12 December 1934[1]

c/o Bombay Congress Socialist Party
Dadabhai Manzil, Congress House
Girgaum, Bombay
12 December [1934]

My dear Naba Babu,
Our solicitor[2] has written to you yesterday to send him a letter, the draft of which he has sent you, authorising Masani & Purushottam to act as your agent in the matter of signing the "Statement" which has to be filed on behalf of the Congress Socialist Publishing Company.[3] I hope you will send the letter required as soon as you can. The Company cannot do business till the "Statement" is filed & a certificate issued to the Company in that respect.

Fraternally yours,
Jayaprakash

[1] *Nabakrushna Chaudhuri Papers* (NMML).

[2] Shantilal Harjivan Shah (1898-1984); imprisoned in 1932, 1939 and 1942 during the freedom movement and spent a total of five years in jail; member, Bombay Legislative Council, 1937-52, Bombay Legislative Assembly, 1952-60, Maharashtra Legislative Assembly, 1961-6, and Lok Sabha, 1967-70; Minister, Bombay Government, 1952-60, and Maharashtra Government, 1961-6.

[3] Congress Socialist Publishing Company was established in 1934 with Lala Shankarlal as Chairman and Shantilal H. Shah as Managing Director. Its Head Office was at Dadabhai Manzil, Congress House, Girgaum, Bombay.

45. Letter to D.L. Pathak and R.A. Khedgikar, 19 December 1934[1]

Ahmednagar
19 December 1934

Dear Comrades Pathak[2] and Khedgikar,[3]
I am enclosing herewith a statement[4] giving the terms of the agreement regarding

[1] *JP Papers* (NMML).

[2] D.L. Pathak; prominent labour leader of Bombay; one of the secretaries of the All India Trade Union Congress, 1934; General Secretary, G.I.P. Railway Workers' Union, 1935, and Secretary, Bombay Provincial Trade Union Congress, 1936.

[3] R.A. Khedgikar (1887-1966); General Secretary, 1935-6, Vice-President, 1937, 1947, and Treasurer, 1943-7, All India Trade Union Congress; member, All India Joint Labour Board, 1935; President, G.I.P. Railway Workers' Union, and its General Secretary, 1938-9; one of the founders of the All India Railwaymen's Federation; member, Railway Workers' Classification Tribunal, and Bombay Legislative Assembly, 1937-45; elected to Bombay Legislative Council in 1952, tendered resignation on Samyukta Maharashtra issue, 1956.

[4] See Appendix 11 for Agreement of the Congress Socialist Party with the All India Trade Union Congress, December 1934.

joint action as settled at our joint meetings. I have signed the statement on behalf of my Party. Please have it signed by a representative of the A.I.T.U.C. also and return one signed copy to me.

Please also see that the agreement is accepted by a proper meeting of the A.I.T.U.C. Executive.

As for the joint meeting on the J.P.C. Report, I have circularised the provincial parties on the subject. We shall meet in Bombay again in a few days to settle the draft of the resolution on the Report.

Fraternally yours,
J.P.
General Secretary

46. Letter to Secretary, National Trades Union Federation, 20 December 1934[1]

Ahmednagar
20 December 1934

To
The Secretary
National Trades Union Federation[2]

Dear Comrade,
I am enclosing herewith two copies of a statement[3] giving the terms of the agreement regarding joint action as settled at our joint meeting. We have made some slight verbal alterations in the terms which I hope will be acceptable to your Committee.

I have signed the "statement" on behalf of my Party. Kindly sign both copies on behalf of your organisation and return one signed copy to me.

Fraternally yours,
JP
General Secretary

C/o The Bombay Congress Socialist Party
Dadabhai Manzil, Congress House
Girgaum, Bombay

[1] *JP Papers* (NMML).

[2] In 1931 a number of railway unions formed themselves into a new central body called the National Federation of Labour with a provisional committee consisting of Jamnadas Mehta, V.V. Giri and others. In April 1933 at a special session in Calcutta the Indian Trades Union Federation and National Federation of Labour joined together and formed the National Trades Union Federation. It merged with the All India Trade Union Congress in 1940.

[3] Not available.

47. New Incentives (1): Article in the *Congress Socialist*, 30 December 1934[1]

Barbara Woolton in her excellent little book, *Plan or No Plan* remarks that "there is very little excuse now for the socialist who cannot say what he means by the terms socialism and capitalism, since the Russians have produced something which by unanimous consent is anyhow not capitalism, it is no longer necessary for the socialist to wander about in the clouds describing the shadowy outlines of mythical worlds . . . 'In my World' said the old-time socialist with exasperating camplacency, 'there would not be poverty or unemloyment or wanton destruction of wealth by greedy profiteers. All this would be changed'. 'Would it indeed?' his realistic opponent would reply and the argument generally ended in a deadlock about the possibility of changing human nature. Today that argument can be carried at least one stage further".

Yes, and therein lies the great historical importance of Russia. Russia is boldly experimenting today with ideas and theories which seemed to those who had not accepted them to be made up more of phantasy than of practical propositions. Therefore, those who are at all serious and earnest about present social problems, whatever be their own convictions, must try to understand what is being done in Russia.

A very common remark about Russia is that it is so difficult to know the truth about Russia. This is in some measure true but it can no longer be held as an excuse for one's not being aware of the major experiments which the Russians have so far, successfully, though frankly admitting and retracting from none too infrequent mistakes, carried out. It can be conceded that even now it is not possible to speak with any certainty regarding such things as particular shooting or a particular trial till long after the event, but it is not possible any longer, except for those who are lazy or dishonest, to adopt the same nothing-can-be-known attitude with regard to the huge and stupendous changes that the Russians have wrought in the social and economic life of their country. Is it any longer possible to doubt the fact of the rise of giant factories and fabulous production without capitalists and entrepreneurs, the rise of huge co-operatives and, most miraculous of all, the growth of collectivised agriculture? Can any one doubt the new freedom, the new spirit of creativity, the new wave of culture? Regarding a detail of administrative policy, regarding a particular incident, regarding a Party "purge", regarding many other things, not all unimportant, there may be mystery, uncertainty, doubt. But with regard to the major policies and achievements of the Soviet Government, is it possible to be in doubt any more? It is possible to take different views of the achievements and praise or condemn them according to your taste, but certainly not to be ignorant about them. There exist too many impartial and scientific accounts today for that.

One of the points which invariably pop up in an argument between a socialist and non-socialist is that which concerns the question of incentives in a socialist

[1] *Congress Socialist*, 30 December 1934.

society. It is argued that the incentives for work and effort have so far been personal reward, personal gain and profit. Industry and commerce flourish and grow only because they are being ceaselessly pushed ahead by the motive of profit. Remove that motive, divorce profit from effort and people would cease to put forth their best. The socialist always argued that profit or money reward was not the only reward, nor individualism, in its narrow selfish sense, an essential attribute of human nature. At the end of his argument, however, he left his opponent, more often than not, doubting the practicability of his alluring but rather phantastic theories.

Today, as Barbara Woolton says, we have advanced a step further. The Russians have given the socialist something more than theories to argue with. They are working today, and have thus worked for the last 17 years—not an inconsiderable period of time even for a social experiment—with new incentives. What are these and how have they worked?

Now, I have never visited the U.S.S.R., nor have I talked to any of the leaders of the country. I shall, therefore, let someone who has visited the U.S.S.R.,—his last visit was the tenth, and who is by no means a "Red"—tell you about this upsurge of new motives which seems to have transformed the face of one-sixth of the world in less than two decades.

48. Letter to President, A.I.T.U.C., Nagpur, 1 January 1935[1]

Dadabhai Manzil
Congress House
Girgaum, Bombay
1 Janaury 1935

To
The President
A.I.T.U.C.
Nagpur

Dear Comrade,
I am enclosing herewith a copy of an agreement[2] regarding joint action on specific issues, apart from trade union work that was arrived at between the representatives of my Party and those members of the A.I.T.U.C. Executives who reside in Bombay. I have already sent two duly signed copies of it to Comrade Khedgikar & Pathak, who doubtless will place it in your hands.

I earnestly hope that your Executive will accept the agreement on behalf of the A.I.T.U.C.

I also wish [to] draw your notice to a statement of which a copy is enclosed

[1] *JP Papers* (NMML).

[2] See Appendix 11 for Agreement of the Congress Socialist Party with the All India Trade Union Congress, December 1934.

herewith issued by the Labour, Sub-Committee of the A.I.C.S.P. defining the latter's policy with respect to the Labour movement & calling for earnest attempts in behalf of Labour Unions Unity in the country. Our plea for unity is clearly set forth in that statement, so I do not propose to repeat it here. It is again my earnest hope that your Executive will give due consideration to the matter and appoint a small Sub-Committee to explore the possibilities of unity.

I further wish to draw your attention to certain misunderstanding which is being created with regard to the agreement that was arrived at between your Executive & the Executive of my Party. Our view of this matter has been clearly explained in the statement to which I have referred above. Here I only wish to repeat that the agreement in question can in no way be interpreted to mean as it is evidently being done by some people, that the A.I.T.U.C. adopted the A.I.C.S.P. as its political party or that it committed itself exclusively to its political programme. Both these interpretations are wrong as a reference to the terms of the agreement will clearly show.

With fraternal greetings,
Very sincerely yours,
JP

49. Letter to Secretary, Bihar Congress Socialist Party, 2 January 1935[1]

Bombay
2 January 1935

To
The Secretary Bihar Socialist Party
Patna

Dear Comrade,
I have gone through the Constitution, Programme etc. of your Party as amended to comply with the requirements of affiliation to the A.I.C.S.P. and find it satisfactory. The requirements have been fulfilled.

I should, however, draw your attention to habitual use of Khadi which your C.O.A.[2] has made a condition of active membership. While I cannot say that technically this condition is inconsistent with the All India Constitution, it is inconsistent with the position taken up by the Party at the Congress. If you recall, the Party took the stand that habitual use of Khadi should not be made a qualification for membership of elected Congress bodies, the plea being that it is an unnecessary restriction & it discriminates against certain genuine anti-imperialist elements in the country, who have as much a right to represent the masses in the Congress as any one else. However, as I have said, technically the step taken by your Party is

[1] *JP Papers* (NMML).
[2] Council of Action.

not contrary to the Constitution or Rules of the A.I.C.S. Party. Nevertheless, I shall make a request to you & through you to the C.O.A. to reconsider the matter again. It is an undesirable condition.

With regard to the power given to District Committees, I desire to say that the phrase "for the conduct of their affairs" is too wide. However, there is no harm in giving them this power, but you should require them to send for approval any such rules that they might make.

Fraternally yours,
Jayaprakash

50. Letter to Secretary, Gujarat Congress Socialist Party, 8 January 1935[1]

All India Congress Socialist Party
Dadabhai Manzil, Congress House
Girgaum, Bombay
8 January 1935

Dear Comrade,
A meeting of the Executive Committee of the All India Party will be held at Nagpur on the 2nd & 3rd of February. In view of the fact that there is no one from your province on the Executive I am herewith inviting your Executive Committee to nominate one of its members to attend the meeting of the Executive. Kindly send me the name of your Committee's nominee as soon as possible and ask him to intimate the time of his arrival at Nagpur to Com. P.Y. Deshpande,[2] Craddock Town, Nagpur, C.P.

Fraternally yours,
Jayaprakash Narayan

[1] *Kamalashanker Pandya Papers* (NMML).

[2] P.Y. Deshpande (1899-1986); Marathi writer, novelist and journalist; left studies to participate in the non-cooperation movement, 1920; member, National Executive, Congress Socialist Party, 1934; Founder-Editor, *Bhavitavya*, 1939-48; Vice-President, I.N.T.U.C., 1946-7; member, Provisional Parliament, 1950-2; recipient of Sahitya Akademi Award, 1962.

51. New Incentives (2): Article in the *Congress Socialist*, 13 January 1935[1]

Dr. Sherwood Eddy[2] is no Marxist, but he observes well. And while it cannot be said of him that he holds no brief for anybody, this subject is sufficiently out of the way of his particular bias to have got coloured by it.

[1] *Congress Socialist*, 13 January 1935.

[2] Dr. G. Sherwood Eddy visited India in 1897 as a Secretary of the Y.M.C.A. for student work.

Sherwood Eddy's latest book on Russia is entitled *Russia Today: What can we learn from it* (London, 1934).

The book is written on the lines of a cash register. There is a debit side and a credit side. On the debit side are three entries (1) Bureaucracy and the Denial of Liberty, (2) Violence and Compulsion, (3) Dogmatism, and Atheism and Anti-Religion. These make communism unacceptable to Dr. Eddy as he himself explains.

On the credit side are eight if not more "possible contributions to human welfare". These are (1) Social Justice and Social Planning, (2) A Classless Society, (3) The Treatment of Criminals, (4) The Care of Children; Youth and Education, (5) New Motives and Incentives, (6) Eliminating Unemployment and Slum Clearance, (7) The Revolution in Agriculture, (8) The New Morality. There are three more, of perhaps less pronounced value to Dr. Eddy: (1) A Unified Philosophy of Life (which is rather a disappointing hash of marxism), (2) The Reformation of Religion, and (3) The Interpretation of History.

I have quoted these chapter-titles not to tell you what the book contains but rather to tell you, in passing, how Dr. Eddy evaluates the whole Russian experiment.

We are concerned here with only one of the chapters, that on New Motives and Incentives.

First a general summing up to the situation: "The Soviets . . . believe that under a planned economy if the worker is relieved of fear of unemployment, sickness and helpless old age, it will have the same beneficial effect upon him that it has upon the employer in other lands. . . . With the saving of the enormous waste of competitive advertising in the selling of the product, with no idle plant, labour or capital, with no waste in the production of useless luxuries, in what Ruskin[3] called 'illth' in contradistinction to true wealth, with an adequate plan for distribution and consumption as well as for production and above all, in the aim of basic justice for all who toil, where labour feels it is sharing in the entire surplus value which it creates, the workers tend to do their best under a system that wins their confidence and loyalty. Where the workers with new solidarity feel that they are working for themselves, they have the same successful motivation that the owners had in the early days of capitalist system."

Now to a more detailed examination. Dr. Eddy says: "Beginning with the lower and more individual incentives, and rising to higher and more social ones, we may distinguish some twelve motivations which are chiefly operative in Soviet Russia today, as follows."

1. *Self-Interest*

This takes the form of differential wages for grades of skill or piece-work, opportunities for adult education, group bonus schemes, prizes and medals, the

[3] John Ruskin (1819-1900); English art critic and writer; wrote on art, architecture and literature, also economic and social problems; advocated national system of education in countrywide lectures, 1855-70; First Slade Professor of Fine Arts, Oxford, 1869-79; publications include: *Modern Painters, Seven Lamps of Architecture, Stones of Venice, Unto this last, Munera Pulveris, Fors Clavigera, The Crown of Wild Olive, Praeterita* (autobiography), *The King of the Golden River, Ethics of the Dust*, and *The Art of England*.

winning for one's factory of an improved social centre, lunch-rooms, entertainment hall, a day nursery for the children, etc.

Not all of these incentives have individual appeal; quite a few are designed to stimulate group effort and consciousness. Let Dr. Eddy explain it.

1. "Objectively, the difference is not in the motive but in the system where the self-interest of the individual is enlisted not for monopolistic private gain but for the common good; where self-interest and social-interest are almost identical. In offering the worker more pay for skilled labour or piece-work, this adds to the production and profit of the whole community in which the worker will have his full share. In doing this the leaders are realistic rather than idealistic. They recognize that the habits of the worker have been warped by the old system under which he has worked. They know that they are not creating an ideal utopia in a vacuum, but building socialism in the midst of a hostile capitalist world which has already opposed them by intervention, invasion, a hunger blockade, adverse competition and propaganda."

2. "Moral Indignation, Hatred and Fear were powerful motivations, especially in the early, destructive stages of the Revolution. There was an outraged sense of justice that burned in the heart of Marx[4] and in all the early revolutionaries. . . . Fear is also a common human motivation, especially in Russia today. Fear of invasion by the capitalist world is constantly played upon by the leaders and the press to unite the population in loyal defense."

3. "Pugnacity, the fighting spirit and the class war are all invoked in the cause of the continuing revolution. . . . In Russia they have been able in a remarkable way to harness this fighting spirit to the creative, constructive and peaceful work which succeeded the dramatic stage of destruction. The whole Five Year Plan was such a constructive undertaking. . . . The factory worker is taught that he is 'a soldier on duty' and is carrying on the fight for socialism against the capitalist world. He is a shock brigade taking part in the industrial and cultural attack. Military metaphors are freely and successfully used."

4. "The will to power, the stimulation of a sense of personal dignity and of self-importance tend to remove the inferiority complex from the workers and to make them feel that they are the messianic class which is to deliver the world. Whether it be true or not, it gives the workers a status, a sense of mission and belief in their own indomitable power that motivates them for tremendous undertaking."

5. "The creative instinct is another powerful motivation. The desire to find satisfaction in excellence of performance, the impulse to create something which many could approve or enjoy was more powerful in early handicrafts and during the Renaissance than after the machine swept this away under system of mass production. In Russia the spirit of youth predominates. . . . It is a moving experience to hear fifty thousand youth shouting in perfect union, as I did in Moscow: 'We are

[4] Heinrich Karl Marx (1818-83); German philosopher and socialist; lifelong partner and friend of Friedrich Engels with whom he collaborated in writing many important works on socialism including *Manifesto of the Communist Party* (1848) and in developing his theories of dialectical materialism; after being expelled from Prussia in 1849 settled in London where he wrote the first volume of *Das Kapital* (1867).

changing the world! We are changing the world!'. . . . In Russia all the parasitic pursuits and privileges of inherited wealth or titles have been destroyed and the ground cleared for creative construction."

6. "Social acquisitiveness gradually takes the place of personal acquisition as a new social order replaces the old artificial, competitive, atomic individualism. . . . The Soviets are learning that the family circle may be widened for the toiler to include his country, his class and the workers of the world; that social acquisitiveness is far more valuable and effective than anti-social individual acquisitiveness. . . . Communists would no more think of commercializing for private profit the necessities of their fellow men for housing, water, gas, electric power, transportation, telegraphs, telephones, radio, moving pictures, or financial credit than they would try to profiteer out of fresh air, or sunshine, or the educational system."

7. "Social competition and the sporting instinct is appealed to constantly and effectively. This seems to be already almost as powerful and far less anti-social than cut-throat individual competition. Williams James[5] maintained that rivalry did nine-tenths of the world's work. All the competition engendered in college athletics and school sports is utilized in Soviet socialist competition. Self-seeking gives place to social serving as in all true team play. . . . The Soviet system co-ordinates the egoistic and altruistic incentives under a scheme of ownership where a man necessarily works for others when he works for himself, and where all share almost equally in the profits. In one aspect the whole Five Year Plan was a supreme achievement in socialist competition. They throw into competition worker with worker, group with group, factory with factory. They compete with their past record, with the goal of the Plan, with the capitalist world."

8. The appeal to the heroic, the dramatic, and to social approval and disapproval.

"In capitalist countries money is power in business, politics and the press. In Russia all success is harnessed to service not profit. This changes the whole atmosphere of the factory, the farm and the school. It will entirely change the character of the moving picture, the radio and the press. In time it alters the psychology of the people as well. There is a transvaluation of ethical values. All exploitation is held to be dishonourable. All using of men as means to another's profit, as powers in a game, or cogs in a machine, or 'hands' in a private enterprise become immoral. Every organization in the Soviet Union from the kindergartens and the youth organizations upward becomes imbued with this spirit. From birth to maturity no other ideal is ever held up before young or old.

"As the visitor passes down the Hall of Fame in any Russian City or park he sees statues and tablets not to generals, admirals or politicians, but to the heroes of industry who have led the way to the success of the Five Year Plan. As Stalin[6] truly

[5] William James (1842-1910); American psychologist and philosopher; taught anatomy, physiology, hygiene, and philosophy at Harvard University; leading exponent of pragmatism; publications include: *The Principles of Psychology, The Will to Believe and other Essays, The Varieties of Religious Experience, Pragmatism, The Meaning of Truth, A Pluralistic Universe, Some Problems in Philosophy.*

[6] Joseph Stalin (1879-1953); Soviet political leader; took part in the Russian Revolution, 1917; General Secretary, Central Committee of the Soviet Communist Party, 1922; succeeded Lenin as Chairman of the Politburo, 1924; became Chairman of the Council of People's Commissars (Premier) and took command of the armed forces, 1941.

said, 'Here in the U.S.S.R. the most desirable course which earns social approval is the possibility of becoming a hero of labour, a hero of the shock movement, surrounded with, the glamour of the respect of the millions of toilers.'

"The dramatic instinct of the Russian and his power to visualize is brought to bear to stimulate the ambition of the workers and to expose their shortcomings."

9. *Mutual Aid and Co-operation*

Dr. Eddy reminds us that in Soviet Russia there are 70,000,000 members of co-operative societies and then adds that "The Soviet Union is building a social environment geared to the higher social motives of co-operation and mutual aid."

10. "Humanitarian and higher ethical ends are increasingly utilized as incentives in Soviet Russia. Their faith in human nature and especially in the common man that he will respond favourably to a favourable environment is validating itself in results. Although Marx undoubtedly idealized the proletariat as a messianic 'remnant', a class that was to deliver the world, his faith in the workers has been rewarded by a vast development of their unsuspected potentialities. We have already seen in their redemption of criminals how these higher motives work in practice.... Such achievements are not only sound in their science, their psychology and their underlying philosophy, but in their humanitarian and ethical motivation as well."

11. The motive of hope, of triumphant optimism, of almost fatalistic conviction in a eschatological future is potent in Russia. "Marx's almost fatalistic faith in the triumph of the proletariat and of the cause of human justice seemed to himself to be an obvious scientific demonstration but it was an undemonstrable and almost religious faith.... Such a faith often becomes creative and builds its dream on the solid earth of reality. For myself, while I see no adequate sign of the tyranny of the proletariat lessening, I must admit that in general the optimistic faith and hope of the communists is tending to actualize and validate itself."

12. "Religious emotion, almost fanatical faith, sacrifice, missionary zeal, and international worldwide objectives which are closely akin to their eschatological hope, are dynamic incentives in Russia today."

These are the new incentives. I cannot say that I agree with the classification followed by Dr. Eddy. There is overlapping and not fine enough analysis to break down the incentives in elementary psychological categories. But anyway these they are, clearly enough set out. They seem to be, by and large, so different from those commonly known in our society that one must wonder, unless one is imbued with the socialist science, that they work so well and are so eminently successful at a time when all human values seem powerless in other parts of the world. Some of them, no doubt, bear resemblance to our own familiar motivations, but one gets the impression that they belong to a transitional stage and that they are there only as a concession to a past which cannot too easily be shaken off. The others are new and their success must give hope and courage to us who have faith in them.

52. Circular to Secretary, Utkal Congress Socialist Party, 16 January 1935[1]

To
The Secretary
Utkal Congress Socialist Party

Bombay
16 January 1935

Dear Comrade,

Re.: Congress Socialist

I am sorry to say that, in spite of my appeals, most of the provincial parties are not discharging their responsibilities towards the central organ of the party. You are aware of the importance of a party organ and the useful work the Congress Socialist has already done. It can do much more: it can become a political force in the country, it can become the vanguard of the whole anti-imperialist struggle, if we all co-operate and build it up.

Every provincial party should do its utmost to enrol subscribers for the *Socialist* and also to organize its sale in the larger cities.

Every active member of the party should get at least five subscribers before the middle of the next month.

You should see that the quota for your province on this basis is fulfilled by that date.

In the cities where single copies can be sold in the streets, it should be desirable to make some arrangement for such sale with a newspaper agent on the usual commissions and terms.

Attempts should also be made by approaching such Swadeshi concerns as insurance companies, publishing houses, soap and oil manufactures, etc., to get advertisements for the *Socialist*. The fact that the paper has an all-India circulation—it sells from Calicut to Lahore—should be stressed while securing advertisements.

Party secretaries should also send reports of the activities of their party and secure contributions for it.

I hope you will set about this work in all earnestness and organize a real good drive for it.

Please let me know how many copies of the *Socialist* are at present being sold through your party and how many subscribers have been made so far by party members.

Re.: Party Organization and Programme of Work

It is a matter of surprise and regret that many party secretaries have not yet replied to my second circular letter.[2] You will recall that the circular dealt with very

[1] *Nabakrushna Chaudhuri Papers* (NMML). The same circular was sent to all the provinical secretaries of the Congress Socialist Party.

[2] See item no. 41.

important matters, namely, the re-organization of the provincial parties and the chalking out of an immediate programme of work. It is to be regretted that even parties which before the last Annual Conference reported a membership of hundreds have shown little sign of activity. With respect to some provinces, when parties were supposed to exist at the time of the Conference, serious doubts have arisen whether in fact there is at all any organization there or not.

I shall earnestly request you, therefore, to inform me accurately the stage of organization your party has reached. In this connection, kindly send me information on the following points:-

1. Does a Congress Socialist party exist in your province on a provincial basis? If so when and how was it formed, who are its office-bearers, what is the strength of its executive, in how many districts of your province are there branches of it, what is its constitution and programme (kindly send me a copy of these)?
2. If a properly organized party on a provincial basis does not exist, what is the form of organization evolved so far?
3. Since the last All-India Conference at Bombay, has any general meeting of your party or of its Executive been held to re-organize the party on the basis of the Bombay decisions? If so, please send me your new constitution and programme. If not so, please call such a meeting immediately for the purpose indicated. In this connection circular letter No. 2 should be consulted for further guidance.
4. How many active and ordinary members are there in your party at present? In this connection, I should like to point out that quality and not quantity should be stressed. Particularly in regard to the active members, every care should be taken to enrol only such members as are really prepared to put in some work for the party.
5. What are the present activities of your party? Please send a report of the work done so far.

I should like to make a few remarks in connection with our work. We should always keep in mind the fact that the Congress Socialist movement claims to be the vanguard of the independence movement. All our activities, therefore, should be such as to justify and further this claim. A tendency has been reached in some places for party members to get involved in little affairs, say, in the organization of employees in petty trades. This is waste of energy. Our resources are very small and we should therefore, use them as effectively as possible.

Our activities fall mainly in three groups: propaganda, labour and peasant.

With regard to propaganda, our first concern should be to influence the rank and file of the Congress. This is very important, because much of the future of our party depends upon our success in this task. Nothing should be done which may antagonize the genuinely nationalist elements and drive them to join hands with the compromise-seeking right wing. Nothing can be worse than adopting such tactics as may divide the Congress into two hostile camps: socialists and anti-socialists. We should, on the contrary, try to take the militant nationalists with us and divide the Congress into the latter and compromising moderates. Our tactics and propaganda should be along these lines.

As for Socialism, there is not the slightest doubt in my mind, that, under present world conditions, it would be at all difficult to bring those who are really fighting for the independence of the masses to accept Socialism. Only patient propaganda and contact are required. Every provincial party should try to produce socialist literature in its own provincial language. It would also be of benefit to organize study classes and get serious Congress workers to join.

With regard to labour, the idea is not to organize any sort of labour. We should first of all concentrate on such fields of labour organization as may be of political advantage. It should be remembered that a general strike is the goal. Naturally, strikes in such places as will affect imperialism and its working, would be the most effective. Railways, mines, the heavy industries should be our first concern. It is not possible to discuss other details in this letter. You should be able yourself to develop the idea. I might say that the other industries and the interests of the labourers are not to be neglected, but in view of our resources, it is better to keep in mind the comparative ultimate effectiveness of our various activities.

Peasant work is really our most important work. As much stress should be laid on this as possible. The work of the Kerala party should serve as a guide in this connection. The attempt merely to form peasant unions is, to my mind, artificial, unless there is a live issue and an agitation to form a basis and incentive for such organization. Our task is to create these issues and develop an agitation around them.

Where our resources or local conditions do not permit the development of a peasant movement, our party members should take up the study of peasant problems in their province, should engage themselves in touring the village for propaganda, should even join the constructive work of the Congress in order to come in touch with the village, if in no other way a contact is possible.

With regard to propaganda among the peasant masses, it may be a profitable thing to establish contacts with sugar mill labourers, because these are seasonal labourers and after the mill closes most of them return to their villages. If these mill workers are organized and propaganda is done among them, the ideas that they may imbibe will find root in the villages. Other seasonal industries may likewise be utilized.

The Congress and our Party

I have already said something about our tactics with regard to the Congress and rank and file.

I wish further to emphasize that we should on no account isolate ourselves from the Congress. It is true that there is hardly anything in the present programme of the Congress which is of interest to us. However, in all those activities with which we have no disagreement, such as enrolment of Congressmen, the campaign regarding the Karachi Resolution, celebration of Independence Day, propaganda against the J.P.C. Report and agitation regarding the Constituent Assembly. (I might inform you in this connection that the party is having a pamphlet prepared on the

Constituent Assembly) we should always be in the forefront.

In closing I shall earnestly request you to send me a detailed reply to this circular, and, if you have not already done so, to circular No. 2 also.

With greetings,

Yours fraternally,
Jayaprakash Narayan
General Secretary

53. Interview to Press on Congress Working Committee Resolution, 19 January 1935[1]

I do not know what is exactly meant by the resolution passed by the Working Committee regarding disciplinary action,[2] a report of which has appeared in the papers.

The phrase 'who deliberately acts or carries on propaganda against the official programme and decisions of the Congress' is too sweeping and ambiguous.

As far as I can see in the new constitution, there is no general provision for taking disciplinary action against an individual Congressman or a subordinate Congress Committee.

Art. V (c) provides for action against those who belong to communal organizations engaged in 'anti-national' activities or in such activities as are 'in conflict with those of the Congress'.

Art. VIII (c) contemplates action against such Provincial Congress Committees which do not comply with the provisions of the New Constitution or the rules framed thereunder by the Working Committee.

Art. XII (d) authorizes the Working Committee to take such disciplinary action as it may deem fit against a committee or individual for misconduct, wilful neglect or default.

These are the only provisions which the new constitution has made for disciplinary action.

The first two provisions are explicit enough and are meant to meet certain definite situations. The first provision even if stretched far enough cannot cover the phrase used by the Working Committee, viz., who deliberately acts or carries on propaganda against the official programme and decisions of the Congress, unless the Working Committee thinks that this is tantamount to misconduct. If that is so all that I can say is that the interpretation is too far-fetched.

[1] *Bombay Chronicle*, 19 January 1935.

[2] Congress Working Committee at its meeting at Delhi on 16 January 1935 passed a resolution deciding upon disciplinary action against any rebel member or committee of the Congress.

Apart from any constitutional provisions the Working Committee's resolution seems to be very unhappily worded. If it is carried out into practice, it would virtually muzzle all criticism, and all such activities which, though not provided for in the official programme, are yet consistent with the object and creed of the Congress.

One only hopes that at a time when Congress leaders are freely issuing invitations to their Liberal friends, who consistently opposed the Congress in the last years of India's critical history, to join the Congress, the vague disciplinary powers would not be utilized to check the genuine, militant elements in the Congress for developing their programme. It should be obvious that such a step would be suicidal for a growing organization like Congress and would be a poor compliment to the political vision of the Congress Command.

54. Letter to Rohit Mehta, 6 February 1935[1]

Bombay
6 February 1935

My dear Rohit,[2]

Your letter. I do not quite see your difficulty regarding the dates of the Nagpur meeting.[3] It would be quite easy for you to reach Meerut on the 20th even if you leave Nagpur on the 18th. Gautam and possibly Firoze Chand[4] are going to Nagpur for the meeting. I might inform you that I changed dates once on account of the anniversary period which was previously fixed in the first week of February.

I do earnestly urge on you the desirability of you being present at Nagpur. If dates be your only trouble, it would not be difficult to solve it—in fact there is no difficulty at all on that account.

Very sincerely yours,
Jayaprakash

[1] Bhaskar Vyas and Bachubhai Sutaria, *A Philosopher's Journey, Reflections on the Times & Values of Rohit Mehta*, Vallabh Vidyanagar, 1998.

[2] Rohit Mehta (1908-95); Secretary, Ahmedabad Youth League, 1928; member, Servants of the People Society, 1929-35; participated in the civil disobedience movement, 1930, 1932, and jailed; Founder-member, C.S.P., 1934, and also member of its National Executive, 1934; Secretary, Gujarat C.S.P., 1934-5; International Secretary, Theosophical Society, 1936-44, and also its General Secretary, Indian Section, 1944-60.

[3] Refers to the meeting of National Executive of the Congress Socialist Party at Nagpur, 16-17 February 1935.

[4] Feroz Chand (1899-1974); participated in the non-cooperation movement, 1921; was one of the first to join the Servants of the People Society, 1921, and was its Vice-President, 1928-37, and President, 1939; edited *Bandematram*, *People*, and *Times of India*; Managing Director, Samachar Bharati; wrote *Lajpat Rai*.

55. Circular to Provincial Secretaries, Congress Socialist Party [before 7 February 1935][1]

[Before 7 February 1935]

To
Secretary
Congress Socialist Party

Dear Comrade,
As announced the Congress will celebrate Feb. 7th as anti-J.P.C. Report Day. I think that it would be inadvisable for our Party members to obstruct or disturb the official programme for that day. We should put forth our point of view on the matter in our speeches, if we are allowed to speak. Further than that we should not go.

The Executive Committee at Nagpur will draw up a programme for our Party with regard to the J.P.C. Report.

The All-India Trade Union Congress is celebrating a Labour Week starting from Feb. 4th. All Provincial Parties and their local committees should give full cooperation to the Trade Union Congress in making the week a success.

Yours fraternally,
Jayaprakash Narayan
General Secretary
All India Congress Socialist Party

[1] *JP Papers* (NMML).

56. Interview to Press on J.P.C. Report, 16 February 1935[1]

It is clear enough that the government suffered a rather ignominous defeat on the J.P.C. Report. Notwithstanding the obliging services of the race-course Prince and the votes of the official bloc, the Assembly decided by a majority of 20 that the All-India Federation was 'bad and totally unacceptable to the people of British India'. 'A real and complete responsible government' at the centre could alone satisfy the Indian people. 'Second Chambers, the extraordinary and special powers of governors, provisions relating to the police', etc., vitiated the scheme of provincial governments and made it disappointing and unsatisfactory.

That a defeat of the government is a victory of the Congress is a rule-of-thumb of Indian politics. Like other such rules it practically never errs. Broadly speaking, the Congress is the only political organization that has effectively challenged the

[1] *Bombay Chronicle*, 16 February 1935. Interview to United Press at Calcutta on the Indian Legislative Assembly's verdict on the Joint Parliamentary Committee Report.

government and if the government suffers a defeat the simultaneity of Congress victory only stands to reason. In this particular instance of a governmental defeat, however, there is an apparent defeat of the Congress too. The Congress Party's amendment calling for a whole-hog rejection of the reform scheme was defeated by 72 votes against 81.

For a self-respecting Indian who by force of a reasoned habit does not count the heads of the officials and the nominees, these figures are a violation of the simple rules of arithmetic. We only know that the Congress Party's amendment was carried by a respectable majority of 26, 61 voting for it and 35 against. The official-cum-nominees bloc, we are told, number 37; we do numerously feel their heavy pressure but otherwise, they are to us an uncognizable non-descript nothing.

However, now that we talk of the verdict of the Assembly, we must take things as they are. In the first instance the Assembly accepted the Communal Award[2] 'until a substitute is agreed upon by the various communities concerned' and, what is more improper, out of the four occasions on which the members divided themselves, two were in regard to the Communal Award. In the second place the Congress Party, in order to defeat the government, had to vote for a review by the government of the whole position in consultation with Indian opinion.

This in itself must be sufficient for every Congressman to rack his brains. Does he want yet another Round Table Conference?

[2] Ramsay MacDonald, the British Prime Minister, made an announcement in the British Parliament on 16 August 1932 regarding communal representation in the legislatures in India. This came to be known as the Communal Award. It recognized the depressed classes amongst the Hindus as a minority and gave them a fixed number of seats with separate electorate. This division of the Hindu community on caste lines was opposed by Gandhi who undertook a fast unto death on 20 September 1932 against the Award.

57. Circular to Members, Congress Socialist Party [after 16 February 1935][1]

[After 16 February 1935]

Dear Comrade,

The Executive Committee decided at its last meeting at Nagpur to levy a monthly tax of Rs. 5/- from its members towards the expenses of the All India Party.

I shall be obliged if you send me your quota for February, March & April, in all Rs. 15/-.

I hope you will send your contribution regularly every month.

Yours fraternally,
Jayaprakash Narayan

[1] *Nabakrushna Chaudhuri Papers* (NMML).

58. Circular to Secretary, Bihar Congress Socialist Party, 23 February 1935[1]

Wardha
23 February 1935

To
The Secretary
Bihar P.C.S.P.

Dear Comrade,
The Executive Committee at its last meeting decided, as you might have learnt from press reports, to observe an All India Detenu Day on March 3.

This question has been rather neglected by the country and during my recent visit to Calcutta I realized how bitter the feeling of Bengal was in the matter. The least that we can do is to remind ourselves of the sufferings of the people of Bengal and give expression to our sympathy for them.

I am sure you will be glad that the lead in this matter has come from our party.

I am trying to get the cooperation of the Congress for the observance of this Day. If I succeed, we shall jointly observe the Day. In that case it might become necessary to change the date to the 10th of March. In the meanwhile, however, kindly make your preparations on the basis of the 3rd. I shall inform you of the postponement, if any, by wire, or through the press.

The programme for the Day would be holding of meetings in the evening at which a resolution, the draft of which I shall circulate later, would be passed and speeches describing the horrors of Bengal and the condition of the detenus would be made.

I shall communicate the other decisions of the Committee as soon as possible. Some of them will appear in the next issue of the *Congress Socialist*.

Fraternally yours,
Jayaprakash Narayan
General Secretary

[1] *JP Papers*. The same circular was sent to all the provincial secretaries of the Congress Socialist Party.

59. Appeal to Observe All India Detenu Day, 24 February 1935[1]

I wish to draw the attention of the country and, particularly of the Congress to the All India Detenu Day, which has been fixed for March 3 by the executive of the All India Congress Socialist Party. Meetings should be held all over the country

[1] *Congress Socialist*, 24 February 1935.

protesting against the imprisonment of nearly 3,000 innocent men—innocent because they have been punished without any charge. On March 3 the whole country should demand the release of these brave patriots or their fair trial in a court of law. I appeal to the Congress to cooperate with us in making the day a success. This is the least we can do for our comrades.

Jayaprakash Narayan
General Secretary
Congress Socialist Party

60. Circular to Secretaries of Trade Unions, 26 February 1935[1]

Wardha
26 February 1935

Dear Comrade,

The Executive Committee of the All India Congress Socialist Party at its last meeting at Nagpur authorized me to convene a Conference of Trade Union representatives for the purpose of discussing ways and means of bringing about unity in the Trade Union movement and to that end to invite the A.I.T.U.C., the N.T.U.F., and the Red T.U.C.[2] to send their representatives to such a Conference.

I propose to convene the Conference in Delhi on March 16 & 17 and I hereby invite your organization to send its representatives to it. The dates are provisional and subject to change, if they do not suit you, in which case kindly suggest other dates. I wish to stress only this that we should like the Conference to meet some time in March, so that the results might be available by the time the annual session of the A.I.T.U.C. meets in April.

To avoid any misunderstanding, I wish to make it clear that my Party does not claim any Trade Union status while convening this Conference. It merely desires to bring the different parties together and to exert whatever influence it has in the interests of unity, for which it has been anxious since its formation. Representatives of the Party have discussed the question with representatives of all the three organizations, which we propose to invite, and it was only the encouragement that we received then that induced us to call this Conference.

I further wish to make clear that this invitation is not bound by any terms whatever. We wish to start on a completely clean slate and our only condition is the desire for unity which, as we discovered from previous consultations, is shared by all the three bodies concerned.

[1] *JP Papers* (NMML).

[2] The Red Trade Union Congress was formed on 6 July 1931 with D.B. Kulkarni as President, S.V. Deshpande, Bankim Mukerjee and S.G. Sardesai as secretaries by breaking away from the All India Trade Union Congress with the help of 12 unions. It merged with the All India Trade Union Congress on 20 April 1935 at the All Parties Unity Conference held at Calcutta.

I shall be obliged if you would treat this letter as urgent and reply at your earliest convenience.

Fraternally yours,
Jayaprakash Narayan

61. Statement on All India Detenu Day Postponement, 3 March 1935[1]

I had issued a statement on March 1, suggesting the postponement of the observance of the Detenu Day, pending consultations with the Congress President for joint observance of the day. I understand that the message did not reach several places in time, and meetings might have been held. No harm is done. After consulting Babu Rajendra Prasad,[2] I shall issue instructions regarding the day and the form of the demonstration and the text of the resolution for adoption throughout the country.

[1] *Bombay Chronicle*, 4 March 1935. Statement issued at Wardha.

[2] Rajendra Prasad (1884-1963); one of the most prominent leaders of the Congress and thrice its President, 1934, 1939, and 1947-8; Minister of Food and Agriculture, Government of India, 1946-8; President, Constituent Assembly, 1946-50; President of India, 1950-62; awarded Bharat Ratna, 1962.

62. Letter to S.V. Ghate [after 12 March 1935][1]

[After 12 March 1935]

Dear Comrade Ghate,[2]
Please excuse me for not replying to your letters earlier.

The Unity affair has been bungled, I am afraid. I wish you had gone to Cawnpore.[3] The decision at Delhi[4] was taken without my knowledge. However, we shall try to

[1] *JP Papers* (NMML).

[2] S.V. Ghate (1896-1970); one of the founders of the C.P.I. and its first General Secretary, 1925; active in Bombay Trade Union movement; arrested in connection with Meerut Conspiracy Case, 1929, and released, 1933; imprisoned, 1940-4, and 1948-50; member, Central Committee, C.P.I., 1943-50; Treasurer, C.P.I., 1953; elected to Central Control Commission, C.P.I., 1956.

[3] Refers to a conference convened by the A.I.T.U.C. at Kanpur on 9 March 1935 to devise ways and means to bring about unity in all the trade union groups in the country. The conference could not be held because of poor response from the representatives of the trade unions.

[4] Representatives of the A.I.T.U.C. met some leaders of the N.T.U.F. at Delhi as a result of which a

set matters right as best we can. The fact that nearly all your Unions have been suppressed, has made the position of your [Red Trade Union] Congress rather weak. I am writing to the A.I.T.U.C. and the N.T.U.F. to invite your representatives also to future meetings of the Joint Committee which was set up at Delhi.

As for the Detenu Day, the thing is still hanging fire. I feel sorry for having asked the Congress to join us. However now I must wait till I definitely hear from the President.

I shall write to you in this matter when the final decision has been reached.

Yours fraternally,
JP

---

statement was issued on 12 March 1935 proposing the formation of a Joint Committee, where representatives of the A.I.T.U.C. and N.T.U.F. could sit and chalk out a programme of joint works in trade union field with mutual understanding that none of the two will indulge in mutual recriminations of each other.

63. Letter to V.V. Giri [after 12 March 1935][1]

[After 12 March 1935]

Dear Comrade Giri,[2]
I am afraid I cannot yet reconcile myself with the constitution of the Joint Committee which was set up at Delhi. I strongly feel that the Red T.U.C. should also be invited to the future meetings of the Committee. It was not the fault of the latter that its representatives were not present in Delhi. It therefore appears to be against the spirit of Unity to leave them out of a body the very purpose of which is to realize that Unity.

I am, accordingly, writing to both the A.I.T.U.C. and the N.T.U.F. suggesting that the representatives of the Red T.U.C. should also be invited to meetings of the Joint Committee.

I hope you are enjoying the Assembly better after the recess.

Yours fraternally,
JP

---

[1] *JP Papers* (NMML).

[2] V.V. Giri (1894-1980); advocate, Madras High Court; gave up practice to participate in the non-cooperation movement; trade union leader; Vice-President, All India Railwaymen's Federation, 1925, and its General Secretary, 1931; President, A.I.T.U.C., 1926, and 1942; member, Indian Legislative Assembly, 1934-7; Minister of Labour, Industries, Cooperation and Commerce, Madras Government, 1937-9, and 1946-7; High Commissioner of India to Ceylon, 1947-51; member, Lok Sabha, 1952-7; Governor, U.P., 1957-60, Kerala, 1960-5, and Mysore, 1965-7; Vice-President of India, 1967-9, and President, 1969-74; publications include: *Labour Problems in Indian Industry*, *Jobs For Our Millions*, *My Life and Times*, Vol. I (autobiography).

64. Letter to General Secretary, A.I.T.U.C. [after 12 March 1935][1]

[After 12 March 1935]

To
The General Secretary
A.I.T.U.C.
209, Cornwallis Street
Calcutta

Dear Comrade,
At a meeting of the representatives of the A.I.T.U.C. and the N.T.U.F. held recently at Delhi, a Joint Committee was formed to explore the possibilities of Trade Union unity. The said meeting was called hurriedly and informally and, as I understand, there was no time to invite the representatives of the Red T.U.C.

I suggest that at future meetings of the Joint Committee the latter should also be invited. This, as you will agree with me, will be in keeping with the spirit of the Unity resolution passed at Nagpur by your Executive.

I am writing a similar letter to the N.T.U.F.

Yours fraternally,
JP

[1] *JP Papers* (NMML).

65. Comment on Subhas Chandra Bose's Statement on Political Situation in India, 24 March 1935[1]

It is a matter of satisfaction to me that a leader of the standing of Subhas Babu,[2] while analysing the present political situation in India,[3] has pointed his finger so unmistakably towards the Congress Socialist Party as representing the next forward step in the evolution of the anti-imperialist struggle in the country and therefore as the party of the future.

[1] *Bombay Chronicle*, 26 March 1935. Statement issued at Banaras.

[2] Subhas Chandra Bose (1897-1945); selected for the I.C.S., 1920, but resigned (1921) and joined the non-cooperation movement; one of the most prominent leaders of the Congress; jailed several times; President, Bengal P.C.C. for several years; elected Congress President, 1938; re-elected, 1939, but resigned owing to differences with Gandhi and the Congress old guard; founded All India Forward Bloc, 1939; escaped to Germany, 1941; organized Indian National Army and Provisional Government of Free India in Singapore, 1943; reported to have died in a plane crash over Taipeh in Taiwan on way to Tokyo.

[3] This refers to Press statement of Subhas Chandra Bose, published in the *Amrita Bazar Patrika*, 15 March 1935. For text see Appendix 12.

As to the misgivings of Subhas Babu regarding our being under Fabian influences, I can assure him that his fears are only due to his lack of contact with the Party, its programme and its work. No one who has even a bowing acquaintance with our programme can for a moment suspect us to be under the influences of that ineffective and discredited school whose high priest has ended in a peerage.

Subhas Babu has mentioned the Constituent Assembly. It is true that we have supported the idea of a Constituent Assembly but we have at the same time made it clear that such an Assembly can be representative only if it is elected by representative Committees of workers, peasants and other exploited classes. The Party will never let matters stand in the way of gaining its objectives.

66. Circular to Secretary, Gujarat Congress Socialist Party, 25 March 1935[1]

Benares
25 March 1935

To
The Secretary
Gujarat Congress Socialist Party

Dear Comrade,

In the issue of 24th of February of the *Congress Socialist* most of the decisions and resolutions of the Nagpur meeting of the All India Executive were published. In addition to them certain other decisions were taken which I am giving below:

Reorganization

1. Whereas in certain provinces Parties which affiliated at the time of the Bombay Conference have failed to function, the secretaries are requested to help in revitalizing such Parties and (1) where there is no properly constituted executive committee in the province or (2) where the Provincial Executive has either communicated its inability to organize the province or where the organization has failed to show signs of life and has lapsed into a mere paper organization, the secretaries are given power in consultation with the active members, if any in the province, to reconstitute such parties by convening Provincial conferences, conducting fresh elections of Provincial Executives and otherwise as may be necessary.

2. The Committee regrets that several Parties have not submitted their Constitutions for approval and appoints Comrades Purushotam and Masani to form a sub-committee for examining Provincial Constitutions and gives them power to suggest modifications in the latter in order to bring them in conformity with the Constitution and Rules of the All India Party. In case their suggestions are not

[1] *Kamalashanker Pandya Papers* (NMML). The same circular was sent to all the provincial secretaries of the Congress Socialist Party.

accepted no general meetings or elections of the Provincial Parties concerned should be held till the next meeting of the All India Executive.

Re.: Resolutions for the A.I.C.C.

It was decided that notice of resolutions on the following subjects should be sent to the A.I.C.C.: (1) The Policy of the C.P.B. (2) War (3) Change in Congress Creed (Party's amendment to article 1 of Congress Constitution) (4) Socialist Objective (5) Indian States (6) The New Government of India Bill.

Re.: National Week

It was decided that in addition to participating in the programme for the National Week as may be fixed by the Congress the Party should give particular attention to the following activities:

(1) Distribution of leaflets in the Provincial languages explaining the Party's objective and programme;
(2) Enrolment of Congress members;
(3) Holding public meetings under the auspices of the Party on the last two days of the week.

Re.: Elections for Local Bodies

It was decided that in the event of the Congress or Congressmen contesting elections to Local Bodies, Party members should press for the acceptance of a socialist programme more or less on the lines of the Bombay Party's municipal programme.

Re.: Party's Attitude Towards Congress

Comrade Sampurnanand's thesis[2] on the subject was considered. It was decided that the line laid down in this connection in the General Secretary's circular letter No. 4 as supplemented by Comrade Sampurnanand's thesis should be followed. The Peasant Committee was asked to recommend ways and means for implementing the proposal made in the said thesis.

So much for the decisions of the Committee. I should like to draw your attention to the questions of organization raised by the Committee. If you have not already sent a copy of your constitution to the Central Office, kindly send one immediately to Comrade Masani.

In connection with organization I wish also to remind you that I have not yet received answers to the enquiries I made in my last circular.

Re.: Central Office

A good deal of confusion has resulted from the fact that so far there has been no Central Office of the Party. Due to the fact of my being constantly moving about you and I have found it difficult to keep in touch. I have therefore decided to set up

[2] See item no. 77 dated 14 May 1935.

a permanent office which will be located here at Benares. From now on please address all communications to the General Secretary, All India Congress Socialist Party, Kabir Chaura, Banares City (U.P.)

Re.: United Front

I am enclosing herewith a copy of the report[3] of the United Front Committee[4] that was submitted at the last meeting of the Executive. The report speaks for itself.

You should get in touch with the local or provincial branches of the organizations which have come to Untied Front agreement with us, viz., the A.I.T.U.C., the N.T.U.F. and the Red T.U.C., and develop joint action with them in your province.

You will please note that joint activity is to be only on specific issues. Where feasible, as it is in large centres where speedy intercommunication is possible, a Joint Committee should be appointed with a representative from each organization for the purpose of arranging the details of joint functions.

If there are any such groups in your Province as are not included in the A.I.T.U.C., the N.T.U.F. and the Red T.U.C., you should attempt to reach an agreement with them also on the lines similar to those evolved by our United Front Committee. It is very important that you should come to a friendly and cooperative understanding with all the radical groups in your Province.

Fraternally yours,
Jayaprakash Narayan
General Secretary

[3] See Appendix 13 for Report of the United Front Committee.

[4] The Congress Socialist Party at its first Conference in Bombay on 21-2 October 1934 authorised the 'Executive Committee . . . to appoint a Sub-Committee to explore the possibilities of joint action on specific issues with the different labour and radical groups in the country'. In pursuance of the resolution a committee was appointed with Purshottam Trikamdas, S.M. Joshi, Sorab Batliwala, Charles Mascarenhas, M.R. Masani and Jayaprakash Narayan (Secretary) as members. This became generally known as the United Front Committee.

67. Circular to Secretary, Bihar Congress Socialist Party, 28 March 1935[1]

Circular No. 8

Kabir Chaura
Benares City (U.P.)
28 March 1935

To
Secretary
Bihar Congress Socialist Party

Dear Comrade,
It is a matter of regret to me that the observance of the Detenu Day had to be

[1] *JP Papers* (NMML). The same circular was sent to all the provincial secretaries of the Congress Socialist Party.

postponed so long. I was hoping that I might get the Congress to join us on this issue. I had thought that the observance would really be made impressive thereby and we would also succeed in getting the Congress actively associated with this question.

However, I am given to understand that the President of the Congress wants to place this matter before the Working Committee, which will meet at the time of the A.I.C.C. meeting. As it would be very inadvisable to delay the 'Day' so long, I am fixing April 7th for the purpose. By a coincidence the date falls in the National Week, which will enhance the importance of the 'Day'.

I am enclosing the draft of a resolution also for the 'Day'.

Yours fraternally,
Jayaprakash Narayan
General Secretary

Resolution

This meeting of citizens strongly condemns the continuous repression that has been going on in Bengal culminating in the detention without trial and in secrecy of a large number of the youth of Bengal torn from their natural surroundings. The meagre news that is given to the public of these detention camps and the news that, in spite of secrecy, percolates out of them fill the public mind with dread and suspicion.

This meeting is further of the opinion that the policy of ruthless repression that is being pursued in Bengal is calculated to overawe and demoralize the public.

This meeting therefore calls upon the Government of Bengal to remove the repressive laws and either discharge the detenus or give them a fair trial through the ordinary courts of law.

This meeting asks Congress members of the Legislative Assembly and others to adopt all possible measures to obtain redress in this matter.

This meeting assures the people of Bengal in general and the detenus in particular of its full sympathy in their suffering and feels that their sacrifice and patriotism would ever remain an inspiration to the whole country.

68. Appeal to Observe Detenu Day, 2 April 1935[1]

As will be recalled, the Congress Socialist Party was to have observed March 3 as the Detenu Day throughout the country. The day was postponed because I was anxious to get the Congress officially to join the Day. I am now given to understand

[1] *Bombay Chronicle*, 2 April 1935. Appeal issued from Banaras.

that the matter must be placed before the Working Committee which is not meeting till the third week of April.

I am, however, glad to say that the Day has been welcomed by large numbers of Congressmen. In Calcutta all the leaders of the Congress joined in an appeal which was published for the observance of the Day. All the Calcutta papers as well as many other nationalist journals elsewhere gave their unqualified support. In several places, including far-off Chandernagore, the 'Day' was actually observed on March 3rd because the notice of postponement had not somehow reached them. Wherever it was observed it was a great success; at the above place the Mayor of the City presided over the meeting.

Now as there will be a good deal of delay in waiting for the decision of the Working Committee, the 'Day' will be observed by the Congress Socialist Party on April 7th which happily falls in the National Week. I appeal to the public, and particularly to Congressmen, to make the Day the success that is ought to be. The minimum programme for the 'Day' should be holding of meetings at which the following resolution should be passed:

> This meeting of citizens strongly condemns the continuous repression that has been going on in Bengal culminating in the detention without trial and in secrecy of a large number of youth of Bengal torn from their natural surroundings. The meagre news that is given to the public of these detention camps and the news that, in spite of secrecy, percolate out of them fill the public mind with dread and suspicion.
>
> This meeting, therefore, calls upon the Government of Bengal to remove the repressive laws and either discharge the detenus or give them a fair trial through ordinary courts of law.
>
> This meeting asks Congress members of the Indian Legislative Assembly and others to adopt all possible measures to obtain redress in this matter.
>
> This meeting assures the people of Bengal in general, and detenus in particular, of its full sympathy in their suffering and feels that their sacrifice and patriotism would ever remain an inspiration to the whole country.

69. Letter to Secretary, Utkal Congress Socialist Party [before 7 April 1935][1]

Kabir Chaura
Benares City, U.P.
[Before 7 April 1935]

To
The Secretary
Utkal Congress Socialist Party

Dear Comrade,
I shall be highly obliged if you would send me the following information.

[1] *Nabakrushna Chaudhuri Papers* (NMML).

1. Names of members of your Executive Committee.
2. Names & addresses of your District Committees with the names & addresses of the Secretaries.

I shall also feel obliged if you could send me periodical reports of the work done in your Province, say, monthly. You would doubtless realize the value of such reports. The reports should be brief and particular. Generalities and vagueness should be avoided.

I hope the Detenu Day will be properly celebrated in your Province.

Yours fraternally,
Jayaprakash Narayan

70. Letter to Shantilal Harjivan Shah, 10 April 1935[1]

Kabir Chaura
Benaras City, U.P.
10 April 1935

My dear Shantilalbhai,

I have not yet had a reply from you. I am anxious to know where the Company's affairs stand. Masani tells me that the 'statement' has been registered. It would be good after this, to put in a small 'ad' in the local papers.

In all, how many shares have been sold? Some shareholders have complained to me that they have not yet received their share certificates.

Have the certificates been printed? If not, please have them printed at once and send them to those who have already bought our shares.

Please also let me know how much I owe the Company, i.e. according to the accounts I submitted to you. I think it was hundred something—thirty or forty.

With best wishes,

Yours sincerely,
Jayaprakash

[1] *JP Papers* (NMML).

71. Appeal to Defeat Government's Plan to Isolate Bengal, 16 April 1935[1]

I have been just informed by friends of Calcutta that as soon as the Detenu Day was announced to be observed on April 7, the Press Officer of the Bengal

[1] *Bombay Chronicle*, 18 April 1935. Statement to Press at Banaras.

Government instructed the local newspapers not to publish any notice, statement or any other information regarding the Day.

People outside Bengal do not know how far things have gone in that province.

The Government have succeeded in isolating Bengal. It is our duty to break that isolation. More specially it is the duty of the journalists of the country to raise such a storm as to defeat the Government's game of isolation.

The Detenu Day was observed as the first step towards breaking this isolation. But one meeting a year is hardly enough. Public men, legislatures and most of all the journalists of the country should take every opportunity to bring the question of Bengal to the forefront and to demand the release of the detenus.

72. Letter to Nabakrushna Chaudhuri, 18 April 1935[1]

Kabir Chaura
Benares City
18 April 1935

Dear Naba Babu,

I must ask your apologies for not writing a personal letter to you for so long. When I read of your accident[2] in the *Congress Socialist*, I wanted to write to you, but somehow I failed to do so. Will you please let me know if you have fully recovered from the injury?

It is a pity that your chances of going to Jubbulpore are very thin. I wish you would come.

I quite understand what you write about your inability to contribute to the All India Fund. Of course, there can be no question of your resigning—that is nonsense.

Well, you do not bother about the contribution.

With kindest regards to you & Mrs. Chaudhuri.[3]

Yours,
Jayaprakash

[1] *Nabakrushna Chaudhuri Papers* (NMML).

[2] Nabakrushna Chaudhuri was stabbed by a Congress worker while he was touring the districts and villages of Orissa in January 1935.

[3] Malati Chaudhuri (1904-98); married Nabakrushna Chaudhuri, 1927; took part in the salt satyagraha and imprisoned, 1930; set up Mahila Bahini along with Rama Devi; joined the C.S.P.; started peasants movement in Orissa, 1935-6; founded *Sarathi*, a magazine; led Gadajata Prajamandal Andolan at Dhenkanal, Talcher and Athamallik, 1938; offered individual stayagraha, 1940; participated in the Quit India movement, 1942, and incarcerated in Cuttack Jail; member, A.I.C.C., 1942-5; joined Gandhi in Noakhali, 1946; President, Orissa P.C.C., 1947; unsuccessfully contested 1977 Assembly election from Dhenkanal constituency as an independent; recipient of Jamnalal Bajaj and Utkal Ratna Award; presented with 'Desikottama' by Visva Bharati University, 1998.

73. Letter to Kamalashanker Pandya, 18 April 1935[1]

Kabir Chaura
Benares City
18 April 1935

Dear Comrade Kamalashanker,[2]

It is a great pleasure to hear that you & Com. Dinkar[3] have seriously taken up the matter of reorganization of the Gujarat Party. I hope you two will be able to infuse new life into it. And I also hope that you will keep one in touch with your activities and send periodical reports.

I have received the money (Rs. 5/8/-) for Detenus relief, though I do not know just where to send it. I am making enquiries from Calcutta and shall send the money there as soon as I find a proper party to handle it.

I agree with what you write about the Constituent Assembly resolution. Before you wrote I had discussed the matter with Sampurnanandji & we had decided to get the amendment made in the forthcoming meeting of the Executive. In the A.I.C.C. it can be, of course, amended only in the manner you point out.

I am sorry to say that I have not been able to appreciate your remarks regarding my views on Provincial Research Bureau. You have been very unkind to me by declaring that any opinion in the matter was pointless.

I shall give you my reasons for my opinion—some indeed were quoted by Asoka[4] in his circular. In the first place, most of the Provincial parties are barely functioning. A Research Bureau would be a sham in these conditions. Secondly, local talent is very scarce. In each province there are not more than a couple or so of comrades with the proper equipment. And two cannot constitute an independent research organization. For this reason, it was desirable to bring together all these scattered elements into one organization, to coordinate their activities, to guide & help them.

[1] *Kamalashanker Pandya Papers* (NMML).

[2] Kamalashanker Pandya (1904-92); participated in the national movement and imprisoned several times; worked for *Bekar, Daily Sun*, 1930, and *Janam-Bhoomi*, 1934; Founder-member, Gujarat Central Youth League, and Gujarat C.S.P., 1934, its Secretary, 1934-5; member, National Executive, C.S.P, 1938; Vice-President, Gujarat Central Youth League, and Central India States' People's Conference, 1939-45.

[3] Dinkar Mehta (1907-89); participated in the Bardoli satyagraha, 1928, and the civil disobedience movement, 1930; Founder-member, Gujarat C.S.P., 1934; joined the C.P.I., 1935; Joint Secretary, C.S.P., 1936-8; worked underground, 1940-2; arrested, 1948; escaped in 1949 and remained underground till 1951; Vice-President, Maha Gujarat Janata Parishad, 1957-60; member, Bombay Legislative Council, 1958-60; after split in the C.P.I. joined C.P.I. (M), 1964; Mayor of Ahmedabad, 1966-7.

[4] Asoka Mehta (1911-84); Founder-member, C.S.P., 1934, and member of its National Executive, 1937-8; Editor, *Congress Socialist*, 1935-9; participated in the individual satyagraha and Quit India movement; jailed, 1940-1, and detained, 1942-5; Chairman, Eighth National Conference of the Socialist Party, Madras, 1950; General Secretary, Socialist Party, 1950-3; member, Lok Sabha, 1954-62, and 1967-70; Chairman, P.S.P., 1959-62; Deputy Chairman, Planning Commission, 1963-6; Minister of Planning and Social Welfare, 1966, and of Planning, Petroleum, Chemicals and Social Welfare, 1967-8, Government of India; arrested, June 1975; released, May 1976; publications include: *Socialism and Gandhism, Indian Shipping, Economic Consequences of Sardar Patel, Who Owns India?, Democratic Socialism, Political Mind of India*, and co-author with Achyut Patwardhan of *The Communal Triangle in India*.

Lastly, it is desirable in my view, to develop a harmonious Party literature, and this could only happen if we had a unified research organization. As far as I am aware, all political parties have a central research & propaganda bureau.

I do not know what has offended you so much in my decision. If you think that I was prompted by a desire to curb local initiative, you are mistaken, because this initiative can be fully developed only under centralised guidance.

Yours,
Jayaprakash

P.S.
Narendra Devji is at Puri. He comes here on the 21st. I shan't be able to see him till I return from Jubbulpore. You write to him about the presidentship.

JP

74. Circular to Secretary, Utkal Congress Socialist Party, 3 May 1935[1]

Circular Letter No. 10

Kabir Chaura
Benares City
3 May 1935

To
The Secretary
Utkal C.S.P.

Dear Comrade,
The Executive Committee of the All India Congress Socialist Party met at Jubbulpore on April 23 and 26.

(1) It was decided that the *Congress Socialist* should be immediately revived and published from Bombay. Com. Asoka Mehta was appointed editor and Com. K.D. Merchant,[2] manager. The old Editorial Board continues but for the change of the editor.

(2) The General Secretary was asked to issue instructions to Provincial Parties re.: enrolment of Congress members and Party conferences.

Instructions Re.: Enrolment of Congress-members

It appears that Party members are not as active in enrolling Congress members as

[1] *Nabakrushna Chaudhuri Papers* (NMML). The same circular was sent to all the provincial secretaries of the Congress Socialist Party.

[2] K.D. Merchant (1903-87); one of the founders of Swadeshi League in Bombay, and its Honorary Secretary, 1930-2; participated in the civil disobedience movement and imprisoned, 1932; member, Executive Committee, Bombay C.S.P., 1934-6; Secretary, Reception Committee, Congress Socialist Party Conference, Bombay, 1934; member, Bombay P.C.C., 1934-5; Vice-President, Bombay Students' Brotherhood, 1934-5.

they ought to be. The Executive felt that in the next month and a half all effort should be concentrated on this work.

I hope you will instruct your members accordingly.

Re.: Party Conferences

It has been found that some Provincial Parties have invited non-Party members to preside over their conferences. This is undesirable as it confuses issues and defeats the task of developing a new leadership.

(3) Among other things considered were resolutions for the All India Congress Committee, statement re.: treatment of our resolutions in the A.I.C.C., the Berar Party Conference which it was decided to postpone.

(4) It was decided to organize a summer school to meet at Almora where Party workers should be invited for study and discussion.

The school will begin in the first week of June and shall last for three weeks. The school will give an opportunity to Party members to know one another well and discuss ideological and organizational problems together.

The place selected is a beautiful one and there will be enough opportunity for recreation and outings. For tired Party members it will be an ideal resting place.

I request you send me the names of *active* members of your Party who may be desirous of attending the school. Members attending will have to pay their travelling expenses to and from Almora, *plus* ten rupees for board.

I suggest that you select at least two people from your province whom you want to send to the school and if the members selected are not in a position to pay their expenses you should ask your Party to find the money for them.

The members selected should be such as are in a position to participate actively in the programme of your Party. Otherwise the expenditure incurred on them would be wasted.

I shall be obliged if you reply soon to this part of this letter.

(5) The next meeting of the Executive will be held at Benares sometime in July.

Yours fraternally,
Jayaprakash Narayan

75. Circular to Members, Congress Socialist Party, 3 May 1935[1]

Kabir Chaura
Benares City
3 May 1935

Dear Comrade,

As you know the *Congress Socialist*, which was our Party's organ, has closed

[1]*Kamalashanker Pandya Papers* (NMML).

down. From the start it was feared that Calcutta would be an unsuitable place for a journal like the *Congress Socialist*. Events soon proved it to be so. Twice our editor received warnings and finally the Press refused to print the paper. Perforce we had to close it down.

The *Congress Socialist* in the brief space of its existence and in spite of great financial and other difficulties, did remarkable service to our movement. It was the only channel for the ceaseless expression of our views and thus an invaluable party-builder. It had already made its mark in Indian journalism and was everywhere looked upon as a serious journal of a high political standard, with something vital to say on current problems and topics.

If our Party is to grow and succeed in its task, one of the irreducible requirements is the publication of a Party organ. *The Congress Socialist must be revived.*

The Executive Committee of the All India Party at its Jubbulpore Meeting decided to publish the *Congress Socialist* again, this time from Bombay. Com. Asoka Mehta was appointed editor and Com. K.D. Merchant, manager. It is expected that the paper would be out within a month.

It is needless to remind you that it is impossible to publish a Party organ without the fullest co-operation of Party members. I have to admit it with regret that the Provincial Parties and Party members generally did not pull their weight when the *Congress Socialist* was being published last.

I hope this time Party members will show greater interest and carry out their responsibilities better.

As soon as the Paper is published again you must undertake its proper distribution. I found last time that even in big cities with large students and professional class population less than a dozen copies were sold. That was inexcusable. I hope, we shall all do better this time.

Yours fraternally,
Jayaprakash Narayan

76. Socialism versus the All India Village Industries Association: A Pamphlet, 1935[1]

Some months back, in an article in the *Harijan*,[2] Gandhiji wrote in reply, if I remember aright, to some question of a friend, that though he had his own views of economic and industrial organization, his scheme of village industries organization

[1] Jayaprakash Narayan, *Socialism versus the A.I.V.I.A.*, Bombay, 1935. This essay was originally contributed to the Press in May 1935 in the form of articles, entitled "Professor Kumarappa's Theory of Centralization and Decentralization". A short chapter was added at the end in reply to the rejoinder of J.C. Kumarappa, published in the *Searchlight*, 26 June 1935.

[2] Refers to Gandhi's article in *Harijan* dated 4 January 1935. See *The Collected Works of Mahatma Gandhi*, Volume LX, pp. 54-5.

was not intended primarily for the experimentation, much less the realization, of those views. His aim was much humbler, he said, namely, that of rendering some economic service to the villager by raising his productivity and income and by making his habitat healthier and less exposed to the exploitation of the cities.

But some of his followers are, in the old French idiom, more royalist than the king. The more enthusiastic of them have discovered in the idea of the Village Industries Association, a fundamental principle of social organization—a principle that transcends all others, including communism, both in its inherent goodness and its value of stability.

Thus we find Sardar Vallabhbhai Patel proclaiming that true Socialism in India can come only through the development of village industries. One wonders if the Sardar will own up to the logical conclusion of his reasoning, namely, that true socialism obtained throughout Indian history—indeed, world history—except during the past century or two.

We have, again, Dr. Pattabhi Sitaramayya[3] growing lyrical in his praise and exaltation of this great idea. To him the A.I.V.I.A. represents the realization of a dream of social reconstruction and cultural regeneration. It is difficult to imagine any one being so completely swept away by his own eloquence as the learned doctor from the South.

However, I am not concerned with these opinions here. My present concern is with a recent interview[4] of Professor Kumarappa[5], given at Patna, which has appeared in several newspapers.

Professor Kumarappa is not a politician and, therefore, is not given to exaggeration. He is a trained economist and a scientific thinker. As the Organising Secretary of the A.I.V.I.A., Mr. Kumarappa is a most responsible exponent of the scheme, the fulfilment of which is his task more than any one else's.

It is natural therefore that great value should attach to his opinions on this subject. And it is for that reason that, finding serious flaws in his thinking, I have felt compelled to present my criticisms to the public.

[3] Pattabhi Sitaramayya (1880-1959); member, A.I.C.C., 1916-52; Founder-Editor, *Janmabhumi*, an English weekly, 1919-30; President, All India States' People's Conference, Karachi, 1936; Working President, All India States' People's Conference, 1946-8; member, Constituent Assembly, 1946-50; President, Jaipur Congress, 1948; Governor, Madhya Pradesh, 1952-7; publications include: *The Redistribution of Indian Provinces on a Linguistic Basis, Socialism and Gandhism, History of the Indian National Congress* (2 Vols.), *Gandhi and Gandhism*, and *Sixty Years of the Congress*.

[4] Refers to the interview of J.C. Kumarappa to the representative of the *Searchlight* at Patna on 1 April 1935 elucidating the object and programme of the All India Village Industries Association and the method of work they intended to follow. For text of the interview see Appendix 14.

[5] J.C. Kumarappa (1892-1957); famous as a Gandhian economic thinker; Editor in charge of *Young India*, May 1930-February 1931, and October-December 1931; sentenced to one year's imprisonment in 1931, and for two years in 1932; was authorized by Bombay Congress (1934) to form, under the guidance of Gandhi, the All India Village Industries Association, became its Organiser and Secretary, and President after Gandhi's death; appointed member of the Committee to formulate a scheme of Basic Education, Wardha, 1937; Chairman, Industrial Survey Committee, C.P. and Berar, 1939, and Congress Agrarian Reforms Committee, 1948; publications include: *Why the Village Movement?*, *Economy of Permanence, Gandhian Economic Thought, Gandhian Way of Life, Public Finance and Our Poverty*, and *An Overall Plan for Rural Development*.

I should like to make it clear at the outset that I am not concerned in this article with the Village Industries Association as an immediate scheme for rural uplift or a scheme for winning Swaraj. Here I wish to examine the Association as representing a scheme of social reconstruction excelling even communism as Professor Kumarappa has claimed.

It is a staggering claim to make.

One wonders what new forces have been discovered by its modern proponents in an economic system which is as old as human civilization. For, after all, village industries are nothing new in the world like collective farms and factory soviets. And therefore when some one comes forward claiming the highest social virtues for a thing which was a commonplace only a century ago, one's curiosity is really aroused.

But is the curiosity fulfilled? I am sorry to have to reply in the negative.

What is Mr. Kumarappa's thesis? It centres round two conceptions—centralization and decentralization (of production). The first he rejects, though not wholly as we shall see, as entailing exploitation and violence. The other he holds up as the ideal cure for all economic maladjustments and injustice.

Mr. Kumarappa, like the communist, is interested in finding out the basis of an economic order that is free from exploitation. He also wants that order to be free from violence. This basis he finds in decentralized production. "If each man", he writes, "is to retain the product of his labour (i.e. to be free from exploitation—J.P.N.) the logical conclusion forces us to adopt decentralization of production as the only way out".

It is of course obvious that if each individual worked for himself with his own tools and consumed what he produced, he would retain the full value of his labour for himself. At the same time it should also be obvious that if a thousand persons *worked together*, not for a third party but *for themselves*, and *consumed together* all that they produced, still each one of them will get the full value of his labour.

Professor Kumarappa accepts the first as the only sound and permanent system (though after making a fatal compromise with the second as we shall see) while he rejects the other—which is the essence of communism—as veiled capitalism; and invokes the picture of galley slaves and other such forms of brutal exploitation to discredit it.

Let us examine this concept of decentralization a little more closely. It should be remembered that under decentralized production, the worker is completely free from exploitation only when he grows his raw materials, owns his tools and consumes his produce himself. If the stage of production has risen above this primitive level and the worker has to buy his raw materials and sell his produce, he at once comes within the orbit of the exploitation of the middleman. To do away with this form of exploitation also it would be necessary either to primitivize further the methods of production or to organize co-operative buying and selling. But the latter solution entails centralization of organization and all those dams of idealism of which the Professor speaks and which we shall examine presently. Will it, therefore, appeal to the Professor? If not, then he must force down the methods of production much lower than he at present contemplates.

Then, there is another from of small-scale production—tilling of the land by individual peasants—which, even though the tiller may be working for himself, may entail exploitation. This exploitation arises from the fact that the land which the peasant tills, is 'owned' by another person; and therefore instead of keeping all his produce to himself, he has to part with a portion of it to that owner. Thus here, in spite of decentralization, there is exploitation.

How does the Professor propose to eradicate this exploitation? The socialist solution is to make the tiller himself the 'owner' of his land collectively with others and to educate him to work on his land as a member of a co-operative or collective organization. This latter method the socialist urges for the purpose of improving agricultural productivity, of bringing agriculture under a planned economy, of developing a social rather than an individualistic outlook among the peasants, of preventing the re-growth of predatory forces in the countryside.

In an agricultural country like India where this curse of landlordism is widespread, economic exploitation would not cease by decentralization of commodity production. The problem of the exploitation of the peasant under landlordism, will have to be faced. Will the A.I.V.I.A.'s solution be different from that of the socialist? I should be thankful to Professor Kumarappa if he would enlighten me on this question.

I have said above that the Professor has made a fatal compromise with centralization—fatal, I mean to his theory.

His picture of the ideal economic organization is a blend of centralization and decentralization, in other words, a blend, if we use his won calculus of valuation, of evil and good, violence and *ahimsa*, capitalism and true socialism.

He accepts centralization in those spheres in which production and management are centralized by their very nature, such as railways, power production, mining, etc. Why does he do so? Either he thinks that centralization in these spheres is free from the evils of exploitation, violence, etc., or, desirous of material advancement and fond of electricity and railways, he is prepared to have them even at the cost of compromising his pure economics.

It is difficult to believe that he thinks that there is no exploitation in these spheres of centralization, if they are on a capitalist basis. Certainly the railway workers—the shopmen, the driver, the booking clerk, the station master—are as much subject to the exploitation of the railway companies as any other industrial worker under capitalism. The same is true of mine-workers and others.

How does Professor Kumarappa propose to do away with this exploitation? He gives us no clue beyond saying that he would have centralization in these spheres.

Till Mr. Kumarappa answers this question, the socialist answer holds the field. Exploitation in these spheres, as in others, can be removed only by abolishing their private ownership and establishing over them the ownership of the community.

If the Professor accepts this solution, he knocks out the bottom from his theory of decentralization. Because if exploitation can be removed by social ownership and management in the sphere of heavy industries why can it not be likewise removed from the rest of the field of production? If, on the other hand, he rejects this solution and fails to produce a better one, he compromises with exploitation along with its brood of attendant social evils and maladjustments. If he allows the

J.P. AS A STUDENT IN THE UNITED STATES

ग.ं. ह.
साबरमती.

1

आरा, ११ जनवरी. '30

S.N. 16351 488

प्रिय बापूजी

सप्रेम प्रणाम।

उस दिन लाहौर से चलकर हमलोग गोरखपुर विश्वनाथसिंह बाबू के यहां दो दिनों के लिये ठहर गये। वहां से हमलोग श्रीनगर गये। अभी प्रभावती वहीं हैं। मैं पिताजी से मिलने के लिये यहां चला आया। अब मेरी इच्छा है कि इलाहाबाद या बनारस जाकर पंडित मालवीय जी से ठीक से बातें कर लूं। उस दिन लाहौर में तो उन्हें फुर्सत ही नहीं थी। मैं उनसे मिलना इसलिये चाहता हूं कि उन्होंने कहा था कि जब उन्हें फुर्सत हो तब उनसे आकर मिलो। दूसरे चूंकि मुझे हिन्दू विश्वविद्यालय में रहने की बहुत इच्छा है इसलिये मैं चाहता हूं कि पंडितजी से कम से कम एक बार बातें तो कर लूं।

मैं इलाहाबाद में पंडित जवाहरलाल से भी मिलना चाहता हूं। उनपर मेरी बहुत श्रद्धा है और मेरे विचार उनसे बहुत कुछ मिलते जुलते हैं, इसलिये यदि किसी प्रकार मैं उनके साथ रह सकूं तो मुझे बड़ा सन्तोष होगा। लाहौर में मैंने उनसे Labor Research Dept. के विषय में बातें की थी जिस पर उन्होंने मुझे इलाहाबाद आने के लिये कहा था। आशा करता हूं कि कल या परसों यहां से इलाहाबाद जाऊंगा। प्रभावती के पत्र का इन्तजार कर रहा हूं।

विशेष कुशल है। मेरी तबीयत ठीक है यद्यपि थोड़ी खांसी हो गई है। आशा है कि आप भलीभांति होंगे। आपके civil disobedience program की बड़ी उत्सुकता से प्रतीक्षा कर रहा हूं। यदि

गांधी संग्रह.
साबरमती.

2 489

S.N. 16351

मुझमें यथेष्ट शक्ति आ सकी तो आशा करता हूं कि इस यज्ञ में अपनी कुछ तुच्छ आहुति भी डाल सकूंगा।

c/o Babu Harsoo Dayal
Revenue Assistant
Arrah (Bihar)

आपका
[illegible]भिलाषी जयप्रकाश

FACSIMILE OF J.P.'S LETTER TO GANDHI

ALL INDIA CONGRESS SOCIALIST PARTY

ORGANISING SECRETARY :
JAYAPRAKASH NARAYAN

July 5th 1934

Dear Comrade Chaudhary,

I learnt from Masani that you are taking keen interest in the organization of a Congress socialist group in Orissa. I have also seen reports in the papers of your activities. I congratulate you for your energetic efforts.

I had asked the office at Benares to send you some copies of the draft Constitution & ~~draft~~ programme of the All India Party. I hope you have received them. I wonder if you have already formed a provincial group in Orissa. If not I should like to request you to act as organizing secretary for Orissa on behalf of the All India Conference. The accompanying letter will be your letter of authority. I am also announcing in the papers that you have been appointed organizing secretary for Utkal.

Please let me hear from you soon. I shall be glad to ~~in~~ give you any information you require in this connection. My address for the next week will be c/o Seth Jamnalal Bajaj, Wardha, C.P.

Yours fraternally
Jayaprakash

P.S.

The procedure for organization of provincial parties is the following:–

1. The enrolment of members on the basis of the programme of the All India Party.
2. Formation of district committees after a certain number of members have been enrolled.
3. Holding of a provincial Conference at which the provincial party should be formed – its committee & office-bearers elected &c.

J.

FACSIMILE OF J.P.'S LETTER TO NABAKRUSHNA CHAUDHURI

J.P. AS GENERAL SECRTARY, C.S.P., c. 1935

'naturally centralized' industries to be in private hands he sounds the death-knell of his scheme.

First of all, the sphere of naturally centralized industries will be much larger than the Professor seems to think, and it will have an insatiable tendency to grow. Secondly, the interests that control these industries will have a dominating voice in the economic organization of the country.

Take the railways, for instance. At present this industry is entirely in British hands. If under Swaraj it is converted into an Indian industry, it alone will require scores of subsidiary industries which must be on a large-scale basis. Iron, steel, coal-mining, wire-manufacture, forestry, building-materials, are some of them. Each one of these will require other subsidiary industries, some of which again in their very nature must be centralized. Mining, irrigation, bridge-building, military industries, telegraph and telephones, ship-building, aeroplane-building, power development, radio, metallurgy, heavy chemicals, are some of the other major centralized industries.

In addition to industries, there are the financial and commercial sides of the economic order which too must be considered. The running of large industries would require banks and large trading houses. These again mean centralization.

Is it not obvious that heavy industries like the ones listed above, banks and large trading houses will dominate the economic life of any community where they exist? And if they are left in private hands, to be run for the profit of those who own them, the entire economic organization will be in the grip of these owners. The urge of profit will reach out and establish the dominion of centralized private production in those spheres too which are according to Professor Kumarappa naturally decentralized—such as spinning and weaving and sugar-making.

The problem of Mr. Kumarappa therefore is not only that of demarcating the spheres of centralization and decentralization. The economic problem is not solved as soon as he says that such and such industries will be centralized and the others decentralized. He must go a step further and face the question: if there is centralization, as he thinks there must be, then should it be under private or social, control and ownership? It would be suicidal for him to say that it matters little to him if a group of big businessmen owns all the mines, the railways and the banks of the country, or if the whole nation owns them. Yet by inference this is exactly what he said when he remarked that capitalism and communism are the same things because they are both centralized.

II

Now let us turn to his criticism of communism. He rejects communism because it is based on centralized production. If Soviet Russia seems to be free from the evils of capitalism, it is only because of the dam of idealism which the Russians have created. Its 'economic structure', to use his own term, is the same as that of capitalism. He therefore argues that it is only necessary to breach that dam for the whole system to collapse; and he warns that "human life is mortal and ideals change; and therefore unless the seed of centralization is taken out of Soviet organization the danger of reversion to type will always be there". He further says: "A change of the personnel at the helm of affairs may convert Soviet Russia of today into a Rockefeller organization of tomorrow." He likens Sovietism to capitalism because in his view "in both organizations the real producer loses his identity and becomes merely tools in the hands of the men at the top"; and adds: "It is with this end in view that our Association is doing all it can to make each individual producer an entity in himself and prevent his being merged into one in a gang of galley slaves. Whether the galley is owned by individuals or the state, makes little difference to the slave himself." Again, he says: "Both capitalism and Soviet Communism have as their basis violence. The galley slaves are driven with a whip for speed and harmony in pulling together."

These are breath-taking statements, and had they not come from an economist like Mr. Kumarappa, I would not have stopped for a moment to examine them.

This view of Soviet society betrays, I regret having to say it, a complete misunderstanding of the basis of socialism on the one hand, and the present trend of capitalist economy on the other.

The Professor indicts Soviet Communism on three counts: (1) only idealism at the top prevents it from being debased into capitalism, because its structure is the same: centralized production; (2) the producer—the worker—loses his identity; and (3) it is based on violence.

The first of these involves the most fundamental error. No one will deny that there is idealism in Russia; and that it is a great driving force. But, firstly, it is not only restricted to a few at the top; and secondly, it is *not* the *basis* of the Soviet economic system.

What is the Soviet economic system? The Professor apparently implies that as long as the dam of idealism lasts and till it 'reverts to type', the system is a valuable one. Had he stopped to examine its nature and its *differences* from capitalism he would have discovered its real social basis.

In the Russian system, first of all, there is no class of individuals who derive profit from the labour of others. Production, which is centralized, i.e. on a large-scale basis, is not for the profit of a small class of capitalists, stopping as the profits cease, but for consumption. Though wages are given, the rule is not to keep them down in order to increase proportionately the volume of profits, but constantly to raise them in correspondence with the total production of the community. Unemployment is not the rule but the rarest exception. (Russia today is the only country in the world where in spite of economic depression there is no unemployment). Security of employment is as definitely assured to every worker as it is to the civil servant in England. Opportunities are equal for all those who work. Social services have reached the highest development as compared with the rest of the world.

Prof. Kumarappa talks of the real producer losing his identity and becoming a tool in the hands of the men at the top, and of the little difference that it makes to the 'slaves' whether he works for a capitalist or the State. This is true of capitalism; but to say that it is also true of the Soviet system is to display utter ignorance of the status of the Russian worker. The whole essence of the Bolshevik Revolution lies in that status. It is not for nothing that the communists speak of the Dictatorship of the Proletariat. The working class is the most privileged class in Russia in the matter of electoral privilege, educational privilege and the privilege to enjoy the fruits of labour and the amenities that the entire community can provide. The factory soviets have vested real power in the hands of workers; the trade unions are the most influential non-Party organizations. Indeed, the worker in Russia is anything but a galley slave, losing his identity in the mass. He is a member of the ruling order; and each individual worker has his voice felt through his soviet or union.

To liken the lot of the worker under capitalism to that under Soviet communism is to miss the meaning of the greatest event of modern history—the Russian Revolution.

It is not only the worker whose status has been radically changed. The peasant too has acquired a new status, second only to that of the worker himself.

Here is the secret of the Russian system, the real basis of Soviet economics. It is this sudden revolution in the position, rights, privileges of these two classes that has been responsible for the stability of the Soviet Government. Were not this broad basis in existence, one could not explain the survival of the Bolshevik Revolution through that terrible period of armed intervention from without and counter-revolution and famine from within. Surely, the revolution had given the people so much that they were prepared to save it at any cost.

Then, we must not forget the Red Army. The revolution revolutionized the class basis of the Russian army as much as it did that of industry and agriculture. The Russian soldier will not accept again the slavery of the upper-classes without a fight. Therefore if the Russian system of economy were to change into capitalism, it would not merely happen by the men at the top deciding to effect that change. For that another all-shaking revolution would be required. The workers and peasants, who have got new privileges and rights will not let them go without fighting. They will not again accept the slavery of the capitalist and the landlords; they will not again give up their palaces for the slums of old; they will not give up their comforts, their opportunities for education and culture, merely because Comrade Stalin, let us say, has decided to hand them over again to the bourgeoisie.

As for the third indictment, that communism is based on violence, it is both true and untrue. It is not true in the sense Mr. Kumarappa means it. He says: 'Both capitalism and Soviet communism have as their basis violence. The galley slaves are driven with a whip for speed and harmony in pulling together.' If this is the sense in which the Professor thinks there is violence in communism, he is entirely wrong.

I have shown that under communism there are no galley slaves. There are workers working together for mutual benefit; and each worker is an individual with rights that are of the highest order existing in that society. There is no violence in this anywhere. There is no whip driving him to work. He works under conditions laid down by himself through his union. The place in which he works is his; its club and recreation grounds are his. It is his initiative that is building up his factory, his soviet, his club, his school and even his theatre. There is no violence in his life.

But there is violence in communism in a different sense, though personally I do not consider it to be violence. The classes which under capitalism constituted the ruling class, and had monopolized all privileges, wealth and position, are deliberately destroyed by force. It is not meant that they are physically exterminated. What is meant is that by legislation they are denuded of their wealth and power. Actual physical violence is only used when these classes organize counter-revolution; when they sabotage and obstruct and undermine the new order. Then they are sent to prison or shot, in accordance with the laws of the land.

In this sense, I am afraid, if Mr. Kumarappa is serious, violence would be inevitable in his scheme too, as I shall try to show below.

I have said above that Mr. Kumarappa's remarks about Soviet economics betray a misunderstanding of the trend of present capitalist society. He declares that "it is but a step from Soviet economics to capitalist organizations". This in fact is just the reverse of reality. Production has reached a stage where Capitalism has failed to organize it. There exist productive powers in the world today and resources to maintain in comparative comfort many times (four times according to Sir George Knibbs[6]) the present population of the world; yet there is everywhere unemployment, scarcity in the midst of plenty, chaos and disorganization.

It was Marx who first pointed out this basic contradiction of modern capitalism. The very forces which gave it birth will be its undoing, he said. The development of productive powers consequent upon the Industrial Revolution ushered in an era of prosperous capitalism. But after it reached a certain stage, serious defects began to show in its working. It began to have periodical setbacks—the economic crises. Since the war it has shown symptoms of chronic disease—the contradiction having begun to have full play.

This contradiction, in brief, is that capitalist production tends to create abundance of goods while capitalist distribution tends to restrict the consumption of the goods created. This has led to the present incurable sickness of capitalism. The result is that everywhere the cry of over-production has gone up and curtailment of production and checking of mechanical advance, even mechanical retrogression, are in evidence all over the capitalist world. Capitalism has ceased to be a progressive force. The age of plenty that has been made possible by present mechanical advance, is being thwarted by capitalism.

Socialism alone is the next step. By solving the problem of distribution, it alone can further develop the productive forces of society. It alone can bring on earth the Age of Plenty, the eternal dream of mankind.

It betrays therefore, as I have already said, an utter misunderstanding of present economic trends, to speak, under these conditions, of capitalism being a step from socialism.

III

So much for a criticism of the Professor's criticism of communism. Let me now turn to his own scheme. I shall formulate my criticism of it in the shape of a question.

How does Mr. Kumarappa expect to realize his scheme? Supposing we have

[6] Sir George Handley Knibbs (1858-1929); Lecturer, Department of Engineering, University of Sydney, 1889-1906; Commonwealth Statistician, 1906-21; President, Australasian Association for Advancement of Science, 1923-4.

our own Government, how does he propose, for instance, to decentralize spinning and weaving and sugar-making? At present most of these activities are carried on in large centralized mills. If Mr. Kumarappa is relying on his Association's ability to drive these mills out of business by pure economic competition, he is obviously mistaken. Hand manufacture cannot compete with machine production. Then again if he hopes to kill them by the effort of his propaganda, i.e. by convincing people that decentralized industry is better, he is again making a mistake. It is not possible to do so. There is no reason to suppose that there will be no propaganda from the other side and that it will not be more effective.

There remains only one course—legislation: placing of such economic handicaps on these industries that they will die out. This, I claim, is in principle, violence of the same kind as that used by communists in declaring a whole class expropriated. If the process is slower in the first case, it hardly alters the principle. The parties concerned would submit to the decrees of Professor Kumarappa only because intimidated by the power of the State to coerce them ultimately.

Suppose Mr. Kumarappa makes a law that no one can employ more than, say, five people in spinning, weaving and sugar-making industries. What would he do with an individual who infringes that law? Would he not use the State's machinery to coerce him, to fine him, even to imprison him? Where then is the difference in this violence and the violence of the Soviet State? As long as there is organization in society, there is violence in this sense. The claim of the communist is that he destroys the violence of the few over the many and establishes the violence of the many over the few. Capitalist property, apart from being theft in the words of Proudhon[7], is also constant violence. Under Communism, at least this form of violence would cease to exist.

But even here, in the matter of legislation, Mr. Kumarappa will come up against a difficulty. If elections are held on the present so-called democratic principle, the centralized industrial classes will certainly try to return as many of their representatives as possible; and, with their resources, they might put up a real good show. At the same time, Mr. Kumarappa will have to find enough supporters of his scheme to put his candidates through. It is difficult to say who will come out victorious in such a contest.

In any case, it is obvious that Mr. Kumarappa, while speaking of this 'great challenge' that Gandhiji has thrown to capitalism and communism, must fight the centralized industries of the present day and decentralize them. Will the A.I.V.I.A. do this? The existence on its Advisory Board of men who are cotton and sugar magnates, does not encourage one to believe that this will happen.

After Mr. Kumarappa has decentralized industry, supposing that he succeeds in it, he will have accomplished only half of his task. The other half would consist in devising plans to prevent centralization again. It must be remembered that cottage industries were in existence everywhere in the world before the Industrial Revolution, and that they were all destroyed by the new productive forces. It should

[7] Pierre Joseph Proudhon (1809-65); French social philosopher and journalist; his writings influenced the development of anarchism and socialism in Europe; chiefly remembered for his pamphlet *What is Property*? arguing that property being based on the exploitation of one person's labour by another is theft.

not be supposed that as soon as machinery appeared on the scene, everyone accepted it cheerfully. There was a long and bitter struggle between machinery and handicrafts; and it was only the combined economic superiority and political power of the new rising industrial class that finally crushed the craftsmen. Machinery is much more powerful economically and politically now than it was in those days; and it would not be very easy for handicrafts to fight it. In a pure economic fight they cannot win. Only if the handicraftsmen permanently hold power in their hands, can they prevent the rise of machinery again. That is, a dictatorship of the small producer would be necessary. Is the Professor prepared to impose such a dictatorship over the country?

To conclude, it is wrong to suppose that centralization under all conditions means violence and exploitation. Centralized production under social ownership and control, eradicates these evils; and, at the same time, by keeping the high productive forces intact and even developing them, it makes unlimited social progress possible.

It is wrong again to suppose, that this socialized production is based on the idealism of a few men at the top. Its real basis is the benefits it confers on the vast masses of the people—the workers, peasants and soldiers. It rests on class interest.

Mr. Kumarappa has confused the economic issues in the present world by posing the problem as centralization *versus* decentralization. The problem in reality is *private* versus *social ownership of the means of production.* The issue is whether factories and mills, banks and mines, trading and business, shall remain in private hands for private benefit, or whether they shall be transferred to society for the benefit of society.

Professor Kumarappa has no reason to reject centralization. And he is guilty of bad logic when he retains it in certain spheres and rejects it in others.

Decentralization, while theoretically solving the problem of exploitation, is a reactionary step and also an illusory hope. It is reactionary because it turns back the productive forces of society. It is illusory because not having a class basis it cannot materialize. Furthermore it means lower standards of living for the people. It means scientific and cultural reaction. It means a medieval and rural outlook. It means military weakness.

IV

At the time Professor Kumarappa published his criticism of my articles, I felt no enthusiasm for 'returning to the charge'. It seemed to me then, as indeed it still does, that the Professor, for some reason best known to him, was anxious to evade the main issues, directing his reply to minor points and superficial observations regarding the U.S.S.R. It did not, therefore, seem useful to continue the controversy.

However, since the articles are being published in a pamphlet form, friends have urged me to write a reply to Professor Kumarappa's rejoinder.

He has picked out eight points from my articles for criticism. I shall first take the minor points.

To begin with, he has argued at some length against my remark that when a system, which was a commonplace till a century or so ago, is trotted out as an economic and political panacea, one's curiosity is really aroused. He labours to show that merely because a thing is old, one need not imagine that it has no undiscovered uses. I agree. And the reader will see that in my original articles, I had nowhere categorically asserted that, since village industries were things of the past, they could have no virtue in them that had not been discovered by past generations. All I had said was that it made one curious to read the claims made on behalf of the A.I.V.I.A. It was for Professor Kumarappa to satisfy that curiosity. I confess that, as far as I am concerned, it still remains unsatisfied.

Secondly, he has criticized my statement that in Russia security of employment is as definitely assured to every worker as it is to the Civil Servant in Great Britain. He writes: "It is an unfortunate comparison as the English Civil Service has built up no reputation for initiative. . . . For the progress of a nation we need initiative." It is unfortunate that such criticism should have come from Mr. Kumarappa.

I referred to the British civil servant while speaking of the security of employment that the Russian State offers every worker. I was not comparing the Russian worker *himself* with the civil servant of Great Britain. Mr. Kumarappa had lumped together, in his original interview, the worker under capitalism and the worker under socialism. In reply to this I was trying to show the difference in the status of the worker under the two systems. One of the important differences that I happened to mention was security of employment. My purpose in referring to the civil servant was merely to give an idea of the security enjoyed by the Russian worker.

Professor Kumarappa talks of a nation's progress depending on 'initiative'. I am sure he will agree that the U.S.S.R. has made astounding progress. Does he believe that all this progress has been due to the initiative of a handful of 'dictators' at the top? Was such progress possible without mass initiative, particularly the initiative of the Russian worker? Professor Kumarappa ought to know that if there is initiative in the 'common' man anywhere on Earth today, it is in the Soviet Republic.

The Professor tries to make another point thus: "Is it necessary to have a class basis for progress? It is no recommendation to say that the workers are the privileged class of Russia. We want no privileged class at all."

These are rather gratuitous remarks. Professor Kumarappa first calls the Russian worker galley slaves, and then when he is told that far from being galley slaves, they are the most privileged class in the country, he turns round and says: "we do not want privileged classes". Surely he knows that what the Russians are trying to do, is not to create a new class of privilege, but to create a classless society, i.e. a society of one class only—the class of workers. Already with 80 per cent of their agriculture collectivized, the Soviets have nearly become a nation of one class.

As for the class basis of progress, it is too long a story to tell here. In any case, it is not vital to our argument. The only time when I made a reference to this theory was when I said that in our society there was no scope for a dictatorship of the small producer; that there was no class basis for it. If this formulation is offensive to the Professor, I shall drop it; and merely say that the small producers cannot be in a position—due to their being scattered, their variety of interests, their small resources, their low competing ability as against machinofacture, their backwardness, and many other causes—to combine and acquire such strength as to be able to fashion society to suit their interests.

The last point he has tried to score against me is in connection with my remark that small industries mean military weakness. This is how the Professor argues: "This, in a way, justifies our scheme as we do not aim at military domination. We are consciously working towards the eradication of all militarism—economic and otherwise. If we make exploitation impossible, we take away the wind from the sails of political and military domination. If we mean 'military weakness' by minimizing group violence, that shall be our national strength."

This, I am afraid, is a little playing to the gallery. And it did not fail to produce the desired effect. The press cutting which is before me of Mr. Kumarappa's article has a streamer headline: 'We Cannot Have An Economic Militarism.' The implication was that I was guilty for having advocated it.

It was not of militarism that I spoke, however. All I meant to do was to point out the simple and rather obvious fact that, in this highly industrialized and mechanized world, a country that is dependent upon village industries is bound to find itself in a weak military position. I did not suggest thereby that we should aim at military domination. The opposite of military weakness is not military domination. It is military strength, i.e. strength to defend one's country against foreign aggression. In speaking of the objective of 'working towards the eradication of all militarism', Mr. Kumarappa has run away from reality. It is a laudable objective to follow, but he should realize that no matter what economic and political views he holds, the defence of the country would be his first responsibility if he were at the head of its government. If he proved indifferent to it, or inefficient, not only his government would go down in a hurry, he would also have the satisfaction of injuring, may be permanently, the country's international position. It should be clear that no manner of economic and political idealism can save a country from outside aggression. To deny it is to indulge in a bit of fancy which has neither reason nor experience behind it.

Let us turn now to the central point under discussion. Professor Kumarappa had held that centralized production leads to exploitation and violence. (In his rejoinder he has stressed lack of initiative and suppression of individualism as other evil results of it.) Judging from his remarks about Russia, one concluded that it made no difference whether centralized production was carried on under capitalism or the Soviet system. "In both organizations, the real producer loses his identity and becomes merely a tool in the hands of the men at the top. Both capitalism and Soviet communism have as their basis violence. The galley slaves are driven with a whip for speed and harmony in pulling together."

My contention was that centralized production means exploitation and violence only when it is run on capitalist lines. Under a socialized economy, it involves no violence and no exploitation and, far from suppressing, encourages initiative. I do not wish to repeat the argument. I shall only attempt to answer briefly the objections that Professor Kumarappa has raised.

He advances mainly three arguments against centralized socialist economy: (1) Working together of large numbers of people is not possible without outside coercion: "If they did so without supervision, they would be highly evolved men and women. What prisoners do in a common kitchen is for themselves. They have supervision too. They do not do things well because the working is wholly for themselves. The moment social coercion on such a large scale has to be applied, methods of violence gain ground"; (2) Individual growth and initiative would be inhibited: "These methods are not calculated to stimulate the individual growth and personality of the citizen. We have to aim at letting every producer have the full benefit of his labour and to develop on his own lines"; (3) Centralized and controlled production vests power in a few hands: "Man seeks after power even more eagerly than wealth. Theoretically we may arrange an ideal organization, but in practice it will resolve itself into an autocracy. England, and the U.S.A. claim to be democratic politically, but are they so in practice? Unless we follow the natural inclinations of man and build our organization on that foundation, our superstructure will not weather the storms of time."

That men would work together only under compulsion is a hypothesis which is neither in accord with experience nor with human ideals. If what Professor Kumarappa says is true, mankind might as well give up all hopes of co-operative life. It should be remembered that this is one of the most cherished hopes of the present generation of humanity throughout the civilized world.

As for experience, may I remind the Professor of Kropotkin's[8] *Mutual Aid*? At a time when Darwin's[9] theory of the 'struggle for existence' was being made into a fetish by enthusiasts, Kropotkin showed with a wealth of evidence drawn from life, that co-operation was perhaps the more important principle of life. It is as important in the case of man as in that of other animals. Any human society, no matter how primitive, shows innumerable forms of co-operation. In fact, the more primitive societies, in which man may be said to be nearer his 'nature', show closer and wider co-operation than those that have ascended the steps of civilization. Co-operation has been narrowed down as private economic interests have come into existence. With the removal of such interests, the socialist hopes that co-operation would once again be established as the rule of life.

Let us look at the question from a more matter-of-fact point of view. What does 'working together' in centralized production mean? Quoting my remarks, Professor Kumarappa writes: "If thousands of people worked together, not for a third party but for themselves, and consumed together all that they produced, still, he (i.e. the present writer) feels each one of them will get the full value of his labour. Here each will work for all (for himself also, at the same time—J.P.N.) If they did so without supervision, they would be highly evolved men and women." I do not exactly know what the Professor means by supervision. There is supervision even in pounding rice. If however by supervision he means coercion as probably he does, judging from his use of the word a little later in the same context, it is not clear why men must be coerced to work together, especially, when the fruits of their labour are to go to themselves. If men have to be highly evolved to do that, they must be much more so to work together in order to make others rich. Yet this is what the workers do under capitalism. Professor Kumarappa would not call the

[8] Prince Peter Kropotkin (1842-1921); Russian explorer, geographer and exponent of anarchism; works include: *Modern Science and Anarchism* and *Terror in Russia*.

[9] Charles Darwin (1809-82); English natural historian and geologist; proponent of the theory of evolution by natural selection; works include: *On the Origin of Species* and *The Descent of Man*.

industrial workers of today evolved beings, yet why do they work together to swell the fortunes of their employers? No one has coerced them to do so. Every one of them is free to quit his job. Yet they do work together. Why? Because the economic organization of the society of which they are members has turned them into property less individuals with no other means of livelihood than their labour for which that organization supplies a market.

Under a socialist economy, the workers will work together not, because driven to do so by that mystic body the 'State', but because only in that manner can they earn, not only their livelihood as under capitalism, but everything good and valuable that their society has to offer—status, honour, comforts. The comparison that the Professor draws with prisoners working in their common kitchen is entirely beside the point. And, if the Professor wishes to see how even prisoners can work together *without coercion*, he should turn to Soviet Russia.

As for inhibition of individual initiative and instinct for creation, it is such a time-worn argument that it need not detain us long. There are two things to remember in this connection. First, that though handicrafts offer opportunities for the exercise of initiative and the instinct for creation, only a small number of craftsmen can have the natural endowment to make use of that opportunity, and further, the level of industry limits severely the scope for creation. Not every craftsman has initiative or is a creator, nor the best of them has the same scope for the use of his powers as, say, an aeronautics engineer.

Secondly, large-scale production, especially under socialized economy, means unlimited scope for creation and initiative in the sphere of science, aesthetics, technology. At the same time, by raising the level of mass culture, by solving the problem of the 'struggle for existence', it releases undying springs of creativity and opens up hitherto unrealized opportunities for *every* individual in society to devote himself to creative work. It is the rule to speak of the instinct for creation in terms of work alone. As society advances, we shall learn more and more to think of it in terms of leisure—leisure that is beyond the reach of over ninety out of every hundred living men and women today.

Turning to Russia we find that the Soviet system, far from suppressing initiative and creativity, has given them an unprecedented stimulus and awakening. Dr. Sherwood Eddy writing on incentives in new Russia in his latest book, *Russia Today*, says: "Where the workers with new solidarity feel that they are working for themselves, they have the same successful motivation that the owners had in the early days of the capitalist system." Again: "In Russia the spirit of youth predominates. . . . It is a moving experience to hear fifty thousand youth shouting in perfect union, as I did in Moscow: 'We are changing the world! We are changing the world!'"

The socialist's claim is that only under his system will the individual have the chance for his fullest development. That is what Lenin meant when he said that every cook should be able to run the state.

The third argument that centralized production vests power in a few hands is equally erroneous. Under capitalism this is so undoubtedly. And when Professor Kumarappa naively points to England and the U.S.A. as being only nominally democratic states, he is over looking the fact, which has so persistently been emphasized by socialists, that in a class society there can be no democracy at all. Only when classes have been abolished that democracy can function. The 'dictatorship' in Russia is far more democratic in reality than the so-called democracies of the West. It is a dictatorship of the many over the few, while the 'democracies' are dictatorships of the few over the many. The outward forms of democracy hide this reality. But the truth comes out every time the least attempt is made to disturb the class-basis of society.

Production under socialism is a process in which the producer, through his factory soviet, continuously plays a dominant role. The individual has an incomparably larger voice in the management of his political and economic institutions under socialism than during any other previous stage of human civilization. It should be remembered that during the days of handicrafts political power everywhere was in the hands of a microscopic feudal oligarchy. Economically also that oligarchy was supreme.

In my original article I had said that the Professor had made a fatal compromise with centralized production. He has replied to that by arguing at length that certain industries are in their very nature centralised. The argument was unnecessary, because I had never questioned or denied it. Though now that he has attempted to make it look so 'natural', I must say that this naturalness was certainly not so clear to the past generations of handicraft societies. I also doubt if to every member of the A.I.V.I.A., the naturalness will be as obvious as to the Professor. However, I have no quarrel with that proposition. What I tried to show in my articles was the consequences of naturally centralized industry. I showed, firstly, that the sphere of such industry is so vast that it will dominate the nation's economy; secondly, that if this industry is left in private hands, the whole scheme as adumbrated by the A.I.V.I.A., would collapse, because the large producing interests would drive the small producer out of existence. The Professor has not replied to the first point. To the second he has given, I am glad to say, an unequivocal answer. He writes: "I have nowhere indicated that private enterprise will be allowed to exploit mines, railways, etc. As I have already said, these services have to be undertaken socially and not by private enterprise."

I do not know how far the views of the secretary of the A.I.V.I.A. represent the views of the Association itself. It is indeed a very significant statement and one should like to know if it is authoritative.

Finally, I had asked in my article how his scheme of small production would save the tenant, who is also a small producer, from being exploited by the landowner. The answer is a complete evasion. "The land question cannot be tackled without legislative power and as we are situated at present, we do not propose to take up this problem just now."

I was amused to read this answer. Our whole discussion has been not about what can be done just now, but about the principles underlying the concept of small industries as freshly interpreted by the A.I.V.I.A. At the very outset of my article I had made it clear that "I am not concerned in this article with the Village Industries Association as an immediate scheme for rural uplift or a scheme for winning *Swaraj*. I wish to examine it here as representing a scheme for social reconstruction—excelling even communism as Professor Kumarappa has claimed."

The Professor was himself conscious of this, because he speaks of "the scheme of a social order adumbrated by the advent of the All India Village Industries Association". Not only that, but his whole argument has proceeded on the basis of a future society ordered according to the principles he was advocating. All that he has said about centralized industry, about military domination, about freedom and initiative, refers to the future. If the land question cannot be tackled without legislative power, much less can the problem of socializing centralized industry.

In conclusion, I repeat that the only development from the present economic stage is towards large-scale production under social ownership; that such production would not only end exploitation and violence but would also raise human life and civilization to an unprecedented level; that all attempts to go back to handicraft economy would end in failure and serve merely to divert men's efforts from being concentrated on the development of society towards its ultimate destiny—socialism. I had asked the Professor how he planned to decentralize already centralized industries and to prevent future centralization. He has not dealt with the question beyond remarking cryptically that "our method generally is to win the co-operation of the people by educative propaganda". We know that more than fifteen years propaganda has had no traceable decentralizing influence upon the cotton (mill) industry of the country. But, I suppose the Professor is speaking in terms of millennia.

77. Statement on Sampurnanand's Circular Letter, 14 May 1935[1]

It has amused me to watch the attempt of the *Pioneer*[2] to create a sensation over an alleged secret Socialist plot. It is a pity that some other papers also have fallen into the trap.

I do not seek to deny the authenticity of the thesis which was in fact circulated by Com. Sampurnanand, not, however, as the *Pioneer* says after our so-called 'crushing defeat' at Jubbulpore[3], which in reality was a moral victory rather than

[1] *Bombay Chronicle*, 14 May 1935.

[2] *Pioneer* was started by George Allen and his son C.T. Allen from Allahabad on 1 January 1865. At first it was published tri-weekly, 1865-9, and became a daily in 1869. It passed into Indian hands in 1933 and its headquarters was shifted from Allahabad to Lucknow. It generally supported the Government's point of view.

[3] C. Rajagopalachari moved a resolution at the A.I.C.C. meeting at Jabalpur on 24 April 1935 congratulating the Congress Parliamentary Party on the 'successful work' done by it in the Indian Legislative Assembly. Speaking on behalf of the C.S.P. Yusuf Meherally opposed the resolution and deprecated the compromising attitude of the Congress vis-a-vis the other groups in the Assembly and not acting according to the Congress stand in the elections. J.P. also criticised the resolution and said that the Congress programme in the Assembly had not been sufficiently revolutionary in character. The contention of the Congress Socialists did not receive much support in the A.I.C.C. and the resolution moved by Rajagopalachari was adopted. However, an amendment moved by Shankarrao Deo (not a

defeat as a large section of the Press has freely admitted long before [the *Pioneer*]. If the *Pioneer* has got a genuine copy, it can easily discover the date given which is February 1935.

It is not my purpose here to offer any apologia for the thesis, which now represents the official view of the Party. Nor do I wish to join in any controversy which has been provoked around it.

I feel, however, that it is necessary to remove certain misunderstandings which have been sought to be created. I have nothing to say about comments like that of the *Hindustan Times*[4] which has likened our methods to those of boot-leggers and highwaymen. The *Hindustan Times* is the voice of Indian capital and, therefore, it strengthens our faith in ourselves when that voice expresses itself in this fashion. The public will no doubt form its opinion about our tactics. Jubbulpore has already opened the eyes of many people.

The *Pioneer's* comments deserve more attention, not because they carry any weight, but because they are intended to mislead the public.

First of all I must condemn the sensationalism indulged in by the *Pioneer*. It has made much of our secret Plot. As a matter of fact there never was any idea of secrecy about Com. Sampurnanand's thesis which by the way has not been published by the *Pioneer*. It is true that it was not meant for publication but it was widely circulated among Party-members and copies were sent through the post. Naturally, the Government must have become privy to its so-called secrets months back because censorship of our mails is rule rather than the exception.

What after all is all this sensation about? The programme of the Party which the *Pioneer* quotes and our plan of action were laid down long ago and published in the Press and our leaflets. Nothing has happened since the formation of the Party which can be any justification for the sensation-mongering, the object of which seems more to provoke the government than anything else.

Com. Sampurnanand's thesis deals only with our tactics towards the Congress. There is nothing sensational about this. It is natural for a left-wing minority group like ours not to rely on its ability to capture the Congress by merely moving resolutions in the A.I.C.C. Looking at the present Congress Constitution and the weightage given to the right wing by the present constitutionalist policy of the Congress it, indeed, seems a remote possibility. It was, therefore, suggested that, along with our day-to-day work of labour and peasant organization which is the foundation-stone of our movement, we must also concentrate our activities on some particular issue and capture the imagination of the masses by a supreme sacrifice. There is no suggestion of trickery or deception in this. It is a clean,

member of the C.S.P.) seeking to omit the word 'successful' from the resolution was accepted. The Congress Socialists considered this as their moral victory. The *Pioneer* and some other newspapers thought otherwise (see *Hindustan Times* and *Bombay Chronicle*, 25 April 1935). J.P.'s contention is, however, supported by the *Indian Annual Register* which described the outcome at the A.I.C.C. meeting as a 'partial victory' for the Congress Socialists (see *Indian Annual Register*, 1935, Vol. 1, p. 30).

[4] *Hindustan Times* was started in 1924 by the Akalis with K.M. Panikkar as Editor. Later it was taken over by Madan Mohan Malaviya and Lajpat Rai, and in 1927 by G.D. Birla who became its Director.

straightforward and open proposal which can only with the respect of those who are genuine anti-imperialists.

It is not worthwhile to take notice of the broad hint the *Pioneer* has thrown to the Government.

Our Party is an open party, with an open membership and a published programme. Our activities too are open. Finally I must say a word about the *Pioneer's* insinuation about our securing funds from Russia. This is a most vicious and mendacious propaganda. Russia is undeniably a great inspiration to us, as it is to all the exploited people but it is mischievous to suggest that we have any such connection with it as the *Pioneer's* insinuation.

78. Letter to Kishori Prasanna Singh, 16 May 1935[1]

Kabir Chaura
Benares City
16 May 1935

Dear Kishori Babu,[2]
Saprem Namaste.

Received both your letters.

The numbers of the circulars mentioned by you are 9 (in which the names of the provincial Executive and District Committee members have been asked for) and 4.

I shall not be able to come to Patna for about two weeks now.

Whatever you have written about Almora seems to be all right, but it will not be advisable to go to hills very late. I think I shall start the camp around 10th June. Let us see what happens. I shall decide after the receipt of letters from other provinces. I may also drop the idea in case there is no response from the provinces. However, from Bihar you, Shyam Nandanji[3] and Awadheshwar Babu[4] must come. It is not necessary that only two comrades come from each province.

[1] *JP Papers* (NMML). Original in Hindi.

[2] Kishori Prasanna Singh (1903-84); left studies to participate in the non-cooperation movement, 1921; associated with *Yuvak* and *Forward*; worked at Sondhu Gandhi Ashram; took part in the salt satyagraha and jailed, 1930; associated with revolutionary activities; arrested in connection with Hajipur train dacoity, 1931; participated in the agitation against chowkidari tax and jailed, 1932, 1933-4; General Secretary, Bihar C.S.P., 1934-40; member, C.P.I., 1940-84, and its National Council, 1973-82.

[3] Shyamnandan Singh (1907-71); took part in the civil disobedience movement, 1931; associated with Kisan movement in Bihar; elected member of Patna District Congress Committee, 1931, Bihar P.C.C., 1933, 1934, and Executive Committee of Bihar C.S.P., 1935; Secretary, Patna District Congress Committee, 1935; member, Bihar Legislative Assembly, 1937-48; organized strike of workers of South Bihar Sugar Mills Ltd., Bihta, 1939; worked underground during the Quit India movement; arrested, 1944.

[4] Awadheshwar Prasad Sinha (1907-89); imprisoned for participating in the civil disobedience movement, 1930; member, Kisan Sabha, 1933-48, Congress Socialist Party, later named Socialist Party,

I have no firm views about shifting of the provincial office to Hajipur. It is for you to decide as to which place would be convenient to you. Rest is fine.

Yours,
Jayaprakash

Perhaps I may not be able to attend the meeting on the 20th.

Jayaprakash

1934-48; Secretary, Bihar Kisan Sabha, 1935-41; President, All India Kisan Sabha, 1941-2; detained, 1942-5; when the Socialist Party decided to ask its members to leave the Congress (1948), he left the Party and chose to function inside the Congress; member, Provisional Parliament, 1950-2, Lok Sabha, 1952-6, and Rajya Sabha, 1956-76.

79. Statement to Press on Bengal Detenus Fund, 17 May 1935[1]

The Congress President has fixed May 19 for collections for the Bengal Detenus Fund. I have no doubt that the country will generously respond to the appeal of the President.

I wish particularly to draw the attention of the members of the Congress Socialist Party to the responsibilities that lie on them in this connection. The creation of the Bengal Detenus Fund is largely the result of our efforts and therefore it is incumbent on us to put forth our best efforts in order to make the fund as big a success as possible.

It should be remembered that collections can never be successful unless a good deal of previous propaganda has been done through distribution of leaflets and notes in the Press.

[1]*Bombay Chronicle*, 17 May 1935.

80. Reply to Critics of the Congress Socialist Party, 3 June 1935[1]

It was with no little surprise that I read in a press message emanating from Bombay the following item: "There appears to be a feeling among a section of Congressmen in Bombay that unless these two wings of the Congress (the official Congress group and the Socialists) are clearly defined, Congress work will become impossible."

[1] *Bombay Chronicle*, 3 June 1935. Statement to Press.

Apparently there is a 'section of Congressmen in Bombay'—whatever that may mean—that is spoiling for action but the cursed Socialists are in its way. Really that is inexcusable. If the Socialists are becoming an obstruction they should be chucked out. I fully agree. I shall be the first to offer to be thrown out if the allegation is proved to be true. I would much rather eat out my heart alone in the intensity of class-hatred than be a stumbling block in the path of the servants of the Motherland—whether that service is performed within the Corporation chamber or amidst the elevating grandeur of Imperial Delhi.

So let us see what the facts are. What is the Congress programme? Mr. Satyamurti, who like the thousand-named Lord of the Hindus, has recently been renamed the 'temptor' announced the other day a very tempting triple programme for his unfortunate P.C.C., which ought to gladden the hearts of the Congress rank and file. Enrolment of Congress members, capture of all local bodies, preparation for Council elections. What an inspiring programme and how ticklish Ministership and all that.

Now, I cannot conceive of Congress Socialists in Bombay or elsewhere obstructing the first activity. In fact, they are as jealous about it as anyone else. As for the second, with the Municipal elections over in Bombay, there is nothing left there to capture. It is a pity that Mr. Nariman's[2] dominions are not as large as those of Mr. Satyamurti. The third, that is, the preparation for coming Council elections, must be causing some anxiety to a section or two of Congressmen in Bombay. Mr. Nariman, however, is too responsible a leader to commit his P.C.C., whatever his personal view, to any programme in this connection. Moreover, he is a member of the Working Committee and till that Committee has taken a decision on this matter, he cannot allow his organization to start any sort of preparation in its furtherance.

Fortunately for us Mr. Satyamurti is not an all-India dictator yet and Bombay might well have a more varied and vigorous programme. The spread of Hindi, I know, is one of its programmes and it has a labour sub-committee. Now, if Mr. Patil has found that the Bombay Congress Socialists are insisting on the spread of Russian instead of Hindi, I shall request him to intimate to me of the same. Hindi being my mother tongue I assure him that I shall use my good offices to persuade my Bombay comrades to transfer their affections from the Russian bear—not a very lovable creature as they too must admit—to the Hindi fairy.

As for labour work, I can imagine differences arising between Congress Socialists and the others. But here too there cannot be any obstruction. Organization of labour is the chief activity of the Bombay Congress Socialist Party and its members would be the last persons to hinder anyone working for the same ends. What the party must be insisting on is the adoption by the B.P.C.C. of a clear-cut labour policy and programme.

[2] K.F. Nariman (1888-1948); gave up practice to participate in the non-cooperation movement and imprisoned, 1921; member, Bombay Legislative Council, 1923-9; President, Bombay Youth League, 1928-9, and All India Youth Conference, Calcutta, 1929; participated in the civil disobedience movement and imprisoned, 1930-2; released, 1933; President, Bombay P.C.C., 1934; Chairman, Reception Committee, Bombay Congress, 1934; Mayor of Bombay, 1935-6; elected to the Bombay Legislative Assembly, 1937, and made an unsuccessful bid to become leader of the Congress Legislature Party.

The position of the Congress vis-a-vis labour is very anomalous. As long as Congress refuses to go beyond Karachi it would be inimical to the interests of labour to come within the ideological influence of the Congress. This is not to say that the working class should keep out of the Congress. No, that would be suicidal for it, as past experience has shown labour must come within the Congress, but it must come with a full political consciousness and on its own programme and with its own leadership. This is the essence of the political policy of the Congress Socialist Party with regard to labour.

As for Trade Union work, here too there may be differences. There is a tendency among Congressmen to form labour associations independent of the existing trade union movement and as appendages to the Congress. This is a disservice to the cause of labour, though it may be the line of least resistance today. Trade unions must be separate from the Congress and part of one countrywide trade union movement. Pandit Jawaharlal Nehru writing on 'Labour and the Congress' (see *Recent Essays and Writings*) says: "I am quite clear that labour should organize itself in the Trade Unions and the like quite separately. Otherwise it will get lost in mixed nationalist groups." In the same article he writes later on: "For Congressmen who are also interested in labour affairs, the course of action should be as follows: They should function separately in labour organizations, trade unions, etc., and help them to develop an ideology and programme of activity as militant as possible, even in advance of Congress programme. In the National Congress they should try to push on an economic orientation in consonance with the labour programme." Evidently Panditji thinks, and rightly, that only those Congressmen should take up labour work who are much in advance of Karachi ideals.

However, these differences on policy are only theoretical. If any work has been done by the labour sub-committee, I have no doubts that the Congress Socialists have been in the forefront.

This leaves only the so-called constructive programme of the Congress. Unfortunately in this respect the position of Bombay Congressmen is rather a difficult one. Bombay is not a village—glorified or otherwise—and therefore its most enthusiastic section of Congressmen cannot find scope for its energies in developing village industries. It can, if it chooses organized stores for the sale of village products. But then in what manner can the Socialists obstruct this work? Surely Masani or Meherally is not going to picket these stores!

The work of the A.I.S.A.[3] follows its beaten path and there is little scope for the general body of Congressmen to meddle in its affairs. However, if the enthusiasm of a section of Congressmen for Khadi disproves this observation, I am sure the Congress Socialists will not organize an inverted Luddite campaign to smash up spinning wheels.

This leaves Harijan work. Mr. Mathuradas Vasanji Khimji[4] may be our sworn

[3] All India Spinners' Association (Akhil Bharat Charkha Sangh) was inaugurated on 22 September 1925 at the A.I.C.C. meeting in Patna under Gandhi's presidency with the object of fostering spinning and use of Khadi in every part of the country. Assests of All India Khadi Board and Provincial Khadi Boards were transferred to the Association.

[4] Mathuradas Vissanji Khimji (1881-1949); Chairman, Bombay Harijan Seva Sangh, and Indian Merchants Chamber and Bureau, 1934; elected to the Indian Legislative Assembly, 1935.

enemy in the capacity of a capitalist but as the head of the 'achhutodhar' movement in Bombay I am sure he can have nothing to say against us. Certainly the repeated failures of Mr. Deorukhkar to go to the Corporation were not due to Socialist obstruction, nor I am afraid, have the Socialists threatened to shun temples polluted by Harijans.

This practically exhausts the list of Congress activities. Bombay may have ten more programmes of which I am not aware. But I have not the least doubt that what is true of the activities I have considered is true also of the remaining. I shall request my friends in the expressive American idiom to cut out the bunk. Let us honestly admit that for those who are really earnest about work there is no obstruction, except from the alien power.

Congress Socialists may not be interested in most of the official activities of the Congress. But that is not the same as saying that they are obstructing in any manner their pursuance by others. If anybody has suggested the latter I have not the least hesitation in branding that suggestion as a mischievous lie.

As far as Bombay is concerned I can imagine one source of friction, which, however—and this is important—has nothing to do with the execution of the Congress programme. The Congress Socialists in the Bombay Corporation may be proving somewhat inconvenient to the Congress bosses there. This is a matter which should be clearly understood. The Bombay P.C.C. not having contested the election itself, its members in the Corporation who excepting the Congress Socialists went there in their individual capacity and not as representatives of the B.P.C.C., cannot now claim to constitute a Congress party in the Corporation and put forth measures and programmes as on behalf of the B.P.C.C. Nor can they seek to apply the whip to the Socialists who in the event of the B.P.C.C. declining to enter the election, contested it 'on behalf of their party with their party programme'. Any programme which the non-Socialist Congress Corporators may have now developed cannot be binding on every member of the B.P.C.C. in the Corporation. The Congress Socialists have every moral and constitutional right and justification for sticking to their own election programme. Any attempt to raise questions of discipline and to accuse the Socialists of indiscipline on this score is, to put it mildly, not playing the game fairly.

A word about the relations between the official Congress and the Congress Socialist Party. The Bombay message says that this relation must be defined forthwith and intimates that when the Congress President visits Bombay next this question will be discussed and the relationship defined. I fail to understand how a discussion between some Congressmen of Bombay on the one hand and the President on the other can result in any authoritative conclusions regarding this matter.

However, I wish to point out that the relationship is not as obscure as the gentlemen who inspired the Bombay message believe. As early as October last the policy of my Party in this regard was laid down by me in my Report of the First Conference of the All India Congress Socialist Party in these words:

> Another problem which faces us is the question of our relation with the Congress. The problem is a simple one and can be easily solved. First of all our organization is within the

Congress. That itself defines our relationship to a great extent. Being part of it, there is no question of any opposition or hostility towards it. 'On the other hand we as Party must participate in the activities of the Congress and consider them our own', except where we disagree with a particular policy of the Congress. At the same time, we must exercise our right as a minority to propagate our views within the Congress to work along our own lines to criticize and even oppose such policies of the Congress as appear to us to be not in the interest of the masses.

This policy has been adhered to since it may be profitable for interested parties to spread misunderstanding, but I should have thought that after such a clearcut expression of our position there was no room left for any doubt or apprehension.

81. Letter to Kishori Prasanna Singh, 9 June 1935[1]

Kabir Chaura
Benares City
9 June 1935

Dear Kishori Babu,
Saprem Namaskar.

Received your letter. I was away from here for about ten days and hence the delay in reply.

I am pleased that the Bihar Party has become active ever since you became the Secretary.

I'll be going to Siwan on 17th and 18th to attend the marriage of Braj Kishore Babu's son.[2] I'll be staying in Bihar for some time after the marriage. During that time we will meet either in Patna or Hajipur. Have lots to talk.

Panna Babu's[3] *Swaraj Kaise Milega* has been printed. It is priced one anna. Tell me how many copies should be sent?

Perhaps, by mistake, the first page of the typed constitution of the party which you sent is left over there. Kindly send that.

One of my friends has promised to pay Rs. 25/- per month for one year to the workers who are working with the kisans. I suggest that we should help our two workers with this amount. The condition is that the person must be a village worker and a member of our party. I have written to Swamiji[4] about this. Kindly have a

[1] *JP Papers* (NMML). Original in Hindi.

[2] Vishwanath Prasad.

[3] B.P. Sinha.

[4] Swami Sahajanand Saraswati (1889-1950); original name Navrang Rai; went to Kashi in 1907 and took sanyas, came to be known as Swami Sahajanand Saraswati; started *Bhumihar Brahman*, a Hindi monthly from Kashi, 1916; also established Bhumihar Brahman Press (Kashi), 1917; joined the Congress, 1920; elected President of Ghazipur D.C.C., 1921; jailed, 1922; Founder-Editor, *Lok Sangraha*, Samastipur, 1927; founded Sitaram Ashram at Bihta near Patna, 1927; organized Western Patna Kisan Sabha, 1927; President, Bihar Provincial Kisan Conference, Sonpur, 1928; participated in the salt satyagraha and imprisoned for six months, 1930; President, Patna D.C.C., 1935, and All India Kisan

word with Swamiji and also have the opinion of Awadheshwar Babu.

Hope your health is fine.

Yours,
Jayaprakash

P.S.

I have dropped the idea of the summer camp. For two reasons. First, except for two or three provinces there was no response from any other place. Secondly, several persons like Narendra Deva and Sampurnanand are not free in the month of June.

This letter was lying for many days. I had kept it because I was about to talk to Sampurnanandji about Deep Babu.[5] Result was that I forgot about this letter. At present I am going to Siwan to attend the marriage. This letter was found lying with the papers. Excuse me for the delay.

Jayaprakash

Sabha, Lucknow, 1936, Comilla, 1938, and Vijayawada, 1944, and its General Secretary, 1936, and 1939-43; jailed for three years for taking part in Anti-Compromise Conference at Ramgarh, 1940; resigned from the Congress, 1948; publications include: *Brahmarishi Vansh Vistaraha, Brahman Samaj Ki Sthiti, Jhoota Bhaiy Mithya Abhiman, Karmakalap, Gita-Hriday, Kranti Aur Sanyukta Morcha, Kisan Sabha Ke Sansmaran, Jharkhand Ke Kisan, Kisan Kya Karen?*, and *Mera Jeevan Sangharsh.*

[5] Dip Narayan Singh (1894-1977); left Bihar Education Service to join the non-cooperation movement; member, Bihar Legislative Council, 1926-9, Bihar Legislative Assembly, 1937-76, and Constituent Assembly, 1946-50; Minister for Irrigation, Power and Information, Bihar Government, 1962-3.

82. Letter to Kamalashanker Pandya, 9 June 1935[1]

Kabir Chaura
Benares City
9 June 1935

Dear Com. Kamalashanker,

I returned yesterday after a week's absence—that is the reason for this delay in answering your letter.

Thanks for inviting me to the Conference. I am afraid, however, that owing to other engagements I shan't be able to attend.

If you have any message for Narendra Devaji, Kamaladevi or any other comrade, I shall advise you to write to him direct, because I am not here regularly & so your message may remain undelivered till it is too late.

Received Rs. 20/- for the Detenus Fund which I am remitting to the A.I.C.C. In future please send all collections for this fund direct to the General Secretary, A.I.C.C.

With greetings & wishing every success to your Conference,

Yours fraternally,
Jayaprakash

[1] *Kamalashanker Pandya Papers* (NMML).

83. Circular to Members of National Executive, Congress Socialist Party, 16 June 1935[1]

Notice of Meeting

Kabir Chaura
Benares City
16 June 1935

Dear Comrade,
I propose to call a meeting of the Executive here at Benares in the last week of July. I suggest a three days' sitting, July 27, 28, 29.

There are a number of important issues which have to be thoroughly discussed and the line of the Party laid down regarding them. Some comrades have prepared these on certain important subjects which need to be examined.

I feel that among us there has been an altogether inadequate contact and exchange of opinions and experiences. It is time that we should meet not to transact formal business but to discuss intimately the problems that have arisen from the experiences of the past seven months.

Some members of the Executive have not attended a single meeting since the October Conference. I hope that the July meeting would be attended by all.

I am giving notice sufficiently early so that you may fix your programme accordingly. As far as possible please avoid asking me to change the dates. It creates confusion.

I shall send you the agenda in a few days.

At the Jubbalpore meeting it was decided, as you may recall, that every member was to prepare a thesis on the problem created by the new Constitution—what should be the attitude of the Congress and of the Party towards it, taking every possible combination of circumstances. I have not received this thesis from any one. Please send yours as soon as possible.

Yours fraternally,
Jayaprakash Narayan

P.S.
I shall be away from headquarters for about three weeks. Com. Sampurnanand will be incharge in my absence. The address remains the same. My address would be C/o *Searchlight*, Patna.

[1] *Nabakrushna Chaudhuri Papers* (NMML).

84. Circular to Secretary, Bihar Congress Socialist Party, 16 June 1935[1]

Circular Letter No. 11

Kabir Chaura
Benares City
16 June 1935

The Secretary
Bihar P.C.S.P.

Dear Comrade,

I regret to inform you that the Summer Camp proposal had finally to be dropped. Firstly, the response it evoked was very poor; secondly, some of the most prominent members whose presence was absolutely essential were not free during this month. July would be unsuitable for the hills. So, the idea had to be given up for the time being.

I wish to remind you that my letter regarding the *Congress Socialist* remains unanswered by you. I hope you will do everything possible to make the *Congress Socialist* a success.

In a previous circular I had pointed out the desirability of monthly reports of Provincial Party activities. Will you be good enough to give your attention to this matter.

Yours fraternally,
Jayaprakash Narayan
General Secretary

P.S.

I shall be away from headquarters for about three weeks. Com. Sampurnanand will be in charge in my absence. The address remains the same. My address would be C/o *Searchlight* Patna.

J.P.

[1] *JP Papers* (NMML). The same circular was sent to all the provincial secretaries of the Congress Socialist Party.

85. Statement on Publication of Socialist Circular by the *Pioneer*, 16 July 1935[1]

The *Pioneer* seems to be on an untiring expedition of discovery. But, it is a sad commentary on its resources and ability that it can do no better than pass off stale documents which have already been published elsewhere, as its original find. The Socialist circular[2] which it claims to have discovered now was issued by me from Bombay on Jan. 16 last, and important extracts from it particularly those which have excited the *Pioneer*'s cheap taste for sensationalism, were published in the *Congress Socialist* of Feb. 10.

I suggest to the learned Editor of the *Pioneer* who must be rather overwhelmed by the worries of discovery that it would much lessen his troubles if he were to secure from us a file of the *Congress Socialist*. He would then be able to unearth conveniently a whole string of secret Socialist documents and plots much to the satisfaction of his masters, the landed nobles of the U.P.

As for the circular itself, I have nothing much to say. We do firmly believe that the Congress cannot become a strong revolutionary body unless the right wing, compromise-seeking elements are driven out of it. I feel strengthened in this view by the recent attempts of some prominent Congress leaders to re-enter the organization which they left rather than share the risks of the deepening struggle for independence.

Finally, I wish to express my gratitude to the *Pioneer* for the publicity it is giving to our Party and our publications. I hope it will continue to oblige us.

[1] *Searchlight*, 17 July 1935. Statement issued at Patna.

[2] Reference is to the extract of the Circular of the Congress Socialist Party published in the *Pioneer* dated 5 July 1935. For the text of the Circular see item no. 52.

86. Statement to Press on Confiscation of M.R. Masani's Passport, 1 August 1935[1]

I find from newspaper reports that the Secretary of State for India,[2] replying to a question in Parliament, said that the reason why the Government impounded Mr. Masani's passport was that he belonged to the Communist Party and moved an amendment at the last Congress session advocating violence. Ignorance on the part of British officials about the conditions in India have always been proverbial.

[1] *Searchlight*, 4 August 1935. Statement issued at Banaras.

[2] Lawrence John Lumley Dundas, Second Marquis of Zetland (1876-1961); member, Royal Commission on Public Services in India, 1912-14; Governor of Bengal, 1917-22; member, First and Second Sessions of Indian Round Table Conference, 1930-1, and of Joint Select Committee on India, 1933; Secretary of State for India, 1935-40; Secretary of State for Burma, 1937-40; publications include: *An Eastern Miscellany*, *The Life of Lord Curzon*, *The Life of Lord Cromer*, *Steps towards Indian Home Rule*, and *Essayez*.

But Lord Zetland has beaten all previous records. Mr. Masani never moved an amendment of the nature the Secretary of State alleges. Nor is he member of the Communist Party. He is one of the Secretaries of the Socialist Party and has been sent to England by that party in response to the invitation of the British Socialist League. I have requested the Congress president to send a wire to Lord Zetland refuting the charge against Mr. Masani.

87. Telegram to Rajendra Prasad, 1 August 1935[1]

Benares
1 August 1935

To
Babu Rajendra Prasad
Maganwadi, Wardha

Refer Zetland's Reply Lords regarding Masani's passport Request cabling Zetland Masani moved no such amendment Bombay Congress as alleged Also request Working Committee pass resolution condemning impounding passport Hope our resolutions considered by Working Committee

Jayaprakash

[1] *AICC Papers* (NMML).

88. Interview to Press regarding Meeting of National Executive, Congress Socialist Party, 6 August 1935[1]

I have already sent the resolutions of the Executive to the President. The long sittings of which you speak were mainly occupied with discussion of policies and reconsideration of certain fundamental positions of our Party. The most important of these was the policy concerning our role and work in the Congress and I am glad to say that the Committee faced the issue boldly and reached very far-reaching decisions. I shall publish a full statement of our new policy in a few days. I take this opportunity however, of briefly stating our position.

First of all the Committee decided that we should endeavour to convert the Congress not to full-fledged Socialism but to the goal of full economic and political freedom for all the exploited classes of the country—the peasants, workers and the lower middle classes. This ideal would no doubt include many items of the socialist programme but instead of being exclusively a working class programme it would

[1] *Bombay Chronicle*, 7 August 1935. Meeting of the National Executive of the Congress Socialist Party was held at Banaras, 27-9 July 1935.

cover the needs of the common class and aspirations of all the classes. In other words the Congress should be converted into an organization of the exploited classes of India which forms the bulk of the population of the country. This alone can mean *Poorna Swaraj* for themselves.

It was further decided that while giving up the stressing of Socialism as such on Congress platforms we must vigorously propagate Socialism among Congressmen and others and build up general sympathy and support for the movement.

With regard to our relation with the Congress the Committee wanted to make it clear that it had never been the policy of the party to attack or weaken the Congress. Our object as a matter of fact has always been to uphold and strengthen the Congress as an ideal and mighty organization. Specific programmes have been criticized and must be continued to be criticized but the Committee enjoined upon its members to avoid use of harsh and unbecoming language.

In the matter of Congress elections, the Committee made it clear that Party's object was not to capture Congress Committees and offices by snatch or manoeuvred votes. The object of the Party is to win over genuine Congressmen, particularly, the rank and file to our views by propaganda and patient work till the great majority of Congressmen become our supporters.

89. Letter to Rajendra Prasad, 20 August 1935[1]

Kabir Chaura
Benaras City
20 August 1935

My dear Rajendra Babu,
A friend from Poona writes that you have been annoyed by our first fixing the Abyssinia Day and then asking the Congress to join us in observing it.

If our friend's information is correct then there has been some misunderstanding somewhere. It was never our intention to ask the Congress to join us on the Abyssinia issue & we did not make any such proposal to the Working Committee.

Of our resolutions, only two (one on the Constitutional issue & the other on the attempt to form alliances with non-Congress groups) requested the Working Committee to consider the issues raised.

I hope that this letter will remove any annoyance that you might have felt.

With kindest regards,

Yours very sincerely,
Jayaprakash

[1] *AICC Papers* (NMML).

90. Letter to Secretary, Gujarat Congress Socialist Party, 31 August 1935[1]

Kabir Chaura
Benares City
31 August 1935

To
The Secretary
Gujarat P.C.S.P.

Dear Comrade,
I have been given to understand that your Party has opened a rival textile union in Ahmedabad. It is strange that I should have no information of this from you.

You know that our Party has always been opposed to the policy of dual unionism; except under extraordinary circumstances. When Com. Masani and I visited Ahmedabad in November '34, this question was discussed between us and Comrade Dinkar Mehta. It was agreed then that the Party should not lend any support to dual unionism (that was in existence at that time) but should form 'cells' among the workers and do political propaganda among them.

I recognize that since then 'extraordinary circumstances' might have arisen necessitating a change in your Party's policy. But a change of this nature which requires the reversal of the All India Party's normal policy should not be initiated by a provincial party without obtaining the sanction of the All-India Party. Questions of this nature are not only of local consequence, but have an All-India bearing.

I do not know how far your Party has gone with the rival union. I should, however, advise you to stay your hands till we have gone into the matter thoroughly.

I suggest the following course:

1. You suspend the activities of the rival union for a month. In the meanwhile we shall examine the matter together and see what can be done. I propose to send one or two representatives on behalf of the All-India Party to Ahmedabad to discuss the matter with you and the Ahmedabad comrades and to generally study the situation there and report.
2. In the first week of October I shall call a meeting of the Labour Sub-Committee of the All-India Party at Bombay to which I shall invite a dozen or so other members of the Party engaged in labour work. At that meeting we shall discuss everything at length and lay down a detailed policy, including the policy to be followed at Ahmedabad.

I realize that it would be difficult for you to suspend the activities of the Union if it is already functioning. But, considering the question from a wider perspective, it seems to be the only desirable course. If you can advise a better course, I shall feel obliged. What is of utmost importance, however, is that the labour policy of

[1] *Kamalashanker Pandya Papers* (NMML).

the Party should be uniform all over the country. You are aware of the mess the Bombay people have made. Therefore, a conference of Party labour workers is essential to lay down a uniform policy which the all India Executive may then accept.

Yours fraternally,
Jayaprakash Narayan

91. Letter to Secretary, Bihar Congress Socialist Party, 31 August 1935[1]

31 August 1935

To
The Secretary
Bihar P.C.S.P.

Dear Comrade,
A meeting of the Executive Committee of the A.I.C.S.P. was held at Benares on July 27, 28, 29 last.

This meeting was called particularly to discuss and decide certain very important questions of policy. The most important of these was that concerning the role, task and tactics of the Party. The others were concerned with Party organization and the Party's attitude towards the New Government of India Act.

The decisions of the Committee regarding the first issue have been embodied in a thesis. I shall send you printed copies of it in a few days. It is necessary that every Party member should get a copy. The thesis embodies decisions of such far-reaching character that every Party member must read and fully understand it.

The policy laid down by the committee regarding the last question, namely, the New Constitution, is embodied in the resolution attached herewith.

As regards Party organization, the Committee discussed the desirability of admitting non-Congressmen into the Party, but decided that no decision be taken at this stage.

Among other decisions and resolutions of the Committee were:

1. (a) This Committee endorses the action of the General Secretary in sending Comrade Masani to England for the purposes of propaganda in response to the invitation of the Socialist League.
   (b) This Committee strongly condemns the high-handed act of the British Government in impounding the passport of Comrade Masani.
2. It was decided to observe an Abyssinia Day and issue a pamphlet on Abyssinia.
3. The Annual Conference of the Party shall be held during X'mas in Delhi.
4. *Labour Policy*—The Committee discussed what should be the labour policy

[1] *JP Papers* (NMML).

of the Party. It noted that there was no uniformity in this regard among Party members working in different centres and felt the need of issuing detailed instructions to Party members in this matter. However, since those members of the Executive who were intimately connected with labour work were not present, it was decided that for the present only the broad lines of the policy should be laid down and the details should be decided at the next meeting of the Committee. In the meanwhile the General Secretary was asked to request Party members working in the labour field to prepare draft theses and submit them to the Executive before its next meeting.

The broad lines laid down were:

(i) There should be uniformity in the labour activities of the Party throughout the country.

(ii) The Party should work in accordance with the principles of 'revolutionary trade unionism' as defined by Marx and Lenin.

(iii) The Party is opposed to the policy of 'rival unionism'.

Note: If any provincial Party finds that it is absolutely essential in the interest of the Labour and political movements to start a rival union in a given industry, it should obtain the permission of the All-India Executive before doing so.

(iv) In the case of 'reformist' unions, Party members must join it, but must work for a change in the policy of the union and should never ally themselves with the reformist workers or those who advocate pure economism.

(v) In any trade union in which more than one political groups are working, the Party should work in cooperation with the group that is nearest to it politically.

5. In view of the policy of the Roy Group[2] as published in the 'Supplement to the Masses' (undated) to enter the Party with the purpose of liquidating it, no individual known to be a member of that group should be admitted into the Party. An explanation concerning the policy should be demanded of such individuals as may already be members of the Party.
6. Comrades Meharally[3] and Ansari[4] who were senior substitute members were appointed full members of the Executive.

[2] The followers of M.N. Roy.

[3] Yusuf Jaffar Meherally (1903-50); founded Young India Society in Bombay, 1925; launched National Militia, 1929; founded *Vanguard*, 1929; jailed during the freedom movement; Founder-member, C.S.P., 1934, member of its National Executive, 1937, Joint Secretary, 1938, and General Secretary, 1940; President, All India Students' Federation (Nationalist Wing), Patna, 1941; Mayor of Bombay, 1942; member, Bombay Legislative Assembly, 1948-50; publications include: *A Trip to Pakistan*, *Leaders of India* (in 2 parts), *The Modern World: A Political Study Syllabus*, and *The Price of Liberty*.

[4] Faridul Haq Ansari (1895-1966); joined the Bar, 1925; member, A.I.C.C., 1927-48; Secretary, Delhi P.C.C., 1929-30, and Delhi D.C.C., 1930-2; participated in the civil disobedience movement, 1930, 1932, and individual satyagraha, 1940; Founder-member, C.S.P., 1934; detained, 1942-5; member, National Executive, Socialist Party, 1948-52, and P.S.P., 1952-8, and its Joint Secretary, 1954-8; member, Rajya Sabha, 1958-66.

Comrades Dinkar Mehta and Gunada Mazumdar[5] were nominated as substitute members.

J.P. Narayan
General Secretary
All India Congress Socialist Party

[5] Gunada Charan Majumdar (1909-92); participated in the agitation against the Simon Commission, 1928; jailed during the salt satyagraha, 1930; Acting Secretary, Bengal C.S.P., 1937; member, National Executive, C.S.P., 1938; detained for two-and-a-half years for participating in the Quit India movement; wrote: *Nachiketar Kahini, Plan Keno?, Amra Ki Karte Pari?, Meyeder Adhikar*, and *Nalkuper Katha*.

92. Letter to Lala Shankarlal, 5 September 1935[1]

5 September 1935

My dear Lalaji,[2]
Thank you very much for your letter of 19th August. It is the first cheerful news from Delhi.

You write that you will do just as we desire. You know the Party's financial position as well as I do. At Delhi, I discussed the whole matter with you frankly and fully. Everything depends on money, you know.

I have no new request to make to you. At Delhi I had requested you to get at least 200 shares of the Company sold and to help us in meeting part of the travelling expenses. You had promised to pay half of the latter. As for the shares I do hope that you will buy at least 50 yourself. I leave the rest to your generosity.

With greetings,

Yours sincerely,
JP

[1] *JP Papers* (NMML).

[2] Lala Shankarlal (1885-1950); involved in Patiala Sedition Case, 1909, and externed; came to Delhi and opened a swadeshi store, 1913; started Home Rule League in Delhi, 1917; General Secretary, Delhi P.C.C., 1918-30, and its President, 1937; participated in the non-cooperation movement and sentenced to three years' imprisonment, 1921; released, 1924; one of the founders of Tropical Insurance Company, 1928; jailed for participating in the civil disobedience movement, 1930-2; Chairman, Congress Socialist Publishing Company; one of the founders of Forward Bloc, 1939; arrested, 1941, and released, 1945.

93. Letter to Kamalashanker Pandya, 11 September 1935[1]

Kabir Chaura
Benares City
11 September 1935

Dear Comrade Pandya,
I am convening a small conference of our Party members who are working in the labour movement for the purpose of discussing and defining the labour policy of

[1] *Kamalashanker Pandya Papers* (NMML).

the Party. At present there is no uniformity in the policy followed by different Party branches. Not only there is lack of uniformity, but also some Party branches have adopted rather unhappy policies on certain occasions. We have been feeling for some time past that it is high time that we should define our policies, tactics, etc., in detail. It is for this purpose that I am convening the conference.

The Labour Sub-Committee of the Party will also be meeting at the same time and we shall have joint conferences.

The decisions of the Conference and the Labour Sub-Committee will of course be recommendatory, for, the final decision on matters of policy rests with the All India Executive and the Annual Conference of the Party. This however, in the present case, will be more a matter of form, because I feel confident that the Executive will accept the recommendations of the Labour Sub-Committee.

The Conference will be held at Bombay in the 1st week of October. I shall announce the dates later. If the time does not suit you, please suggest other dates.

I hope you will not fail to attend the conference.

With fraternal greetings,

Yours sincerely,
Jayaprakash Narayan

94. Interview on Acceptance of Ministerial Offices by Congressmen, 14 September 1935[1]

It has been a matter of genuine surprise to me that the question of acceptance of ministerial offices has so rapidly become a matter of practical Congress politics. A year ago, I think, most Congressmen would have been scandalised at the mere suggestion of it. I take this change of mentality as an evidence of serious deterioration of the spirit of the Congress under the ministrations of the Parliamentary Party.

As the Working Committee resolved at Wardha this question can be decided only at the open session of the Congress. I do not understand, however, how opinions on this knotty and complicated question can be made to suddenly crystallize overnight at the Congress session.

A question of such an importance must needs be discussed thoroughly months beforehand, so that the public and particularly the would be Congress delegates, may form their opinion in the matter. It is incumbent especially on our leaders to take the public in their confidence and place before it their arguments for and against.

I am therefore, not in the least in sympathy with the ban the Congress President has imposed on the members of the Working Committee not to express their views in this matter. This amounts, in my humble opinion, to shirking of responsibility. The fact that there is acute difference of opinion in the Working Committee on this question is the more reason why both sides should be given full liberty to agitate on behalf of their respective views.

[1] *Searchlight*, 18 September 1935. Interview at Patna.

Sardar Sardul Singh[2] has taken a courageous step by resigning from the Working Committee. His resignation, I understand, was not due to difference of opinion but to the fact that he wanted the 'keep mum' ban to be lifted. I think that the Congress President will soon find that his fear of disruption of the Working Committee in case he allowed free expression of views would become much more real if he continues the ban. Sardar Sardul Singh's resignation points which way the wind will blow.

It is a matter of great satisfaction to those of us, who are opposed to the ministerial programme, that the Sardar Saheb has promised fullest support to our campaign. Our movement has been greatly strengthened by the support of such an eminent Congress leader. We hope to secure the support of other equally eminent leaders.

[2] Sardul Singh Caveeshar (1886-1963); Secretary, All India Sikh League, 1920, and President, 1921; Secretary, Punjab P.C.C., 1921; participated in the non-cooperation movement and Akali *morchas*, 1921-2, and imprisoned; presided over the Punjab Provincial Conference, 1925; member, Congress Working Committee, 1928; acted as Congress President in 1932, 1933, and sentenced four times in connection with the civil disobedience movement; resigned membership of A.I.C.C. on office acceptance question, 1935; President, Forward Bloc, 1941-8.

95. Presidential Address at the Bengal Congress Socialist Party Conference, Calcutta, 21 September 1935[1]

Comrades,

I am grateful to you for the honour you have done me by inviting me to preside over this conference. Being the first Provincial Conference of your Party, it possesses a unique importance. Much of the future of our movement in this province will depend upon the lead that this conference gives. I, therefore, wish that you have entrusted the responsibility of conducting its proceedings to abler and more experienced hands. However, I hope that with your co-operation I shall be able to discharge my duties to your satisfaction.

Bengal, of all the provinces in India, has occupied a premier political position. It has been in the vanguard of the country's freedom movement since the beginning. In suffering and sacrifice it is easily the first province in the country. Even at the present moment, whole districts of the province are subject to virtual martial law. Thousands of Bengal's youngmen—some of them with the promise of the most brilliant careers—lie wasting in jails, without as much as a charge having been framed against them in a court of law. The Bengal Government enjoys the unique but doubtful reputation of depriving its citizens of their liberty without having proved their guilt. And yet the Governor of the province, Sir John Anderson,[2] remarked the other day that it was ignorance that prompted people to demand the release or trial of the detenus. It is true that the public does not possess the facts that the Secret Service has made available to Sir John. But that is no reason why

[1] Jayaprakash Narayan, *Towards Struggle: Selected Manifestos, Speeches and Writings* (Bombay, 1946). Edited by Yusuf Meherally.

[2] Sir John Anderson (1882-1958); Governor of Bengal, March 1932-November 1937; member, British Parliament, 1938-50; Lord President of Council, 1940-3; Chancellor of the Exchequer, 1943-5.

the public should condone acts which offend against all canons of civilized law. If Sir John Anderson is so sure of his facts, why does he not produce them in a court of law and have them established? As long as his Government refuses to do this, the public will continue to condemn its action and to demand the release of those who have been deprived of their liberty without any known cause. In the words of Babu Rajendra Prasad, the President of the Congress, the Government "have no reason to complain if the public are not prepared to accept their view, subversive as it is of all recognized principles of civilized jurisprudence".

The demand for justice being done to the detenus has been brushed aside by the Governor of Bengal as ignorance or pro-terrorism. Under the latter pretext, all efforts in behalf of the detenus have been suppressed in this province, thanks to the black laws with which the executive has provided itself here. Outside Bengal where the black laws have no jurisdiction, the detenu agitation is disposed of on the plea of ignorance. Official effrontery never before presented itself in a more brazen form. It is well that the Government should realize clearly and once for all that the demand for the release of the detenus has nothing to do with terrorism nor is it based on ignorance. It is based, as a matter of fact, on one of the most elementary principles of civilized society, viz., that no person should be deprived of his liberty without due processes of law. The country's case in this connection cannot be put better than in these words of the President of the Congress:

> The Governor of Bengal in his address to the Bengal Legislative Council divided those who pressed for the release or in the alternative for the trial of Bengal detenus into two classes, viz., those who were in secret sympathy with terrorism and therefore should be regarded as out of court and those who though well-meaning were ignorant of the real state of affairs and therefore deserved no consideration. He ignored the third class which I believe, is the largest in the country and which has among it persons holding diverse political views and belonging to diverse parties. That third class comprises persons who hold the liberty of person as sacred and who strongly believe that none should be deprived of his or her liberty except as a result of a trial openly held in accordance with canons of civilized law.

The country has only recently begun to realize the gravity of the detenu question. Till practically the middle of last year we were in the midst of a great national struggle. Every province at that time had its own troubles, its own share of repression. Bengal, though being incomparably the worst sufferer of all, remained, therefore, a provincial issue. But not entirely so. Even during that period such eminent leaders as Pandit Jawaharlal Nehru showed considerable concern for the Province and you are all aware that it was for pleading your case that he was imprisoned.

When the Satyagraha movement was withdrawn, the strain of the struggle left us unprepared to take up immediately any such issue as that of Bengal. Gradually, however, the Bengal question, particularly the question of the detenus, rose to prominence. It has now become a countrywide issue, though much remains to be done.

It should be a matter of satisfaction to us that our Party has played a considerable part in bringing this issue to the fore. The Detenu Day which we observed last March in a way marked the beginning of this agitation on an all-India basis.

It should also be a matter of satisfaction for all of us that the President of the Congress, Babu Rajendra Prasad, has been giving his particular attention to this question since he assumed office.

But, as I said above, there remains a great deal to be done yet. The demand for the release of the detenus is still very feeble. Much more publicity is required to be given to this question than it has received so far. And the publicity should be extended to foreign countries also, particularly to England. Mr. C.F. Andrews[3] has already led the way in this direction. He must be followed up by others.

On behalf of my Party I assure the people of Bengal, and the detenus particularly, that we shall always stand by them and do all we can to help them.

The question of the detenus is not the only outstanding problem in Bengal. Under the pretext of putting down terrorism, the Bengal Government has made all national and mass activities impossible. Many Congress bodies, Khadi organizations, trade unions, peasant organizations, student associations, presses and publications have been placed under a ban. Those which are not actually banned have to live under the perpetual surveillance of the Secret Service.

To strengthen my assertion I shall quote again from the statement of the Congress President. "But today they are bent on perpetuating the lawless laws", runs the statement, "depriving people of personal liberty, liberty of association and liberty of expression of views on the platform and through the press at the will of the executive, and they have been enforcing such laws with all their rigour and not unoften misapplying them to conditions for which they were never intended. Consider the number of presses and newspapers which have been penalized, the number of Associations, including Labour organizations and Congress organizations which are banned, the number of individuals who have been deprived of their liberty without any of those being tried and condemned by a court of law, and it becomes clear to what extent the Government can go even when things are more or less quiet."

There is no need of my going into the details of this question. You who belong to this province know them much better than I do. The real question before us is, what can we do in the matter? It is clear that Bengal alone is helpless. The other provinces must come to its aid.

As in the case of the detenus, publicity is the chief remedy here also. The public does not know all the facts. I believe that if all that was happening in Bengal was

[3] C.F. Andrews (1871-1940); Fellow and Lecturer, Pembroke College, Cambridge, 1899; Vice-Principal, Westcott House, Cambridge, 1900-4; came to India as member of Cambridge Brotherhood, 1904; friend of Gandhi and Rabindranath Tagore; taught at St. Stephen's College, Delhi, 1904-14; went to South Africa to help in Smuts-Gandhi Agreement, 1913-14, and to Fiji regarding abolition of indentured Indian labour, 1915 and 1917; joined Santiniketan, April 1914; Adviser to Indian Delegation at Kenya Conversations, London, 1923; went to South Africa to help in Indian-Union Agreement between South Africa and India, January 1927; Correspondent of *Manchester Guardian, Cape Argus, Natal Advertiser, Toronto Star*, and *Hindu*; Vice-President, Santiniketan, 1939-40; wrote *The Renaissance in India, Zaka Ullah of Delhi, India and the Simon Report, What I owe to Christ, Sadhu Sunder Singh, India and Britain—A Moral Challenge, The True India*, and edited *Letters to a Friend, Thoughts from Tagore, Mahatma Gandhi's Ideas, Mahatma Gandhi—His own Story*, and *Mahatma Gandhi at Work*.

made known to the country and to the civilized world outside, such a storm of protest and condemnation would be let loose that even the Bengal Government would be compelled to bend down before it.

This cannot be done, however, unless there is an organization which takes it up as its sole activity. I wish to place before you a suggestion in this regard, though I must tell you that I am not its author. Bengal, though suffering the most from the evils of an arbitrary rule, is not alone in its suffering. The whole country is in a manner subject to it; and acts of high-handedness and unlawful victimization are not uncommon elsewhere even in normal times. Most of these acts would not be committed if the public were a little vigilant and if there were some organization, the task of which was to bring such acts to light and put up a fight against them, through the law-courts, the legislatures, the press and the platform.

It is, therefore, suggested that a non-political association should be formed, the business of which should be to defend the ordinary right of citizenship—rights that are enjoyed by every member of any civilized society. You have heard of the Civil Liberties Union of the U.S.A., which under the able leadership of Mr. Roger Baldwin has done extremely valuable work. There are also many international organizations for the protection of the working man's rights and interests. This association which is suggested here should also be on similar lines. It should be formed not of political workers but of leading jurists of the country; eminent publicists and journalists; women workers (for women are the worst sufferers); social workers, like some of those of the Servants of India Society,[4] and so on. It should be an all-India body and should have intimate contacts with kindred foreign organizations. It should collect facts; publish literature; organize legal defence, raise funds for sufferers; do foreign propaganda; cause questions, resolutions, etc., to be asked or moved in the legislatures and so on. Is it not a pity that in spite of all that has happened in Bengal, there is not even one pamphlet published which gives even the bare facts? Such a pamphlet should have been placed in the hands of every public man in India, every member of Parliament, every organization in Europe and America that is interested in the civil liberties of the people. If we turn the merciless lights of publicity on every act of official excess, we shall be able if not to totally stop them, at least, to reduce them greatly.

There has been recently some talk of foreign propaganda. It may be true that general nationalist propaganda in the West is not very fruitful; but I have no doubt that a propaganda which exposes specific acts and measures of official terrorism will prove effective. I may add that its efficacy will be in proportion to the accuracy and regard for truth that the Association shows in its work.

I think that there is ample material in the country to form such an association. The first step is to find a competent individual, with a status in public life, who has travelled in the country and abroad, to take the initiative. Such an individual must give his whole time to the association and should be paid by it. I do not think that

[4] The Servants of India Society was founded by Gopal Krishna Gokhale in Poona on 12 June 1905 to train selfless public servants for the welfare of the people and service of the country. The president, assisted by a council of three ordinary members, was in charge of the affairs of the Society. Its branches were founded in Madras, 1910, Bombay and Nagpur, 1911, and Allahabad, 1913. The Society grew in strength under V.S. Srinivasa Sastri and H.N. Kunzru after Gokhale's death.

the cost of running such an association would be more than Rs. 5000/- per year—a sum which can be easily raised for a cause such as this. I do hope that some one from Bengal would come forward and take up the work.

I hope you will not misunderstand me and take me as saying that this Association alone will be sufficient to deal with the problem. The Association will do very valuable work, but not the whole of it. I have already suggested other necessary measures.

I shall take up next certain other issues which loom large on the political horizon of Bengal.

II

The first of these is the communal problem. Bengal is one of those provinces, the minority community of which is said to have been wronged most by the so-called Communal Award. While non-Hindu minorities have been given special treatment elsewhere, the Hindu minority of this province has been particularly discriminated against. The Hindu politicians of the province are naturally in a flurry over this and have formed a party which is called, paradoxically enough, the "Nationalist Party".

Let us look at this question little more closely.

The question whether the Communal Award is good or bad is one which admits of no controversy. There cannot be two opinions about it. For me it is sufficient reason to condemn it that it is an award of the British Premier. That high executive of imperialism could not have been allowed to commit such a grave public lapse as to do India a good turn. The Communal Award was deliberately calculated to exploit the communal tension in the interests of imperialism. Subsequent events have borne this out. We shall have further proofs when the New Constitution begins to work. That a few individuals of this or that community have benefited or will benefit by it does not alter the basic reality. The Communal Award is the greatest single anti-national factor in our political life today.

And that brings us to the real problem. Granted that the Communal Award is bad, what should be our attitude towards it? Shall we be foolish and play into the hands of the imperialists or shall we be wise and foil their attempts?

When we say that the Communal Award is bad, what do we mean? Where does its badness lie? Does it lie in the fact that so many seats have been given to the Muslims and so many to the Hindus, or in the fact that it has become an instrument of communal discord? From the nationalist point of view, it matters not a whit how many seats Muslims or Hindus have got. They are both Indians, and, granting that seats do any good, whichever community benefits, the nation benefits. The real mischief of the Communal Award is in its potency to take advantage of our foolishness in sowing seeds of discord. If that be so, are we acting in the national interest if we deliberately aggravate that mischief? If the Muslims or Sikhs get a few more seats than the Hindus, India is not the loser; but if we fall out and quarrel among ourselves, we not only lose heavily but we do so to the tremendous profit of the outsider. To fight over the Communal Award is like the serpent swallowing his own tail.

The exasperated "nationalist" may cry: "what is the solution, then?" The solution of what? I shall ask him. If he is looking for a solution which will set right the disproportion between Hindu and Muslim representation in the Bengal Legislative Council, I am afraid, I have no such solution for him. I am not even interested in the question. A few seats more or less for this or that community is not of the least consequence to our struggle for freedom.

If, however, he is looking for a solution which will bring both Muslims and Hindus in their full strength into the freedom movement, I do have an answer for him and I believe, the only answer.

The communal question in Bengal as in other parts of the country is largely an economic question and has resulted from the fact that the Muslims are nearly all tenants, and the landlords are nearly all Hindus. There has always been a serious conflict between the Bengal tenant and landlord; and peasant uprisings have been quite frequent here. But since the class division nearly coincides with the communal division this conflict and these clashes have often been given a communal colour. It is well-known that religious fanaticism and economic radicalism often go hand-in-hand among the Muslim masses of the province. Just as the Irish under Protestant Britain clung fanatically to their Catholicism and the Czechs under Catholic Austria turned free thinkers, so the Muslim peasants of Bengal under Hindu landlords are as easily susceptible to communal passion as to the idea of the abolition of zamindaris.

In a modified form this is true even outside Bengal. Where the class and communal divisions cross each other, instead of coinciding, the communal question is confined to the upper layer of the social stratum—to men who are desirous of posts and positions, seats and titles.

This being the background of the communal problem, how is it to be solved?

It is clear that if we continued to wrangle for seats in the legislatures, we shall only aggravate the malady. The masses, whether Muslim, Hindu or of any other community, have no interest in the communal distribution of these seats. It may be that today they are persuaded by demagogues into supporting this or the other proportion of communal representation, but their basic interest lies in an entirely different manner of representation. The Hindu labourer and the Muslim labourer have identical interests and if they are made conscious of them, they would forthwith denounce and repudiatc communal representation and demand the representation of their common economic and political interests.

The communal question, as it exists today, affects only a small class, the class which is directly interested, purely for the gratification of personal ambitions and desires, in legislative elections and jobs and employments in the departments of the Government. This class taking advantage of broader causes of communal conflict such as exist in Bengal due to the economic circumstances, I have already mentioned, seek, and unfortunately succeed, to give to their claims and wranglings a much wider sanction than they would have otherwise possessed.

What is the duty of the "nationalist" in these circumstances? In my humble opinion there are only two courses he must follow, if he genuinely desires to solve the communal problem. Let me remind him again that that problem consists not in amending the percentages of communal seats so as to suit better the claim of this or the other community—which invariably means the self-seeking upper fringe of that community—but to endeavour to bring all the various communities wholeheartedly into the freedom movement.

The courses that suggest themselves to me are: firstly, a total withdrawal from the wrangling for legislative seats; secondly, the linking up of the freedom movement with the economic struggle of the masses.

My first suggestion would seem to cut the ground from under the feet of the Bengal Nationalist Party, which, I do not wish to deny, enjoys a great popularity among the Hindu population of the Province. The popularity rests, however, not so much on the issue being a popular one, as in the fact that the educated upper class in this province has taken advantage of its prestige and of the estranged relations between the two communities to arouse popular sentiment on this entirely false issue. For, the issue is a false one. The millions of the Hindus of this province cannot in any manner gain by a few more Hindu seats in the Bengal Legislative Council. Nor do those millions have interests which are different from the interests of the Muslim millions.

The Bengal Nationalist Party, unlike such parties in some other provinces, is formed of genuine, even militant, Congressmen. I ask these friends if they are in any way helping the freedom movement, the cause of the people of the country, by generating the hostilities, the suspicions, the bickerings, which must be the natural issue of their policy. I ask them if they are not weakening the movement for independence, if not diverting it into fruitless, nay, dangerous channels?

The Congress exists and Congressmen exist not to fight the Communal Award but the system whose instrument it is.

I now come to the second course. I have said that we must link the freedom movement with the economic struggle of the masses. This, of course, is a basic tactics with us. But just now I have to discuss it only as a solvent of the communal problem. Later I shall return to it to consider it as a technic of mass action.

The communal problem exists, i.e. we fail to draw, let us say, the Muslim masses, into the national struggle, because we fail to inspire confidence in them. Our movement is not a mass movement. It is not the problem of the masses that we discuss, that guide our action, that determine our social philosophy. Our outlook is yet limited by middle class ambitions and desires. That is why the distribution of seats looms so large on our horizon. If we were leading a genuine mass movement, the masses of all communities would gather round our banner; in other words, the communal problem would have ceased to exist.

As an instance of how we fail to inspire confidence among the masses let me remind you of how the Bengal Swaraj Party years ago caused a Tenancy Bill to be passed through the Legislative Council in the teeth of the opposition of the ryots. You will recall that Muslim opinion was bitterly hostile to that Bill. Consider for a moment what would have been the effect had the Swaraj Party brought in, as it would have if it were a mass party, a Bill which was in the interest of the ryots. It would have secured the unstinted support of the Muslim community—at least, of the 98 per cent of it. But, as it happened, the Swarajists only succeeded in creating the impression that the Congress was a Hindu and Zamindar organization. This, as every one can see, was a fatal impression as far as creating confidence was concerned.

It is clear from this incident that if we adopt a programme which is in the interest of the masses, if we participate in their struggle for economic emancipation, we shall have no difficulty in getting their support and following. And when we do that, the communal problem disappears, because the masses include all communities.

I, therefore, suggest that if Bengal Congressmen want to solve the communal problem, they must, first, unequivocally declare for the abolition of the Zamindari system, and, second, they must seriously set out to enquire into the present difficulties of the tenants and organize them for their removal. A tenants' movement, with the slogan of abolition of zamindaris in the foreground, is the best and only solution of the communal problem in Bengal. Besides liquidating this problem, such a movement will also prepare the masses for the achievement of independence—political and economic.

III

Now I shall touch a little upon the subject of unemployment in Bengal. Unemployment among the poor is a chronic ailment all over India. But middle class unemployment is perhaps the most acute in Bengal.

If there is any social phenomenon more responsible than another, for turning men's minds to the examination of existing society and to proposals for the creation of a better one, it is unemployment. There is no more forceful argument against it than the *status quo*.

What is the solution of the unemployment problem? Is it provincialism, nationalism?

It is strange that in such an intellectually progressive province as Bengal, provincialism should be considered in certain sections, as a solution of problem, the roots of which are very much deeper. It is not a problem which admits of such an easy solution. Unemployment results from the maladjustment between production and consumption which is an irremovable feature of capitalist society. It can be cured only when this maladjustment is cured, i.e. when society is reorganized on a socialist basis. We see this being demonstrated in the present world. While every capitalist country is suffering from unemployment, Soviet Russia, which is yet only on the road to Socialism, is entirely free from it.

It follows from what I have said that not even national independence will be able to remove unemployment. We have only to look at the independent countries of the world to be convinced of this. Socialism is its only cure.

Therefore, I shall say this to my unemployed comrades: Come and join us. You might reply that we have nothing but an idea to offer you. Yes, but, I assure you, the other parties and persuasions have nothing more; and their ideas will not be of the least service to you.

IV

Now I wish to consider with you the attitude that we should adopt towards the New Constitution that has been forged for us by the imperial power.

You recall that the Working Committee of the Congress decided at Wardha that this question should be settled only at the Lucknow Congress. The final decision always lies with the annual session of the Congress. What the Working Committee really meant to say was that it was not prepared to express its opinion yet. The Working Committee not only refused to express its opinion as a committee; it also placed a ban, through its President, on its members from expressing their individual opinions. The result is that the country is deprived of the guidance of these leaders in discussing, analysing, examining this complicated question. It is not clear to me how this state of things has been considered desirable by our leaders. Unless the question is previously discussed threadbare and unless the opinion of the Congress leaders is known beforehand, it would not be possible to reach an intelligent and democratic decision at Lucknow. A few speeches cannot be expected to consolidate opinion in a few hours at the Congress Session.

Perhaps the President was anxious to maintain the unity of his cabinet. But, the reported resignation of Sardar Sardul Singh shows that that policy too has its dangers.

You are all aware, I expect, of the move made to convene a conference of those Congressmen who are opposed to the policy of acceptance of ministerial offices under the new constitution which has been advocated by certain Congress leaders. We expect that this move will help to mobilize opinion on this issue and give the much desired lead. In this connection, I am happy to note that the Bengal Nationalist Party has already decided against acceptance of offices and, if I mistake not, your Dinajpur Political Conference[5] also reached the same decision.

I take this opportunity to place my views and the views of my Party before you in this regard.

What is the situation before us? Briefly, that the imperialist power is attempting to force upon us a device for the further perpetuation of its domination. I need not describe that device to you with all its traps and dangers. It has been fully analysed in the Indian Press and it has declared that it would rather struggle under the existing order of things than have the new dispensation. The new dispensation will however be upon us in a few months, in spite of our rejection.

The question is what should we do with it?

Before going into details, let us consider some broad principles of policy. Remember, I am discussing the issue from the point of view of the Congress, i.e. trying to discover what should be the policy of the Congress in this regard.

The first course that suggests itself is to work the constitution for what it is worth. This is the policy that the Liberal Party would adopt, notwithstanding its severe condemnation of the constitution. In doing that the Liberal Party would be acting logically; mind you, I do not say correctly. Logically, because the Liberal Party knows only one method of political work—constitutionalism.

Now, the Congress long ago gave up its belief in constitutionalism and embraced direct action as its basic policy. The respective strengths of the Liberal and Congress parties show which has been the more fruitful and correct of the two.

Direct action and constitutionalism are incompatible. The Congress cannot truthfully profess its faith in the former, if it agrees to work the constitution. I need not dilate on this point because I think no Congressman will be found to disagree

[5] The Bengal Provincial Political Conference was held at Dinajpur on 19 April 1935.

with it. I doubt if even the great ministry-enthusiast, Mr. Satyamurti will disagree.

But there is a catch in this agreement. While the ministerialists, by which term I mean those Congressmen who favour holding of ministerial offices, hastily agree that the Congress cannot even contemplate holding of offices, the proposals they put forth virtually amount to the same thing. But we shall examine this question later.

So, if it is agreed that we cannot work the constitution, what must we do? What policy should the Congress accept? Our answer is that where possible, i.e. where the Congress has a majority, we should make its working impossible. The Working Committee in its resolution on the J.P.C. Report said that "the Joint Parliamentary Committee scheme designed as it is to facilitate and perpetuate the domination and exploitation of this country by an alien people under a costly mask is fraught with greater mischief and danger than even the present constitution". And, further on, that "this Committee is of opinion that the said scheme should be rejected well knowing that the rejection must involve the necessity of struggling under the present constitution, humiliating and intolerable as it is".

Such being the opinion of the Congress, does it not follow as a natural corollary that the Congress policy should be to carry out the decision of rejection, by forcing the Governor to continue the administration by the exercise of his special powers?

Lest this policy should be considered futile and barren, I quote some very interesting remarks of a British statesman. Captain Wedgewood Benn,[6] writing on the 'Outlook on the Indian Reforms' in the *Political Quarterly* for July-September 1935, hazards some guesses about the policy that the Congress would be likely to follow with regard to what he has termed the Indian Reforms.

He begins by asking: "The most powerful, the best organized and the most important of all Indian National parties is the Congress. What will they do?" He thinks that "in all, but a few of the Provincial Assemblies, they (Congress candidates) will secure a victory". Then he goes on to say that, and this is interesting, "the Congress candidates, if elected, will undoubtedly attempt to wreck the constitution".

Discussing the underlying principle of Congress policy he says: "The issues they (Congress members of Legislatures) will present will not be offered as local at all. Everything will be put into the guise of opposition to the hated British Domination. *The issue which they wish to keep before the public, that of British versus India, will be most clearly presented of course.*" I want you to take special note of this, "*if they can force the Governor into the use of autocratic powers which he now possesses in an unprecedented degree*". This is a most significant statement, coming as it does from such high quarters. Capt. Benn adds: "The technique of the Irish, which has been closely studied in India, will be copied, possibly with success."

Looking at the present drift of Congress policy, one doubts, if it will be.

However, Capt. Benn has gone to the root of the problem. If there is any issue which it is the duty of the Congress to keep perpetually before the public, it is that

[6]William Wedgwood Benn (1877-1969); member, British Parliament, 1906-27, 1928-31, and 1937-42; Secretary of State for India, 1929-31; Vice-President, Allied Control Commission for Italy, 1943-4; Secretary of State for Air, 1945-6; President, Inter-Parliamentary Union, 1947-57.

of Britain versus India, as he puts it. And by forcing the Governor to continue his administration without the aid of ministers this issue is kept alive.

To elucidate this point further, as it does not seem to be clear to many of us, it is better to look for a while at a very important aspect of the new constitution, which I am afraid has not been kept before the public eye as prominently as it ought to have been. The new constitution, without transferring any real power to the ministers, creates the fiction of responsible government in the provinces. The British Power withdraws itself into the background keeping all the leading strings in its hands. This means that the issue, Britain versus India, is covered up by this subterfuge. The issue, in fact, is turned into "the people versus the party in office", in other words, one part of the people versus the other part. This from the British point of view is a master stroke of political craft. By thus blurring the issue, the British politicians wish to destroy the directness and keenness of the Indian struggle. They further seek to shift the responsibility of carrying on an unpopular administration to the shoulders of Indian ministers, thus hoping to dull the edge of popular resentment against them.

There is a difference between Indian ministers and "members of Government" of the present, and the ministers of the new constitution. At present the position is that the foreign power is able to secure the services of individual Indians, who in return for a title and a consideration carry on the administration for the British. Under the new arrangements, ministers will represent parties, which in turn will represent a section of the electorate. For the actions of the ministry, a party, and ultimately a section of the people itself, will be responsible, at least in theory—and not the British Government. What use a clever governor will make of this situation can well be imagined. Of course, it is obvious what will happen. It has often been said that imperialism has attempted through this constitution to strengthen itself in the face of gathering mass of discontent by rallying around it the vested interests in the country. These "responsible" ministries would be the constitutional mechanism through which this plan would be put into practice. The vested interests will become a facade behind which imperialism will continue its rule. But I am digressing.

To return to the original point, I was saying that the issue of India versus Britain can most clearly be brought out only by forcing the suspension of the constitution, where this is possible.

This is a course desirable for another reason also. We rejected the J.P.C. Report. After that Report has been made a fact in the new constitution, shall we drop our policy of rejection? Remember that the British have always been counting on the constitution being worked. It is with that belief that they went on, most cynically disregarding the counsel even of their Indian friends, with their reactionary measure. The Government members in the Legislative Assembly have often mockingly replied to the Opposition that however much it may howl against the 'reforms' every one would come back and work them.

Under these circumstances it is the duty of the Congress party wherever in a majority, to defeat the objects of the foreign power and to foil their well-laid plans by showing that the constitution they have laboured so long to perfect is a broken reed and that Governor must carry on the administration himself. The impression that this will create in India and abroad would be infinitely superior to anything that can be achieved by any other tactics. From the point of view of keeping up the spirit of the Congress, which after all is the thing that matters, there can be no better course to follow.

It is said that there will be no popular enthusiasm for this policy, because it will not enable the Congress party to throw any crumbs to the people. This is a pathetic plea.

The manner in which the electorate responds depends entirely on the manner in which the issue is presented to it. If we go to it in a defeatist, apologist frame of mind, it is clear we shall fail to inspire confidence. If, on the other hand, our campaign is marked with vigour, our case presented aggressively, the electorate is bound to respond. Suppose that on this constitutional issue a whirlwind propaganda is carried on, raising the one issue of wrecking the constitution, on the ground that it has been thrust on us forcibly and is a michievous device for our further enslavement. I feel sure that in that case we shall be able to arouse sufficient enthusiasm to be returned every time in a majority. Even if we don't we shall have done excellent political propaganda during the election campaign which will prove its utility when we resort to direct action again. For, all our efforts must lead to that.

There is another important aspect of this policy which makes its acceptance well-nigh imperative by the Congress. In its resolution on the J.P.C. Report the Working Committee declared that "the only satisfactory alternative (to the constitution adumbrated in the Report) is a constitution drawn up by a Constituent Assembly". I might remark parenthetically that it is curious to note that since the half-hearted reference to the Constituent Assembly made at the last Assembly elections, there has been no talk about it again. Indeed, a member of the Working Committee, Dr. Pattabhi Sitaramayya, has in a recent interview[7] poohpoohed the whole idea as applied to current politics. "To talk of the latter (the Constituent Assembly)," he concludes his interview, "in our retreat is to cover it up with undue hope, if not bluff." One wonders if the Working Committee was bluffing when it made the solemn declaration I have just quoted. At any rate, I wonder if the President's ban on his colleagues is only in regard to the ministry question or also on making light, in the manner of the Andhra Doctor, of the considered decisions of his cabinet.

However, if the only satisfactory alternative to a constitution devised in Westminster is a constitution drawn up by a Constituent Assembly, is it not our duty to raise the slogan of the Constituent Assembly during the coming election and place it before the electorate as the only alternative, as we have said in our resolution? It may be urged that the Constituent Assembly is a distant prospect and therefore it is mere bluff, as Dr. Pattabhi says, to talk of it as an alternative to any current political measure. Is the Constituent Assembly more distant than independence, and yet have we not 'declared' independence from a thousand platforms? Moreover, why, if it is a distant prospect, was it made a slogan at the

[7] Refers to the interview of Pattabhi Sitaramayya to the United Press in which he expressed the view that the Congress demand for a Constituent Assembly was not only futile but also irrational. See *Bombay Chronicle*, 9 September 1935.

last Assembly elections? In its resolution from which I have quoted before, the Working Committee expressed pleasure that the "demand for a Constituent Assembly has been endorsed in a clear and unambiguous manner by the country, at the recent general election to the Legislative Assembly". That demand was put forward as an alternative to the J.P.C. scheme which we were asked to reject. Now when that scheme is actually being foisted on us, should it not be our policy to raise the issue of the Constituent Assembly still more vigorously?

But if we do that on the one hand, we must say on the other that, where we can, we shall wreck that constitution by making its working impossible. Just as when the constitution was in the making and we were asked to consider it, rejection and the Constituent Assembly were complementary parts of a whole policy, so now when the constitution is an accomplished fact and we are asked to work it, wrecking and the Constituent Assembly are again the inseparable complements of any self-respecting policy that we may adopt. The slogan of the Constituent Assembly cannot be part of any election programme which contemplates acceptance of offices under the new constitution. Its counterpart can only be the slogan of wrecking.

Let us now consider the alternative proposal. I have said before that an objection is raised to this policy on the ground that the electorate would lose interest in it because it would not get any concrete and immediate benefits from it. Suppose that we adopt such a programme of benefits. If we really wanted to give benefits, we would have to remain in office as long as possible, because going out in that case would be a barren policy. At the same time it is well-known how much scope for ameliorative measures the constitution provides. In other words, we will have to work the reforms, and will have the satisfaction of finding at the end of the term of our ministries that very little has been done for the people—so little, indeed, that they have become as much dissatisfied with us as with the British. We shall also find that we have succeeded in killing that mentality of fight against government which is the soul of the Congress movement and in its place have taught the people to look for loaves and fishes to it. The argument of not being able to do anything for the people if we follow a wrecking policy, leads inevitably to constitutionalism. There is no half-way house.

I have considered so far only our tactics in case the Congress has a majority. What should be its policy where it fails to be so successful?

Before taking up that question, let me examine briefly the case of those who are advocating acceptance of offices. First of all, we note that they absolutely overlook all the considerations I have urged. All the underlying principles of our movement, its psychological foundations, our past commitments—all these are given the go-by.

It is interesting to recall in this regard the old policy of the Congress when it decided in 1926 to contest elections: The A.I.C.C. laid it down that "Congressmen in the legislatures shall refuse to accept offices in the gift of the government until, in the opinion of the Congress, a satisfactory response is made by the Government". I wish to draw your attention particularly to the condition for accepting offices. The Government must make a satisfactory response. Considering the objectives of the Congress of those days, it was an honourable and self-respecting decision, consistent with the spirit of the times. The present Congress has travelled far away from its old objectives and it no longer looks for a "response" from the British Government. Is it not regretful therefore that Congressmen should advocate acceptance of offices under the present circumstances, and with no qualifications. It might be said that the offices are no longer in the gift of the Government. That would be a very superficial view of the matter. There is no popular sanction behind the constitution. The whole thing is a gift of the Government—withal a most unwelcome gift.

Thus the first thing the ministerialist seeks to do is to destroy a valuable psychological aspect of Congress policy.

What does it offer in return? It is difficult to say, because this point has not been made clear yet. Mr. Satyamurti and certain others have spoken of benefits and ameliorative measures; of clothing the services in khadi; of flying the national flag over government buildings and so on. A rather doubtful fare. The Congress which has stood for large measures cannot forsake them and seek to appeal to the electorate with a programme of petty reforms. If the Congress did so, it will divert the public mind from the basic and fundamental issues and teach the electorate and the people to look to the government for petty favours. This would mean the diverting of mass energy into fruitless channels and therefore the weakening of the national movement.

At the same time, it is obvious that if the Congress adopts a programme consistent with Congress policy and objective, it will be of such a far-reaching character that no Congress ministry would be allowed to carry it out. A Congress ministry can only be a very short-lived experiment under these conditions, leading us nowhere and greatly damaging some of our basic ideas and principles.

Here, I wish to pause a little to consider the suggestion that Mr. C.R. Reddy[8] has made in a recent speech[9] in the south. He suggested that there was a midway house between wrecking and working the constitution. The Congress Party should seek election on a proper Congress ticket and, if returned in a majority, it should take office, and try to work out its programme. If obstructed by the Governor, it should resign and seek re-election on the issue which created the deadlock.

This kind of political strategy can be suggested only by one who is used to thinking on constitutional lines alone. Consider, what this strategy does; it drops the slogan of basic opposition to the new constitution, of rejecting and wrecking it, of the Constituent Assembly; it destroys the valuable mentality that has been generated in the course of our struggle of always looking at the government as an opponent; it creates illusions in the people's mind regarding the capacity of ministries to solve their difficulties; and so on. Let us look at the other side of the

[8] C.R. Reddy (1880-1951); joined Maharaja's College at Baroda as Professor and Vice-Principal, 1908; shifted to Maharaja's College at Mysore, 1909, and was its Principal, 1916-17; Inspector-General of Education, Mysore, 1918; joined Justice Party, 1921; member, Madras Legislative Council, 1921-6, and 1935-46; Vice-Chancellor of Andhra University, 1926-30, and 1936-49; President, Chittoor District Board, 1935-6; Pro. Chancellor, Mysore University, 1949; publications include: *Musalamma Maranamu*, *Congress in Office*, *Democracy*, and *Bharata Artha Saastramu*.

[9] Refers to the presidential speech of C.R. Reddy at Tuticorin Political Conference on 7 September 1935, where he had urged upon the A.I.C.C. to give the country a right lead and made a passionate plea for the removal of ban on the acceptance of offices. See *Bombay Chronicle*, 9 September 1935.

shield. What does it achieve? Nothing except that a few Congressmen occupy the seats of government for some time—the time will depend on how soon Mr. Reddy considers the ground to have been prepared for a spectacular walk-out. The constituents would not have "benefited", at all, because the deadlock would prevent the ministers from benefiting them. In other words, this strategy does not even have the merit of the *pucca* constitutionalist who gives the people what tiny benefits he finds possible to give. On the other hand the fight against the governor takes place not on the fundamental issue of India versus Britain but on something of much lesser importance. Mr. Reddy's suggestion is as dangerous as any other.

I do not wish to devote much more time to this question. However, let me mention a few more dangers and risks that lie hidden in the programme of the ministerialists.

Take the election campaign itself. If it is decided that Congress should accept offices, then every attempt would be made by the Congress Party to secure a majority. This would inevitably lead to compromise with non-Congress groups and the modification of the Congress programme in such a manner as to allow non-Congress and vested interests to join the Congress campaign. It was a genuine surprise to me when I came across a Hindi manifesto of the U.P. Congress Parliamentary Committee, issued over the signature of its assistant secretary during the last Assembly election, setting forth reasons why the landlords of the province must support the Congress candidates. The manifesto, in short, tried to make out that the Congress has always stood for and defended the rights of the landlords. It is interesting to note that the spirit of this manifesto runs wholly counter to another of the same committee, issued in English for the general voter. It is also interesting to recall that in this same province, a few years ago, a resolution was passed by the Provincial Political Conference advocating the elimination of all middlemen between the tiller of the soil and the State.

I have brought up this matter merely to show how the exigencies of winning a majority leads to watering down, vulgarizing and distorting of even the present Congress ideals, moderate as they are. I do not for a moment believe that U.P. was an exception in this regard. This sort of thing must have happened everywhere.

So we see that at the very outset of this policy in the election campaign itself, there is compromise and a drift to the right. Whereas the election campaign should be utilized for raising fundamental issues, for educating the masses, for organizing them, we will be led to make compromises and to give up the more revolutionary slogans and programmes.

Then the dangers after the ministries have been actually formed are not negligible—the dangers, I mean, of demoralization, leading in the end to constitutionalism on the one hand and serious disruption of the Congress ranks on the other.

So far I have discussed with you only the policy which should be followed in the case of the Congress securing majorities. I have taken so much of your time in discussing this question because I felt that of all present issues it is of the greatest significance to the growth of the freedom movement.

Now, I shall briefly touch upon the policy the Congress Party should follow where in a minority. The policy of the old Swaraj Party was "one of determined resistance and obstruction to every activity, Governmental or other, that may impede the nation's progress towards Swaraj" coupled with enactment of ameliorative measures. We suggest an improvement upon this. Mere obstruction will not be sufficient. We must also use the legislatures as tribunes for voicing the people's grievances, their rights and demands. The most effective form of legislative activity is one which brings the struggle that is waged outside into the legislative chamber. This means that the Congress must attempt to develop mass activity in the shape of an economic agitation of peasants, workers and other exploited groups, and use the legislature to further that activity. Without linking up in some such manner legislative work with an agitation outside, the former becomes utterly sterile and ineffective.

I need not dilate on this point any further. The policy in cases where the Congress is in a minority is not difficult to determine. There are also a number of instances in history to guide us in this regard.

In concluding my remarks on the constitutional issue, I should like to state, as a résumé of what I have said already, the underlying principle of our entire policy in the matter of legislative work. We believe that legislatures have to be used only in order to strengthen and support the revolutionary work outside. For us there is no parliamentary work, as such. I remember Mr. Rajagopalachari[10] saying at Jubbulpore, in his speech[11] on our resolution concerning the work of the Congress Party in the Assembly, that when we go to the legislative chamber we must do what is customarily done there. What he meant to say was that we must work there on approved constitutional lines. According to him our insistence, for example, on the slogan of the Constituent Assembly having been raised in the Assembly chamber, was misplaced tactics. That was a slogan which had to be raised outside at the proper time.

Our whole conception of legislative activity is opposed to this. We hold that when we go to the legislatures our purpose should be not only to inflict constitutional defeats on the Government, but also to raise fundamental slogans for the purposes of propaganda, to relate the work within to the day-to-day struggles of the masses outside, to expose Imperialism to obstruct its working. This, of course, means that the Congress while sending its members into the legislature must simultaneously engage itself in organizing the grievances of the masses outside. A strong labour and peasant movement outside coupled with revolutionary use of legislatures—that is the principle which ought to govern the constitutional policy of any fighting

[10] C. Rajagopalachari (1878-1972); one of the most prominent leaders of the Congress till 1959; joined satyagraha campaign against Rowlatt Bills, 1919; General Secretary, Congress, 1921-2; member, Congress Working Committee, 1922-42, and 1946-7; Editor, *Young India*, 1922-3; Premier, Madras, 1937-9; Minister, Interim Government, 1946-7; Governor, West Bengal, 1947; Governor-General of India, 1948-50; Minister without Portfolio, 1950, and Minister of Home Affairs, 1951, Government of India; Chief Minister, Madras, 1952-4; awarded Bharat Ratna, 1954; one of the founders of Swatantra Party, 1959; publications include: *A Jail Diary, Plighted Word, The Way Out, Reconciliation: Why and How, Ambedkar Refuted, Mahabharata, Bhagvad-Gita, Towards a Responsible Press, Ramayana, My Inconsistencies*, and *Satyam Eva Jyate*.

[11] Refers to the speech of C. Rajagopalachari while moving a resolution on the work of the Congress Party in the Indian Legislative Assembly at the A.I.C.C. meeting, Jabalpur, 24 April 1935.

organization like the Congress. Its details will depend on leadership, but its principles are there.

V

I do not know if I have bored you. You doubtless expected me to speak about Socialism. As members of the Congress Socialist Party, I wish you to remember, however, that the most important role that we have to play at present is in connection with the freedom movement. It was for this reason that I have examined at length certain problems which happen to be of great immediate importance to that movement. I shall devote the rest of the time I have, to a few remarks regarding our party and its policy and work.

You know, the first and main task of the party is to develop the anti-imperialist movement. There are two aspects of this task, both of which I wish to consider with you. The first relates to our work with the Congress and the other to our work among the masses. The two spheres of work are complementary.

Our work within the Congress is governed by the policy of developing it into a true anti-imperialist body. It is not our purpose, as sometimes it has been misunderstood to be, to convert the whole Congress into a full-fledged socialist party. All we seek to do is so to change the content and policy of that organization that it comes truly to represent the masses, having the object of emancipating them both from the foreign power and the native system of exploitation.

There are some who ridicule this whole idea. Their view is that the Congress is a bourgeois body with absolutely no chance of being influenced in the direction I have indicated. We do not subscribe to this view. The Congress at present is dominated by upper class interests and its leaders are uncompromisingly opposed to admitting into its objective any programme aimed at the economic emancipation of the masses. Yet, within the Congress there is a very large body of opinion which would welcome such a programme. Only, this body which had worked under the old leadership has to be convinced that the programme we advocate will not weaken the national struggle by dividing, as they have learnt to think, the nationalist forces. If we seek to influence them—and without influencing them no group of pure and brilliant theorists can develop an anti-imperialist movement in this country—it is not sufficient to abuse the leadership or to produce learned theses. What is needed is a demonstration in actual practice that our programme is more dynamic and effective. I will take up this point more fully when I come to the second part of our task.

So if within the Congress there is a very large anti-imperialist body—I believe numerically it is a majority body—is it not imperative for a party like ours to work actively within that organization? And, with what object and tactics are we to work? Not to disrupt the Congress, not by denouncing the Congress. We should work rather with the object of bringing the anti-imperialist elements under our ideological influence through propaganda and work among the masses, so that finally they come to accept a proper anti-imperialist programme. I am not saying that by working in this manner we shall win the right wing to our programme and thus "convert" the Congress. The Congress as it is constituted at present cannot hold together very long. The more successful we are in pushing our programme, the nearer the day when a split will occur in it. The right wing will doubtless say that we are disrupting the Congress. But, in reality, it will be a ripening consolidation of anti-imperialist forces. The Congress has faced such splits before and has come out stronger each time. Another split would take it to another, and I expect, the last stage of its anti-imperialist existence.

There is another direction in which we must develop the Congress. This concerns its internal organization and constitution. The basis of individual membership on which the Congress is at present organized is very unsatisfactory. It becomes an artificial body, representative not of the masses, but of a handful of members. We must endeavour to change this constitution in such a manner as to make the Congress a direct representative of the people. In my view this can best be done by developing a system of group representation. Members who constitute a primary committee of the Congress should be representatives of class and group organizations. They should represent tenants, farmers, labourers, merchants, the professions and so on. The actual details of this plan may be difficult to draw up, but the principle is simple enough, and, to my mind, most just and proper.

It should be obvious that such a constitution would remain a paper document till the class and group organizations are actually brought into existence. The demand for such a constitution would therefore remain unreal and unheeded till this is done. It must, therefore, be accompanied by the creation of these organizations.

Lest I should be misunderstood, I wish to make it clear that I do not for one moment flatter myself into believing that we are, or shall be, the only political group working towards this consummation—I mean the development of an anti-imperialist movement. There are various other socialist groups following different methods and tactics, but basically working for the same end. It is sad to reflect that all of us are not able to work together, but I have no doubt that the efforts of the other groups will have an undoubted share in the ultimate result. Only, if a common line of work was agreed upon, we would be more successful.

I must add that I naturally feel that the line that the Congress Socialist Party has been following is the most correct of all the tactics that are being used, and that, having an organic relation with the Congress movement, our efforts are bound to be more fruitful. Had not the radical elements left the Congress in 1929, just on the eve of the great national upheaval of 1930, the radicalization of the Congress would have gone much further and we would have been much nearer our goal today.

This process of development of the anti-imperialist forces that I have mentioned just now, cannot be brought about, as I have already said, by mere ideological propaganda. We must at the same time work among the masses. After all, the anti-imperialist movement will consist not only of ideologues, but of workers, peasants, the impoverished middle-classes. To work among these classes, to develop their political consciousness, to organize their economic struggle—this is our main and fundamental task. I must admit that we have not been able to make the desirable headway in this direction. However, the nucleus of work has been formed in many provinces. In the labour movement, our task is not so difficult, because there we have only to join hands with other radical groups and strengthen the dynamic labour movement. But in the sphere of peasant work, we have to do pioneering work in most of the provinces. Here in Bengal there has been a certain amount of economic agitation among the peasants and a nucleus might already exist. If it does, your task is made somewhat easier.

In Bengal, you have almost a limitless field for activity. Both the peasantry and the working class offer ideal spheres of work. Perhaps nowhere in India is the plight of the peasants so pitiable as here and perhaps nowhere are the class issues so distinct. The Bengal Congress movement is greatly dominated by zamindari interests. It is the top-layer, however, which reflects those interests. The rank and file and the lower strata of leadership are, I have no doubt, opposed to them. But, because they lack a programme and an ideology, they have willy-nilly to follow the present leadership.

It will be the task of the Bengal Party to offer the required programme and ideology. If it does so, I have no doubt that it will soon gather around it the great majority of Congress workers of the province and thus pull the Congress movement out of the rut of inaction.

In my talks with village Congress workers—genuine men with fullest sympathy with our ideals—I have found it difficult to explain to them one programme of work among the peasantry. The question I have found most difficult to drive home is how an economic agitation which is naturally aimed immediately against indigenous vested interests can become a force against imperialism. The answer, of course, is that the masses are not directly concerned with imperialism—I am using the term here merely in the sense of the foreign power. What they are faced with is a system of economic exploitation which is daily grinding them to poverty. If they, in their millions, will fight anything, it is this system of exploitation. But this system is an integral part of imperialism and a fight against it becomes a fight against imperialism itself. This point can be elaborated greatly and all its various aspects discussed; for instance how does it apply to those parts of the country where the zamindari system does not exist. But I need not go into all that here. As far as Bengal is concerned its application is obvious.

To return to the village Congress worker, who I have said has, in most cases, the fullest sympathy with our ideals. It is my experience that it will take something more than an argument, however forceful, to carry conviction with him on this score. He has had no experience with the kind of work we are advocating, though, in provinces like Bihar, Bengal, the U.P., he has ample evidences of class struggle. He has so far worked through *ashrams*, hospitals, khadi centres. He does not know what an economic approach to the peasant is. But I am sure that if we show him the way he will be sure to follow.

I have described to you in brief what the main task of the Party is. Now I wish to tell you as briefly as possible my idea of its development. It is fulfilling today a dialectic need. And as the situation develops and changes we must adjust our policies accordingly. I do not believe, for instance, that we shall remain, or ought to remain, separate from the other socialist forces in the country. That would not be in the interest of the ideals for which we stand. I firmly believe that unless there is a fusion of the forces which I have mentioned, our common objectives will remain unrealized. I shall therefore warn you against sectionalism and futile controversies and exhort you to develop the greatest possible co-operation with the groups that are, except for minor differences, working for the same objects as ourselves. I shall take this opportunity to appeal to these also to follow a like policy. I do not ask them to give up criticism, nor do I myself forswear it, but I entreat them to work together in the promotion of identical ideals, keeping in mind the day when we shall all come closer and merge into one organization. I shall not hazard an opinion at present on the nature of that organization, nor indeed there is an occasion for it now.

Now, I wish to take your leave. In concluding, I shall only say that I am fully alive to the difficulties which you have to face in your work in this province. Please remember, however, that we cannot expect the other party to make things easy for us. If our methods are elastic we should be able to work under any conditions.

I thank you all for giving me your willing attention and hope you will excuse me for having taken so much of your time.

96. Statement on the Nagpur Divisional Political Conference, 17 October 1935[1]

Certain prominent Congress leaders of this province, with the approval of the Provincial Congress Committee, have declared the Nagpur Divisional Political Conference which is being organized by left-wing Congressmen and Labour and other anti-imperialist workers as being anti-Congress. After having gone into the matter and read the statement that was issued on behalf of the Provincial Congress Committee and the manifestos of the organizers of the Conference, I have come to the conclusion that to have declared the Conference as being anti-Congress was without the least justification, and was, to my mind, a move which will lower the prestige of the Congress. Among the organizers of the Conference are names which have men of Congress history in the province and who can in no circumstances be expected to entertain anti-Congress feelings.

The Conference has already attracted widespread support from mofussil Congressmen. The purpose for which the Conference is to be called was published by the organizers at the very beginning; and at no time was there any indefiniteness about it. The Conference will discuss the situation created by the passing of the Criminal Law Amendment Act[2] and the general policy of repression followed by the Government; the question as to how effectively to reject the new Constitution and the war danger that is more imminent now than ever.

It is difficult to understand how a Conference of anti-imperialist workers, called to discuss these questions, can be regarded as anti-Congress. If such a Conference will strengthen the Congress, i.e. as far as its anti-imperialist character is concerned,

[1] *Bombay Chronicle*, 19 October 1935. Statement issued at Nagpur on his way to Madras, 17 October 1935.

[2] The Criminal Law Amendment Act was passed in December 1908 to expedite the trials of cases against persons involved in terrorist crimes and anarchist conspiracies and to end the existence of certain volunteer organizations by declaring them unlawful.

if the creation of political consciousness among the public on such questions as repression, war and the slave constitution is anti-Congress activity, then we might as well bury the Congress and bury it deep.

I notice that for some time past there has been a good deal of talk about disciplinary action in certain official Congress quarters. The Congress leftists seem to be in the danger of being put out of the pale any day. When the Bombay leftists wanted to convene a Conference to consider the war danger and means of rejecting the new Constitution, Sardar Vallabhbhai Patel lost no time in calling that a breach of discipline. Certain officials of the Bombay Congress Committee have been itching for disciplinary action for the past some months. The proposal to convene a Conference only whetted their appetite.

It is amusing to recall that when the Congress Nationalists openly flouted Congress discipline by fighting the candidates of the Congress, these voices of disciplinary action were not even heard from any quarter. In 1923 when Pandit Motilal Nehru and Mr. C.R. Das[3] carried on a raging and tearing campaign against the clear decision of an annual session of the Congress, no one even dared to talk of disciplinary action.

Some Congress leaders may feel that by suppressing expression of opinion they are consolidating their leadership. History points to the contrary.

I urge upon not only Congress Socialists but every Congressman of the Nagpur Division to lend his fullest support to the Nagpur Divisional Political Conference, and thereby not only assert their right to freedom of opinion but also infuse fresh life into the Congress and the forces of freedom in the province.

[3] C.R. Das (1870-1925); leading barrister, Calcutta High Court; one of the most prominent leaders of the Congress; President, Bengal Provincial Conference, Bhawanipore, 1917; member, Congress Punjab Inquiry Committee, 1919-20; gave up legal practice to join the non-cooperation movement, 1921; President, Gaya Congress, 1922; founded the Swaraj Party in collaboration with Motilal Nehru, 1922; started an English daily, *Forward*, 1923; leader of the Swaraj Party in the Bengal Legislative Council, 1923-5; President, A.I.T.U.C., Lahore, 1923, and Calcutta, 1924; Mayor of Calcutta, 1924; President, Bengal P.C.C., and Bengal Provincial Conference, Faridpur, 1925; published books of poems: *Malancha, Mala, Sagar-Sangeet, Antaryami,* and *Kishore Kishori.*

97. Letter to C.M. Mehta, 16 November 1935[1]

Kabir Chaura
Benares City
16 November 1935

Mr. C.M. Mehta, Esqr.
The Hospet Sugar Mills Ltd.
Hospet
M.S.M.Ry. (Madras)

Dear Sir,
We are greatly indebted to you and Mrs. Mehta[2] for buying one hundred shares of

[1] *JP Papers* (NMML).
[2] Radhabai C.M. Mehta.

our Company. We have already received Rs. 100/- from you on account. I am writing this to request you to remit the remaining amount of Rs. 400/- to us. You can make out the cheque payable to the Managing Director of the Company, Mr. Shantilal Shah, and send it direct to him. His address is as below.

Shantilal H. Shah, Esqr.
C/o Bhaishankar Kanga & Girdharlal
Solicitors & Notary Public
Albert Buildings
Hornby Road, Fort
Bombay

Wishing to remain.

Yours faithfully,
J.P.

98. Letter to Shantilal Harjivan Shah, 18 November 1935[1]

18 November 1935

My dear Shantilal,
I am sorry I could not meet you in Bombay. I went twice to your office but I was told you were out of town. I had so much to discuss with you regarding the Company.

I am sending you herewith the accounts of the Company. If you want any more details please let me know immediately.

At Delhi I met Lala Shankarlal. He was enquiring if all legal requirements have been fulfilled by the Co. I could not give him any definite answer. You must have heard from him. Please reply to him and see that no legal obligation remains unfulfilled.

Mr. C.M. Mehta of the Hospet Sugar Mills has bought 10 shares of the Co. for his wife. You have already received Rs. 100/-. He promised to Kamaladevi that he would pay up the rest whenever asked to do so. I wrote to him yesterday to send you a cheque for Rs. 400/-. You should expect it in a week or two.

Mr. S.N. Mitra[2] of Calcutta who is a Director of the Co. complained to me when I met him at Calcutta sometime ago that some months back he wrote you a letter making certain enquiries and got a reply to the effect that you were going out of

[1] *JP Papers* (NMML).

[2] Sailendra Nath Mitra (1906-41); participated in the non-cooperation movement and jailed, 1921; chief of the propaganda committee of All Bengal Students' Association and edited its magazine *Chhatra*; practised at Calcutta High Court.

Bombay and would answer his enquiries after returning. He told me that he did not hear from you since then. Will you be good enough to write to Mr. Mitra and give him the information he wants.

Please reply soon.

Yours sincerely,
J.P.

P.S.
I am sending you 16 share applications.

J.P.

99. Letter to R.A. Khedgikar, 21 November 1935[1]

Kabir Chaura
Benaras City
21 November 1935

Dear Com. Khedgikar,
I am glad to inform you that the 2nd Annual Conference of our Party has been fixed to meet at Meerut on Dec. 30, 31 and Jan. 1. I understand that the A.I.T.U.C. Exec. and a Textile Conference are meeting at Nagpur during X'mas. I am writing this to request you to so fix the dates of the A.I.T.U.C. Exec. meeting that they do not clash with our Conference dates and allow sufficient time to delegates to reach Meerut from Nagpur. I have written to Com. Ruikar also about this.

I am sorry I did not send you the monthly donation I promised the A.I.T.U.C. I shall send tomorrow Rs. 10/- by m.o.

I congratulate you on your amicable settlement of the G.I.P. tangle. That is the spirit. I am sure our Party will gain strength if it always shows such revolutionary spirit.

With kindest regard,

Yours sincerely,
Jayaprakash

P.S.
The Surma Valley (Assam) C.S.P. has organized the Surma Valley Labour Association which it wants to affiliate with the A.I.T.U.C. The Secy. of the Party writes that he has written to Ruikar about it. Will you kindly put yourself in touch with Sjt. Suresh Chandra Deb,[2] Secretary Surma Valley Congress Socialist Party, Karimganj, Sylhet, Assam?

[1] *AITUC Papers* (NMML).

[2] Suresh Chandra Deb (1893-1981); participated in the non-cooperation movement and jailed, 1921; Headmaster, National High School, Karimganj, 1925-9; took part in the civil disobedience movement and imprisoned, 1930-3; member, C.S.P., 1934-8; Manager, *Swadhikar*, a weekly, 1936-7; member, Lok Sabha, 1952-7, and Rajya Sabha, 1957-66.

100. Letter to Secretary, Bihar Congress Socialist Party, 7 December 1935[1]

Kabir Chaura
Benares City
7 December 1935

To
The Secretary
Bihar C.S.P.

Dear Comrade,

Conference Dates

The dates of the Annual Party Conference which I had provisionally fixed have been found to be unsuitable for a number of provincial parties have asked me to extend the dates to a more suitable time. After consulting Comrades Masani and Narendra Deva who happened to be here, I am fixing finally the following dates: The Conference to meet on Jan. 19 and 20; the Subjects Committee on Jan. 18 and the Executive of the All India Party on Jan. 15, 16 and 17. These dates are final because if the Conference is to meet at all before Lucknow, no further change is feasible.

Subjects Committee

The Subjects Committee shall be constituted in the following manner: a provincial party entitled to send 10 or more delegates (depending on the membership of the party concerned) to the Conference shall send three members to the Subjects Committee; a party entitled to send from 5 to 9 delegates shall send two members to the Subjects Committee; and a party entitled to send from 1 to 4 delegates shall send one member to the Subjects Committee.

Members of the All India Executive shall be ex-officio members of the Subjects Committee.

Resolutions for the Conference

It is desirable that resolutions, if any, should [be sent] in advance by provincial parties. . . .[2] I suggest that resolutions and suggestions [be sent to] me by December 31.

Delegation Fee

A fee of Re. 1/- per delegate will be charged. The fee will be collected at the Party's office at Meerut.

[1] *JP Papers* (NMML). The same circular was sent to all the provincial secretaries of the Congress Socialist Party.

[2] Not legible, moth-eaten.

Affiliation Fee

Members of a provincial party which has not remitted its contribution of 25% of its membership fee to the All India Party as provided in the Constitution shall not be allowed to participate in the Conference.

Yours fraternally,
Jayaprakash Narayan
General Secretary

101. Letter to Kishori Prasanna Singh, 9 December 1935[1]

Kabir Chaura
Benaras City
9 December 1935

Dear Kishori Babu,
Received your card.

We had to extend the date of our Conference owing to the change in the date of the Congress elections. A circular has been despatched; you'll come to know all the details from it.

The Bihar Party Conference should be postponed for the present. First, there should be some organization there, I had told everyone in Patna. The Conference may be held some time in February or at the end of January. At present you do just one thing, you arrange the election of delegates for the Meerut Conference. You write to every district Committee (wherever there is a party committee) that according to its membership, they should elect one representative on every 20 members. Discuss this matter with other comrades too.

Send a hand-written receipt for Rs. 150/-.

How is Suniti Devi's[2] health now? Do write more.

Your comrade,
Jayaprakash

[1] *JP Papers* (NMML). Original in Hindi.

[2] Suniti Devi (1913-36); married to Kishori Prasanna Singh in 1927; joined her husband in the national movement; took part in the agitation against chowkidari tax in Hajipur, 1930; did not keep good health because of the hard life she led during the national movement.

102. Letter to Lala Shankarlal, 9 December 1935[1]

9 December 1935

Dear Lalaji,
I do not know if Lohia saw you at Calcutta. I understand his uncle was seriously ill, so he might not have had found it convenient to see you.

As you must have learnt already we are bringing out our weekly from the 21st of this month. Everything is settled. I am writing to you to be good enough to (1) send a cheque for Rs. 500/- as your share in the Publishing Co. immediately to Shantilal Shah, C/o Messrs Bhaishankar Kanga Girdharlal & Co., Solicitors, Hornby Road, Fort, Bombay. (2) send the advertisements that you had promised to Asoka Mehta, Editor, *Congress Socialist*, Dadabhai Manzil, Congress House, Bombay. (You had promised me long ago that you would secure 'ads' from 6 insurance companies to the value of Rs. 50/- per month.) Both these things you must immediately do.

Please also send me the hundred for this month.

With kindest regards,

Yours very sincerely,
J.P.

P.S.
Have you written to Srinivas Iyengar?[2]

[1] *JP Papers* (NMML).

[2] S. Srinivasa Iyengar (1874-1941); started practice at Madras High Court, 1898; member, Senate, Madras University, 1912-16; appointed Advocate General of Madras, 1916, resigned, 1920; gave up practice to join the non-cooperation movement, 1920; President, Madras Provincial Conference, Tinnevelly, 1920; President, Gauhati Congress, 1926; member, Indian Legislative Assembly, 1926-9, and Deputy leader of the Swaraj Party in the Assembly; organized boycott of Simon Commission at Madras, 1928; author of *Law and Law Reform, Swaraj Constitution, Problems of Democracy in India, Mayne's Hindu Law*, and *Stalemate and Reorganization*.

103. Greetings to the Editor, *Congress Socialist*, 13 December 1935[1]

Dear Comrade Editor,[2]
I send you warmest greetings on behalf of our Party on the eve of the reappearence of our Party organ, the *Congress Socialist*. While we all regret that our former editor, Comrade R.M. Lohia, is not in a position to continue in the office which he had filled with such distinction, it is undoubtedly our good fortune that we have

[1] *Congress Socialist*, 21 December 1935.

[2] Asoka Mehta.

been able to secure your services. I hope the Party as a whole will cooperate with you in making the paper a success.

Since the closing of the *Congress Socialist* some months back, our work has suffered a great deal. A Party organ is above all a party builder. And it was in the sphere of organization that I felt most the need of reviving our weekly. I trust therefore that its reappearance will prove an invaluable aid to the Central Executive in organizing, shaping, and consolidating the Party.

While the *Congress Socialist* must remain an organ of our Party, I wish that you will take care to keep it away from sectarianism. It should be so conducted that it becomes a natural channel for the expression of all radical thought. Above all it must become the rallying centre, the unifying agency, of the entire socialist movement in the country. Only then it will fulfil the aims of the Party which it speaks.

The All India Congress Socialist Party
Benaras, 13 December

Jayaprakash Narayan
General Secretary

104. Letter to Secretary, Bihar Congress Socialist Party, 14 December 1935[1]

Kabir Chaura
Benaras City
14 December 1935

Secretary
Bihar C.S.P.

Dear Comrade,

As you have already been informed, the *Congress Socialist*, the weekly organ of our Party, resumes publication from December 21. I need hardly point out the value of such a paper for our work.

Every Provincial Party and every Party member bears an immediate responsibility towards the *Congress Socialist*. It is your paper and it cannot be run without your support.

When Com. Lohia was editing the paper from Calcutta he had much to complain about the attitude of Provincial Parties towards the paper. Com. Asoka Mehta, our present editor, is already complaining of the poor response he is getting from the provinces. This is regrettable. I hope you and your Party will lose no further time in rendering as much assistance to the paper as possible. You should pay your particular attention to the following:

[1] *JP Papers* (NMML). The same circular was sent to all the provincial secretaries of the Congress Socialist Party.

1. Every member of your Party should get a certain number, say five, subscribers for the paper.
2. In every city, in every university and college you should arrange for the distribution of the paper through agents.
3. Regular reports of the activities of your Party must be sent to the editor.

You should write immediately to Comrade Asoka Mehta for copies of the *Congress Socialist*. Every Provincial party should be able to buy at least 100 copies to begin with.

Yours fraternally,
Jayaprakash Narayan
General Secretary

105. Letter to Shantilal Harjivan Shah, 19 December 1935[1]

19 December 1935

Dear Shantilal,

I clean forgot to endorse the cheque. Returning it herewith duly endorsed.

In your last letter you wrote that Masani told you that I wanted the Company to proceed on the present basis and that you were acting accordingly. This is rather strange. What I told Masani was that I did not want it to be turned into a private company. Excepting that there were important changes in the present basis that were agreed upon. They were: (1) Converting the 5 rupee shares into 25 rupee ones; (2) Changing the Company's name to something non-political.

Please let me know if these changes are feasible. If they are, please circularize the directors and secure their approval.

I have several pamphlets in the press. They must all come out as the publications of the Company. Are we now, legally, in a position to proceed with their publication?

I am glad that you are taking keen interest in the *Congress Socialist*. I hope you will be able to bring it out on the 21st. Tell Asoka to send me 100 copies every week.

Hoping to hear soon from you.

Yours sincerely,
JP

[1] *JP Papers* (NMML).

106. Statement on Pact between Congress Socialists and Communists, 25 December 1935[1]

The whole story that a pact has been reached between the Congress Socialists and Communists, which was published in a Lucknow paper,[2] is untrue and is calculated to embarrass our Party.

There is no truth in the statement that we are thinking of separating from the Congress, nor any resolution suggesting such separation has been tabled for the Meerut Conference by our Party.

The very fact that the party since its inception voluntarily banned the acceptance of offices on the Congress Executive by its members shows how ridiculous is the suggestion of the paper that we are tired of playing second fiddle to Congress leaders.

[1] *Bombay Chronicle*, 26 December 1935. Statement issued at Nagpur.

[2] Refers to the story of secret pact between Congress Socialists and Communists published in the *Pioneer*, 22 December 1935.

107. Fifty Years: Article in the *Congress Socialist*, 28 December 1935[1]

Only twenty-eight years separated 1857 and 1885. Yet, the one was an open and armed struggle for sovereign power, while the other an act of petitioning for a Royal Commission, for simultaneous examinations for the I.C.S., for admission of elected members into the 'Councils', and for such other petty demands. Only twenty-eight years and such a change in national ideals! It is not odd, that the prayer should be called the first cry of Indian nationalism? Looking back at that event, I cannot help remarking that far from being the beginning of any movement of national liberation, it signalized the beginning of a new stage in the country's political life—the stage of acceptance of foreign rule and of adaptation to it.

I am aware that Mrs. Besant[2] is not alone in the characterization of the first session of the Indian National Congress as the 'beginning of the formulation of India's demands'. Even to this day, fifty years after that session, we look upon 1885 as the birth-year of Indian nationalism. My remarks above may therefore appear blasphemous to devoted Congressmen.

What did that change mean?

[1] *Congress Socialist*, 28 December 1935.

[2] Annie Besant (1847-1933); came to India from U.K., 1893; translated the *Bhagvadgita* into English, 1895; established Central Hindu College, Banaras, 1898; President, Theosophical Society, 1907-33; founded Home Rule League, 1916; President, Calcutta Congress, 1917; started Women's Indian Association, 1917; author of many publications including, *Reincarnation*, *Autobiography*, *Karma*, *Shri Ramachandra*, and *The Story of the Great War*.

An easy, but an extremely unintelligent, explanation is that 1857 represented no national movement at all, that it was merely a feudal *coup*; whereas the seventy-two gentlemen who met at Bombay in the winter of 1885 spoke the voice of the nation. This view is based merely on the fact that the gentlemen who founded the Congress put forth their demands as being those of the nation as a whole, while the princes who fought in 1857 did so for *their* own territories. This is a very superficial view, as it would be apparent to any one who thinks about it.

The organization of society in 1857 was such that the opposition against foreign aggression—i.e. the 'nationalist' movement—could take the shape only of wars between the Indian princes and the foreigners. Nor were these wars entirely lacking in a unity of purpose as was evidenced by the attempt to put the Moghul throne in the foreground. On the other hand, the demands of 1885, were those of a small class of people, to whom the very idea of opposition to the foreign rule was alien and unintelligible. Not that the forces which still desired freedom were dead, but they lacked the agency which could organize them and put them into action.

Till the British conquest, Indian society was organized on a feudalistic basis (though India's feudalism differed in many details from European feudalism). The feudal chiefs or princes were the leaders of society, which was so organized as to support and maintain them at the top. The foreign aggression struck directly at this organization, which meant against the princes. The princes struck back. By a combination of circumstances they were beaten, however, 1857 was their last attempt.

Their defeat meant that, as society was organized those days, there was no other element left in society which could give battle to the foreign power. The existing organization of society determined that the issues involved be either submission or freedom, that the form of opposition be armed battle, that the princes be at the head of such battle. With the princes crushed, society lost its leader, the forces of freedom lost their purposive, directive principle. When no princes came forth to fight and lead the forces of discontent that were widely created by the miseries that followed in the wake of the foreign rule in the territories conquered, they became disorganized and were eventually dissipated. Craftsmen, merchants, peasants—all of them suffered greatly; but with their princes gone they were helpless.

Thus ended the first phase of opposition to foreign rule—the feudalist opposition.

The second phase of opposition did not begin till after the World War and it culminated in the movement of 1932-4. Till the post-war period there was no question of opposition to the alien power.

Opposition required, as its *sine qua non*, the appearance in Indian society of a social class which fulfilled three conditions: firstly, the economic interests of which were such that they demanded freedom from the foreign system for sheer self-development; secondly, which was destined to play the leading role and become the ruling class in the society to be established after the attainment of that freedom; thirdly, which is able to gather sympathy and support of the wider masses of people in its struggle.

It is clear that those whose demand it was that more jobs should be given to them could not be the class which would strive for freedom from the system which has those jobs at its disposal. Freedom cannot be their class demand. They have no interests that are independent of the foreign system and which require for their development the abolition of that system.

The Indian National Congress was founded by just such people. They were not in reality a social class proper. They were only a group of educated Indians, extracted mostly from the upper agrarian strata. As long as they held sway over the Congress, which was over thirty years, the demands of the latter were no more than better jobs, more representation in the so-called legislatures, permanent settlement, and some civic rights.

The masses had naturally no interest in those things and the Congress remained, as the British so persistently declared, an organization of the educated middle classes without a mass following.

That did not mean that the masses were quiescent or satisfied. Recurring famines could not have generated a love of the British power in them. But in the society of those days they lacked leadership. So, their discontent could issue forth only in local, unorganized risings. The Congress satisfied itself only by demanding an enquiry into the causes of famines. It took no steps—it could take no steps—to organize and canalize the discontent and lead the peasants to any sort of struggle with the ruling powers. The masses in their turn had little use for the tactic of 'fighting' by passing resolutions, particularly when the resolutions dealt with things that must have seemed frivolous to them! The masses know only one form of struggle—direct action. And, as I have said above, the forces which could lead the masses to direct action had not yet appeared in Indian society; in any event they had not acquired sufficient strength.

During and after the War a number of things happened in India. The foremost of these was the extraordinary growth of Indian industry. The growth was particularly noticeable in the rates of profits of industrial capital. Indian capitalism took on a heretofore unknown exuberance. At the same time the War and the events following in its wake, such as the Russian Revolution, had shaken up the whole country; there was an unprecedented 'awakening'.

The rise of an industrial class in India provided the basis for the rise of the independence movement. This class, with its other capitalist allies, satisfied, though very weakly as we shall see, the conditions I have pointed out above as being the *sine qua non* of opposition to the foreign power. The Indian bourgeoisie had interests which did require freedom from outside interference; it did have the socio-economic position to take the place of the foreign power as the ruling class in the country; it did have the capacity, though limited, to rally some mass support around it.

Before the foreign conquest India was, as we all know, a feudalist country. British imperialism subdued feudalism and destroyed the socio-economic relations of which it was built up. As in the West, the next step after feudalism in India too was bourgeois democracy. The new capitalist class in India was destined to be the ruling class in the future India—in a free India. At least, so it seemed to that class and to all those who breathed in the atmosphere created by its growth.

Till the bourgeois class grew up in the country, the picture of a free India remained dim and unrealistic. Its growth gave meaning to independence, the conception of which had not yet been freed from feudal idealization, such as of Rana Pratap.[3] The 'national' movement was suddenly raised to a higher plane—the plane of opposition, of direct struggle against the foreign power.

But just as a combination of circumstances brought about the defeat of Indian feudalism, so a set of other circumstances had, from the very beginning, placed such disabilities on this new class that it too was destined to lose, rather, to retire from battle.

The circumstances, briefly, were these: Indian capitalism was not united in its opposition to imperialism. A large section of it served as the middleman of imperialism and even its self-interest did not demand that the *status quo* should be changed. The industrial bourgeoisie was the one section of it that required for self-development the breaking of the shell of imperialism. But at the same time, its growth in the present depended so largely on the help and facilities given by imperialism that it was not in a position to engage in an uncompromising struggle against it. It was nearly completely at the mercy of imperialism and could develop only under its tutelage. So the opposition of even this section of the Indian bourgeoisie could go no further than encouraging the petit-bourgeoisie to do the fighting. And even that encouragement was withdrawn when the fight took an ugly turn.

If the Indian bourgeoisie could prosper independently of imperialism, or if it could rely on some foreign support, like the Irish bourgeoisie, the history of the Indian nationalist movement, particularly of the fateful years, 1930-4, would have been entirely different. Its fatal handicap, owing to its economic position, has been, and is, two fold: (1) Its incapacity for any class-action against imperialism; (2) Its incapacity of leading the petit-bourgeoisie to revolutionary action.

Both of its incapacities were demonstrated during the civil disobedience movements. Let us take the first. I still remember most vividly a meeting of Congress leaders at Benaras some time in the middle of 1932, when I had the privilege of acting as the General Secretary of the Congress. The meeting was convened to consider a programme which would give fresh impetus to the already slackening movement. Some of the topmost notches of the Congress were present. After two days discussion a statement embodying the programme was prepared, which was later circulated and published over the signature of the Acting President. The most important item on the programme—it would be, rather, more correct to say, practically the whole of the programme—was *boycott*. Not that the idea of boycott was put before the country for the first time. The programme was already there, not only in 1932, but also in 1930. What the statement did was to point out the importance and the effectiveness of boycott and to exhort the public and Congress bodies to concentrate on it above everything else.

Now, an economic boycott in its very nature is a programme which can be used

[3] Rana Pratap (1540-97); Rajput king of Mewar (1572-97) who successfully resisted the efforts of Mughal Emperor Akbar to conquer Mewar.

most effectively only by the bourgeoisie; in other words, it is bourgeois class action *par excellence*. A fine instance of it was the economic boycott of Japan by the Chinese bourgeoisie some years back. Here, the Indian bourgeoisie, if anything, sabotaged the boycott which was artificially kept up for some months. Thousands of youngmen had to suffer imprisonment not for fighting imperialism but for *picketing* at the doors of the Indian bourgeoisie.

As for the second incapacity—the incapacity for leadership, it is implicit in the first. If the bourgeoisie is not in a position to take class action against imperialism, i.e. if it is not revolutionary as a class, it cannot, naturally, lead the other classes into action. This is true, however, only of active leadership, i.e. leadership in action. The bourgeoisie can still exercise, as it has and is still doing, an ideological leadership over the nationalist movement. That is, the development of this class in India has thrown up such national ideals—both political and economic—as are the normal ideals of a bourgeois society. We accepted those ideals in a natural course and called them nationalism and fought for their realization. In this sense the Indian bourgeoisie has been the leader of Indian nationalism (especially of its post-war phase).

The above analysis provides to my mind, the best clue to the failure of the 1930-4 movements. *It was the failure not of the Indian masses, as it has been commonly supposed, but of the Indian bourgeoisie.* As such, 1934 marked the end of the second phase of Indian opposition to imperialism—*the bourgeois phase.* 1857 had marked the end of the first phase—the feudal.

We have already entered the third phase. What are its characteristics? Who will be its leaders? What will be its programme? These are questions which we must learn from the fifty years of our political experience. If the Congress Jubilee means anything to us, it must not be mere futile sentimentalization, mere wooden worship. It must mean restless questioning, ruthless evaluation and—a bold leap ahead. What we need today is not the encrusted loyalty of age, but the iconoclastic courage of youth. It seems to me that we will have to fight the old idols and tear up part of what we have built up so that we may build higher.

Before I take up the problems of the third phase it is necessary to dwell a little longer on the second—the bourgeois phase. When I said above that 1934 marked the end of this phase, I meant that it did so only *objectively*. The next phase of our struggle will not be under bourgeois hegemony—either active or ideological. This does not mean that this hegemony has ended subjectively. Neither the bourgeoisie has decided to withdraw its influence from the Congress, nor have Congressmen understood the debacle of 1934 in the light I have presented. They continue to be governed by the conceptions of bourgeois society. In fact, just at present, as a result of the cessation of direct action, bourgeois influence is on the ascendant. The influence of a revolutionary bourgeoisie would have meant advance. The influence of the Indian bourgeoisie, with its limitations, can only mean, as it has already meant, restraint, compromise, defeat. To destroy the ideological hold of the bourgeoisie over the Congress worker is, therefore, of the utmost necessity. [incomplete]

108. Dissemination of Sound Sex Knowledge [undated][1]

The few courageous young men who are organizing the Marriage Reform League[2] deserve the fullest support of every progressive individual or group in this province. They have launched forth upon a bold and laudable programme with the characteristic frankness of youth and I sincerely hope youth as ever will win. I need hardly add that their success would mean the removal of some of the most mischievous evils from our society.

The objects of the League[3] have appeared more than once. It has been found, however, that a good deal of misapprehension has been created in the mind of the public with regard to some of the objects. Perhaps one most readily misunderstood is that which aims at spreading among young people a sound knowledge of sex. The members of the League have, therefore, asked me to explain to the public this particular item of their programme.

Before I begin with my explanation, however, I should like to address a few introductory words to the critics of the League. I wish to tell them at the outset that the subject of sex requires not so much keenness of thought as the courage to think—the courage to be willing to question one's prejudices, the courage to be willing to question even the fundamentals of one's faith. There are people, and these constitute the majority of the population, for whom most of the vital and intimate aspects of social and individual life are a closed topic, on which the final word was said generations, perhaps, centuries ago. They refuse to think afresh about them.

I am reminded by this of a very fine saying of Anatole France[4] full of that deepest, wisest irony of which he alone was capable: "It is a great infirmity to think. God preserve you from it, my son, as He has preserved His greatest saints and the souls whom He loves with special tenderness and destines to eternal felicity." Commenting upon it Mr. Upton Sinclair[5] writes, "Now it is possible to conceive of a Catholic Bishop or a Methodist missionary or a Kleagle of the Ku Klux Klan[6]

[1] *Sri Jayaprakash Narayan Sixtyfirst Birth Day Celebration Commemoration Volume*. Jayaprakash Narayan wrote this article in the early 1930s as a member, Board of Advisers, Marriage League, Patna.

[2] The Marriage Reform League was started at Patna in 1931 and the same year a branch was opened at Banaras.

[3] The objects of the Marriage Reform League were to encourage selection of wife and husband by the partners themselves, remove the custom of dowry, encourage inter-marriage, discourage early marriage, disseminate sound sex knowledge among young persons, and work for abolition of purdah.

[4] Anatole France, pseudonym of Jacques-Anatole-Francois (1844-1924); well known French writer and novelist; awarded Nobel Prize for Literature, 1921.

[5] Upton Beall Sinclair (1878-1968); eminent American writer and social reformer.

[6] An extremist right-wing secret society, originally founded in 1866 in the southern states of the U.S.A. to oppose the new rights being given to Afro-Americans during the Reconstruction after the Civil War. Members disguised themselves in white robes and hoods in order to carry out acts of terrorism and intimidation against Afro-American and their supporters. The original Klan was outlawed by Congress in 1870-1, but a similar, much more powerful, organization emerged in 1915. It was very active in the period 1922-30, showing hostility towards Afro-Americans, Roman Catholics, Jews, immigrants and also trade unionists. A burning cross became the symbol of this organization. Although temporarily disbanded in 1944, it became active again in the 1950s and 1960s.

who might be too stupid to understand this remark; but it is difficult to conceive how, understanding it, he could withhold the tribute of a smile. Into this remark the great master of words has distilled the essence of civilization, the precious flavour of centuries of culture. There are only thirty-four words in it and yet you can afford to meditate upon it for a long time". I have only to add to this an invitation to my complacent friends to take a tip from Mr. Sinclair and do the bit of meditation that he suggests.

The Marriage Reform Leaguer is often asked by his impatient critics "Why on earth does one have to know about sex?" Yes, why on earth? I repeat. Is not man a beast? And does the beast read ponderous lines on sex; or essays on clinic researches? It is difficult to imagine a more difficult question.

Sex is poison some wiseacres exclaim. The wonder is that though they don't appear to have shunned the poison they have managed to escape death. Or is it perhaps that sex brings moral death alone? May be; we shall see. Anyhow luckily for us, there don't seem to be running amock such great flocks of depraved creatures as we are given reasons to expect.

The fact of the matter is that sex is neither poison nor tonic; it is both. It all depends upon what you make of it. And in order to make anything out of it you must first understand it. It is not a thing to be ignored or trifled with. For good or for evil it matters profoundly and it matters as profoundly to the individual as to the group. It is one of the few things, in fact one of the two things, which have constituted the dynamics of social evolution. Sex and hunger have together been the most potent forces dominating and directing human life and civilization. The whole of man's culture, his art, religion, industry and government bear the impress of sex. Sex has been equally potent in its influence on the life of the individual as well. It is one of the irresistible urges which drive man to action and dominate and mould his life. Since the time it makes itself felt in early adolescence, it continues to colour and permeate his life in a manner more intimate than anything else. It begins by asking perturbing questions, raising violent uprisings of feeling and continues through life, ceaselessly revealing its kaleidoscopic content and ends by conferring upon us either spiritual and physical happiness or the opposite of it. Depending upon how we handle it, it sometimes inspires us to lofty ambition, goads us to noble adventures, makes us create beauty and song and sometimes leads us to shameful depravities, nameless abominations. Surely the man who claims that there is no need of knowing anything about sex not only illustrates his stupidity but also betrays the civic responsibility that lies on him by virtue of his being a member of society. Man is essentially a beast. It has taken him thousands of years to bring himself to the present level of humanity and even yet he runs loose sometimes and lapses into barbarity at times in whole masses as in the last war, or at times in single instances as in the case of frequently reported murders, rapes and robberies. Man to be human must first of all control himself. For that he must understand himself. Just in order to control nature he must understand it, must discover its laws, in order to elevate himself from the level of the brute he must discover and learn the laws of life.

I have said that man is essentially a beast. In some respects he is worse than a beast. The sexual life of the beasts and of all animals generally is regulated and controlled by instinct. They have all their appointed seasons for mating and are free from evils of over-indulgence and perversity. Man on the other hand, is completely at the mercy of his reason or unreason. In his inherited psychological make-up there is nothing that corresponds to the animal's instinct of self-control. All seasons are mating seasons for him and all hours are mating hours. He has no inherent inborn instinct that can save him from the danger of sex—from over-indulgence and perversity, nor any instinct which can enable him to realize its glories. If sex can mean anything more to him than mere bestiality—and boundless bestiality—at that he must understand it. He must take full advantage of the rich experience of his race. He must learn how to fulfil the great primordial appetite so that it may result in the physical and mental well-being of himself, his spouse and his offspring. The sexual experiences of our race have been many and varied and man being distinguished from the beast by the possession of a civilization, these experiences have been recorded, analysed and interpreted by those of our fellow-beings who are fortunate enough to possess the required ability for the task. Nor is the interpretation of sex experience a Western phenomenon. In the East, and particularly in our own country great Rishis devoted their time and intellect to the science of sex. As a result we have available today a healthy, enlightening, and extremely useful literature.

APPENDICES

APPENDIX 1

Report on Civil Disobedience, December 1931[1]

Preface

Since the inauguration of the swadeshi campaign by the Calcutta and Nagpur Congress and after the special emphasis laid on the spinning-wheel by the Bezwada Programme, people are asking if it is within the purview of practical politics to have a complete boycott of foreign piece-goods and yet to have the normal wants of the country satisfied from indigenous resources. The object of this leaflet is to show with the help of the statistics collated from Government records that if the Indian people make but an effort, it is not only possible but also practicable to boycott foreign piece-goods and to make India self-sufficing in this direction. People who are now the loudest in declaiming the campaign were the first to pioneer such a campaign for swadeshi in all directions when the Empire was in the grip of war. In fact the very object of the Munitions Board was to tap all the indigenous resources for satisfying the wants and requirements of India in war-time. It was proved during the period that even though no foreign stuff came to this country, India was able to maintain herself and to contribute a big quota to the winning of the war. If India could put forward herculean efforts at that time for winning the war for the Empire, there is no reason why she cannot put forward similar, if not greater, efforts to win Swaraj for herself.

For much of the statistical portion given in the first section of this leaflet we are indebted to the comprehensive letter contributed to the *Times of India* by the Honourable Sir D.E. Wacha on the 27th May 1919. We also express our thanks to Mr. Thakorelal H. Desai for the help he has given in collating statistics.

[1] *AICC Papers* (NMML).

Foreword

The year nineteen thirty was the *annus mirabilis*, the year of great deeds and great sacrifices of the Indian people; and it more than fulfilled the promise of the Lahore Congress. To write the report of Congress work for this year is to write the history of the Indian people during a heroic period of their existence. It is to recount the long tale of their sacrifices in the cause of India's freedom, the indomitable spirit with which millions of our brothers and sisters rallied to India's flag and faced, without flinching, every manner of suffering and hardship. It was a year in which every day brought news of a firing or a lathi charge or barbarous behaviour of the police or jail authorities; and every day also brought news of the peaceful and organized defiance of the laws and ordinances made by the alien authority to suppress the campaign. During a great part of the year the Congress was outside the pale of the law, its membership was a crime, its property was forfeited; but the Congress flourished as never before in the five and forty years of its life. The future historian may make a record in cold print of these heroic deeds. But we, who have been privileged to see, and to take our humble part, in common with our countrymen and countrywomen, in the making of history, find it difficult to deal adequately with this great subject.

. . . .[2] In the end, we have given a number of appendices which members of the A.I.C.C. might care to refer to.

We would add that the province of Burma has not been included in this report. Although an integral part of the Congress organization, there were practically no Congress activities during the period under report, and no attempt was made to extend the civil disobedience movement to it. Burma was for the greater part of the year, and is still, in the grip of her own troubles. These have been tragic enough, but as they were not connected with the civil disobedience movement, we have not referred to them.

The resolutions of the A.I.C.C. and the Working Committee passed during the period under report have already been published separately and are therefore not included in the appendices to this report.

We would like to express our gratitude to Shri Jaya Prakash and Shri Raghubir Sahay, who have collected the material for this report and have helped in drafting it.

December 1931

Syed Mahmud
Jairamadas Doulatram
Jawaharlal Nehru
General Secretaries
All India Congress Committee

[2] Not legible, moth-eaten.

CHAPTER I

A Survey of the Campaign

At the stroke of midnight of December 31, 1929, as the old year passed away and 1930 was ushered in, bearing the message of hope and freedom on its youthful brow, the Lahore Congress passed the resolution of Complete Independence. And the delegates of the Congress, who had taken the fateful decision to free their ancient and well-beloved country, and on whom the burden of the coming struggle was largely to fall, assembled together at that midnight hour to celebrate the coming of the new year by hoisting the Flag of India and pledging themselves to its service.

Soon after this declaration by the Congress, the nation confirmed it. On January 26th Independence Day was celebrated all over the country, in accordance with the directions of the Working Committee, and at thousands of mass meetings in cities and in villages the pledge of Independence was solemnly taken. The challenge thus given and repeated was followed by preparation for the campaign that was imminent. Members of the Central and Provincial legislatures resigned in large numbers in obedience to the mandate of the Congress. Congress committees re-organized themselves for action, and the air was heavy with expectation of what was to come. The Working Committee gave authority to their trusted leader Gandhiji to inaugurate the campaign of civil disobedience with colleagues of his choice, who believed in non-violence as an article of faith. Early in March, Gandhiji sent his first letter to the Viceroy announcing his intention to disregard the provisions of the salt laws. Salt immediately became the word of power, the symbol of the fight to come. Some ridiculed it in their ignorance. They learnt soon that their ridicule was premature and misplaced. Soon after, began Gandhiji's two hundred mile march to the sea with his chosen band. But even before this began Sardar Vallabhbhai Patel was arrested and convicted. Earlier still, Shri J.M. Sen-Gupta and Shri Subhas Chandra Bose and other leaders of Bengal had been lodged in prison.

For three weeks the nation watched in evergrowing enthusiasm and excitement the great march of their leader to Dandi. And as they watched they prepared for his word of command. Satyagraha committees and "War Councils" grew up in provinces and districts and volunteers were enrolled. The A.I.C.C. authorised the provincial committees to undertake civil disobedience as soon as the word for it was given, and the President was given the power to nominate his successor, in case of arrest, as well as to fill vacancies in the Working Committee caused by the arrests and convictions of members.

On April 5th Gandhiji and his band of satyagrahis reached Dandi village on the sea coast and on the next day they committed breaches of the salt laws. Permission to disobey the salt laws was also given to the rest of the country and, with the rapidity of a prairie fire, civil disobedience spread throughout the country. Everywhere the salt laws were broken and salt made or collected from sea water or salt earth or the salt mines. Millions participated in this satyagraha and it seemed that the country had thrown away the burden of the salt laws.

Government took swift and heavy action. People were arrested and beaten and tortured to give up the salt they had gathered. The Congress treasurer, Seth Jamnalal Bajaj, was sentenced to two years' rigorous imprisonment and a fine for a breach of the salt laws. Police raids took place on Congress offices to destroy the accessories of salt manufacture; and police lathis, which were to play such a prominent part in the campaign, came on the scene and were used on satyagrahis and onlookers alike. Congress volunteer camps were broken up and destroyed and volunteers beaten till some of them fainted. Women were not spared.

On April 14th Jawaharlal Nehru, who was President of the Congress during the year, was arrested and convicted for a breach of the Salt Act. In accordance with his nomination, the late Pandit Motilal Nehru became the Acting President of the Congress. Two days later Jairamdas Doulatram a member of the Working Committee received a gunshot wound in his abdomen when the police opened fire without warning at a crowd in Karachi.

A week later, on April 23rd, took place one of the outstanding occurrences of the campaign—the Peshawar firing in which hundreds were killed and wounded. This tragedy and the sorrow at the death of so many brave comrades was almost overshadowed in the triumphant pride at the heroism of the gallant Pathans who had faced death without flinching and without turning back, perfectly peacefully and with almost reckless courage. The news was kept back by the Government, but it trickled through and it sent a thrill throughout the country. It proved how widespread and all embracing was the freedom movement and how the masses had grasped the lesson of non-violence. It proved, as nothing else could have done, how the Muslims had thrown in their lot with their other countrymen. It proved, to the amazement of many, how even the warlike Pathan had understood the basis and the peaceful technique of the struggle. Peshawar was but the first of many tragic and heroic episodes in the Frontier province. And Peshawar witnessed yet another outstanding deed of heroism. Two platoons of the Royal Garhwal Rifles when called upon to fire upon their unarmed and unresisting brethren, refused to do so, well knowing the consequences of such refusal. They were court-martialled and sentenced to long terms of imprisonment, but they had demonstrated to the country and to the Government that in the heart of the Indian soldier, mercenary as he was now, was the spark of patriotism. Peshawar Days and Garhwali Days were celebrated throughout the country and as a result thousands more went to prison and thousands suffered injury from the policeman's lathi.

On April 25 Shri Vithalbhai J. Patel resigned from the presidentship of the Legislative Assembly.

On the 4th of May Gandhiji wrote another letter to the Viceroy. But before it could be sent he was arrested and imprisoned without trial. The arrest of the leader gave the final drive to the campaign and thenceforward it was a mass struggle on a vast scale, the revolutionary energy of the people finding outlet in a variety of ways. But almost invariably the masses remembered his oft repeated advice to carry on the struggle peacefully and to suffer violence without retaliation.

Some places stand out. Dharasana, where the salt raids took place and where Shri Abbas Tyabji and Shrimati Sarojini Naidu successively took the place of Gandhiji and suffered arrest, and where the police committed all manner of barbarous outrages on the bodies of the volunteers. Contai, in the District of Midnapore in Bengal, where volunteers were disgustingly maltreated and even the women were assaulted and subjected to shameful indignity. Sholapur, where the crowd, greatly provoked by police firing that killed a boy, forgot for a while the lesson of non-violence, attacked the police and set fire to some Government buildings, and later had to put up with a reign of terror under Martial Law, when even carrying a national flag meant a sentence of ten years' rigorous imprisonment. Bardoli, and many other taluqas of Gujarat, where the peasants took a solemn pledge not to pay land revenue till Gandhiji and Sardar Vallabhbhai told them to do so, and carried on their no-tax campaign in spite of confiscation of property and destruction and all manner of oppression, till large numbers of the peasantry forsook their homelands and trekked to adjoining State territories. Delhi, where firing took place inside the Sisganj Gurudwara and thus demonstrated to the Sikhs, to their great indignation, that even their sacred places of worship were not safe from the firing and the boots of the police and military. Borsad, where bloody assaults were made on a huge procession of women and 160 women were wounded. And above all Bombay. Week after week and day after day, the men and women of Bombay challenged the might of the British Empire and challenged it successfully, even though thousands were grievously wounded by the brutal lathi and great new hospitals, which grew up at a word from its generous citizens, were filled to overflowing by the victims of police violence.

These are but a few names of places out of a host through the length and breadth of India which vied with each other in the great struggle—Agra and Lucknow and Shamli in the district of Muzaffarnagar and Bihpur in Behar and Peddapuram in the East Godavari District, and Sargodha in the Punjab and the sixty odd places where firing took place, and so many others. It is difficult to mention all the cities even, and it is impossible to refer to the thousands of remote villages, which, far from newspapers and publicity or outside help, bore the brunt of oppression and hardship. For it must be remembered that brave as was the part of the towns and cities, the burden of the struggle fell on India's innumerable villages and on the long suffering peasantry who form the real India.

As the struggle developed, in spite of oppression and terrorism, Government brought into play all the weapons in its well-stocked armoury of repression. Finding these insufficient many an illegal method was tried. But the national movement continued to prosper. Additional laws were then forged by the Executive and ordinance after ordinance was issued by the Governor-General-in-Council. Eleven such ordinances were issued, and as each came out the Congress welcomed it as affording a new opportunity for satyagraha. The Congress itself was declared illegal and yet the Congress prospered as it had never done in its previous history and its power grew. It became obvious to the world that it was the Congress, illegal as it was supposed to be by the alien government, which commanded the willing allegiance of India's millions. Nationalist newspapers were stopped or not allowed to function except under strict censorship; letters and telegrams were not delivered; the telephone was interfered with; Congress notices could not even be printed at any press. Apparently no means of communication were left open to the Congress. But the Congress continued to flourish and the whisper of the Congress went further than the ordinance of the Viceroy. Presidents and secretaries went to prison in an almost unending procession, the Working Committee was arrested *en bloc*, but the Congress continued to function.

At an early stage in the campaign, the Working Committee authorized other forms of civil disobedience, besides the salt satyagraha. In Gujrat there was non-payment of revenue; in Behar and Bengal and Utkal non-payment of the chowkidari tax; in the Central Provinces and Berar and partly in the U.P. breach of the forest laws. Non-payment of revenue was also recommended in all ryotwari areas. In Bengal proscribed literature was read out at public meetings. Stress was also laid on the boycott of intoxicating drugs and all foreign cloth. The boycott of liquor resulted in heavy loss in excise revenue to Government. The foreign cloth boycott developed rapidly and became a powerful incentive for the additional production of handspun and handwoven khaddar and of Indian mill cloth. It became an effective weapon against foreign countries exporting cloth to India, specially England, which had so far controlled the piece-goods market in India. Largely on account of the efforts of Pandit Motilal Nehru, arrangements were made with Indian textile mills, according to which the owners or managers of these mills accepted various Congress conditions and were thereupon placed on the approved list of mills. This help given by the Congress to the textile mills saved many of them at a time when all industry had to face a crisis due to worldwide depression. Foreign cloth in retail shops was largely sealed up. An ordinance of the Governor-General against picketing helped greatly in adding to the strength of the boycott.

Apart from cloth, a boycott of British goods also became effective and caused considerable injury to British trade in India, particularly in Bengal. On the constructive side this gave a great impetus to the swadeshi movement.

An ordinance issued by the Governor-General against newspapers gave another opportunity for satyagraha and large numbers of unauthorized news-sheets, usually cyclostyled, came out and had extensive circulations. Every effort was made to suppress them but many continued to appear regularly right through the campaign.

The refusal of the Garhwali soldiers to fire at the peaceful crowd in Peshawar led the Working Committee to pass a resolution defining the rights and duties of soldiers. The Government thereupon issued another ordinance against any instigation of the military or the police. This led to satyagraha again in the shape of repeating publicly the Working Committee's resolution on the subject.

Section 144 of the Criminal Procedure Code was as usual applied in an astonishing variety of ways to suppress or prevent all manner of things. Indeed it appeared that so long as Section 144 was conveniently available, there appeared to be no necessity for any other law or ordinance. The use of this section in the south was particularly extensive. It was even sought under its all embracing authority to prevent the wearing of Gandhi caps and the payment of Congress monies by banks, as at Masulipatam.

All these methods were employed to suppress the movement. About a hundred thousand people were put in jail, and the treatment in jail of most of these has been brought out in all its horror in the Visapur and the U.P. jail enquiry reports; firing on unarmed people became a frequent occurrence, and a lathi charge almost an every day affair. But the movement seemed to thrive on repression and terrorism and progressed and went deeper and deeper into the villages. In the United Provinces in October 1930 a no-tax campaign was formally started and it spread rapidly in many districts. This no-tax campaign had, unlike the Gujrat campaign, an economic basis as the tenantry were in great distress owing to the phenomenal fall in prices. It became a no-rent campaign and the centre of gravity of the civil disobedience movement in the U.P. gradually shifted from the towns to the villages.

The civil disobedience movement of 1930 worked many a miracle, but there was no greater miracle than the part of the women in this campaign. How deeply it had affected the people and touched the mainsprings of Indian society was evidenced by the social revolution it brought about silently and without apparent effort. The shy and retiring woman of India, unused to the rough and tumble of politics, came out of the shelter of her home and insisted on being in the forefront of the struggle. When her menfolk went to prison she did not flinch, but shouldered the burden and exhibited not only her wonderful powers of sacrifice and endurance, with which she is endowed in such rich measure, but surprising powers of organization and initiative. Many played a brave part in the deeds of 1930 and many are entitled to a measure of credit for the achievement that came. All classes, in greater or less degree, joined in the struggle—Hindus, Muslims, Sikhs, Parsis, Christians, Jews, etc. But all recognise and admit that the real credit and glory of achievement belongs to the womanhood of India. From the very beginning, picketing and the boycott of foreign cloth and liquor were placed by Gandhiji in their charge and, as the campaign developed, they assumed more and more responsibility and largely directed the movement. Over one thousand of them went to prison. In most cities their Kesari saris were familiar sights—emblems of gentleness and firmness, of courage and of sacrifice. Equally familiar were the Vanar Senas and the Bal Sabhas, organizations of children, which played a brave and notable part in the struggle.

The civil disobedience campaign went on and, aided by new ordinances of Government, it added to its fronts and its activities. Presidents of the Congress came and disappeared for a while behind prison bars, but the Congress continued. Pandit Motilal Nehru in spite of age and ill health shouldered the heavy burden of the leadership of the movement at its most critical stage. He did not spare himself or others and just when his health was breaking down, he was arrested and convicted. In prison he became weaker and his illness grew till his condition became such that Government had to discharge him. But the time for recovery was past and even in his last and fatal illness he continued to serve the cause he loved.

Sardar Vallabhbhai Patel who had just come out of jail, was the third President. On his return to prison, Maulana Abul Kalam Azad became President and then Dr. M.A. Ansari, who was followed by Chaudhri Khaliquzzaman. Jawaharlal Nehru, having completed his six months of imprisonment, came out to take charge immediately of the presidentship. But this lasted eight days only and he went back to Naini Prison. Shri J.M. Sen-Gupta then became the acting President and on his return to jail Sardar Vallabhbhai Patel took charge again. He was followed by Shri Rajendra Prasad. Lastly, Jawaharlal Nehru on his discharge again assumed charge of the presidentship.

An attempt was made in July and August 1930 to bring about a compromise between the Congress and the Government by Sir Tej Bahadur Sapru and

Mr. M.R. Jayakar who visited Gandhiji in Yervada jail and Pandit Motilal Nehru and Jawaharlal Nehru in Naini jail. In order to enable the Congress leaders to confer together those in Naini jail were transferred to Yervada where a meeting took place at which Gandhiji, Pandit Motilal Nehru, Shrimati Sarojini Naidu, Sardar Vallabhbhai Patel and the three signatories of this Report were present. A joint reply on behalf of all these was sent to Messrs. Sapru and Jayakar. The attempt to bring about peace failed and the civil disobedience movement and Government repression continued unabated.

In January yet another attempt at peace was made. The 26th January was the anniversary of the Independence Day and the Congress had decided to celebrate it on a nationwide scale. In spite of various disabilities attaching to an illegal organization, the denial of postal and telegraph facilities and no publicity by newspapers or notices, the day was celebrated on a vast scale all over the country, the pledge of Independence was repeated and an identical Resolution of Remembrance, recommended by the Working Committee, was passed everywhere. On this day original and substituted members of the Working Committee were released by the Government to enable them to confer together. They came out of prison to find Pandit Motilal Nehru striken down by mortal illness. He had given his all to the mighty cause he served, and even while illness gripped him and he lay in the shadow of death, he fought against it so that he might serve India still and see her come out free and victorious through the struggle. Ten days later, on February 6th, he passed away. But he died with the happy conviction that India's freedom was assured.

The peace talks continued and as a result of prolonged conversations between Gandhiji and Lord Irwin a Provisional Settlement was arrived at in Delhi on March 5th between the Congress and the Government of India. Government, *inter alia*, agreed to discharge the satyagrahi prisoners, to repeal the ordinances; to permit the manufacture of salt by individuals for personal use and not to interfere with peaceful picketing of foreign cloth or liquor. Congress agreed, *inter alia*, to stop civil disobedience and the boycott of British goods as such. So ended the first phase of the civil disobedience campaign, almost twelve months after Gandhiji started on his fateful march to the sea.

Government, it would lapse, and the Congress would then stand for the independence of India. The offer was not accepted, and, inevitably, the Lahore Congress resolved to make Complete Independence the immediate objective of the country. By a curious and remarkable coincidence this resolution was finally passed at the exact moment when the year of grace ended—at midnight of December 31st 1931.

The resolution authorized the All India Congress Committee to launch a campaign of civil disobedience whenever it deemed fit to do so. The A.I.C.C. did not meet till March 21, but the Working Committee started preparing the ground for the campaign immediately after the conclusion of the Lahore Session of the Congress. On January 2, 1930, the Committee met in Lahore and called upon all members of the Central and Provincial Legislatures to resign their seats and devote their attention to the prosecution of the Independence programme. The committee also fixed the 26th January 1930 as Purna Swarajya Day—Independence Day—to be celebrated all over the country, so that the message of Complete Independence might be carried to the remotest village in India. A committee to enquire into the special laws and regulations in the North West Frontier Province, which were said to be particularly oppressive, was also appointed. This committee consisted of Dr. S.D. Kitchlew, Lala Duni Chand of Ambala and Syed Mahmud. The Committee was unable to function. When it attempted to go to the Frontier Province it was stopped on the way and immediately after the Peshawar tragedy and Martial Law put an end to all attempts at investigation.

The call for the boycott of legislatures was immediately responded to. The late Pandit Motilal Nehru, who was then the leader of the Swaraj Party in the Legislative Assembly, sent in his resignation soon after the Lahore Congress and asked his colleagues to do the same. Swarajist members of the Central and Provincial Legislatures obeyed the Congress mandate in large numbers, 172 of them resigning in January. A few such members disobeyed the mandate and the Working Committee took disciplinary action against them. It was resolved that no such person would be eligible for membership of any elective Congress Committee.

The celebration of Independence Day on January 26th took place on a vast and unprecedented scale throughout the country. The Working Committee issued a special Pledge of Independence for the occasion which was read out and adopted in the language of the province at the mass gatherings which were held everywhere.

Instructions were issued that there should be no speeches at these gatherings and only the pledge of Independence was solemnly adopted, often by the whole audience repeating it word for word. Tens of thousands of towns and villages took part in these celebrations by holding meetings and taking out huge processions. In the large cities like Calcutta and Bombay and Delhi over a hundred thousand persons took part. In rural areas the celebration was held even in remote villages, the villagers walking many miles to attend it. In some districts there were as many as a hundred meetings. Many municipal buildings and large numbers of shops and private houses, displayed the National Flag. Thus millions participated in these mighty demonstrations and the people of India put their final seal of approval on the Congress resolution on Independence, and pledged themselves to work for it and achieve it.

Independence Day was celebrated not only in what is known as British India, but also in some Indian States and even in some foreign countries where Indians live, such as England, the U.S.A., Japan, Australia, Canada and Ceylon.

Independence Day celebrations passed off as a whole without any serious mishap. Many people were sentenced to small terms of imprisonment. In some places attempts were made to remove National Flags. In a Punjab Municipality a vice-chairman was removed from his office by Government because he had hoisted the Flag on the Municipal building. In the Indian States particularly there was considerable interference with the celebrations and a large measure of victimisation of the participants. In one State some participants were convicted and sentenced to one year's imprisonment.

Even before Independence Day a number of Bengal leaders had been sentenced to a year's imprisonment for the offence of leading a procession in Calcutta. Syts. Subhas Chandra Bose, J.M. Das Gupta, Kiran Sanker Roy were among those so sentenced.

Having felt the temper of the country by the demonstrations on Independence Day, and heartened by the disciplined enthusiasm shown, the Working Committee took the next step. The Committee met at Sabarmati on February 14, 15 and 16. Civil disobedience was now envisaged as a thing of the immediate future and the Committee therefore gave authority to Gandhiji "and those working with him, who believe in non-violence as an article of faith" for the purpose of achieving Purna Swaraj, "to start civil disobedience as and when they desire and in the manner and to the extent they decide". The Committee wanted to begin the movement cautiously but it looked forward to its developing into a mass struggle and hoped "that in the event of a mass movement taking place all those who are rendering voluntary cooperation to the Government, such as lawyers, and those who are receiving so-called benefits from it, such as students, will withdraw their cooperation or renounce benefits, as the case may be and throw themselves into the final struggle for freedom". The Committee well knew that as soon as the campaign started the leaders would be removed by the Government and so the Committee trusted "that in the event of the leaders being arrested and imprisoned those who are left behind and have the spirit of sacrifice and service in them will carry on the Congress organization and guide the movement to the best of their ability".

The Working Committee was not authorised to begin civil disobedience. That authority had been given by the Congress to the All India Congress Committee. But in view of rapid developments in the country the Working Committee decided to take this vital step and convened a meeting of the A.I.C.C. to confirm it.

With the authority of the Working Committee behind him, Gandhiji immediately set to work to lay down the plan of action. On March 2nd he addressed a letter to the Viceroy in which he announced his intention to proceed with his co-workers "to disregard the provisions of the salt laws" if the Viceroy offered no solution of the problems raised by him in the letter. The letter contained a strong indictment of British rule, which Gandhiji called a "curse" for India. He laid special emphasis on the "terrific pressure of land revenue", the so-called "debt" of India, and the high cost of administration. He added that "the plan through civil disobedience will be to combat such evils as I have sampled out. If we want to sever the British connection it is because of such evils".

The Viceroy's reply to Gandhiji was short and formal. No attempt was made in it to answer the points raised by Gandhiji. Civil disobedience thus became the only course, and the attention of the whole country was fixed on these developments which, like the events in a Greek tragedy, were leading us on inevitably and inexorably to the predestined end. Gandhiji's announcement that he would begin with colleagues of his choice a two hundred mile march to the sea coast to break the salt laws sent a thrill throughout the country.

Ever since the Lahore Congress, Congress Committees had been reorganizing themselves and preparing for the coming fray. As the struggle seemed to come nearer the preparations became more intense. There was full realisation of what was to come.

On March 7 Sardar Vallabhbhai Patel was served with an order at Ras in Borsad Taluqa prohibiting him from delivering a speech. The Sardar refused to obey the order and was thereupon tried and sentenced immediately to three months' imprisonment and a fine of Rs. 500/-.

On March 12 Gandhiji started from his Ashram at Sabarmati with his chosen band of 80 satyagrahis on his famous march to Dandi, a sea-coast village in the district of Surat. His departure was the occasion for an amazing demonstration in Sabarmati and Ahmedabad. Vast numbers of people gathered at the Ashram the evening before the March and spent the night in the open anxiously waiting for the hour of departure. Early next morning as the satyagrahi column, headed by Gandhiji, marched onwards hundreds of thousands of people lined the route and accompanied them till Gandhiji had to ask them to go back. It was a wonderful and spontaneous manifestation of national feeling which none that saw can ever forget.

Sabarmati was not the only place where these demonstrations took place on that fateful day. At the suggestion of the President the 12th of March was celebrated throughout the country as a great day and mass meetings and processions were held in town and village alike to wish Godspeed to Gandhiji and his noble band. The march to Dandi became the symbol of the country's march to Swaraj, and all knew that the great pilgrimage had begun and that it would continue, whatever the hardship and suffering might be, till the goal of Independence was reached.

All along the route followed by Gandhiji there were scenes of enthusiasm similar to those witnessed on the day of his departure. Meetings were held at every halting place and during the course of this march large numbers of village officials resigned their posts. Government introduced a censorship of news of the march and even cinematograph films of it were proscribed.

All over the country the march was followed with breathless interest, and everywhere there was preparation and organization and consolidation. Most of the provinces and many districts set up special satyagraha committees or "War Councils" invested with full powers to take action whenever the word for it came. Salt became the mystic word which was to open the gates of Swaraj, and people started learning the methods of salt manufacture, so that they might be able to break the salt laws effectively. Some people affected to ridicule the idea of individual salt manufacture, not realising that it was but the symbol of a nation's defiance of an alien power. They learned the lesson soon enough and their ridicule and sarcasm gave place to astonishment and admiration.

During the period of the march, the A.I.C.C. and the Working Committee held their deliberations at Ahmedabad in order to give the final lead to the country for the great struggle that was already darkening the horizon. It was the first A.I.C.C. meeting since Lahore and it was also the last of the year. Henceforth the great majority of the members of the A.I.C.C. found a safe lodgement in prison. The A.I.C.C. endorsed the resolution of the Working Committee authorising Gandhiji to initiate and control civil disobedience. Further, it authorised the Provincial Committees to organize and undertake civil disobedience. Salt was to be the first point of attack but authority to start other forms of satyagraha was also given. The A.I.C.C. however issued definite directions that civil disobedience should not be started in any province till Gandhiji had reached Dandi and committed breach of the salt laws and given the word. In case of Gandhiji's previous arrest the provinces were free to act.

The A.I.C.C. made further preparation for the campaign by authorising the President to nominate his successor upon his arrest and to fill up all vacancies in the Working Committee caused by the arrests and convictions of members.

Thus all the preliminaries were complete, all the necessary steps taken, before Gandhiji reached Dandi. The Congress had fully prepared itself and was ready for all emergencies.

Meanwhile the Government had also taken action and many arrests had been made in various parts of the country. Shri J.M. Sen-Gupta, a member of the Working Committee, was arrested and convicted. So also were three A.I.C.C. members from Behar and one from Bombay. Several editors of newspapers were also sentenced to various terms of imprisonment. In Masulipatam the president and secretaries of the District Committee and the captain of the volunteers and six other prominent workers were convicted; in Rae Bareli district in Oudh as many as 36 Congress organizers were sentenced under Sec. 107 Cr.P.C. in March; and many Congressmen of Delhi, Lahore, Jaranwala, Multan and Sheikhupura were convicted. All these convictions preceded the civil disobedience movement.

Another event happened in March which added to the enthusiasm and spirit of sacrifice of the country. On March 21 Pandit Motilal Nehru announced the gift of his old house and grounds, long known as Anand Bhawan, to the nation. The ceremony of dedication was performed by Shrimati Swarup Rani Nehru on April 11 when she named the house "Swaraj Bhawan". The office of the A.I.C.C. was later removed to Swaraj Bhawan.

CHAPTER II

Civil Disobedience Begins

Gandhiji reached his destination on April 5th. On the morning of the following day he committed technical breach of the salt laws by collecting a handful of muddy salt from the sea from which he later prepared pure salt. Knowing Gandhiji's plans, Government had taken pains to destroy previously all free salt on the coast by thoroughly mixing it up with dirt and mud.

After Gandhiji had collected his handful of salt he formally authorised the country to start civil disobedience by preparing, collecting, or selling contraband salt. There was immediate and unbounded response to Gandhiji's call. In every province except Assam, where there are no facilities for salt-making, salt began to be prepared in hundreds of places amidst great popular enthusiasm. As first batches of chosen volunteers, after passing in procession through the streets of towns and villages, assembled at appointed places and actually went through the process of salt manufacture, surrounded and cheered by thousands of citizens. Where the seacoast or other large salt sources were accessible the breach of the laws was not confined to chosen volunteers alone. Immediately it became a mass movement and whole populations took part in it. Gandhiji himself participated in such mass disobedience a couple of days after the initiation of the movement. In Bombay hundreds of thousands of men and women went to the beach to fetch sea water which they evaporated into salt in their homes. In areas where salt could be prepared with difficulty, batches of volunteers toured through villages, carrying accessories of salt-making. Meetings were held by them in village after village and salt prepared, many of the villagers participating. Thus they spread the movement far and wide.

Apart from the demonstrational salt-making described above, salt was also prepared in private homes for domestic consumption. In many families, in fact, market salt was replaced with home-made contraband salt.

Simultaneously with the beginning of the movement Government repression, which had already begun, assumed a fiercer aspect. It soon transcended even the bounds of its own laws. Immediately after the launching of the movement such prominent Congressmen as Seth Jamnalal Bajaj, treasurer of the A.I.C.C., Messrs Manilal Kothari and K.F. Nariman were arrested and convicted. Seth Jamnalalji was specially singled out for Government vindictiveness. For the offence of a breach of the salt laws he was sentenced to 2 years' rigorous imprisonment and a fine of Rs. 300/-.

Before the first week of satyagraha was over reports came of deliberate maltreatment of satyagrahis. Forcible wresting of salt from the hands of volunteers, sometimes resulting in the drawing of blood, became a common occurrence not only in Gujrat but everywhere. At one place boiling saline water (from which salt was subsequently to be prepared) was poured over the body of a satyagrahi. Only two days after the eventful 6th of April, while volunteers were preparing salt in Delhi, a force of policemen appeared on the scene and caught hold of the volunteers and dragged them away over thorny brambles and stony ground. The same day while salt was being prepared the third time the police repeated this behaviour. As a result of this, all the volunteers were bleeding and badly bruised, five of them fainting. Two days later, on April 10th, Bombay witnessed the first instance of police violence of which it was to have so much experience later. Among the victims were cultured ladies like Shrimatis Perinbai Captain and Kamala Devi Chattopadhya. The occasion was the raiding of the Congress House by 300 policemen and the attempt to destroy forcibly accessories of salt manufacture that had been collected there. On the same day about 200 policemen and 50 armed Gurkhas led by the Dist. Magistrate and the Superintendent of Police attacked the satyagraha camp at Kalikapur in Bengal. The police used their lathis indiscriminately, even injuring villagers who were mere onlookers. About a dozen volunteers were pushed into a canal after being well beaten and half a dozen of these were dragged out later in an unconscious state. While one section of the guardians of law and order was thus trying to restore order and enforce the law, another section of it was engaged in an endeavour to destroy private property, with the result that the satyagraha camp was soon changed into a heap of ruins. Worse than all this was the attack the police made on the Congress Red Cross volunteers. The volunteers were not only beaten but medical aid articles were broken and destroyed.

Just eight days after the initiation of the movement Jawaharlal Nehru, who was then President, was arrested on April 14 at Chheoki while entraining for Raipur, C.P. He was tried the same day in the Naini Central jail on a charge under Section 9 (c) of the Salt Act and was sentenced to six months' simple imprisonment. Complete hartal was observed in the country upon news of the President's conviction. Huge processions were taken out and meetings were held everywhere.

In accordance with the President's nomination the late Pandit Motilal Nehru became the acting President of the A.I.C.C.

On April 16 Jairamdas Doulatram, then a member of the Working Committee, received a gunshot wound in his abdomen when the police opened fire at a crowd in Karachi which he was trying to control and pacify. The firing which was begun without warning and without any warrant, cost the lives of two brave men, Shri Menghraj Lula and Shri Yaswant Dattatreya.

A few days later, on April 23, occurred the Peshawar tragedy, which stands out even in this year of heroic deeds and barbarous atrocities. Hundreds of unarmed and peaceful men were done to death in Peshawar city by the military and the brave Pathans faced armoured cars and machine guns with amazing courage, although their comrades lay dead and dying all around them.

For some time past there had been a general awakening of the people of the Frontier province. Many of them attended the Lahore Congress as delegates or volunteers and they returned, deeply stirred and with the determination to carry on the work of the Congress with redoubled energy. Men of action, unused to empty talk, they set about re-organizing Congress Committees, and soon the Government began to look upon their activities as a serious menace to British rule and apparently decided to put an end to all Congress organizations in the province.

On the 5th April, the Peshawar District Congress Committee decided to picket forthwith the liquor shops in the city. Upon the request of the dealers, however, they were given in 15 days to dispose of their stocks. This period was to expire on April 23rd. On April 22, the Enquiry Committee appointed by the Working Committee to investigate into the special laws and grievances in the province was due to arrive and a large crowd assembled at the railway station to welcome it. But the Committee was stopped at Attock and refused admission into the province. Upon receipt of this news in Peshawar a huge procession was taken out and a mass meeting held to protest against the order of the Government. It was also resolved at this meeting, in accordance with the previous decision, to start picketing the liquor shops the following day. Early next morning, however, nine prominent Congressmen were arrested. At 9 a.m. two more arrests were made. The police lorry conveying them having some tyre trouble, the two Congressmen offered to present themselves at the police station of their own accord. The police officer accompanying them agreed. The two leaders then started for the police station on foot with a large crowd following them. On reaching the police station they found the gates closed and they were not opened till the police officer who had arrested them also arrived. They then entered the police station, the crowd meanwhile shouting national slogans. As the crowd was dispersing two armoured cars suddenly came from behind without blowing horns or giving any intimation of their approach. The cars ran over some people but the crowd continued to remain peaceful in spite of this provocation. In backing, one of the cars appears to have collided against a motor bicycle the rider of which, an Englishman, fell down and was also run over. The car then seems to have caught fire accidentally. Firing was ordered and although many were killed and wounded, the crowd did not disperse and was not willing to do so till it was allowed to carry away the dead and wounded and till the armoured cars and military were removed. The authorities were not prepared to agree to this and firing was again resorted to. This firing lasted off and on for three hours. The number of persons proved to have been shot dead during these firings was 125 but it was estimated that a much larger number, perhaps exceeding 200, was killed.

After these firings the authorities, for some unexplained reason, or simply because of an attack of nerves, removed not only the military but even the ordinary police force from Peshawar city for a few days. During this period the Congress volunteers stood guard at the city gates and maintained order. Soon however the police and military returned and Martial Law was proclaimed.

On May 31, another tragedy, resulting in many deaths, occurred in Peshawar. Sardar Ganga Singh, a Government official and Superintendent of the Government Dairy Farm, was going in a tonga with his wife and children. He noticed some British soldiers in the window of a building. Immediately after shots were fired wounding his wife and killing his son, aged three, and daughter aged nine. A funeral procession was subsequently taken out. This was met by a party of British soldiers and, without any provocation or warning, these soldiers fired on the procession. Ten men were killed by this firing and twenty were wounded.

The Peshawar occurrences were enquired into by a Committee appointed by the Working Committee presided over by Shri Vithalbhai J. Patel. The Patel Committee in spite of every obstruction put in their way by the Government carried out a careful enquiry and published a valuable report which was proscribed by Government. The facts stated here in brief have been taken from this report.

Peshawar was not the only sufferer. The Patel Committee writes that "Methods no less atrocious are being pursued in other parts of the Peshawar district and also in other districts of the province where the Congress has influence. All the Congress organizations, youth leagues and allied organizations have been declared illegal. In spite of all this the spirit of the people has remained unbroken and strict non-violence has been observed."

News of the Peshawar incidents was withheld by the Government and only garbled versions were given to the public. Part of the truth leaked out, however, and this electrified the whole country. The courage and the non-violent spirit of the war-like Peshawaris became famous and earned for the whole province a unique place in the history of the struggle. Peshawar Day was celebrated all over the country to commemorate the brave deeds of that city.

At Peshawar, on the tragic 23rd April, another heroic deed took place which demonstrated that the great national awakening was not without its effect on the Indian Army, mercenary as it was. The peaceful crowds on that day, it has been stated above, were fired upon from an armoured car. Armoured cars had to be summoned when two platoons (Nos. 1 and 4) of the 2/18 Royal Garhwal Rifles refused to fire upon or use their bayonets on unarmed and unresisting crowds, which included many children. The brave Garhwalis did this deliberately and cheerfully took the consequences without expressing regret for their action.

The Garhwalis were court-martialled, as a result of which the seventeen officers of the two platoons were given various terms of imprisonment, with or without transportation, and the privates were dismissed from service. Four of the officers were transported—one *havildar* for life, another for fifteen years, and the other two, who were *naiks*, for ten years. The rest of the officers were imprisoned in India for terms varying from eight to three years.

The bravery and patriotism of the Garhwali soldiers were deeply appreciated by the whole country and Garhwali Days were celebrated in a large number of places. In Bombay on that day as many as 800 persons were wounded from police lathis. In this manner India showed its appreciation of these brave soldiers.

On April 25 Shri Vithalbhai J. Patel resigned from the presidentship of the Legislative Assembly. In his letter to the Viceroy he stated that the manner in which the principle of Imperial Preference had been "forced down the throat of an unwilling Assembly" by the Government showed that the Assembly was meant merely to register the decrees of the executive and could not safeguard the vital interests of the country. He could not therefore continue to lend false prestige to such a body by presiding over its deliberations. He further stated that he had been disillusioned about the intentions of the Government and their recent policy had shown that instead of recognising India's claim they were trying to crush the aspirations of the people.

Meanwhile the satyagraha campaign was going on in full swing. It had gained both in strength and extent. In Bombay city salt was being prepared in many a home. In parts of Gujrat contraband salt was being publicly sold, at one-twentieth the price of Government salt. In almost every province salt manufacture was being daily carried out in public meetings, and, at not a few places, under a shower of lathis. A "salt victory" was celebrated in Bombay by a huge procession half a mile long, when funeral honours were paid to the Salt Act.

Disobedience of salt laws was not, however, the whole of the movement even at this stage. By this time boycott of foreign cloth and of liquor had also become an important part of it. Even the boycott of British goods had appeared on the programme of certain Provincial Committees, notably on that of Bombay. The boycott of liquor had already proved a great success in Gujrat, where along with picketing of liquor shops, toddy trees were being cut down. This cutting down of toddy trees was a feature in some other provinces also, particularly in Behar and Utkal. Picketing of foreign cloth shops had by this time become widespread and effective. At the suggestion of Gandhiji, women were everywhere, and specially in Bombay, Gujrat and Delhi, taking a prominent part in it. In Bombay the Desh Sevikas had made their appearance by the end of April. Many mercantile associations took the swadeshi pledge. Many private professions, such as the medical profession, also took the vow to use professionally only swadeshi or non-British articles. There was also in some places, notably in Gujrat, a boycott of Government officials.

The Government on their side were active enough. As far as using the ordinary law against the satyagrahis was concerned they had reached the end of their resources. The movement had acquired such proportions that the ordinary processes of the law were rendered wholly impotent in dealing with it. Unable to cope with the movement by legal means the Government encouraged hooliganism. Lathi charges became common. There were lathi charges in Bombay, Calcutta, Madras and several other places. There was also more firing, for instance, at Madras, Calcutta and Neela in Bengal. Shri J.M. Sen-Gupta and Shri Subhas Chandra Bose were severely assaulted even inside the Alipore jail where they were prisoners. There was also looting and pillaging by the police. In Bengal paddy fields were burnt and edibles forcibly taken away from houses. A vegetable market in Gujrat was raided because the dealers would not sell vegetables to officials.

Madras had a grim experience at an early stage of the campaign. There had been assaults and beatings of volunteers, and an "all parties" monster meeting, in which even those not taking part in the civil disobedience movement participated, was held on Triplicane Beach on April 27th to protest against these beatings. At the close of the meeting the police charged at the crowds. Lights were put out and the crowds were chased and beaten in the dark. One, Manickam Chetty of Choolai, was trampled to death by a mounted sawar. The police opened fire and Shri E.K. Govindsamy, an advocate of the High Court and an officer of the St. John's Ambulance Corps, who had nothing to do with the meeting was shot and killed.

But worse than the lathi charges, and firing, and looting was what Gandhiji called the "violation of the body" of satyagrahis. At Viramgam and other places volunteers were not only assaulted and abused but were also deliberately hit and tortured in their private parts. It was this violation of the body, this unclean means of warfare, that made Gandhiji decide about the so-called "raid" of the Dharasana salt depot. On the 26th of April at Charavada Gandhiji spoke out his intention of marching with his comrades to the Dharasana Salt Depot and demanding possession of it. In his letter to the Viceroy which was written on May 4th, but published after his arrest, he gave his reasons for intending to take such a bold step. After recounting the injustices and horrors perpetrated by Government he wrote "Before the reign of terrorism that has just begun overwhelms India, I feel that I must take a bolder step, and if possible, direct your wrath in a cleaner if more drastic channel." The cleaner channel was the using of guns against the satyagrahis. He wrote on April 24: "If the Government do not stop this brutal violation of the body, they will find the satyagrahis presently compelling them to use the guns against them. I do not want this to happen. But if the Government will have it, I have no hesitation whatsoever in giving them the opportunity. They must not physically interfere with the bands of civil resisters manufacturing salt, they may arrest every man, woman and child if they wish. If they will neither arrest, nor declare salt free, they will find people marching to be shot rather than be tortured."

On May 4th Gandhiji wrote his letter to the Viceroy about Dharasana. The same night, or rather on the morning of the 5th, for it was just a little after midnight, he was arrested while sleeping in his camp at Karadi. He was arrested under an ancient Regulation more than a century old. From Karadi he was taken straight to Yeravda Central Jail near Poona where he was imprisoned without trial as a state prisoner. The text of the warrant issued for his arrest was as follows: "As the Government view with alarm the activities of Mr. M.K. Gandhi they direct that he should be placed under restraint under Regulation XXV of 1827 and suffer imprisonment during the pleasure of the Government and he be immediately removed to the Yeravda Central Jail."

The news of Gandhiji's arrest flashed like lightning throughout the country. There were hartals, meetings and processions on a larger scale than ever before. Several members of the legislatures resigned in protest. The determination of the people to win Purna Swaraj became even firmer. At the same time there were protests made by non-Congress bodies and individuals against Gandhiji's arrest. Particularly, the action of the Government in incarcerating Gandhiji without any trial and for an indefinite period aroused indignation not only in India, but also among progressive circles all over the world.

CHAPTER III

After Gandhiji's Arrest

In accordance with the resolutions of the All India Congress Committee and the Working Committee, Gandhiji continued to lead the campaign till his arrest. After his arrest the burden of guiding the civil disobedience movement and giving continuous lead to the country devolved upon the Working Committee. The Committee discharged this duty effectively right through the campaign in spite of being declared an illegal organization and despite the repeated arrests of its members.

The first meeting of the Working Committee after Gandhiji's arrest was held on May 12, 13, 14 and 15 at Anand Bhawan, Allahabad, under Pandit Motilal Nehru's presidentship. The Committee had to face an unparalleled situation and a grave responsibility rested on it. The spirit of peaceful revolt against the British Government had spread all over the country; civil disobedience was spreading far and wide; and the country looked to the Committee for guidance at that critical stage when their trusted leader had been removed.

The triple programme of disobedience of the salt laws, and the picketing of foreign cloth and of liquor shops was being followed everywhere with great zeal. Wholesale piece-goods merchants cabled to England and other foreign countries cancelling their indents. Huge processions paraded the streets advocating the boycott of British goods. Women had joined the movement in large numbers and had become the main pillars of the boycott programme. Non-violence was being meticulously observed by Congress workers and, except for a few instances of outbreaks of violence under severe provocation, was being observed even by the public at large.

The campaign for the non-payment of land revenue which had been started in Ras soon after Sardar Vallabhbhai's arrest became more widespread after Gandhiji's incarceration. The Bardoli Taluqa started it immediately after. The solemn pledge that the peasants of Bardoli took at that time is worthy of note:

> We the inhabitants and farmers of the Bardoli Taluqa take this pledge today that we will not pay a single pie of land revenue to the Government unless and until Sardar Vallabhbhai and Mahatmaji bid us to do so; and that we shall cheerfully endure lathis, imprisonment, attachment and destruction of our property and will even meet death if need be.

It was also about this time that the annual sessions of the Jamiat-ul-Ulema, the premier organization of Muslim divines, was held at Amroha (U.P.) to determine what lead they should give to Muslims in regard to participation in the civil disobedience movement. After three days' strenuous discussion the Jamiat resolved "that under the present circumstances there is no reason why Muslims should keep themselves aloof from the Congress". It further appealed to the Muslims "that for the sake of the freedom of the country and to protect from outrage the Islamic personal law, they should, in cooperation with the Congress, carry on the non-violent struggle for freedom with courage, zeal and determination". The Working Committee in a resolution expressed its appreciation of the patriotic act of the Jamiat.

As civil disobedience grew in intensity, police violence and terrorism kept pace with it. On May 6, while Delhi was celebrating Gandhiji's arrest, there were brutal assaults on women and unwarranted firing and lathi charges by the police. These resulted in two deaths. During this firing the Sisganj Gurudwara was made a target by the police and this aroused great indignation among the Sikhs. Later Sec. 144 Cr.P.C. was applied to the whole city of Delhi. At Viramgam and Agra there were also assaults on women and in the Midnapore district of Bengal a reign of terror began which lasted for several months. In this district there was firing, assaults and destruction of property, and even of medical appliances, by the police.

A graver situation than that at Delhi or elsewhere developed at Sholapur on May 8th. Since Gandhiji's arrest there were daily processions in that city. On the morning of the 8th the usual procession was taken out. After the procession had dispersed some volunteers proceeded to cut down toddy trees. A large crowd followed them. The police appeared on the scene and arrested some people from the crowd. The crowd unfortunately was not in a proper temper. It demanded the return of the arrested men. A sergeant at this stage fired a shot which killed a boy. The mob became infuriated and the police replied by firing at the crowd. Some people from the crowd marched into the city and set fire to some Government buildings. The civil authorities thereupon handed over the city to the military and there was indiscriminate shooting the whole of that day. A lorry load of soldiers drove through the streets shooting indiscriminately with the result that no less than 25 persons were killed that day. On May 12, when the city was returning to normal and when quiet and peace were established, Martial Law was declared. This meant a reign of terror and amazing and fanciful punishments were given for trivial acts. It is sufficient to say that during those days even the carrying of the national flag was punishable with 10 years' rigorous imprisonment. Maharashtra replied gallantly to this by initiating a flag satyagraha at Sholapur. Many volunteers carrying national flags were sentenced to heavy terms of imprisonment and many were severely beaten and maltreated. The authorities hit upon unique methods for harassing the volunteers. The latter would be told, for instance, to abuse Gandhiji, or the vegetarian Brahmins among them would be asked to take meat, and upon refusal would be beaten and spat upon!

It was in such a setting that the Working Committee commenced its deliberations at Anand Bhawan and took command of the operations. The Committee began with congratulating Mahatma Gandhi "on the phenomenal success of the movement throughout the country resulting in the universal defiance of the salt laws". It placed on record its grateful appreciation "of the lead given by Mahatma Gandhi and his incomparable generalship in the conduct of the great campaign of civil disobedience inaugurated and carried on by him up to the moment of his arrest". The Committee also reiterated "its abiding faith in civil disobedience" and resolved "to carry on the struggle during the incarceration of Mahatma Gandhi with redoubled vigour". To this effect the Committee issued a call to "students, lawyers and other professional men, the workers and peasants, merchants, industrialists and government servants and all others to contribute to the success of the fight for freedom by making all the sacrifice they are capable of".

The Committee passed several other important resolutions also. It condemned the declaration of Martial Law at Sholapur, the firing at Delhi, the "cowardly assaults" upon ambulance workers and the destruction by authorities of medical appliances, stretchers, etc., in Bengal, and the assaults upon women at Agra, Delhi and Contai in Midnapore. It also considered separately the several fronts at which the fight was going on and defined the plan and the method to be followed at each. It directed the Provincial Committees to continue and extend manufacture of contraband salt for sale or consumption, to continue the technical breaches of the salt laws and to organize public breaches of those laws on every Sunday as a mark of the country's disapproval of them.

With regard to foreign cloth the Committee passed an important resolution. Picketing of foreign cloth was at this time going on vigorously all over the country. Cloth dealers were, however, resenting it at many places and were desiring some sort of arrangement which would have allowed them to dispose of their existing stocks in return for an undertaking not to import or indent any more foreign cloth. They were accordingly approaching the P.C.Cs and the acting President, with their various proposals. It was in view of this situation that the Committee passed the following resolution:

> After giving full consideration to the different aspects of the question of boycott of foreign cloth and to the representations of foreign cloth dealers, this committee is of opinion that in the interest of the country it is essential to carry out a complete boycott of foreign cloth throughout the country without delay and for that purpose to take effective steps to prevent sales of existing stock, secure cancellation of orders already placed and prevent the placing of future orders.
>
> This Committee therefore calls upon all Congress bodies to carry on intensive propaganda for the boycott of foreign cloth and to organize the picketing of shops dealing in foreign cloth.
>
> This Committee while appreciating the efforts of Pandit Madan Mohan Malaviya to help the boycott movement regrets that it cannot endorse any agreement or understanding with the dealers whereby their shops are not to be picketed and the sale of existing stock is to be permitted in return for promise made by them not to import or order foreign cloth for specified periods.
>
> This Committee directs all Congress organizations to be no party to any such or similar agreements or understandings with dealers or importers of foreign cloth.

The Committee also passed a resolution authorising "the acting President to enter into negotiations with the Indian Mill Owners with a view to devise means to prevent unfair increase in the prices of swadeshi mill-cloth and the manufacture of khaddar and generally to take steps to promote the boycott of foreign cloth". Thus were laid the foundations of the formidable movement of boycott which paralysed British trade and shook the very basis of British rule in this country.

No less important than the resolution on foreign cloth was the Committee's resolution on non-payment of taxes. The resolution is given below:

> This Committee is of opinion that the time has arrived for the inauguration of a no-tax campaign by non-payment of specified taxes in certain provinces and is further of opinion that a beginning should be made by non-payment of the land tax in provinces where the

ryotwari system prevails such as Gujrat, Maharashtra, Karnatak, Andhra, Tamil Nad and the Punjab and by the non-payment of the chowkidari tax in provinces where it is levied such as Bengal, Behar and Orissa. It therefore calls upon such provinces to organize campaigns for non-payment of land tax or the chowkidari tax as the case may be, in areas to be selected by the Provincial Congress Committee concerned. The Committee warns the tax payers not selected by the Provincial Congress Committee against embarking on a campaign of non-payment of land revenue or chowkidari tax as such action is likely to interfere seriously with the conduct of the general campaign of civil disobedience.

The Committee also urged the people to make earnest attempts to bring about an effective boycott of British goods at an early date. It also appealed strongly to the public "to boycott all British banking, insurance, shipping and similar other institutions".

The acting President had previously allowed the Provincial committees of the Central Provinces to take up the breach of forest laws, so far as they affected grazing, as a part of their civil disobedience programme. The Committee confirmed this action of the acting President and further resolved "that other provinces where similar laws are in force may organize the breach of such laws with the sanction of the Provincial Congress Committee".

Finally the Committee, "having regard to the increasing difficulty in holding meetings of this Committee caused by the repressive policy of the government" passed a resolution delegating to the acting President all its powers in order to enable him "to deal with urgent matters in connection with the campaign" if in his opinion it became impossible or difficult or undesirable to call a meeting of the Committee.

After Gandhiji's arrest, and the meeting of the Working Committee, the campaign became so widespread and so multiformed that it is very difficult to trace its daily developments and present a systematic account of its growth. The nation was on the move and every step of it was bitterly contested and, although non-violence was the creed and policy of the civil resisters, they were sought to be suppressed by every species of violence. The law was a convenient handmaiden of the government, and new laws were framed overnight by a stroke of the pen by the irresponsible authority that sought to impose its will on an unwilling people who had openly discarded their allegiance to it. But even its own laws, which it could make and unmake at pleasure were not obeyed by the government. Free licence was given to the police, and sometimes to the military, to do what they pleased to terrorise and break the spirit of the people. The events that occurred in the larger cities found some publicity in a garbled form in the newspapers. Of the occurrences in thousands of villages little was known and much that happened there will remain unrecorded. Nationalist newspapers soon felt the heavy weight of the Government. Some ceased to exist; some continued under a strict censorship and the publication of any police atrocity or even of a Congress notice of meeting became a crime.

It is proposed therefore to refer in this report only to some outstanding events. An attempt will be made to group them and to classify the various aspects of the campaign, and to deal with the measures taken by the government for the suppression of the movement. The progress of the campaign will be considered in its relation to the decisions of the Working Committee on the one hand and to the ordinances of the Governor-General on the other. Round these two pivots the movement revolved and progressed; each followed the other and was in part an answer to it. While the Working Committee continued to lead and direct the campaign, it received no little help from the ordinances which were meant to suppress the movement, but which gave further and welcome opportunities to the Congress for civil disobedience.

CHAPTER IV

The Progress of Civil Disobedience

Breach of the salt laws. The manufacture of contraband salt and formal breaches of the salt laws continued all over the country till the setting in of the rains. It was not possible to continue this manufacture during the monsoon. But in many provinces demonstrational breaches of these laws were continued on a certain day of the month or week. This practice was followed up till the signing of the Delhi truce.

Gandhiji had decided on a "raid" of the Dharasana salt depot just before his arrest. On his incarceration Shri Abbas Tyabji became the leader of the salt satyagrahis in Gujrat. He was arrested with his batch of volunteers on May 12 and Shrimati Sarojini Naidu succeeded him. The first "raid" at Dharasana took place under her leadership. Many other "raids" followed her arrest. These "raids" were remarkable for the barbarous behaviour of the police and the peaceful manner in which the satyagrahis bore all manner of assault and indignity without desisting from the task they had set before themselves. Neither food nor water was allowed by the police to reach Shrimati Sarojini and her band for a long period and for hours they remained in the hot sun of an Indian summer without any relief. But much worse was to come after Shrimati Sarojini's arrest.

The Dharasana raids began on May 12 and lasted for about 3 weeks. During this period 2640 volunteers mainly from Gujrat and some from other provinces, participated in the raids. Out of these 1333 were wounded, four met their death and 328 were sentenced to various terms of imprisonment. The wounds received by the volunteers were on practically every part of their body—on head, face, eye, ear, neck, shoulder, arm, chest, abdomen, back, thigh, leg, scrotum, anus. There were cases of fractures, internal haemorrhage, dislocations, vomiting of blood, injuries from horse's hoofs.

Shrimati Mirabai (Miss Slade) who visited Dharasana during the raids enumerates the following types of atrocities perpetrated upon the person of non-violent satyagrahis.

1. Lathi blows on head, chest, stomach, joints.
2. Thrusts with lathis in private parts, abdominal regions, chest, etc.
3. Stripping of men naked before beating.
4. Tearing off of loin cloth and thrusting of stick into anus.
5. Pressing and squeezing of the testicles till a man becomes unconscious.
6. Dragging of wounded men by legs or arms, often beating them the while.
7. Throwing of wounded men into thorn hedges or into salt water.
8. Riding of horses over men as they lie or sit on the ground.
9. Thrusting of pins and thorns into men's bodies sometimes even when they are unconscious.
10. Beating of men after they had become unconscious.

"And other vile things too many to relate besides foul language and blasphemy, calculated to hurt as much as possible the most sacred feelings of the satyagrahis."

The Working Committee after surveying the atrocities committed at Dharasana and other places held "that high British and Indian officers of Government are directly responsible for these inhuman acts by having permitted or failed to stop them" and it warned the Government "that it is only driving the iron deeper into the soul of the people whose determination cannot be shaken by the cruelest forms of torture".

Besides Dharasana the salt depots at Wadala, Shiroda and Sanikatta (Karwar District) were also raided. Incidents similar to those witnessed at Dharasana occurred at these places also; with this difference, however, that in the raids at these places not only volunteers but even the general public took active part and also that hundreds of maunds of salt were removed from the pans. At Wadala, particularly, thousands of citizens participated in the raids. There was even a batch of ladies raiding the depot and also a batch of Mohammadans. One person named Pasu died on May 29 from injuries received in one of the Wadala raids. At Shiroda the very first day volunteers were able to remove as much as 526 maunds of salt from the depot. These raids showed the great faith that the people had in non-violence and bore testimony to the capacity of the people for heroic sacrifice.

Thus the breach of the salt laws was countrywide and Government were unable to cope with it. Contraband salt was for a time the only salt used in many areas, specially on the seacoast. Some provinces report that in many areas people had equipped themselves with a whole year's supply of contraband salt.

Non-payment of Taxes

Land Revenue and Rent. The first province to take up non-payment of taxes was Gujrat. Mention has already been made of the resolution adopted by the farmers of Bardoli after the arrest of Gandhiji. Even earlier the village of Ras, in the taluka of Borsad, had resolved, upon the arrest of Sardar Vallabhbhai at Ras, to withhold payment of its land revenue. The echo of Ras was heard in the villages around, and within a short time fourteen villages had resolved to follow its lead.

On June 30th, the Kheda District Peasant's Conference was held which decided that the whole district should join the campaign. The taluka of Bardoli had already joined a month before. Other talukas followed, some joining the fight as late as December 1930. It appears from the report of the Gujrat P.C.C. that the districts of Surat and Kheda were foremost in the fight. And in these districts the talukas of Bardoli and Borsad occupied the first place; Nadiad, Anand and Jalalpur also taking prominent part. In other talukas the movement was not widespread or acute. The talukas of Jambusar, Dholka, Viramgam, the Panchamahals, Kalol and Godhra, however, took some part in the campaign.

The story of the no-tax campaign in Gujrat is a simple story of suffering and sacrifice. The authorities trying every means in their power to realise their revenue and the farmers adamantly refusing to pay in spite of being subjected to all manner of hardships, losses and indignities. They were beaten and tortured, their property was seized and destroyed, they were abused and some of them were jailed. Attempts were made to corrupt them and set them against each other, and false propaganda was resorted to by Government. The authorities of Borsad even took to publishing a highly propagandist and mendacious periodical which, as irony would have it, was called the *Satyanivedan*. The provincial report cites an instance, which is presumably typical, in which a Mamletdar summoned Khatedars and showed them false receipts and book entries in order to bring home to the Khatedars the fact that their co-farmers had already paid up their dues, whereas in fact none had paid them! But these methods met with little success.

Mr. Brailsford the well-known English journalist visited the no-tax area in Bardoli during the movement and his accounts were published at the time. His testimony is that of an impartial observer. In one of his articles he states as follows:

> My note-book is full of the complaints of the peasants with whom we talked on this tour. I could seldom verify their stories, but I questioned them carefully, and do not doubt their word. These notes with names and dates shall go to the superior officials. One village was haunted every night by a gang of roughs, who fired guns, wore veils, and on one occasion murdered an old peasant with an axe. When the villagers asked for protection a high police official is said to have answered: 'You shall have it when you pay your tax.' Most of the complaints were of unprovoked beating by the police with their formidable lathis (staves).
>
> One scene I managed after much questioning to reconstruct. It happened in the abandoned village of Afwa. Here some peasants who own no land had remained behind, and with them were some who had returned from Baroda to cultivate their fields. On October 21st, about 3 a.m. a car arrived with ten policemen under a certain sub-inspector. The police found these men sleeping in the fields, they beat them, and then demanded the tax. They were then brought before this sub-inspector, who beat some of them with his own hands and kicked others. One was still limping and the other showed a painful swelling. The heads of two brothers he knocked together. They were then taken in the lorry to the lock-up in Bardoli. There the sub-inspector threatened, with unprintable details, 'to make them useless to their wives'. That threat told and the younger brother, though not himself a landowner, paid the tax on his father's farm. In another case a passer-by from another village was seized and beaten, and the money in his pocket picked. A receipt was given in the name of a local tax payer, and the stranger was told to recover it from him. This sub-inspector was a person who combined ingenuity with brutality. Finding in the village another stranger, a man from Surat, he appropriated his gold ornaments, and tried to force some of the villagers to buy them, a species of summary destraint. But I might continue this narrative indefinitely, and still it would record only the morning of this officer's activity. I might have hesitated to believe these peasants, had I not happened to meet this person in the flesh, and caught him out, in a ludicrous and palpable lie. By such hands far from the heights of Simla and the serenity of Whitehall, is law and order dispensed to the silent millions.

But the severest weapon—severer even than the lathi—in the Government's armoury was the confiscation, loot and destruction of property. Loot and destruction were extra "legal" methods, but were for that matter not the less used. The losses suffered by the peasants due to these measures, excepting confiscation and sale, are difficult to calculate. The loss suffered by Borsad alone as estimated by the Gujrat P.C.C. comes to Rs. 9,96,257. The loss of Bardoli has been put at Rs. 7,93,581. The P.C.C. has made the following analysis of the losses: losses due to (1) Japties, (2) premature harvesting of crops, (3) failure to irrigate the farms properly, (4) crops attached, (5) crops looted and destroyed, (6) inability to harvest the rabi crop, (7) damage to water pumps, (8) the fact that the farmers were constrained to sell their crops and cattle at very reduced prices owing to the exigencies of the movement, (9) houses gutted when the farmers were away after their emigration.

The above analysis and the above figures do not include losses due to the confiscation and sale of land. It appears from the Gujrat Report that in Borsad 784 acres and 31 gunthas of land were confiscated and sold. Ordinarily the value of these lands would have been something like Rs. 7,00,700. The price for which the lands were actually sold, however, was Rs. 8,533. This money went to the Government in payment of the outstanding revenue dues. Thus the farmers had a net loss of over seven lakhs from the confiscation of their lands alone. Likewise in Bardoli 855 acres and 37 gunthas were confiscated and sold. The price realised by Government was Rs. 8,328, whereas the real value of the lands must have been in the neighbourhood of over four and a half lakhs.

There were corresponding losses in other talukas.

The farmers, especially those of Borsad and Bardoli, put up bravely with every Government offensive. When the destruction and confiscation of property became too excessive for them they emigrated where opportunities for such emigration were available to non-British areas, particularly to the Gaikwar's territory. The peasants of Borsad and Bardoli were fortunate in this respect because of their proximity to Baroda. It was, however, no easy thing for the farmers to leave their homesteads with their families and shift to improvised huts in strange territories, leaving their immovable property and their standing crops, which were sometimes very valuable, especially in the tobacco areas, at the mercy of government officers and any chance person who chose to help himself to them.

Some figures, showing the collections made by the authorities in some leading talukas during the course of the movement, will give an idea of the success of the no-tax campaign. In Bardoli at the time when the campaign was seriously taken up there were Rs. 4,63,500 to be collected. Out of these the authorities were able to collect only Rs. 26,500 till the signing of the truce. Even this small collection was made mostly through the sale of land, movable property and standing crops. In Borsad out of Rs. 3,91,198 outstanding only Rs. 1,78,475 could be collected. In Jalalpur out of Rs. 3,66,000 only Rs. 31,000 were realised.

The only other province where non-payment of the land tax was taken up on a considerable scale was the U.P. But there was a fundamental difference between the movement in Gujrat and in the United Provinces. In Gujrat the basis of the movement was purely political; in the U.P. the economic motive was added on to the political. In Gujrat the land belongs to peasant proprietors dealing directly with the Government; in the U.P. as also in Bengal and Behar, the zamindari system prevails and the peasants are mostly the tenants of large landholders. Owing to this zamindari system and very heavy rents and other exactions the condition of the tenants in the U.P. is pitiable in the extreme and compares very unfavourably with that of the peasant proprietors in Gujrat or the Punjab. The catastrophic fall in the prices of agricultural produce hit these tenants hardest and it became very difficult for them to pay any substantial part of their rents. A no-tax campaign therefore fitted in with the agrarian distress and was immediately responded to. But it could not have succeeded in the large measure it did but for the strength of the Congress organization in the affected rural areas and the close association of this organization with the interests of the tenants. The peasants in the U.P. had taken a prominent part in the purely political salt campaign and large numbers had already gone to prison for it. For them Swaraj was, as it should be, synonymous with the relief of the many burdens they suffered from. When therefore the U.P. Provincial Committee inaugurated the no-tax campaign in October 1930, there was an immediate and enthusiastic response. The Committee did not call for a no-rent campaign only. It asked the zamindars also not to pay their revenue to Government. But, while few of the larger zamindars had the courage to risk losing their lands by non-payment of revenue, the tenantry gladly welcomed the new phase of the movement. Thus in effect the no-tax campaign became a no-rent campaign. In its aggressive form it was confined to some districts only: Allahabad, Rae Bareli, Agra, Partabgarh, Cawnpore, Etawah and Fatehpur. But all districts were affected by it and in effect payment of rents stopped in the greater part of the province. And as rents were not forthcoming, revenue payments by landlords also became difficult.

Coercive processes and repression were resorted to by Government to break up the no-tax front. But the movement grew and took root in the rural areas and by the end of the year 1930 the U.P. was a stronghold of the civil disobedience campaign, and was indeed stronger than it had been at any previous time during the year. The great cities of the province had played and continued to play a prominent part, but the centre of gravity of the movement had shifted to the countryside and it was the village that henceforth occupied pride of place in the campaign. The tenants suffered greatly by the usual methods of repression. There was firing and lathi charges and assaults and looting of villages and punitive police. But the combination of the political and economic motives was too powerful to be easily shaken.

As the no-rent campaign was largely based on the agrarian distress, the coming of the truce after the Delhi Settlement did little to relieve the tension. And the sufferings of the tenants during the period of the truce have been even greater than before. But that is beyond the scope of this report.

It might be mentioned that a no-tax campaign was also begun in a few villages of Delhi district. But it does not appear to have been pressed, except in two of them where it had some success.

Non-payment of Chowkidari Tax. This form of satyagraha was taken up in Behar, Bengal and Utkal, the three provinces where this tax is levied.

The Behar P.C.C. had from the very beginning raised the question of non-payment of this tax. The Working Committee in its resolution No. 17 of May 12-15 allowed Behar to take up this form of satyagraha. Accordingly preparations had been made for it in several districts. After the Instigation Ordinance was promulgated the Provincial Committee acting under the instructions of the Working Committee, authorised the districts to take up this programme. Champaran, Saran, Bhagalpur and Muzaffarpur were particularly well prepared. The amount of tax that was yet to be realised was very small, and these were mostly dues on account of arrears. However, the defiance of law involved was very real and the sufferings of the people were quite considerable. There was the inevitable lathi and in addition punitive police and punitive taxes; detachments of Pathans were posted in particularly recalcitrant villages. Property was destroyed, seized and looted. The value of property attached, not the real value, which was much greater, but the value realised, was always many times the amount of arrears outstanding. It is not possible to form any estimate of the loss suffered by the people on account of the illegal destruction and removal of property.

In Bengal non-payment of the chowkidari tax was made early an item of its programme by the Bengal Council of Civil Disobedience. Towards the end of May preparations for it were started by the Council in Midnapore (particularly in Tamluk and Contai); in Arambagh (Hughly); in Bishnupur (Bankura); in Balurghat (Dinajpur) and in a few other places. The campaign actually began some months later and was most successfully pursued in Contai and Tamluk. As in Behar, valuable property was destroyed and looted. The district of Midnapore became famous for the atrocities committed there in connection with the movement for the non-payment of chowkidari tax.

In Utkal the movement was confined to only one union of the district of Balasore and was attended with the usual consequences.

Non-payment of other taxes. Special taxes to pay the cost of punitive police were also levied in many places and were usually resisted and not paid. They were partly realised by confiscation of property, but with the coming of the truce the outstanding amounts were written off in accordance with the terms of the settlement.

The U.P. P.C.C. when it started the no-tax campaign also called upon income tax payers not to pay it. But most of such payments for the year had previously been made and the next occasion would have come seven or eight months later. The truce intervened before this time came. Pandit Motilal Nehru, however, had not paid his tax and he announced that he would not pay it. There were also other isolated cases of refusal to pay income tax.

The Breach of the Forest Laws

The resolution of the Working Committee permitting satyagraha against grazing laws has already been given. The movement was initiated in the Hindi Central Provinces on May 30 in the district of Jubbulpore by sending volunteers to cut grass in the Government reserve forests. This phase of the campaign became very popular and soon became widespread in both the C.P.s., Maharashtra and Berar. In fact in these four provinces it was the major movement. This rapid development and success were due to the resentment felt by the masses at the restrictions on the grazing of cattle in the forests, on cutting grass, collecting firewood, etc. Large numbers could easily participate in committing breaches of the forest laws and it was not unusual to see ten to fifteen thousand persons taking part. In Maharashtra when the Forest Satyagraha was initiated under the auspices of the Sangamner Satyagraha Camp it is estimated that nearly a hundred thousand persons participated. The C.P. Marathi War Council organized a mass disobedience of the forest laws on August 25, and it is stated by the P.C.C. that no less than three hundred thousand took part in this in various parts of the province. In Berar Shri M.S. Aney initiated the movement and it soon became the chief form of satyagraha.

Besides grazing cattle, collecting wood and cutting grass, the P.C.C.s also organized picketing of the annual forest auctions. This resulted in considerable losses to Government.

The Maharashtra P.C.C. states that as a result of the forest satyagraha many village patels resigned their posts. In Belgaum Taluka alone, District Nasik, out of 245 patels as many as 200 are reported to have resigned.

In addition to the four provinces named above where Forest Satyagraha was practised on a mass scale, mention must also be made of the U.P. and Gujrat. But in these two provinces the movement was restricted to some districts only, in the U.P. to Dehra Dun, Pilibhit, Etawah and Lakhimpur, and in Gujrat to the district of Panchmahal.

The usual methods which Government had adopted for resisting the civil disobedience campaign were applied to Forest Satyagraha also.

Boycott of British Goods

The boycott of British goods was no part of the original satyagraha programme nor was any stress laid on it at the beginning. For some years past the Congress had passed resolutions in favour of this boycott and some propaganda had been done in its behalf. But at no time previously had it become a major plank in the Congress platform. As civil disobedience developed, however, the boycott of British goods grew spontaneously and spread rapidly and it was only later that the Working Committee made it one of the principal grounds of attack. In the larger cities like Calcutta and Bombay specially and in many other cities British trade was brought almost to a standstill and British goods were often sealed up in retail shops. In particular, the sale of British made cigarettes, which was assuming alarming proportions, was affected by this boycott.

This boycott was meant for goods other than textiles. So far as textiles were concerned there was no question of boycotting British cloth only. All foreign cloth was boycotted, but as it happened most of the foreign cloth that came to India came from Lancashire.

The constructive side of this boycott was swadeshi or the preference for home-made articles. The swadeshi movement had been inaugurated, together with that of the boycott of British goods, in Bengal in 1905. After some time both had languished. The boycott was then dropped from the Congress programme to be revived again in a mild form after the non-co-operation movement of 1920-21. But swadeshi had continued as the Congress policy all along and had made steady, though not very startling, progress. With the recrudescence of the boycott of British goods in 1930, the swadeshi movement marched forward rapidly. Stress was always laid on buying Indian-made articles, and only in case of essential articles not made in India were foreign goods other than British recommended.

The boycott of British goods was formally suspended by the Delhi Settlement of March 1931.

Other Forms of Satyagraha

As the campaign of civil disobedience developed and Government tried to counter it and suppress it by ordinances, resistance of these ordinances gradually became the major part of the movement. This is dealt with more fully in the next chapter.

But there were many other forms of satyagraha practised locally, which, though of minor importance from an All-India point of view, developed temporarily into major occurrences. The spirit of disobedience was in the air, but it was strictly limited and circumscribed by the basic conditions laid down by the Congress. Disobedience was to be civil and peaceful and disciplined, and in the vast majority of cases these conditions were adhered to.

The elections to the Legislative Assembly and Provincial Councils held in September 1930 were boycotted and a very small proportion of the electors went to the polls.

A boycott of the All-India census was suggested by Shri C. Rajagopalachari and was later endorsed by the President. It was taken up in some parts of the country and some municipalities, notably the Ahmedabad Municipality, refused to co-operate with Government in census work. This boycott did not spread much or become intensive owing to the prolonged negotiations between the Government and the Congress which ultimately led to the Delhi Settlement.

Section 144 of the Criminal Procedure Code was frequently used or misused by the Government for all manner of strange purposes, and it was as frequently disobeyed. Among the strange orders passed under this section was the ban on the wearing of the Gandhi cap in Guntur. This order was later cancelled by the Madras High Court. In Masulipatam Sec. 144 was used to prevent withdrawal of money from the banks by the Congress. Women were frequently to be found among those who defied the orders under Sec. 144.

Police orders interfering with processions, meetings, etc., were also frequent and were often defied. Such defiance sometimes led to serious situations, such as in Bombay and at Patna, and large scale and persistent satyagraha resulted, accompanied by lathi charges and the like.

Another form of satyagraha practised, particularly in Bengal, and also to some extent in the C.P. and in parts of the U.P., was the reading of proscribed literature at public meetings. Such meetings were often dispersed forcibly by the police. The Patel Enquiry Report on the Peshawar tragedy was also proscribed by Government but the Report continued to be sold to the public.

The resolution of the Working Committee on the duties of the police and the military was also proscribed. The resolution was not originally meant as a measure of civil disobedience. It merely stated the recognised law on the subject and how far the military and police were entitled to refuse to obey illegal and unjustified orders. But, fearful of the effect that truth would have on their armed forces, the Government proscribed the resolution and thereby gave it greater publicity. The Working Committee took the challenge and had hundreds of thousands of notices containing the resolution distributed among the public as well as the police and military. The resolution was also read out in public places.

A number of Government officials resigned from their offices, and joined the movement. These included assistant magistrates and teachers, but most of those who resigned were village officials. Reference has already been made to the very large number of patels and village officials who resigned in Gujrat, specially during Gandhiji's march. Altogether 3028 village officials resigned in Gujrat but some of these went back to their posts later. In the Karwar District of the Karnatak

144 patels resigned. In a taluqa of Nasik District in Maharashtra 200 out of 245 patels resigned.

Some lawyers also suspended their practice during the movement but the number was not great. Many of those who had suspended practice during the non-co-operation movement had not gone back to the courts since then, and they took prominent part in the campaign.

The response from students in Government or aided schools or colleges was not great, although at one time special efforts were locally made in some provinces. A considerable number of students went to prison as a result of satyagraha but there was no large scale suspension of studies or withdrawal from state or state-aided educational institutions. Of state-aided institutions probably the biggest contribution for satyagraha came from the Benaras Hindu University, the revered Vice-Chancellor of which, Pandit Madan Mohan Malaviya, himself going to prison as a member of the Working Committee.

If the response from official and semi-official educational institutions was not remarkable, the response from the national schools and colleges was certainly remarkable. The Gujrat Vidyapith, the Kashi Vidyapith and the Behar Vidyapith specially threw their entire resources into the struggle and almost all their professors and students took part in it.

CHAPTER V

The Ordinances and How They Were Met

Throughout the entire civil disobedience campaign the form of activity that consumed the greatest energy of the people was the defiance of the Governor-General's ordinances. Every fresh ordinance provided an additional opportunity for civil disobedience and added to the strength of the movement. It may indeed be said that the Governor-General fed the movement with his ordinances. The immediate objective of the movement was to provide the masses with suitable opportunities for breach of the laws framed by the Government. For this purpose laws had to be carefully chosen as such laws as were good in themselves could not be made the subject of attack. But the ordinances, which were executive decrees to suppress the movement, were ideally suited for this disobedience. They were new and were all additional encroachments on the liberty of the people, and their advent one after the other provided a novelty which gave a fillip to the campaign and prevented it from becoming stale.

The Governor-General promulgated eleven ordinances. Two of these were not directly connected with the movement. These were the Bengal Criminal Law Amendment Ordinance and the Lahore Conspiracy Case Ordinance. The former, it was stated, was intended to deal with outbreaks of violence in Bengal, but in practice it was used against peaceful Congress workers and to suppress the Congress organization, the latter with the trial of Shri Bhagat Singh and his comrades. Two other ordinances were promulgated to provide for the proclamation and regulation of Martial Law in Peshawar district and in Sholapur. The declaration of Martial Law in Peshawar was, according to the Governor-General's explanatory statement, intended to deal with the situation created by the Afridi offensive. But there can be little doubt that it was also meant to suppress the Congress in the Frontier Province, and in effect Congressmen suffered considerably under it.

The Sholapur Martial Law was, as shown above, a direct outcome of circumstances created during the course of the movement. These circumstances were not, however, the creation of Congress workers; nor were they of such a serious nature as to justify the declaration of Martial Law. The Working Committee condemned the declaration and the continuation for a long period of Martial Law at Sholapur. For a while Sholapur was numbed by the barbarous treatment of its people by the military. But soon the Maharashtra P.C.C. organized Flag Satyagraha in defiance of the order forbidding a display of the National Flag.

The remaining seven ordinances gave wider scope for disobedience; but the two that were made the centre of the movement were the Prevention of Intimidation Ordinance and the Unlawful Instigation Ordinance. The last one was promulgated a second time after the expiry of its first term of life. This was the last ordinance to be promulgated and was in force at the time of the truce.

Both the Intimidation and Instigation Ordinances were promulgated on May 30th. They were a reply, a counter-offensive, to the offensive launched by the Working Committee during its session at Anand Bhawan, Allahabad, on

May 12-15. The Governor-General stated in his introductory statements to both of these ordinances that they were made necessary as a result of the resolutions passed by the Working Committee. We quote the following extracts from his statements:

At the meeting of the Working Committee of the All India Congress Committee held recently at Allahabad a resolution was passed to the effect that the time had arrived for the inauguration of a no-tax campaign by non-payment of specified taxes in certain provinces. Previous to the passing of this resolution a movement for the refusal of the payment of land revenue had been started in certain districts of Gujrat in the Bombay Presidency, and attempts had been made in several other provinces to persuade revenue and tax payers to withhold the payment of their liabilities. The decision above referred to clearly contemplates a wide extension of the civil disobedience movement in the shape of an appeal to the masses which must if successful involve grave reactions upon the administration and stability of the state.

The taxes against which the movement is at present aimed are sources of provincial revenue, and their non-payment would deprive Local Governments of a considerable part of the resources on which they depend for the efficient conduct of the reserved and transferred departments. . . .

Having regard to these considerations and to the necessity of firm and prompt action against a movement, the object of which is to bring the administration to a standstill, I have deemed it necessary to promulgate an Ordinance, by which Local Governments may, as the necessity is established, be invested with powers to deal effectively with persons who instigate others to withhold the payment of certain lawful dues.

And again:

From the beginning of the civil disobedience movement it has been part of the programme of the Congress to use for various purposes the methods of picketing in order to make their will prevail. At the recent meeting of the Working Committee of the All India Congress Committee held at Allahabad resolutions were passed which urged the adoption of such methods on more intensive lines.

The Viceroy went on to state that the exigencies were such that they necessitated an ordinance to stop intimidation and molestation of those who were carrying on their trade in foreign cloth and liquor.

The Working Committee was not slow in replying to the counter-offensive of the Government. At the session of June 4-7 held at Allahabad it resolved that:

Whereas the Governor-General has recently promulgated three ordinances, namely the Press Ordinance, the Prevention of Intimidation Ordinance and the Unlawful Instigation Ordinance, the first of which has killed free and independent nationalist journalism and the last two have made it criminal to organize peaceful picketing of liquor and foreign cloth shops, social boycott of Government officers participating in various kinds of excesses and to carry on propaganda for non-payment of taxes not voted by the representatives of the people.

And whereas the statements issued by the Governor-General justifying these ordinances contain allegations which are contrary to facts, showing that the Governor-General is either kept in complete ignorance of the actual happenings in the country or is intentionally ignoring them.

Now therefore this Committee calls upon the country to meet the situation thus created, by publicly disobeying the three ordinances aforesaid with calm and unflinching courage and strict observance of non-violence under the gravest provocation as heretofore, and carry out fearlessly all the resolutions of the Congress, the A.I.C.C. and the Working Committee, regardless of the said ordinances.

In particular the Committee advises the people to carry on with redoubled vigour the peaceful picketing of liquor and foreign cloth shops, social boycott of Government officers known to have participated in unjustifiable assaults on satyagrahis and others and to extend the campaign for non-payment of land tax to parts of Gujrat, Maharashtra, Karnatak, Andhra and Tamil Nad where it has not yet been started, and also to intensify and extend the campaign of non-payment of chowkidari tax in Bengal and start it in Behar and Orissa.

The country rallied to this call and carried out the directions of the Working Committee. Picketing of foreign cloth shops was the one item in the programme which was carried out with splendid thoroughness in spite of ordinances and wholesale arrests of pickets. The large foreign cloth markets were specially made the centres of attack and with remarkable success. Stocks of foreign cloth were sealed in the presence of Congress authorities and removed from the sales rooms. Pickets stood guard the whole day and sometimes till late in the night. At some places they even remained on duty for all the twenty-four hours. Godowns, banks and railway stations were also picketed in some of the larger cities. The picketing was thorough but stress was always laid on non-violence. There was to be no compulsion if a person wanted to buy foreign cloth. The picket succeeded because he had public opinion on his side and it must be admitted that even the merchants, who stood to lose by the boycott, often cooperated with the Congress in furthering the boycott. Boycott pledges were taken by them and local associations of cloth dealers were formed which helped to detect any breach of the pledge. Occasionally over-zealous volunteers formed cordons in front of shops or round motor trucks carrying foreign cloth. But this was discouraged and just prior to the Delhi truce the Working Committee issued explicit and stringent directions to the effect that picketing must be perfectly peaceful and there must be no compulsion of any kind. In Bombay a tragedy occurred in connection with foreign cloth picketing. A young volunteer Babu Ganu determined to prevent the removal of foreign cloth by a motor lorry, lay down in front of it. The lorry however was taken over him and killed him. Bombay was deeply stirred by this self immolation and the boycott movement was given an impetus by this sacrifice.

But the burden of carrying on the boycott fell most heavily on the women of India. In compliance with Gandhiji's wishes they made the two boycotts of foreign cloth and liquor their own special work and it was due to their remarkable perseverence and sacrifice that success came in such large measure.

Picketing of liquor and other intoxicating drugs was also carried on with great success throughout the country and excise revenue was seriously affected thereby. The ordinances of the Governor-General against the no-tax campaign was ineffectual insofar as payment of taxes were concerned. But they were effective in filling the jails and in causing great suffering to the people concerned.

The remaining ordinances, except one, provided for the control of the press and the suppression of the numerous Congress bulletins and satyagraha Samachars that were being issued all over the country. The Working Committee advised the nationalist newspapers to defy the ordinances or to cease publication. Some of the newspapers appearing in the Indian languages accordingly suspended publication. But the great majority of the newspapers in English did not act up to the Working Committee's direction. A very few suspended publication only to reappear again some days later. Several continued to appear without any leading articles or editorial matter.

The Working Committee's many resolutions and directions, far-reaching as they were and involving defiance of laws and consequent suffering, had been acted up to by the country with an amazing discipline and loyalty. It is noteworthy therefore that this resolution about newspapers was not obeyed in any large measure. It was the sole exception. The public was hungry for news and it was difficult for the newspaper man to desist from supplying it even though this meant a large measure of humiliation under the ordinance. The few that obeyed the Working Committee's direction found their customers going to other newspapers. It is highly likely that if most of the newspapers had simultaneously suspended publication, as the Working Committee desired, the situation created would have been such as to compel the hands of Government to repeal the Press Ordinance. A general suspension of newspapers in the middle of the campaign would have resulted in the circulation of wild and exaggerated rumours which the Government could not have welcomed.

Three newspapers continued to defy the Press Ordinance right through the campaign and it was in the fitness of things that they should do so. They were Gandhiji's *Young India*, *Navajivan* and the *Hindi Navajivan*. The Navajivan Press in Ahmedabad where all these three were printed, was consequently seized and dismantled by Government. *Young India* continued to come out regularly in a cyclostyled form. It had a large circulation as it was re-cyclostyled in many centres for further distribution.

If Government met with a measure of success in terrorising many newspapers into a submissive and moderated activity, it failed completely in regard to unauthorised and cyclostyled news-sheets. Large numbers of these cyclostyled newspapers in English and Hindi and other languages used to come out and commanded an extensive circulation. Occasionally the duplicators and cyclostyling machines were seized by government but it was found impossible to put down these unauthorised news-sheets. Special mention might be made of the Congress Bulletin issued regularly by the Bombay Congress Committee. Many of its editors went to prison, many of the office-bearers responsible for its publication were arrested and sentenced, but the Bulletin came out with unfailing regularity and the newsboys who sold it were almost mobbed by an over-eager public. Searches would take place regularly for this bulletin and even while the search was going on it would be openly sold within a few yards of the search party.

On October 10th the "Unlawful Association Ordinance" was promulgated. But long before this the government had adopted the practice of declaring Congress Committees unlawful bodies. The first Congress Committees to be so declared were those of Peshawar District. This was done on May 3rd. Many other committees, provincial and local, were subsequently declared unlawful as also youth leagues and similar organizations. The Hindustani Seva Dal, the Congress Volunteer organization, was also declared illegal. In Bombay the Rashtriya Stree Sabha, a purely women's organization, and their volunteer organization, the Desh Sevika Sangh, were declared unlawful on the 15th October at the same time as the Bombay Provincial Congress Committee. The Stree Sabha and the Sevika Sangh were the first women's organizations not only in the history of the civil disobedience campaign but probably in the history of India, to be declared illegal. They well deserved that honour.

The Working Committee itself, the executive of the All India Congress Committee, with whom rested the leadership of the entire campaign, was declared illegal in several provinces. Even previous to this, many presidents and members of the Committee had been arrested and their places had been filled by nomination of the acting presidents, under the authority given to them by the A.I.C.C. After the President for the year had been sentenced to imprisonment, Pandit Motilal Nehru had taken his place. On June 30th the U.P. Government, in consultation with the Government of India, declared the Working Committee an unlawful association. This declaration was communicated by telephone to the local officials at 4 a.m. in the morning. At 5.30 a.m. of the same day before any one else knew of the declaration, Pandit Motilal Nehru and Syed Mahmud, who was then as now one of the General Secretaries of the Congress, were arrested as members of an unlawful association. Sardar Vallabhbhai Patel became the next President and on his arrest Maulana Abul Kalam Azad took his place. Dr. M.A. Ansari was the next president, but only for a few days, and Chowdhry Khaliq-uz-zaman followed him. On his release from jail after completing his six months term, Jawaharlal Nehru assumed charge, but he had only eight days of freedom. Shri J.M. Sen-Gupta then became president. He was followed by Shri Rajendra Prasad. On the discharge of all members of the Working Committee on January 26th Jawaharlal Nehru again took charge of the presidentship and he remained in office till the Karachi Congress.

Pandit Motilal Nehru was discharged from jail early in September, before his term expired, owing to ill health. The heavy burden of leading the movement during its most critical days, from April to the end of June, had fallen on him and in spite of advanced age and weak health he had not spared himself. His health was reaching breaking point when he was arrested. He went to prison, ill and worn out, and prison life made his condition worse. He came out prematurely, but the illness had got firm hold of him and was past cure. He did not assume charge of the presidentship but even from his bed of mortal illness, in spite of the entreaties of his doctors, he continued to guide the movement and to give his best to it.

Early in August the Working Committee met in Bombay. While the Committee was in session a procession organized by the Bombay P.C.C. was stopped by the police near the Victoria terminus and a vast concourse of people gathered there. The Committee, being informed of this situation, immediately went to the spot and put themselves in a body at the head of the procession which had been banned. All night long the members of the committee, including Pandit Madan Mohan Malaviya, and the processionists and large number of sympathisers and sightseers kept vigil in the open in spite of rain and inclement weather. In the morning the committee members were arrested and removed and, immediately after, there were brutal lathi charges on the procession and the crowd. Ever since, the place is known as "Lathi chowk" in Bombay.

The Working Committee continued to meet in spite of the declaration of its illegality. On August 25th the Delhi Government declared the Committee unlawful and two days later at its meeting held in that city, all the members present, including the President Dr. M.A. Ansari, but excluding two women members, were arrested *en bloc*.

The object of the "Unlawful Association Ordinance" was thus not to enable government to declare the Congress illegal. They had already done this and were doing it. The object was in the words of the Governor-General to enable "Government to take effective measures for the occupation of immoveable property and for forfeiture in certain conditions of moveable property used for the purpose of any association declared unlawful under the Criminal Law Amendment Act". This ordinance was enforced with great rigour and sometimes with much injustice. But the Congress found scope for satyagraha even in its wide folds. As Congress offices were occupied by the police and Congress workers and volunteers arrested or evicted new offices came into existence. In some cities after the declaration of illegality scores of houses put up sign boards that they were Congress offices and it became difficult for the police to raid all of them or to know which was the real office. In the smaller towns and in rural areas Congress offices were sometimes established in the open under trees and thus every opportunity was given to the police to arrest.

Another form of satyagraha was resorted to in some places. Volunteers tried peacefully and openly to regain possession of the premises from which they had been evicted by the police. This again led to further arrests and a long drawn out satyagraha was the result.

The ordinance failed signally to suppress the Congress. It demonstrated that while ordinances might come or go, the Congress would go on and Congress work would be carried on. The occupation of Congress offices could make little difference when every house could be turned into a Congress office; nor could arrests or lathi charges produce much effect, except to strengthen the movement, when the supply of those who were willing and eager to be arrested was practically inexhaustible.

The ordinances, bad as they were, were made worse in their application. Very flexible interpretations of their provisions were made by the courts. There was no uniformity in these interpretations and every magistrate decided for himself as to what constituted peaceful picketing. In Rajahmundry the police inspector declared a committee of lawyers about to take evidence as an unlawful assembly liable to dispersal, on the ground that the recording of evidence of witnesses as to police excesses encouraged civil disobedience. The District Magistrate of Guntur officially called upon the Municipal councillors to cancel a resolution to fly the national flag as this encouraged the operations of an unlawful association and made the councillors liable to prosecution.

The existing criminal law and the ordinances gave almost unlimited scope to the Government and their officials for any kind of repressive action. But the magistracy, and even more so the police, went even further and became laws unto themselves, knowing full well that they would be protected by their superiors. In the rural areas especially they had the fullest licence. They were not mistaken in the support they expected from higher quarters. Demands for enquiries into police excesses were not agreed to and every official from the Viceroy and the Provincial Governors downwards, and Ministers and prominent members of the British Parliament gave continuous and fulsome praise to the police.

CHAPTER VI

The Campaign Continued

Month after month went by, and Ordinances came, and people went to jail in an unending succession, and lathi charges became the commonest of occurrences, and firings ceased to surprise any one; and as horror succeeded horror, it was matched by greater courage and sacrifice. But civil disobedience went on, and the iron entered deeper into the soul of the people. And the face of India changed and those who knew her of old could hardly recognise her in her new-found youth and strength.

Life seemed to become outwardly one long round of processions and prabhatpheris and Flag salutations and monster meetings and hartals, and picketing and civil breach of the law and lathi charges and assaults and firings and arrests and long, sometimes rather lonely, spells in prison. But behind all this was the passionate urge to freedom and the grim resolve to gain it at whatever cost. The leader and author of the campaign lay in prison. But the inspiration he had given remained and his oft-repeated advice was not forgotten. To a remarkable degree this great mass movement stuck to its original pledge of non-violence and demonstrated to the world that our fight was clean and straight.

It is difficult to give an account of this period of the campaign. At an early stage nearly all prominent workers had been arrested. It was not the policy of the Government to arrest indiscriminately. They had had some experience of this in 1921 and they knew that such a policy was bound to fail as millions were ready to court arrest. Only the chief workers therefore were to be arrested and the others were to be dealt with by lathi charges. The lathi thus played a prominent part in 1930-31, and as lathi-raj spread, large and well-equipped Congress hospitals grew up in the bigger cities to treat the thousands of victims of police assaults. But arrests also continued and batch after batch of office-bearers and members of Congress Committees went to prison till all the old workers and thousands of new ones had been removed. The whole movement was thus in its second and subsequent stages in the hands of newcomers. In particular, women were coming into it and beginning to control it.

Everywhere there was a new life and everywhere women were in evidence. With rare devotion and courage they had thrown themselves into the struggle and had shamed many a man into following them, and sometimes, while men paused and considered, women acted. The leadership of the movement in provinces and local areas gradually passed to them and women "dictators" were to be found in many provinces. In Bombay specially the Desh Sevika Sangh played a memorable part and both their name and their "kesari" saris spread throughout India and became synonymous with service and disciplined sacrifice. One of their number, Shrimati Perin Captain, the inheritor and bearer of an honoured tradition, became the first woman dictator of the Bombay P.C.C. After her arrest Shrimati Hansa Mehta was dictator, and later Miss Sofia Somji functioned for a while before she too was arrested and sentenced. In Tamil Nad Shrimati Rukmani Lakshmipathi was the

2nd dictator and she was followed by Miss Pichumuthu Ammal. In the Punjab Shrimati Ladorani Zutshi was "dictator"; in the U.P. Shrimati Uma Nehru; in Berar Shrimati Durgavati Joshi; and in Kerala Shrimatis Aaron, Eswari Ammal, and K. Kunhi-Lakshmi Ammal; and in Utkal Shrimati Rama Devi. In Delhi province also there were women dictators.

In particular women took charge of the boycott programmes and the picketing. Gandhiji had specially appealed to them in an open letter addressed to the women of India which appeared in *Young India* of April 10, 1930. He did not wish them to confine themselves to the salt campaign as "there will be in it no suffering for which they are thirsting". But picketing must be a matter of "conversion" and not "coercion" and "who can make a more effective appeal to the heart than women?" The response to this call was beyond expectation. Everywhere, even where the custom of "parda" prevailed, women came out in the sun and in the rain to picket foreign cloth shops and liquor shops and face the wrath of the representatives of "law and order". Apart from making the boycott successful, women lent a peculiar grace and balance to the movement. Their presence in the front ranks of India's peaceful army of freedom and their readiness to suffer raised the tone of the struggle and made it adhere still more firmly to its foundation of non-violence. Many an ugly development was prevented by the timely intervention of women. Even official violence felt to some extent the restraining influence of the women in "kesari".

The Desh Sevika Sangh of Bombay was perhaps the largest and most prominent women's organization in the movement. The Sangh was organized in 1930 as the volunteer department of the Rashtriya Stree Sabha. The membership of the Sangh reached 500 and during the height of the movement no less than 300 Sevikas were on active service from day to day. Similar Desh Sevika Sanghs sprang up in other parts of the country. Among other women's organizations were the Naree Satyagraha Sangh of Calcutta, the Swayam Sevika Sangh and Stree Swarajya Sangh of Gujrat, and the Desh Sevika Sangham of Kerala. The Bombay branch of the Hindustani Seva Dal also organized a strong women's corps which took part in the campaign.

Accurate figures of arrests and convictions of women are not available for all provinces. In Bombay 200 women went to prison, in Bengal 200, in Delhi 221, in Gujrat 109 and in Punjab 100. The total number for all India must be between 1000 and 1500.

Even young boys and girls and little children played a noble part in the struggle and inspired their elders by their own enthusiasm. They formed Vanar Senas and Bal Sabhas and their processions, flag in hand, singing national songs, were familiar and pleasing sights in the cities. They took their full share in the sufferings that came. One of them, Rajpal, a young boy of about 12, met his death in Lahore. Many were sentenced to imprisonment and many were injured in police charges.

It is extraordinarily difficult to obtain accurate figures of convictions. The figures given by Government in answer to questions in the Legislative Assembly are patently incomplete. Large numbers of civil resisters who were arrested and convicted under the ordinary criminal law are not included in these statistics. The Provincial Congress Committees have supplied the following figures for convictions:

Province	*No. of convictions*	*Province*	*No. of convictions*
Ajmer	150	Delhi	4500
Andhra	2878	Gujrat	3549
Assam	1459	Karnatak	1900
Behar	14251	Kerala	450
Bengal	15000	Maharashtra	4000
Berar	1750	Punjab	12000
Bombay	4700	Sind	724
C.P. Hindustani	2255	Tamil Nad	2991
C.P. Marathi	907	U.P.	12651
		Utkal	1009
	Total 87,124		

The Frontier Province is not included in this list as complete statistics have not been received from there. A communication received from the N.W.F.P.C.C. in November 1930 put the total number of arrests at that time at 2328. There can be no doubt that this figure went up considerably by the time of the Delhi truce and must have reached at least 4000. This brings up the all India total to 91,124. Even this figure is likely to err on the moderate side as information from rural areas was difficult to obtain. It may be stated therefore without exaggeration that the total number of convictions in connection with the civil disobedience movement was about one hundred thousand. Burma is not included.

This hundred thousand is only a small part of the large numbers, running into many millions, who took some part in the campaign. The movement represented the effort of the whole nation in which all the different groups and communities and vast numbers of individuals took more or less share. The Hindus, being in a great majority in the country, naturally took a predominant part so far as numbers went. The Muslims' share was also marked. It is estimated that about 12,000 of them went to prison. Reference has already been made to the Frontier province where the whole burden of the fight fell on the Muslims. In the Punjab and in Bombay and Delhi prominent part was taken by the Muslims. The Jamiat-ul-Ulema, the respected organization of Muslim divines, officially co-operated with the Congress in the campaign and many of its office bearers went to prison. Of the acting presidents of the Congress during the year three were Muslims and two of these went to jail.

Sikhs gave notable support in the campaign specially in their home province, the Punjab, and large numbers of them went to prison. The Parsis, though small in numbers in the country, played a conspicuous and distinguished part. Of the other smaller communities, the Christians and Anglo-Indians and Jews, all had their representatives in the ranks of India's peaceful fighters.

Of the different classes all contributed to some extent. Specially worthy of mention is the part of the merchants specially in Bombay, who, often at considerable loss to themselves, threw themselves into the struggle. The success of the foreign cloth boycott and the British goods boycott was largely due to their co-operation. The industrialists also helped in the boycott but this resulted in helping their own mills at a time of great depression. The agreements entered into by them with the

Congress, through the instrumentality of Pandit Motilal Nehru, put the boycott and swadeshi movements on a firm and rational basis. The Federation of Indian Chambers of Commerce and Industry, the most important organization of Indian commercial and business interests, allied itself to the national movement by boycotting both the Assembly and the first Round Table Conference.

Many classes and groups helped. The industrial workers took a real and effective part in many factory areas. The man in the street was even to the fore in taking his part in the struggle and in getting his share of lathi blows. But the real burden of the struggle fell on the peasantry. As the struggle developed the village began to play a more prominent part than the town. Most of the volunteers came from the rural areas, and while the leadership remained largely with the towns, the strength and backbone came from the villages.

Effects of the Boycotts

Some statistics may help in appreciating the effects of the boycott of foreign cloth and liquor. It must be remembered, however, in regard to the former that there was a worldwide wave of depression and the foreign cloth trade might have been reduced to some extent because of this.

Imports of Piece-goods	*Quantity in yards*			*Total*
	United Kingdom	Japan	Other countries	
1926-27	1,466,874,209	243,587,199	77,482,000	1787944386
1927-28	1,543,110,423	323,053,458	107,216,008	1973379889
1928-29	1,456,092,130	357,343,077	123,325,305	1936760512
1929-30	1,247,539,321	561,965,625	109,841,566	1919346512
1930-31	523,431,001	320,694,043	45,844,862	889969906

Import of Piece-goods	*Value in rupees*			
1926-27	447375113	65755166	37020723	550150952
1927-28	427423486	82474783	41425392	551323661
1928-29	404301889	88928981	44907917	538138787
1929-30	336539600	126956110	39015126	502510836
1930-31	125729210	59279780	15481029	200488028

Import Duty on Cotton Piece-goods and yarn		
		Rs.
1928-29	-	6,50,29,000
1929-30	-	6,28,79,000
1930-31	-	4,03,48,000

Note: Duties were increased on cotton piece-goods in March 1930 and accordingly the Government of India estimated to receive Rs. 7,66,80,000 instead of which they only received Rs. 4,03,480.

Imports of Merchandise

There was a drop of $31^1/_2$ per cent in the value of private imports of merchandise which decreased from 238.9 crores in 1929-30 to 163.6 crores in 1930-31. The largest decreases were in cotton yarn and manufactures (from 5949 to 2525 lakhs); metal-iron and steel (from 1720 to 1088 lakhs); machinery (from 1935 to 1513 lakhs); sugar (from 1578 to 1096 lakhs); and vehicles other than locomotives (from 1085 to 731 lakhs).

Imports of wheat from Australia fell from 498 to 215 lakhs. Imports of cotton from East Africa and America went up from 296 and 20 lakhs to 515 and 83 lakhs respectively.

Fall in Excise Revenue

Province	*Excise Revenue in 1000's of rupees*		
	1929-30	1930-31	Loss in 1000's
Madras (including Coorg)	5,96,17	5,27,63	68,54
Bombay	4,02,06	3,01,56	1,00,50
Bengal	2,26,25	1,80,36	45,89
United Provinces	1,29,86	1,11,82	18,04
Punjab	1,13,73	1,14,88	
Burma (including Shan States)	1,28,31	1,08,55	19,76
Behar & Orissa	1,90,81	1,42,11	48,70
Central Provinces and Berar	1,25,45	86,29	39,16
Assam	66,23	58,37	7,86
Total	19,78,87	16,31,57	3,48,45

Deficits of Central and Provincial Governments
(In lakhs of rupees)

	Revenue	*Expenditure*	*Deficit*
Central	123,44	136,12	12,68
Bombay	13,43	14,62	1,19
Bengal	9,82	11,56	1,74
Madras	17,25	17,81	56
United Provinces	12,30	12,80	50
Punjab	11,31	11,41	10
Behar & Orissa	5,43	6,14	71
C.P.	5,00	5,22	22
Assam	2,62	2,79	17
Burma	10,11	11,09	98
		Total	18,85 lakhs

CHAPTER VII

Repression

Civil disobedience was sought to be crushed by the Government by violence and methods of terrorism. As the freedom movement gained strength the violence of government against the civil resister increased. Repression began by the arrest and conviction of noted leaders and workers. From the very beginning however the lathi played a prominent part and the use of it became progressively more brutal. In Bombay the Congress hospital alone treated 1300 indoor and 2500 outdoor victims of lathi charges. A number of eminent Bombay doctors issued a statement giving statistics of the injuries caused by the lathi in Bombay and showing how injuries on the head and other vital parts were increasing with each subsequent charge. Probably many more thousands than were treated in the Congress hospital were injured in Bombay. On the Garhwali Day in Bombay 800 were injured and on the Tilak Jayanti Day 500 received injuries. During the Dharasana raids 1333 persons were wounded. In Behar on one day—the Jawahar Day celebrations—over 900 were wounded. In Barisal a single day's lathi charge resulted in 500 persons being injured. These are instances of what occurred all over India with increasing frequency for many months. Even ambulance workers, spectators and press correspondents were not spared. It might be mentioned that many mourning processions which took place on Pandit Motilal Nehru's death were forcibly dispersed in many places. It is quite impossible to collect full statistics of the total number injured, specially in the numerous organized assaults by the police in rural areas. Many a city in India has given new names to its public squares and open spaces in memory of these lathi charges—lathi chowks, Azad maidans, etc.

Some instances of Government violence and methods of terrorism have been mentioned in previous chapters of this report. There was a great variety of such methods—from personal violence and indecent handling of men and women and ill treatment in prisons, to martial law in some and firing in many places. In Madras on Jan. 27, 1931 Shri K.N. Bhashyam, a leading lawyer of the High Court was individually attacked with lathis and chased along the street, while peacefully picketing a foreign cloth shop. Punitive police was stationed generally in rural areas and military columns were marched through the countryside. The police entered private houses and belaboured the inmates and often destroyed charkhas and household goods. Volunteer camps were destroyed and their property taken away or looted. Congress offices were being continually raided. National flags were publicly burnt and prominent citizens of villages were sometimes taken to the market place and, to add insult to injury, were publicly beaten with shoes. In Midnapore district people were forced to prostrate themselves and rub their noses on the ground.

The usual means of communications by post or telegram or telephone were denied as a rule to Congressmen, and newspapers were threatened with dire penalties if they gave publicity to Congress news or reports of police atrocities. Printing presses were also under the same ban.

In Andhra and in Midnapore and in Shamli in the district of Muzaffarnagar and in many other places people appearing in Gandhi caps in the streets were assaulted by the police and the caps were forcibly removed. At Guntur the District Magistrate passed an order against the wearing of Gandhi caps. At Bezwada and Vellore railway stations these caps were regularly seized by the police from passengers who might be wearing them. At Angalur in Andhra the keeping of charkhas and *taklis* and the wearing of khaddar were prohibited. Khaddar clad people were frequently attacked in rural areas. At Tirupati and Antarvedi, in Andhra, where religious festivals are held in January, all Gandhi cap wearers were prohibited from taking part in these festivals. Those who refused to give up their caps were beaten.

In Bezwada a blind old man of about 80 was sentenced to 2 years' imprisonment. In Bombay a highly respected Muslim lady, 65 years of age, the daughter of the late Mr. Justice Badruddin Tyabji, was sentenced to four months' rigorous imprisonment for peaceful picketing of a liquor shop.

Treatment in Jails

Assaults were not confined to people outside the walls of prison. Lathi charges took place even on the political prisoners even inside jail in a large number of prisons, notably in Calcutta, Allahabad, Lucknow, Monghyr, Bhagalpur, Purulia, Anmer, Patna, Cannanore, Trichinopoly and Balasore. During such a charge in a Calcutta jail even Shri J.M. Sen-Gupta and Shri Subhas Chandra Bose were not spared. In the Allahabad District Jail organized and brutal assaults were made on the political prisoners repeatedly.

The provincial reports, and specially the reports of the Visapur Jail Enquiry Committee and a committee appointed by the U.P. P.C.C. give numerous instances of ill treatment of political prisoners. Prisoners were divided into three classes—A, B, and C. Many Congressmen objected to this differential treatment which was often a source of irritation and friction. The vast majority of prisoners were in class C and were supposed to be treated like ordinary criminals. In practice, they were often treated worse and were singled out for difficult tasks. Attempts were made in many places to force satyagrahis into tendering apologies and printed forms were prepared for the purpose. The jails were over-crowded and even the release of thousands of ordinary convicts to make room for the satyagrahis did not relieve the tension. Vast new camp jails were then hurriedly erected and these seldom contained even the conveniences which the ordinary jails possessed.

Ordinarily the satyagrahi prisoners willingly submitted themselves to the discipline of the jail. But wherever it was felt that humiliation was intended or that any practice was degrading, there was often a refusal to submit to it. This refusal gave rise to most of the assaults and punishments in jail. In Assam and Behar and Utkal prisoners were made to call out "Sarkar salam" during parade. This was strongly objected to as being humiliating and after much trouble the order was withdrawn. "Parade" was also a fruitful source of trouble in most jails because of other causes.

In the Lucknow District Jail satyagrahi prisoners were severely beaten and forcibly locked up for refusing to go into the barracks in the evening owing to excessive heat. Some of the injuries were serious. Shri Mohanlal Saksena, a leading Congressman, was punished with solitary confinement and forfeiture of remission for preparing a list of the injured and requesting the Superintendent to institute an enquiry.

In the Amraoti Jail a satyagrahi under high fever was given a heavy task. He died as a result of this. In Bijapur Jail also a satyagrahi prisoner, Ram Chandra Pande, who was suffering from a severe attack of dysentery, was made to work at stone-breaking. He succumbed soon after. His aged mother was not allowed to see him and his dead body was not given to his relatives. In Aligarh a prisoner was dragged by his fetters when he refused to join the morning parade. His left leg was badly hurt but fetters were kept on for eight or nine days and he was not removed to hospital. He was later released and had to be operated upon in the leg.

The Inspector General of Prisons in the U.P. issued a circular to the Superintendents of Prisons authorising them and indeed encouraging them to resort to flogging in the case of any breach of jail discipline. This was specially meant for political prisoners and as a consequence satyagrahis were flogged in Mirzapur, Ghazipur and Allahabad. This circular gave rise to great indignation among the satyagrahi prisoners and the general public and the lathi charges in the Allahabad District Jail were caused because of the friction resulting from it. The circular was subsequently withdrawn.

The U.P. P.C.C's Jail Enquiry Committee's report reveals an even more revolting attempt to humiliate and degrade the prisoners. It states that juvenile satyagrahi prisoners were placed with habituals, some of whom had been convicted for unnatural offences, and the latter were encouraged to molest them. This was done in order to force them to apologise and give undertakings not to take part in political activities in the future.

The Visapur Jail Enquiry Report reveals such an extraordinary state of affairs that the full report is being given as an appendix to this Report.

Complaints of bad and sandy food and insufficient covering during the winter months, resulting frequently in illness and sometimes death were very common throughout the jails. Bars and fetters and solitary cells were frequent punishments. Occasionally satyagrahi prisoners resorted to the hunger-strike as a method of protest.

Firings

The police and occasionally the military, fired at peaceful crowds on numerous decisions. The most fatal of these firings was at Peshawar in April 1930 to which reference has already been made. In Sholapur there was also indiscriminate shooting. In the N.W.F.P. firing took place on many occasions. In most other provinces, and specially in Bengal and the U.P. there was repeated firing. At Mymensing firing took place on pickets of liquor and ganja shops on May 14, 1930 and as many as 90 persons were injured. At Seoni in C.P. Hindustani a peaceful group of 25 liquor pickets were fired upon and five persons were killed. Of these three were women.

At Chirnur in the Pannel Taluq of Maharashtra an extraordinary instance of firing took place in which besides 14 others the Magistrate himself was shot dead.

Fifty persons were injured. As no member of the public had a fire arm it is clear that the police shot their own magistrate either accidentally or intentionally. About 5000 persons had gathered for forest satyagraha and wood was being cut. The police arrested 15 or 20 persons and handcuffed them. Some people protested against the handcuffing and thereupon the handcuffs were removed under the magistrate's orders. Later as the people were returning some kind of scuffle seems to have taken place and firing was suddenly resorted to. No one knows who gave the order for firing. An independent enquiry was demanded but was refused by Government. An unofficial enquiry committee was not permitted to visit the place. This incident illustrates the irresponsible manner in which firing often took place and how Government tried to suppress the truth. It was usually alleged when firing took place that the police had been attacked but the police did not seem to suffer from such alleged attacks. At Chaukraden in Nasik District the villagers were fired upon and 12 were killed. The allegation was that they had attacked the police but not the least injury was caused to any policeman.

The provincial reports give the following figures showing the number of places in each province where firing took place:

Andhra	2
Behar	5
Bengal	10
Bombay	4
C.P. (H)	4
Delhi	2
Gujrat	2
Maharashtra	2
N.W.F.P.	Many places and repeated at the same places
Punjab	Several places
Sind	1
Tamil Nad	6
U.P.	10
Utkal	1

Other Instances of Repression and Terrorism

Mention has already been made in this chapter as well as in previous chapters of this Report to acts of repression and terrorism perpetrated by officials of the Government in their attempt to crush the civil disobedience movement. Some further typical instances are given below:

(1) On 22nd December 1930 in Peddapuram in the East Godavari District a picnic party was given by a zamindar to his friends. The gathering was a social one and was in no way political. Neither the host nor most of his guests were connected with the civil disobedience campaign. While the guests were having refreshments a police party with lathis suddenly appeared and without any warning started beating the bewildered guests with their lathis. The picnic party dispersed soon enough but even the departing guests were beaten. Among the wounded was a lady guest.

(2) On 25th May 1930 there was a severe lathi charge on a procession in Lucknow. Many onlookers were injured. Among these was a young boy who had his head broken. He was taken to a house nearby. His mother and aunt were washing his wounds when a police officer came and started beating both the ladies in spite of their protests and weeping.

(3) The Congress office at Bihpur in Behar was occupied by the police on May 1, 1930. Thereupon jathas of volunteers used to go daily to the office to demand possession. They were beaten and sometimes arrested. On the 9th May Shri Rajendra Prasad, Prof. Abdul Bari and other well-known persons went to the place to see how these jathas were being treated. A large crowd of spectators also collected but all of these stood a hundred yards away from the jatha. The jatha, contrary to usual practice, was quietly arrested. The police then hurried to the crowd and the Superintendent of Police shouted "*maro sale ko*". According to Shri Rajendra Prasad the crowd was absolutely peaceful and would have dispersed soon. The attack on it was wholly unprovoked and the leaders present were specially singled out by the S.P. and the police. Prof. Abdul Bari was badly injured and even after he sat down with blood flowing from a gaping wound in the head, he continued to be beaten. Shri Rajendra Prasad was also beaten, as also many other prominent persons present. As a result of this incident at Bihpur 150 chowkidars and 6 presidents of chowkidars' unions resigned. Five newly elected members of the Legislative Council also resigned.

(4) The district of Midnapore in Bengal had to submit to a reign of terror for many months. A non-official committee enquired into some of the occurrences at Contai. Their findings are given in an appendix to this report. The following extract from a statement addressed to Gandhiji, which appeared in *Young India*, gives an idea of the state of affairs in that part of the country.

> The tortures at Contai and its sub-centres are daily becoming more and more heartless and barbarous. Every day the officials and the constables beat mercilessly in one or the other centre. They take away caps, tear away shirts and cane the satyagrahis severely. They give blows and kicks in the lower abdomen till many drop down senseless. I could not believe when I first heard that a stick was thrust into the rectum of a volunteer when he was lying senseless, but the statement of a doctor friend (an ex-I.M.S.) who examined the satyagrahi set all my doubts at rest. They adopt many mean tactics. They spoil the food when the volunteers are dining or when it is being cooked or is just ready. They throw away rice and dal or take it away to their camps. The volunteers often have to go without food.
>
> They follow three methods (1) keep the leaders away from the field; (2) torture the satyagrahis so that they may run away and leave the movement; and (3) terrorise the masses to remain aloof so that it may not develop into a mass upheaval. Therefore, whichever villager openly helps the satyagrahis is severely dealt with. Sometimes the constables surround the houses of those that are in sympathy with us, terrorise them and do not even spare the ladies.

(5) Shri Satish Chandra Das Gupta gives the following instance of torture in *Young India*.

> One old man was taken and wrapped in a woollen *kambal* was made to sit on a hot brick under a blazing sun for hours. Then he was whipped, no water being given till he became

senseless through beating. He was then given water to revive only to be whipped to unconsciousness again.

(6) The following instance is from Viramgam in Gujrat. Some volunteers had been confined at the railway station within a police cordon for a long time. It was a hot summer day and they were given no water. When information reached the town that the volunteers were fainting for want of water a large number of women rushed to the station with jugs of water. After giving water they were returning when the mounted police came and beat them with their lathis. Some women fell down and were also injured by the horses' hoofs. One of the injured women has given the following statement:

> Women came out after giving the men water and began to move out slowly. Then came dazzling lights of a motor car on them and about 20 mounted police rushed in and ran their horses among them beating them with lathis saying, 'Beat them, beat them'. One woman with a child was running, and in so doing she dropped the child. She cried out that her child had fallen down. At this time the mounted police were running their horses and were freely using lathis. I was at that time very near, so I ran to rescue the child and to hand the child over to her, but she in fright had run away. As I lifted up the child one mounted policeman gave me a lathi blow on my right hand. . . . The child was about four months old.

(7) In Champaran a volunteer had a long needle pierced through the palm of his hand in several places. In Saran district a volunteer named Sunderlal died as a result of beating by the police.

(8) A young boy, aged 10 or 12, was caught picketing in Shahabad district and was tied to a bundle with a rope, suspended into a well, taken out and asked if he would do picketing again; the process was repeated several times, and ultimately he was branded with red hot pice at several places and then let off.

(9) In Calcutta there were daily lathi charges for some time on students picketing the University and boys were beaten till many fainted. Girl picketers were taken far out in a motor car and left by themselves in the wilderness.

During a visit to Calcutta by Shrimati Mira Bai a procession was organized in her honour. This was charged with lathis. Police sergeants and constables also entered the Ashutosh Building in College Square and beat teachers and students indiscriminately while university classes were actually being held. The Vice-Chancellor visited the place soon after and found the blood marks on the floor and walls. The university authorities protested strongly against this brutality.

(10) In Hubli even a public library—the Tilak Grantha Sangraha—was declared unlawful.

(11) In Kerala a student, P.K. Panikkar, while addressing a public meeting was beaten and dragged away by the police. He was brutally assaulted in the lock-up. He fainted several times. On regaining consciousness he was beaten again. He died some months later.

(12) In Kerala also, Shri Sankaran Nambiar, a prominent worker of North Malabar, was invited by the sub-inspector of police to his house and was assaulted and beaten when he went there. This was because he had criticised the police the previous day in a speech.

(13) In the Tamil Nad Shri C. Rajagopalachari marched with 100 satyagrahis to

the seacoast at Vedaranyam to inaugurate the salt satyagraha campaign. En route at Tanjore the District Magistrate issued a notice that any one giving food, shelter or assistance to the satyagrahis would be prosecuted under the Penal Code. His order however had little effect on the public who welcomed the satyagrahis. At Vedaranyam there were lathi charges on the volunteers and individual satyagrahis were brutally beaten. Three volunteers were almost beaten to death and left on the prickly pear bushes on the outskirts of Vedaranyam. Later, the whole camp was demolished and all volunteers were arrested.

(14) The Congress hospital in Madras was raided by the police and the manager, the cook and the ward attendants were all arrested.

(15) At Berhampur in Utkal the salt satyagrahis were brutally attacked on 25 April 1930. Sixty were rendered unconscious and were left untended on the hot sands. On the 25th May 1930 there was another lathi charge at Berhampur in which 200 persons were wounded, including the representatives of two newspapers—*The Hindu* of Madras and the *Statesman* of Calcutta.

(16) At Sholapur during the Martial Law period, apart from indiscriminate firings, every attempt was made to humiliate and terrorise the inhabitants. Amazing sentences were passed for trifling offences. For an alleged offence of evading arrest the sentences passed ranged up to seven years' imprisonment plus Rs. 10,000 fine. Four young men—Malappa Dhansheti, Shri Krishna Sarda, A. Qurban Husain and Jagannath Sindhi—were sentenced to death although they were believed by everyone concerned to be wholly innocent. Representations from all over India were made for their reprieve but they were rejected. The four young men were hung in Yervada jail in January 1931 and there were many demonstrations of sympathy resulting in lathi charges.

(17) In the North West Frontier Province conditions were very different from those prevailing in other parts of India. For some time there was martial law, but even the ordinary law there is but a variation of martial law.

Even the lathi charges were of a special kind. Villages would be surrounded at dead of night and all inhabitants turned out of their houses and then attacked. While the military and the Frontier constabulary surrounded the village, the police would loot the houses.

The raid on the office of the Khudai Khidmatgars was typical. Eight hundred British troops, a regiment of Indian cavalry and 300 Shia soldiers were posted outside the village. There were also many Lewis and machine guns. Then there was raiding and plunder and brutal assaults and the office was burnt down.

(18) The following instance is typical of the methods used to realise chowkidari tax. In village Gokulnagar in Tamluk in Bengal a sum of Rs. 11/4 was due from the whole village. To recover this over 30 houses and several granaries were burnt down. The total value of the property destroyed was not less than Rs. 10,000/-.

(19) In Tamluk also the police raided the house of Upendra Chandra Maity, the leading lawyer of the town, who was then in jail. The women were ordered to be taken out of the house. They were escorted out by Dr. Mahendra Maity. When Dr. Maity returned he was abused in a filthy manner and then whipped till the blood came out of his wounds. He was also spat upon. Finally he was taken to the house of a neighbour, Ishwar Maity. Armed constables were placed on either side

of him and he was forced, on threat of being shot down on the spot, to set fire to his neighbour's house. The house was burnt down.

(20) In the village of Mohanpur, district Midnapore, the chowkidari tax had been withheld. On June 20, 1930, the Additional District Magistrate, the Excise Superintendent and 25 armed policemen under a sub-inspector came to the village and went to the house of Shri Hrishikesh Ghose, a leading resident and vice-president of the Union Board. Shri Ghose was not in the village nor were any other male members of the family present. The police entered the house, put all the ladies under custody and then broke open the boxes and even destroyed part of a wall where they suspected treasure was hidden away. They took away Rs. 3700 in cash, 4 tolas of gold and 100 tolas of silver, ornaments, a bicycle, a harmonium and many other articles worth about Rs. 1000. They broke into pieces the brass and other utensils and destroyed large stores of provisions by pouring kerosene oil on them after mixing them together. Documents and other papers were torn and thrown away.

(21) In September 1930 a Circle Officer with policemen visited Chorpolia in Midnapore district. A large number of villagers went in deputation to them and stated with folded hands that they were unable to pay the chowkidari tax owing to their poverty. They asked for remission or for postponement. The villagers were thereupon attacked by the police from two sides simultaneously with lathis and about 200 of them were thus forced into a tank as there was no other way of escape. As the men in the water struggled to the bank and tried to come out they were hit with lathis and pelted with hard sods and thus driven back. Many were seriously injured. The next day five dead bodies were found floating in the tank. . . .[3]

. . . .[4] On Nov. 16 Jawahar Day was celebrated all over the country and the speech for which he had been sentenced was read out at public meetings and adopted. Meetings and processions were prohibited in most places, but despite these prohibitory orders, they were held. The day was celebrated at 384 places. There was one firing and numerous lathi charges. One person was killed, 1500 were wounded and 1679 were arrested on that day. Behar had the most widespread celebration and suffered most, 987 persons being injured and 584 arrested, besides one killed.

(25) In Borsad Shrimati Lilavatiben led a procession on January 15, 1931 in defiance of an order under Section 144 Cr.P.C. She was arrested and almost dragged to the lock-up. On her refusal to give her address she was slapped on the face several times by the sub-inspector of police who then pulled her by the hair and threw her down on the ground. She fainted and remained unconscious the whole night.

(26) The news of Lilavatiben's ill treatment raised a storm of resentment and the Kheda D.C.C. fixed the 21 January 1931 as a day of protest. A large women's gathering was arranged at Borsad. About 1400 women gathered from all parts of the taluqa. Even before the time for their procession and meeting, the police went to the bazaar and ordered the shopkeepers to close their shops. The shopkeepers

[3] Last few lines of para (21) missing. Paras (22) and (23) also missing.

[4] First few lines of para (24) missing.

were beaten even as they were closing their doors. Some people running away entered a library nearby. The police chased them inside the library and beat every one they found there, including the librarian. The shopkeepers had done nothing aggressive which might offend the police, nor had there been the slightest disturbance.

Later a group of women started in procession. The police charged them with lathis and attacked. . . . [incomplete].

APPENDIX 2

A Socialist Syllabus, January 1934[1]

Foreword

This syllabus obviously is meant to be [n]either complete [n]or exhaustive. On socialism there is quite a vast literature. A very large portion of this literature, however, is polemical, repetitious, fragmentary and now, in the light of the present collapse of capitalism and democracy and the success of Russia, hopelessly out of date. This portion of the socialist literature therefore is simply not worth bothering about, except to gain a knowledge of the historical development of socialist thought. This knowledge can be gained even from one single good book on the history of socialism. Laidler's *History of Socialist Thought* for instance is a fine book for this purpose though written from a non-Marxian point of view. As far as the understanding of socialism is concerned the best rule is to go to Marx-Engels and Lenin and to follow closely the Russian experiment—which by the way, seems to have definitely grown out of the experimental stage, now, though yet growing and changing. Marx and Engels were the founders of scientific socialism and Lenin its greatest and most successful exponent and Russia is the only country in the world today where a serious attempt is being made to build up a socialist society. Therefore, for one wishing to understand socialism it is just as necessary to know what is being done in Russia as to read these great teachers of socialism.

Perhaps it is well to warn the beginner against a common danger—the danger of falling into a futile and academic controversy. Before the World War and to some extent even after it there used to rage in socialist camps a great but worthless controversy which may be briefly described as "revolutionism vs. evolutionism". The whole controversy has become entirely beside the point now. Democratic institutions are crumbling everywhere. There is no question today of a gradual evolution to socialism. Every one today realises that what is required is swift and resolute action. Capitalism threatened with extinction is nowhere in a mood to let socialists slowly and pleasantly (for everybody) clip its wings and chop off its limbs bit by bit. Today it is in a desperate mood and will not allow any monkeying.

[1] *JP Papers* (NMML). The syllabus was prepared by the Socialist Research Institute, Patna, January 1934.

A Socialist Syllabus
For the Guidance of Persons Interested in Socialism
Prepared by the Socialist Research Institute
For Beginners

General

1. Marx and Engels: *The Communist Manifesto.*
2. F. Engels: *Socialism Scientific and Utopian.*
3. T. Kirkup: *A Primer of Socialism.*
4. Joseph E. Cohen: *Socialism for Students.*
5. Charles H. Vail: *Principles of Scientific Socialism.*
6. Charles C. Hitchcock: *The Socialist Argument.*
7. Harry W. Laidler: *Socialism in Thought and Action.*
8. N. Bukharin and E. Preobrazhensky: *The A.B.C. of Communism.*

Books that help in understanding Marx

1. Max Beer: *The Life and Teachings of Karl Marx.*
2. Max Beer: *Guide to the Study of Marx.*
3. Lenin: *The Teachings of Karl Marx.*
4. Julian Borchardt: *The People's Marx.*
5. A.D. Lindsay: *Karl Marx' Capital.*
6. E.B. Aveling: *The Student's Marx.*
7. Karl Kautsky: *The Economic Theories of Karl Marx.*

Books by Marx

1. *The Communist Manifesto.*
2. *Wage-Labour and Capital.*
3. *Value, Price and Profit.*
4. *Civil War in France.*

Recent Books on Marxian Economics

1. Bogdanoff: *A Short Course of Economic Science.*
2. Tracts on Economics published by Martin Lawrence for the 'Marxist Study Course', Parts I to XI (6d. a part).

Books on Lenin

1. J. Maxton: *Lenin.*
2. R. Palme Dutt: *Lenin.*
3. N. Bukharin: *Lenin as a Marxist.*

Books by Lenin

1. *State and Revolution.*
2. *Imperialism.*

3. *What Is To Be Done.*
4. *Socialism and War.*
5. *The Revolution of 1905.*

Miscellaneous

1. Karl Kautsky: *The Class Struggle.*
2. Karl Kautsky: *The Social Revolution.*
3. Ernest Untermann: *The World's Revolutions.*
4. Paul Lefargue: *The Evolution of Property.*
5. Paul Lefargue: *The Right to be Lazy.*
6. Maurice Dobb: *Development of Capitalism.*
7. Emile Burns: *Modern Finance.*
8. Varga: *The Process of Capitalist Decline.*
9. Leonard Woolf: *Economic Imperialism.*
10. J.A. Hobson: *From Capitalism to Socialism.*
11. Emile Burns: *Capitalism, Communism and the Transition.*
12. R. Palme Dutt: *Fascism.*
13. G.D.H. Cole: *The World of Labour.*
14. R.W. Postgate: *The Workers' International.*
15. Bertrand Russel: *Proposed Roads to Freedom.*
16. C.E.H. Joad: *An Introduction to Modern Political Theory.*
17. H.J. Laski: *An Introduction to Politics.*
18. Shaw, Laski and others: *Where Socialism Stands To-day?*
19. John Strachey: *The Coming Struggle for Power.*
20. P.H. Box: *Russia (A Short History).*
21. N. Mirsky: *A Short History of Russia.* (?)
22. John Reed: *Ten Days that Shook the World.*
23. John Reed: *Humanity Uprooted.*
24. H.N. Brailsford: *How the Soviets Work.*
25. (?) *Moscow Has a Plan.*
26. Y.A. Yakovlev: *Red Villages.*
27. R. Bishop: *From Peasant to Collective Farmer.*
28. Maurice Hindus: *The Great Offensive.*

For Advanced Reading

A. General

1. T. Kirkup: *History of Socialism.*
2. Harry W. Laidler: *History of Socialist Thought.*
3. William Morris and Ernest B. Bax: *Socialism, Its Growth and Outcome.*
4. Max Beer: *History of British Socialism*, 2 volumes.
5. Robert Hunter: *Socialists at Work.*
6. W.E. Walling: *Socialism as it is, a Survey of the World's Revolutionary Movement.*
7. S.P. Orth: *Socialism and Democracy in Europe.*

8. George Plekhanov: *Anarchism and Socialism.*
9. G.D.H. Cole: *Guild Socialism Restated.*
10. National Guild League: *Guild Socialism.*
11. Harry W. Laidler and Norman Thomas: *The Socialism of Our Times.*
12. G.B. Shaw: *The Intelligent Woman's Guide to Socialism.*

B. Books by Marx and Engels

1. *The Eighteenth Brumaire of Louis Bonaparte.*
2. *Peasant War in Germany* (Engels).
3. *Revolution and Counter-Revolution in Germany* (Engels).
4. *A Critique of the Gotha Programme.*
5. *The Holy Family.*
6. *The Poverty of Philosophy.*
7. *Feuerbach: The Roots of Socialist Philosophy* (Engels).
8. *The Revolutionary Act* (Engels).
9. *Landmarks of Scientific Socialism (Anti-Duehring)* (Engels).
10. *A Contribution to the Critique of Political Economy.*
11. *Capital*, 3 volumes.

C. Books Dealing with Different Aspects of Marxism

General

1. Louis Boudin: *The Theoretical System of Karl Marx.*
2. Lenin: *Marx-Engels-Marxism.*
3. Maurice Dobb: *On Marxism To-day.*
4. Sydney Hook: *Towards the Understanding of Marx.*
5. V.G. Simkovitch: *Marxism Versus Socialism.*
6. J.M. Rubinow: *Was Marx Wrong? A Critique of "Marxism Vs. Socialism".*

Philosophical

1. George Plekhanov: *Fundamental Problems of Marxism.*
2. Antonio Labriola: *Socialism and Philosophy.*
3. Karl Kautsky: *Ethics and the Materialist Conception of History.*
4. F. Engels: *Feuerbach, The Roots of Socialist Philosophy.*
5. F. Engels: *Landmarks of Scientific Socialism.*
6. Lenin: *Materialism and Empirio-Criticism.*
7. John Mac Murray: *The Philosophy of Communism.*

Sociological

1. N. Bukharin: *Historical Materialism.*
2. Antonio Labriola: *Essays on the Materialist Conception of History.*
3. Benedetto Croce: *Historical Materialism and the Economics of Karl Marx.*
4. Karl Kautsky: *The Class Struggle.*
5. Karl Kautsky: *The Social Revolution.*

Economic

1. Karl Kautsky: *The Economic Theories of Karl Marx.*
2. Emmet: *The Marxian Economic Book.*
3. Benedetto Croce: *Historical Materialism and the Economics of Karl Marx.*
4. N. Bukharin: *The Economic Theory of the Leisure Class.*

D. An Excellent Text Book on Economics

1. J. Lapidims K. Ostrovitysnov: *An Outline of Political Economy.*

E. Books by Lenin

1. *Left Wing Communism, An Infantile Disorder.*
2. *The Paris Commune.*
3. *Two Tactics.*
4. *The Proletarian Revolution and Kautsky the Renegade.*
5. *The Imperialist War.*
6. *The War and the Second International.*
7. *Towards the Seizure of Power.*
8. *On the Road to Insurrection.*
9. *Marx-Engels—Marxism.*
10. *Collected Works.*

F. For an Able Summary of Lenin's Views

1. Joseph Stalin: *Leninism*, 2 volumes.

G. Biographies

1. Wilhelm Liebknecht: *Memoirs of Karl Marx.*
2. Max Beer: *The Life and Teachings of Karl Marx.*
3. D. Ryazanov (ed.): *Karl Marx, Man, Thinker and Revolutionist.*
4. D. Ryazanov: *Karl Marx & Friedich Engels.*
5. A. Labriola: *Karl Marx.*
6. Karl Kautsky: *F. Engels, His Life, His Work and His Writings.*
7. R.W. Postgate: *Karl Marx.*
8. N. Mescheviakov: *Life of Marx.*
9. M. Mirsky: *Lenin.*
10. J. Maxton: *Lenin.*
11. R. Palme Dutt: *Lenin.*
12. Martin (?): *Lenin.*
13. N.K. Krupskaya: *Memories of Lenin*, 2 volumes.
14. M. Gorky: *Days with Lenin.*

H. Books on Imperialism

1. J.A. Hobson: *Imperialism.*
2. Moon: *Imperialism and World Politics.*
3. Lenin: *Imperialism.*
4. N. Bukharin: *Imperialism and World Economy.*
5. Michael Pavlovitch: *The Foundations of Imperialist Policy.*
6. R. Fox: *Colonial Policy of British Imperialism.*
7. Labour Research Departments Pamphlets on Imperialism in various countries.
8. Scott Nearing and Joseph Freeman: *Dollar Diplomacy, A Study in American Imperialism.*

I. Books on the Present World Crisis

1. G.D.H. Cole: *The Intelligent Man's Guide Through World Chaos.*
2. John Strachey: *The Coming Struggle for Power.*
3. M.J. Bonn: *The American Experiment.*
4. G.D.H. Cole: *The Intelligent Man's Guide to Modern Europe.*
5. Bernard Fay: *Roosevelt and His America.*
6. John Strachey: *The Menace of Fascism.*
7. R. Palme Dutt: *Fascism.*
8. Albert Einstein: *The Brown Book of the Hitler Terror.* (Chairman of an International Committee responsible for the book).
9. John S. Munro: *Through Fascism to World Power.*
10. Paul Einzig: *The Economic Foundation of Fascism.*
11. Harold J. Laski: *Democracy in Crisis.*
12. Shaw, Stafford-Cripps and others: *Where Socialism Stands To-day.*
13. E. Burns: *Capitalism, Communism and the Transition.*
14. Guy Aldred: *At Grips with War.*
15. S. Pankhurst: *Fascism, Its Origin and Development in Italy and Germany.*
16. *World Economic Survey (1931-32)*, League of Nations.
17. L. Dennis: *Is Capitalism Doomed?*
18. J.G. Smith: *Facing the Facts.*
19. R.S. Brookings: *The Way Forward.*
20. F. Gay and H.V. Mitchell: *Recent Economic Changes*, 2 volumes.
21. H.V. Hodson: *Economics of Changing World.*
22. E. Burns: *The Only Way Out.*

On Russia

1. Fullop Muller: *Mind and Face of Bolshevism.*
2. N.M. Pokrovsky: *A Brief History of Russia*, 2 volumes (Translated by N. Mirsky.)
3. W. Astrov (ed.): *An Illustrated History of the Russian Revolution*, 2 volumes.
4. L. Trotsky: *History of the Russian Revolution*, 2 volumes.
5. Maurice Dobb: *The Economic Development of Soviet Russia.*

6. A.R. Williams: *Through the Russian Revolution.*
7. N. Berdyanev: *The Russian Revolution.*
8. A.L. Strong: *The First Time in History.*
9. Badayev: *The Bolsheviks in Tsarist Duma.*
10. (Russian Government Publication): *The Land Without Unemployment.*
11. M. Dobb: *Russian To-day and To-morrow.*
12. Wm. H. Chamberlain: *Soviet Russia.*
13. W.P. Coates: *Anti-Soviet Lies Nailed.*
14. Julias F. Hecker: *Moscow Dialogues.*
15. G.T. Grinko: *The Five Year Plan of the Soviet Union.*
16. Russian Delegation to the International Planned Economy Congress, Amsterdam, 1931: *Socialist Planned Economy in the U.S.S.R.*
17. Anna L. Strong: *Red Star in Samarkand.*
18. Calvin B. Hoover: *The Economic Life of Soviet Russia.*
19. Walter Duranty and others: *Red Economics.*
20. G. Dobbert: *Soviet Economics* (Same thing as no. 19).
21. Lancelot Lawton: *An Economic History of Soviet Russia.*
22. International Labour Office (1925): *Co-operation in Soviet Russia.*
23. R. Bishop: *From Peasant to Collective Farmer.*
24. Lili Korbev: *Life in a Soviet Factory.*
25. Maurice Dobb: *Soviet Russia and the World.*
26. M.M. Litvinov: *The Foreign Policy of Soviet Russia.*
27. Louis Fischer: *The Foreign Policy of the Soviet Union.*
28. Henri Barbusse: *The Soviet Union & Peace.*
29. H. Kohn: *Nationalism in the Soviet Union.*
30. Fannina Halle: *Women in Soviet Russia.*
31. E. Winter: *Red Virtue.*
32. Hebe Spaull: *The Youth of Russia Today.*
33. Klans Mehnert: *Youth in Soviet Russia.*
34. Julias F. Hecker: *Religion and Communism.*
35. Will Durant: *The Lesson of Russia.*
36. Molotov: *Results of the First Five Year Plan.*
37. J. Stalin and others: *From the First to the Second Five Year Plan.*

Books on the Labour Movement

1. Paul H. Douglas, C.N. Hitchcock and W.E. Atkins: *The Worker in Modern Economic Society.*
2. Sidney and Beatrice Webb: *History of Trade Unionism.*
3. R. Hedges: *The Legal History of Trade Unionism.*
4. David J. Saposs: *Readings in Trade Unionism.*
5. The International Federation of Trade Unions: *The Trade Union Movement in Various Countries* (Separate monographs on different countries).
6. A. Losovsky: *The World's Trade Union Movement.*
7. The International Labour Organization (The First Decennial Report of the International Labour Office, League of Nations.)

8. Published by The Trade Union Congress: *The Story of the Trade Union Congress.*
9. Published by The Trade Union Congress: *The General Council of the Trades Union: Its Powers, Functions and Work.*
10. Published by The Labour Research Department (L.R.D.): *Labour International Handbook, 1921. Supplement, 1923.*
11. G.M. Stekloff: *The History of the First International.*
12. R. Palme Dutt: *The Two Internationals.*
13. J. Clunie: *The Third International: Its Aim and Methods.*
14. R.W. Postgate: *The Worker's International.*
15. P. Blandshard: *An Outline of British Labour Movement.*
16. G.D.H. Cole: *History of the British Labour Movement.*
17. Mary R. Beard: *A Short History of the American Labour Movement.*
18. E.E. Cummings: *Labour Problem in the United States.*
19. Wm. Z. Foster: *Bankruptcy of the American Labour Movement.*
20. Robert Dunn: *Americanization of Labour.*
21. A. Losovsky: *Trade Unions in Soviet Russia.*
22. Joseph Freeman: *The Soviet Worker.*
23. Sen Katayama: *The Labour Movement in Japan.*
24. L.R.D. Publication: *The Meaning of May Day.*
25. Communist Party of Great Britain (C.P.G.B.): *The Fight of the Miners.*
26. R. Page Arnot: *The General Strike, 1926.*
27. R. Palme Butt: *The Meaning of the General Strike.*
28. Robert Dunn: *Company Unions.*
29. Jay Lovestone: *Government Strike Breaker.*
30. Bertram D. Wolfe: *Class Collaboration.*
31. Robert Dunn, C. Tead and Others: *New Tactics in Social Conflict.*
32. A. Lovosky: *Marx on Trade Unionism.*

Miscellaneous

1. R.H. Tawney: *The Acquisitive Society.*
2. Sidney and B. Webb: *The Decay of Capitalist Civilisation.*
3. Toynbee: *The Industrial Democracy.*
4. J.A. Hobson: *Evolution of Capitalism.*
5. Henri See: *Modern Capitalism.*
6. Hilferding: *Finance Capital.*
7. J.A. Hobson: *Unearned Income.*
8. G. Lowes Dickinson: *Causes of Industrial War.*
9. S. and B. Webb: *Industrial Democracy.*
10. Margaret Miller and Douglas Campbell: *Financial Democracy.*
11. Carl D. Thompson: *Public Ownership.*
12. Heinrich Strobel: *Socialization: Theory and Practice.*
13. Harry F. Ward: *The Profit Motive, Is It Indispensable to Industry?*
14. J.A. Hobson: *Incentives in the New Industrial Order.*
15. Thorstein Veblen: *Absentee Ownership.*

16. Ernest Beaglehole: *Property, A Study in Social Psychology.*
17. Paul Einzig: *Finance and Politics.*
18. Charles Beard: *Economic Basis of Politics.*
19. Charles Beard: *Economic Interpretation of the Constitution.*
20. L.R.D.: *Capital in Parliament.*
21. Marshal Brown: *Prosperity, The New Socialism.*
22. C.T. Cramp and Others: *The Worker's Point of View, A Symposium.*
23. G.D.H. Cole: *Payment of Wages.*
24. Fraz Oppenheim: *The State.*
25. Penmann: *The Irresistible Movement of Democracy.*
26. Leonard Woolf: *After the Deluge, A Study of Communal Psychology.*
27. Carlton Hayes: *Essays on Nationalism.*
28. H.J. Laski: *Nationalism.*
29. G.P. Gooch: *Nationalism.*
30. Hans Kohn: *A History of Nationalism in the East.*
31. L. Trotsky: *Literature and Revolution.*
32. L. Trotsky: *Whither England.*
33. L. Trotsky: *My Life.*
34. N.L. Mecheriakov: *The Peasantry and the Revolution.*
35. Heinrich Strobel: *The German Revolution.*
36. L.E. Mathaei: *Germany in Revolution.*
37. E.R. Pease: *History of the Fabian Society.*
38. H.J. Laski: *Communism.*
39. Edward Bellamy: *Looking Backward.*
40. Frank Arkwright: *The A.B.C. of Technocracy.*
41. R.H. Tawney: *Equality.*
42. The Russian Delegation to the International Science Congress: *Science at the Cross Roads.*
43. Levy: *The Universe of Science.*
44. Reinheld Niebuhr: *Moral Man and Immoral Society.*

APPENDIX 3

Resolution of the Bihar Socialist Party, May 1934[1]

Resolution

This Party considers it essential that all those Congressmen who hold socialist views should place, through those of their comrades who are its members, united proposals before the A.I.C.C. when it meets at Patna on 18th and 19th May. This Party further considers it to be high time for the socialists of this country to make united and organised efforts for the promotion of the socialist cause.

With these objects in view the Party considers it desirable to hold an All India Conference of socialist Congressmen at Patna on the 17th of May, so that an agreed line of action with regard to both of these objects may be evolved.

[1] *Kamalashanker Pandya Papers* (NMML).

APPENDIX 4

Agenda suggested by the Bihar Socialist Party for the Congress Socialist Conference at Patna, May 1934[1]

The Bihar Socialist Party

Resolved that the following agenda for the proposed Socialist Conference be circulated among the invitees together with the proposals of the party with regard to items on the agenda:

Agenda

I. Consider plans for creating an All India Socialist Movement within the Congress.
II. Consider proposals to be placed before the A.I.C.C.

Proposals of the Party

With regard to item no. I:

In the view of the Party it would be premature to form an All India Socialist Party or group at present. It would be better in the opinion of this Party to appoint an Organising Committee, with regional secretaries, to prepare the ground for an All India Party; the regional secretaries being wholly responsible for the work, as prescribed by the Organising Committee, in their region. The Organising Committee to meet from time to time.

In the view of this Party the following course of action should be prescribed for the regional secretaries:

(a) To get in touch with the Left Wing Congressmen and induce them to form, depending upon their strength, socialist nuclei, groups or parties.
(b) To organise propaganda on behalf of socialism in their region—particularly among Congress, Labour and Kisan workers.

With regard to item no. II:

First, a resolution committing the A.I.C.C. to a socialist point of view must be moved. The following draft resolution is suggested:

> This Committee (the A.I.C.C.) declares that the interests of the exploited mass of India cannot be served nor their economic, political and social salvation be secured by the achievement of political freedom unless it is accompanied by fundamental changes in the existing economic and social structure of society.

[1] *Kamalashanker Pandya Papers* (NMML).

In the view of this Committee such changes can be brought about only if the following programme is adopted by the free Indian State when it comes into being:

(1) Socialisation of key and principal industries (e.g. Steel, cotton, jute, railways, shipping, mines, banks, public utilities) with a view to the socialisation of the entire economic life of the country.
(2) Development of the economic life of the country to be planned and controlled by the State.
(3) Elimination of princes, zamindars, talukdars, landlords, capitalists, moneylenders and all other parasitic and exploiting interests.
(4) Redistribution of land so that no one may possess more land than is necessary for the maintenance of an average family on an average standard of living.
(5) Liquidation of agricultural indebtedness.
(6) The State to encourage and promote co-operative and collective farming with a view to the ultimate collectivisation of all agriculture in the country.

Second, a resolution committing the A.I.C.C. to the idea of organising the masses on the basis of their economic interests must be moved. The following draft resolution is suggested:

In the opinion of this Committee the only effective method for creating a mass movement is to organise the masses on the basis of their economic interests and accordingly this Committee calls upon Congressmen to take up the work of organising *kisan and mazdoor sabhas*, or entering such *sabhas* where they exist, with a view to participate in the day-to-day struggles of the masses and lead them eventually to their final goal.

Third, with regard to the proposal to revive the Swaraj Party this Party suggests the following draft resolution to be moved in the A.I.C.C.:

In view of the Lahore Resolution calling upon Congressmen to boycott legislatures and in view of the fact that the said resolution is still binding on Congressmen this Committee is of opinion that only a full session of the National Congress is competent to decide the question of Council Entry. This Committee, therefore, strongly disapproves of the attempt being made by certain Congressmen to revive the Swaraj Party independently of the Congress and it calls upon Congressmen to desist from all such attempts.

APPENDIX 5

Joint Statement by Narendra Deva, Jayaprakash Narayan, Sri Prakasa and Sampurnanand on Congress Working Committee Resolution, 22 June 1934[1]

The resolution of the Working Committee regarding the Congress Socialist movement came as a painful surprise. We were certainly not prepared for this deliberate offensive. The Working Committee speaks of loose talk on our part. If there has been any loose talk it is the Working Committee which has indulged in it. The committee talks of confiscation of private property and the necessity of class war as being the programme of the Congress Socialists. In the programme that was adopted at the Patna Conference there was no mention of confiscation of private property with or without any just cause. What the Patna programme speaks is the progressive socialisation of means of production, distribution and exchange. This does mean a gradual abolition of private property in the spheres named. It does not mean abolition of all private property. As for the first cause, the welfare of the greatest number and the human society as a whole is sufficient a just cause for us. As regards class war, to speak of the necessity of creating a thing which is ever present is meaningless. The question is not of creating a class war but of deciding which side we should take in that war, the side of the oppressed or the oppressor. There is no other alternative. The Socialists aim at the ultimate abolition of all class struggles by having a classless society.

The Working Committee is further of opinion that confiscation and class war are contrary to the Congress creed of non-violence. This is the most surprising assertion which, we feel, it will be difficult for the majority of the Congressmen to accept. The creed of the Congress is the attainment of Purna Swaraj through legitimate and peaceful means. There is nothing in our programme, as adopted at Patna, which in any sense whatever can be said to be contrary to this creed. We too aim at the attainment of independence and the very fact that we are within the Congress means that we accept the principle of using peaceful and legitimate means. Now, we ask, how does the idea of a class war offend against the creed in question.

As for confiscation, we have already made it clear that our aim is the socialisation of industry, commerce, etc. The programme as distinctly laid down in the Patna resolutions is meant to be brought in force by the Indian State after the political freedom has been achieved. This enforcement naturally will be through legislation. We fail to understand how a legitimate act of a free Indian State can be said to be against the creed. Does the Working Committee mean to say that the creed of the future Indian State will also be non-violence? This is a doctrine that cannot be

[1] *The Indian Annual Register*, 1934, Vol. 1, January-June 1934. The statement was issued from Banaras regarding the Congress Working Committee resolution on the Socialist Programme adopted at its meeting held in Bombay, 17-18 June 1934.

subscribed to by anyone except by the religious devotees of non-violence. Here it is worthwhile to remind the Working Committee that even the Karachi resolution advocates state ownership of the key industries. How does the Working Committee reconcile this confiscation of property with its high conception of non-violence? How do we who merely want to extend this principle of nationalisation to other economic activities become rebels against the Congress creed?

The Working Committee says that it is contemplating a wiser and more just use of private property, to stop the exploitation of the landless poor. We shall await the results of its contemplation and in the meantime want to warn the masses [that] there can be no solution of their problems and no end to their exploitation unless the economic organization is brought under social control. There can be no adjustment of class interests. There is no party in the society which can bring about and maintain this adjustment. Finally, we appeal to all Socialist Congressmen to muster strong at Bombay and put forth their best efforts to get our programme accepted.

APPENDIX 6

S.K. Patil's Article on the Formation of the Congress Socialist Party, 10 August 1934[1]

In these days we hear a good deal of noise in India about Socialism and Socialists. The formation of a Socialist Party within the Congress ranks has created a situation in Indian politics, which must exercise the minds of many people. After everything is said and done, the one question which still remains unreplied is: What in God's name is the cardinal difference between the perspectives of the Congress on the one hand and those of the Socialist Groups on the other? Are these differences of such a fundamental nature as can never be mutually adjusted. If they cannot, then, in my humble opinion, a Socialist Party within the Congress is a meaningless thing. If in the long run these differences can be adjusted then, also, it seems to me that the existence within the Congress of a separate party with a separate programme becomes a needless superfluity. Some how or other there is a feeling that things are moving in a direction which does not bode any good either to the Congress or the Socialists.

Some of us who in the heart of their hearts have never any doubt that the Indian National Congress claiming to represent the toiling masses of India was bound to develop on socialistic lines as its activities and popularity expanded, were mad with joy when Pandit Jawaharlal, with his characteristic impatience about things he has set his heart upon, made an open declaration on the future economic policy of this country and the part which the Congress was expected to play in it. Gandhiji's reply to this outspoken move on the part of Jawaharlal was in no way discouraging and looking to their personal relations, most of us thought that a stage was unalterably set in the Congress politics for an economic programme based on the broad principles of Socialism. So long as the strings of the situation were in the hands of Jawaharlal and Gandhiji, everyone confidently believed that all that was happening was happening for the best. Neither the Congress as represented by Gandhiji was averse to basic principles of Socialism nor was Jawaharlal opposed to India evolving an indigenous socialism suited to Indian conditions. A blend of Gandhi-Jawahar philosophy with a proper admixture of economism and spritualism would have been as many people thought, an ideal solution of India's peculiar problems. For a number of years Jawaharlal was known to be a Socialist of confirmed views. One could see his hand in the shaping of many resolutions with an economic bearing but he never despaired of success to a point where the formation of a new party would become a necessity. His creative mind backed by his forceful personality would have certainly avoided a split within the Congress ranks.

With the incarceration of Jawaharlal came a chaos and confusion which is growing every day and with disastrous consequences. The formation of Socialist Groups professedly within the Congress fold has put an enormous strain on many people's loyalty to the Congress. There has been such a wild confusion of thought

[1] *Bombay Chronicle*, 10 August 1934.

that very few people can really distinguish between the objectives of both. Then came the two resolutions of the Working Committee and the repercussions of these in the socialistic circles. All this is tending to aggravate the situation and make the gulf between the two more impassable. One is, indeed, staggered by the turn that the events have taken. In all propagandist squabbles, Jawaharlal's name is so cleverly exploited that it should provide one more excuse to Government for his continued incarceration. Why should they release him if that release would mean a certain reunion between the two wings of the Congress? Government is never known to be doing things in that way. The whole position has become so awkward that it is time every thinking man and woman within the Congress rank, did some serious thinking of the issues involved.

The first question that presents itself to a thinking man in the progress of mental criticism is: Has Congress at any time after it came under Gandhiji's influence shown the slightest tendency to oppose or bring any obstacles in the way of socialised national economy? I do not for a moment argue that Karachi resolution embodies all basic principles of socialism. It is only a turn in that direction with about 25 per cent of socialism in as much as it advocates the nationalisation of the key-industries and ensures a decent standard of life to toiling millions. And yet the Congress even in the flush of victory did not demand any more and whatever was demanded was granted without the slightest demur. I cannot understand for the life of me why the tendencies of our socialist friends should be activated by an utter want of faith in the Congress to do the right thing by the masses. The inevitable inference is that either the differences are radical in which case the socialists are untrue to themselves in remaining a part of the Congress or they are too superficial to justify the existence of a separate party within the Congress. In either case the attitude taken by the Socialists does them little honour.

Socialism is not a new invention in any sense. In a variety of experiments, it is before the civilized world for over a century and a half. The West has tried it for decades and has yet come nowhere near success. The reaction of several of these experiments can be seen in the emergence of a new political tendency known as "Fascism." All these things are as old as our Congress, if not older, and that takes away from them the element of novelty if any was claimed in its favour. There is no tailor-made pattern of socialism anywhere in the world which India can adopt while at the same time evade its consequences. The mere expression of "Socialism" leads us nowhere. It neither expropriates the rich nor brings any bread to poor man's table. As Gandhiji told the student deputationists of Calcutta, India can find an original solution in the light of the world experience, for liquidating the differences between Capital and Labour and evolving a socialist economy based on socialistic principles. For over a decade, Sweden has professed Socialism as a State programme and yet has not advanced an inch farther beyond publishing voluminous brochures on various unsuccessful socialistic experiments. Russia is still in the whirl, while Italy and Germany have set the hands of the clock in the opposite direction. Which then is the pattern which our Socialist friends want us forthwith to put into practice? Cannot we improve on all these experiments?

The latest election manifesto of the Bombay Socialist Group I am afraid, does not bring us a jot nearer any practical suggestion. It is discreetly silent on many points. The establishment of an "Independent State" will be a noble achievement indeed. But cannot Congress do it? Have the Socialists got any scheme of direct action which the nation can be persuaded to accept in preference to Gandhiji's movements? The sponsors of the Socialist Groups will agree with me that in the interest of all concerned the issues involved ought to be clearly elucidated so that they can make a convincing appeal to the intellect. The thought-confusion must go. So far as the theories of class war and confiscation of private property go, the Socialist claim in regard to these "vis-a-vis" Congress solution has got to be carefully examined. This examination will show that our differences are in no way of a fundamental character.

APPENDIX 7

Constitution, Programme and Resolutions of the First Conference of the Congress Socialist Party, Bombay, 21-2 October 1934[1]

The Second All India Congress Socialist Conference, which was also the first Conference of the All India Congress Socialist Party, met in Bombay at Readymoney Terrace, Worli, on October 21 and 22, 1934, the Subjects Committee deliberations having commenced on October 20.

There were 137 delegates present representing 13 Provincial Congress Socialist Parties. The delegates from each such Party were as follows:

> U.P. 28, Gujrat 16, Bombay 15, Maharashtra 14, Andhra 13, Bengal 12, Kerala 10, Behar 9, Delhi 7, Berar 6, C.P. (Hindi) 3, Utkal 3, Ajmer 1.

The Subjects Committee was formed of not more than three representatives from each Provincial Party *plus* the members of the Drafting Committee which was appointed by the First All India Congress Socialist Conference (Patna, May 17, 1934).

Votes in the Open Session were taken according to the bloc system, each provincial delegation or bloc having 3 votes, which were cast in a manner so as to give proportionate representation to minority views.

The Conference commenced with the address of the Chairman of the Reception Committee, Comrade Purshottam Tricumdas. Thereafter Comrade Sampurnanand was unanimously elected as Chairman of the Conference, Comrade Kamaladevi Chattopadhyaya having withdrawn her name. The Chairman, after making a few introductory remarks, called upon the Organizing Secretary, Comrade Jayaprakash Narayan, to read his report. After the report had been read the Conference proceeded to discuss the draft Constitution and Programme of the proposed All India Congress Socialist Party, which was submitted to the Conference by the Drafting Committee referred to above. After prolonged discussion the Constitution and Programme were adopted with amendments. The Conference then passed the following resolution which ushered into life the All India Congress Socialist Party:

> Resolved that the All India Congress Socialist Party be hereby formed on the basis of the Constitution and Programme just adopted by the Conference.

The Chairman thereupon invited delegates from the Provincial Parties to affiliate their Parties to the All India Party. The following Parties were affiliated:

> Ajmer, Andhra, Bengal, Berar, Behar, Bombay (City), C.P. (Hindi), Delhi, Gujrat, Kerala, Maharashtra, U.P. and Utkal.

With the formation of the All India Party the Conference, hitherto a Conference

[1] *All India Congress Socialist Party. Constitution, Programme and Resolutions of the First Conference of the Party and Report of the Organizing Secretary, 1934.*

of representatives of autonomous Provincial Parties, automatically turned into a Conference of the Party, its decisions becoming the decisions of the Party.

The first day's session concluded with the election of Office-bearers and of members of the Executive Committee of the Party. The following Committee was elected:

1. Jayaprakash Narayan, *General Secretary*	
2. M.R. Masani	
3. Mohanlal Gautam	*Joint Secretaries*
4. N.G. Gore	
5. S. Nambudiripad	
6. Narendra Dev	
7. Sampurnanand	
8. Kamaladevi Chattopadhyaya	
9. Purshottam Tricumdas	
10. P.Y. Deshpande	
11. Ram Manohar Lohia	
12. S.M. Joshi	
13. Amarendra Prasad Mitra	
14. Charles Mascaranhas	
15. Naba Krishna Choudhury	
16. Achyut Patwardhan	
17. Yusuf J. Meherally	
18. Sorab Batliwala	
19. Rohit Mehta	*Substitute Members*
20. Farid-ul-Haq Ansari	
21. Rambriksh Benipuri	

The second day's proceedings began with consideration of resolutions from the Subjects Committee. After these had been disposed of other resolutions which had been received in time to be moved in the Open Session were taken up. The Constitution and Programme and the resolutions passed are published herein.

Upon an announcement by the General Secretary that another session of the Conference might be called after the sessions of the Indian National Congress if the Executive Committee considered it necessary, the Conference was adjourned *sine die*.

In view of the fact that the basis of delegation was membership of the Provincial Parties and that such parties were in existence in only 13 out of the 20 provinces, it was encouraging to find that as many as 137 delegates attended the Conference. It showed what progress the movement had made since the first Conference was held at Patna only six months back. The discussions that took place in the Conference also showed the keen interest of the delegates in the problems that were before them. It was clear that the issues before the Conference were not of mere academic interest but had great practical and living value for the delegates.

This Conference had a unique significance, held as it was on the eve of the sessions of the Indian National Congress. Its decisions had a direct bearing on those of the Congress and one of the main purposes for which it was held was to give a lead to the Congress rank and file and rescue it from the back-sliding politics of the Congress leaders. It is a matter of gratification that the Conference by raising fundamental political issues and giving a clear verdict on them succeeded to a considerable extent in this task.

Constitution

Name

The name of the Party shall be the All India Congress Socialist Party.

Objects

The objects of the Party shall be the achievement of Complete Independence, in the sense of separation from the British Empire, and the establishment of a socialist society.

Membership

The Party shall consist of members of the Indian National Congress who are also members of a Provincial Congress Socialist Party affiliated to the Party, provided that they are not members

(a) of any communal organization or
(b) of any other political organization whose objects and programme are in the opinion of the Party inconsistent with its own.

Organization

There shall be an affiliated Congress Socialist Party in every Congress Province, including the Indian States.

The Provincial Parties shall be affiliated on their acceptance of the objects and programme of the Party except that they shall have freedom to make such additions and alterations in the immediate demands of the Party as are necessary in view of local conditions.

Provincial Parties shall have power to frame rules for the conduct of their affairs provided such rules are not inconsistent with the Constitution of the Party.

Every Provincial Party shall levy a membership fee of one anna per year of which it shall contribute 25% to the funds of the Party.

Annual and Special Sessions

The Party shall meet annually. The time and place shall be fixed by Executive Committee.

The Secretary shall call a special conference of the Party when directed to do so by the Executive Committee or on the requisition of at least three Provincial Parties.

The time and place shall be decided by the Executive Committee.

Decisions of the Annual and Special Sessions of the Party shall be binding on all affiliated Parties and their members.

Delegation

Provincial Parties shall be represented on the basis of one delegate for every twenty members or fraction thereof and the delegate or delegates attending shall have the right to cast the number of votes to which their Parties are entitled, in such manner as to secure proportionate representation to minorities.

Executive Committee

The Executive Committee of the Party shall be elected by the Annual Conference and shall consist of one general and four joint secretaries and eleven other members. Five substitute members shall also be elected to take the place of absent members in rotation. Vacancies during the year shall be filled up by the Executive Committee.

Quorum of the Executive Committee

Eight members shall form of the quorum of the Executive Committee.

Auditing of Accounts

The Secretary shall submit audited accounts of the Party to the Annual Conference. The Auditor shall be appointed by the Annual Conference.

Disciplinary Action

The Executive Committee shall have power to take disciplinary action by way of suspension of a Provincial Party or any member thereof, subject to ratification by the next Conference of the Party, provided that such decision is taken by a two-thirds majority.

The Annual Conference of the Party shall have power to disaffiliate a Provincial Party or expel any member thereof.

Constitutional Amendments

Amendments to the Constitution or the programme of the Party can only be made at a Conference of the Party by a two-thirds majority.

Programme

Objective

1. Transfer of all power to the producing masses.

2. Development of the economic life of the country to be planned and controlled by the State.
3. Socialisation of key and principal industries (e.g. Steel, Cotton, Jute, Railways, Shipping, Plantations, Mines), Banks, Insurance and Public Utilities with a view to the progressive socialisation of all the instruments of production, distribution and exchange.
4. State monopoly of foreign trade.
5. Organization of co-operatives for production, distribution and credit in the unsocialised sector of economic life.
6. Elimination of princes and landlords and all other classes of exploiters without compensation.
7. Re-distribution of land to peasants.
8. Encouragement and promotion of co-operative and collective farming by the State.
9. Liquidation of debts owed by peasants and workers.
10. Recognition of the right to work or maintenance by the State.
11. 'To everyone according to his needs and from everyone according to his capacity' to be the basis ultimately of distribution and production of economic goods.
12. Adult franchise on a functional basis.
13. No support to, or discrimination between, religions by the State and no recognition of any distinction based on caste or community.
14. No discrimination between the sexes by the State.
15. Repudiation of the so-called Public Debt of India.

Plan of Action

1. Work within the Indian National Congress with a view to secure its acceptance of the objects and programme of the Party.
2. Organization of peasant and labour unions, and entry into such unions where they exist, for the purpose of developing and participating in the day to day economic and political struggles of peasants and workers and intensifying the class struggle of the masses and of creating a powerful mass movement for the achievement of Independence and Socialism.
3. Organization of, and participation in Youth leagues, Women's organizations, Volunteer organizations, etc., etc., for the purpose of getting their support to the programme of the Party.
4. Active opposition to all imperialist wars and the utilisation of such and other crises for the intensification of the national struggle.
5. Refusal to enter or any stage into negotiations on the constitutional issue with the British Government.
6. Convening after the capture of power of a Constituent Assembly elected by local committees of deputies of workers, peasants and other exploited classes for the purpose of formulating a Constitution for the Indian State.

Immediate Demands

POLITICAL

1. Freedom of speech and of the Press.
2. Freedom of association and combination.
3. Repeal of all anti-national and anti-labour laws.
4. Re-instatement of all farmers and tenants deprived of their lands owing to their participation in the movement or restraint on political grounds.
5. Release of all political prisoners detained without trial and withdrawal of all orders of externment, internment or restraint on political grounds.
6. Free and compulsory primary education and the liquidation of adult illiteracy.
7. Drastic reduction, by at least 50% of the military expenditure of the Government of India.
8. Regulation and control of religious endowments.

ECONOMIC

9. Municipalisation of Public Utilities.
10. Control of usury, direct and indirect.
11. Liquidation of debts owed by workers and peasants.
12. A steeply graduated tax on all incomes including incomes from agriculture, above a fixed minimum.
13. Graduated death duties.

CONCERNING LABOUR

14. Freedom of labour from serfdom and conditions bordering on serfdom.
15. The right to form unions, to strike and to picket.
16. Compulsory recognition of unions by employers.
17. A living wage, a 40-hour week and healthy quarters and conditions of work.
18. Insurance against unemployment, sickness, accident, old age, etc.
19. One month's leave every year with full pay to all workers and two months' leave with full pay to women workers during maternity.
20. Prohibition against employment of children of school-going age in factories, and women and of children under sixteen underground.
21. Equal wages for equal work.
22. Weekly payment of wages whenever demanded.

AGRARIAN

23. Elimination of landlordism in zamindari and talukdari areas without compensation.
24. Encouragement of co-operative farming.
25. Liquidation of arrears of rent.
26. Complete exemption from rents and taxes of all peasants with uneconomic holdings.

27. Reduction of rent and land revenue by at least 50%.
28. Abolition and penalisation of all feudal and semi-feudal levies on the peasantry.
29. Penalisation of illegal exactions and forced labour.
30. Freedom from attachment in execution of rent or money decrees of homestead, agricultural resources and that portion of a peasant's holding which is just sufficient to maintain an average peasant family.

Resolutions passed by the 1st Conference of the All India Congress Socialist Party

Meaning of Complete Independence

1. This Conference declares that the Congress goal of Complete Independence must mean the establishment of an Independent State in which power is transferred to the producing masses and that such an objective involves refusal to compromise at any stage with British Imperialism.

India and the next War

2. This Conference considers that in view of the international situation and the danger of the sudden outbreak of a war in which the British Empire may be involved, it is necessary for the Congress to declare its opposition to the participation by India in any war in which the British Government may be involved and to undertake forthwith the preparation of the entire Indian nation to resist actively the utilisation of Indian men, money and resources for the purpose of such a war and to utilise such a crisis for securing Swaraj.

Congress and the Indian Princes

3. Inasmuch as the Indian States constitute a political and military support to British Imperialism and a source of feudal backwardness and reaction, this Conference declares that the interests of the people of the Indian State are as much the concern of the Indian National Congress as those of the people of British India and that the abolition of the rule of the Indian Princes can alone assure Complete Independence for the whole of India and it invites the people of the Indian States to fight side by side with the people of British India in the struggle for Independence.

Socialist Solution of the Communal Problem

4. This Conference is of opinion that all attempts made so far to solve the communal problem, including those made by the Congress, and the position taken up by the Congress Working Committee on this question, have been on a wholly false basis of recognition of rights belonging to religious groups and is of opinion that the problem can effectively be liquidated only by the struggle for the economic emancipation of the masses.

This Conference condemns the formation of the so-called Nationalist Party on the issue of the Communal Award as a communalist and anti-national move which has started a futile controversy over an issue which is of no importance to the masses and which has distracted attention from the real task of their emancipation from exploitation.

Reactionary Policy of C.P.B.

5. (A) This Conference takes note of the concerted attempts of the right wing to take back the Congress to the discredited path of constitutional agitation and to convert it into an instrument of the Indian upper classes in their bargains with British Imperialism. This Conference is emphatically of opinion that these attempts run counter to the creed of the Congress and to the fundamental principles and policies it has been following since 1920. This Conference, therefore, resolves to resist these attempts and to rescue the Congress from the hands of the right wing by educating and organizing the rank and file on the basis of a clear-cut programme of national revolution and to carry on a consistent propaganda for the exposure of the reactionary aims, policies and programmes of the right wing.

(B) This Conference is of opinion that parliamentary activities conducted by the Congress shall be based on the theory of revolutionary use of legislatures with the following as its essential principles:

(i) Congress candidates shall go into the legislatures as the representatives of the exploited masses of India and in no other capacity;
(ii) Parliamentary activity inside the legislatures shall be closely linked up with the activities of the exploited masses outside, on the basis of their immediate economic and political demands;
(iii) Every issue coming up before the legislatures shall be approached and dealt with from the point of view of the masses, their economic and political emancipation forming the only criterion;
(iv) The least betrayal of the cause of the exploited masses shall forthwith meet with expulsion and merciless exposure;
(v) No elected Congress candidate shall accept ministerial offices because:

 (a) The legislative, executive and judicial machinery, present and forthcoming, is the creation of British Imperialism and is intended solely for the purpose of facilitating and intensifying the exploitation of the Indian masses;
 (b) Acceptance of ministerial offices will create the dangerous illusion that the imperialist State machine can be utilised for the good of the masses, while its essential structure is so designed as to automatically result in their exploitation;
 (c) A mass organization that stands for complete independence as its immediate objective must necessarily remain in the opposition until complete independence is an accomplished fact;
 (d) Economic and political emancipation of the masses is incompatible with the imperialist and capitalist structure of state and society.

(C) Whereas the decision of the A.I.C.C. at Patna for contesting the present Assembly elections was not on the lines indicated above, it should be rescinded and the candidates standing on behalf of the Congress should be withdrawn.

Socialists and Assembly Elections

6. (a) This conference calls upon members of the Congress Socialist Parties (i) to decline nomination as Congress or Independent candidates for the Assembly election and to withdraw their candidatures if already nominated; (ii) to decline to serve as members of the Parliamentary Boards, Central or Provincial, or any Committee formed for the electoral campaign.

(b) This Conference further calls upon Provincial Parties to take disciplinary action against such of their members as may contravene the terms of part (a) of this resolution.

Conditions for Acceptance of Congress Offices

7. This Conference is of opinion that no member of a Congress Socialist Party should become an officer-bearer in any Congress organization except where (1) the Party is in a majority or (2) the organization concerned has resolved to carry out the immediate programme of the Provincial Party and the Executive Committee of the Party concerned gives previous permission to accept office, and calls upon those Congress Socialists who are office-bearers in any Congress organization, except such as those indicated, to resign their offices.

The Party in the Congress Session

8. All members of the Party shall support resolutions or amendments moved on behalf of the Party in the Subjects Committee or the Open Session of the Congress.

Fundamental Principles of the Future Indian State

9. This Conference is of opinion that to enable the masses to appreciate what 'Swaraj' as conceived by the Congress will mean to them, it is desirable to state the position of the Congress in a manner easily understandable by them. In order to end the exploitation of the masses, political freedom must include real economic freedom of the starving millions. The Congress should therefore declare that the future Constitution of the Indian State shall be based on the following fundamental principles:

1. Transfer of all power to the producing masses.
2. Development of the economic life of the country to be planned and controlled by the state.
3. Socialisation of the key and principal industries, e.g. steel, cotton, jute, railways, shipping, mines, banks and public utilities.
4. State monopoly of foreign trade.

5. Organization of co-operatives for production, distribution and credit in the unsocialised sector of economic life.
6. Elimination of princes and landlords and all other classes of exploiters without compensation.
7. Redistribution of land to the peasants.
8. Liquidation of debts owed by peasants and workers.
9. Provision by the State of
   (i) Work to every able-bodied adult.
   (ii) Insurance against unemployment, old age, sickness, accident, maternity, etc.,
10. "To each according to his needs and from each according to his capacity" to be ultimate basis of distribution and production of economic goods.
11. Adult franchise on a functional basis.
12. No support to, or discrimination between, religions by the State and no recognition of any distinction based on caste or community.
13. No discrimination between the sexes by the State.

Organization of Workers and Peasants

10. The Conference is of opinion that the daily struggles of workers, peasants and other exploited classes for their immediate economic and political demands are an integral part of the struggle for Independence. The Conference therefore resolves that the workers and peasants and other exploited masses, including those of the Indian States, should be organized for the immediate realisation of the following among other demands and for the creation of a powerful mass movement for the achievement of Independence:

1. Freedom of speech and of the press.
2. Freedom of association and combination.
3. Repeal of anti-national and anti-labour laws.
4. Release of all political prisoners and prisoners detained without trial and withdrawal of all orders of externment, internment or restraint issued on political grounds.
5. Re-instatement of all farmers and peasants deprived of their lands owing to their participation in the movement for National Independence.
6. Free and compulsory primary education and the liquidation of adult illiteracy.
7. Drastic reduction, by at least 50%, in the military expenditure of the Government of India.
8. Municipalisation of public utilities.
9. Control of usury, direct and indirect.
10. A steeply graduated tax on all incomes, including incomes from agricultural sources, above a fixed minimum.
11. Graduated death-duties.
12. Liquidation of debts owed by peasants and workers.
13. Freedom of labour from serfdom and conditions bordering on serfdom.

14. The right to form unions, to strike and picket.
15. Compulsory recognition by employers of workers' unions.
16. A living wage, forty hours' week and healthy quarters and conditions of work.
17. Equal wages for equal work.
18. Weekly payment of wages whenever demanded.
19. Insurance against unemployment, sickness, accident, old age, etc.
20. One month's leave every year with full pay to all workers and two months' leave with full pay to women workers during maternity.
21. Prohibition against employment of children in underground mining and hazardous occupations.
22. Elimination of landlordism in zamindari and talukdari areas without compensation.
23. Abolition and penalisation of all feudal and semi-feudal levies on the peasantry.
24. Encouragement of co-operative farming.
25. Introduction of scientific agriculture at State cost.
26. Liquidation of arrears of rent.
27. Complete exemption from rent and taxes of all peasants with uneconomic holdings.
28. Reduction of rent and land revenue by at least 50 per cent.
29. Freedom from attachment in execution of rent or money decrees of homestead, agricultural resources and that portion of a peasant's holding which is just sufficient to maintain an average peasant family.

The Constituent Assembly

11. This Conference asserts that the right of framing the constitution is the sovereign right of the Indian people and declares that the supreme authority which should promulgate the constitution of India is the National Constituent Assembly.

This conference further declares that the National Constituent Assembly cannot meet as the result of a compromise with Britain but must rise as a consequence of a victorious capture of power by the Indian masses.

The Conference is of opinion that the Constituent Assembly should be elected by Local Committees of deputies of workers, peasants and other exploited classes and that the said Committees will arise out of the daily struggles of the oppressed masses for the enforcement of their immediate economic and political demands.

This Conference resolves that a mass campaign for raising the fundamental issue of self-determination and to agitate for the Constituent Assembly be immediately started incorporating the immediate economic demands of the oppressed and exploited masses.

United Front Against Imperialism

12. In view of the urgent necessity of carrying forward the fight for Independence and preventing a further spread of demoralisation, it is resolved that the Congress Socialist Party shall forthwith commence work with the object of putting its

programme into effect, irrespective of the acceptance or rejection of its programme by the Indian National Congress.

For this purpose the All India Congress Socialist Party desires to act in cooperation with other Parties having similar aims, within or without the Indian National Congress, and this Conference authorises the Executive Committee of the All India Congress Socialist Party to appoint a Sub-Committee to explore the possibilities of joint action on specific issues with the different labour and radical groups in the country.

Mahatma Gandhi's Retirement

13. This Conference condemns the tactics adopted by the right wing of the Congress of trying to focus public attention on personal or sentimental issues arising out of Mahatma Gandhi's statement and proposals and to sidetrack the fundamental struggle for Independence.

Amendments to the Congress Constitution

14. This Conference desires that the present Constitution of the Indian National Congress be amended in the following manner:

1. In Article 1
   (a) After the work "Independence" add the words "meaning the establishment of an Independent State in which power is transferred to the producing masses".
   (b) At the end of the clause add: (Note: The above object involves the refusal to compromise at any stage with British Imperialism).

2. In Article 7 (i)
   After the words "Art. 4" omit the words "and paying a subscription of annas four per year in advance, or 2000 yards of evenly spun yarn of his or her own spinning".

3. Delete Art. 7 (ii).

4. In Art. 7 (iii)
   Omit all the words after "March 31st".

5. In Art. 7 (iv a)
   Delete the words "and does not habitually wear khaddar".

6. In Art. 8 para 5
   Delete the word "fifty" and add in its place "hundred".

7. In Art. 8 para 5
   After the word "electorate" delete the words "and shall prescribe the procedure to be adopted for securing the proportional representation by a single transferable vote or by any other method".
8. At the end of Art. 19 para 3

Delete the full-stop and add the words "in the following manner: The members of the District Congress Committee (or when the District Congress Committees are primary organizations the members of their Executive Councils) shall form an electoral college".

9. Delete Art. 19 para 5.

10. Delete Art. 22.

11. In Art. 24 delete the words "the President".

12. In Art. 24 at the end add a new para:
The Annual Report of the Working Committee shall be submitted to Provincial Congress Committees not less than one month before the annual session of the Congress.

13. In Art. 26, at the end add the words:
Which shall be circulated to the members of the Subjects Committee not less than one week before the first date of the meeting.

14. Add new Art. 34:
All elections shall take place according to the system of the Single Transferable vote.

Class Struggle and Confiscation of Property

15. This Conference is of opinion that the resolutions passed by the Working Committee of the Indian National Congress at Bombay and later at Benaras concerning class war and confiscation of property were uncalled for and misleading.

This Conference claims that participation in the class struggle and advocacy of expropriation of property are not in any way inconsistent with the Congress creed.

Government's Reign of Repression

16. (a) This Conference emphatically condemns the campaign of repression and terror now being conducted by British Imperialism in India: in the form of special legislation in Bengal under which the death penalty can be inflicted for minor offences and a regime of martial law can be established over whole districts, thousands of people detained without trial and many other outrages committed against the public without restraint; in declaring illegal the Khudai Khidmatgars, the Communist Party of India, the Naujavan Bharat Sabha, the Kirti Kisan Sabhas, the Anti-Imperialist League, Youth Leagues and Seva Dals; in promulgating the Emergency Powers Act under which freedom of speech and organization and more specially of the press has been ruthlessly suppressed, labour leaders have been imprisoned and deported; in suppressing the strike movement of the workers and peasants by the use of armed force; and finally in passing the Trades Disputes Conciliation Act for the more effectual suppression of the rising working class movement.

(b) This Conference resolves to launch an immediate and countrywide agitation, in co-operation with other organizations having similar objects, and to organize mass opposition to this regime of terror.

Repression in the Indian States

17. This Conference condemns the action of the Travancore, Baroda, Rewa and other Native States which have taken repressive measures against Congress, labour and States, Peoples' Organizations and movements.

Bihar Tenancy Amendment Act

18. This Confernece is wholly opposed to the recently enacted Bihar Tenancy Amendment Act and condemns the action of the Government of Bihar in siding with Zamindars and sacrificing the interests of the tenants.

Solidarity with Workers and Peasants

19. This Conference extends its fraternal greetings to all class organizations of workers and peasants in the country and declares its solidarity with them in their day to day struggles.

Greetings to Pandit Jawaharlal Nehru

20. This Conference sends its greetings to Pandit Jawaharlal Nehru whose absence from its midst is keenly felt and extends its sympathy to him on the grave illness of Smt. Kamala Nehru during his term of imprisonment and condemns the Government for continuing his incarceration in such circumstances.

M.N. Roy's Release

21. This Conference learns with deep concern that Com. M.N. Roy is seriously ill in jail and demands his immediate and unconditional release on the grounds of health.

The "Congress Socialist"

22. This Conference resolves that the report of the sub-committee which was appointed at Benaras regarding the *Congress Socialist* be referred to the Executive Committee for necessary action.

Party's Membership

23. This Conference resolves that the Executive Committee shall have power to frame rules regarding the enrolment, nature, classes and powers of members of Provincial Parties.

Sub-Committees

24. (a) This conference directs the Executive Committee of the Party to appoint the following Sub-Committees:

    (1) Propaganda Sub-Committee.
    (2) Peasant Sub-Committee.
    (3) Labour Sub-Committee.

(b) This Conference also recommends that the Propaganda Sub-Committee should conduct an organ of the Party in English as well as in Hindi and publish literature on Socialism.

APPENDIX 8

Rules and Recommendations framed by the Executive Committee of the Congress Socialist Party, 1934[1]

Rules Framed by the Executive Committee

In pursuance of the resolution of the Conference empowering the Executive to frame rules regarding the enrolment, nature, classes and powers of members of Provincial Parties the following rules were framed:

1. There shall be in each Provincial Party two classes of members: (1) Active (2) Ordinary.
   Active members shall be those who work actively for the Party; Ordinary members shall be those who accept the objects and programme of the Party.
2. The Executive Committee of the Provincial Party shall prepare and from time to time revise the lists of Active and Ordinary members.
3. The number of delegates to the Conference of the All India Party shall be determined on the basis of the total membership of the Provincial Party.
4. The delegates shall be elected by all the members of a Provincial Party from amongst its Active members.

It was resolved that the Executive Committee of Provincial Parties should submit their Constitutions to the All India Executive Committee within one month for its approval. Amendments made in the provincial Constitutions should also be similarly submitted to the All India Executive within one month of their adoption.

Recommendations of the Executive Committee

1. The Executive Committee of the Provincial Party should be elected from amongst its Active members half by the Active members and half by all the members.
2. Provincial Constitution should be amended only by Active members.
3. Provincial Executive Committees should reserve the rights to refuse applications for membership without giving reason and to expel members.
4. Any one who the provincial Executive is satisfied is a member of the "Official" group of Communists should not be admitted as a member. (Attention is drawn to the membership clause in the Constitution.)

[1] *Nabakrushna Chaudhuri Papers* (NMML).

APPENDIX 9

Joint Statement by C.B. Kantak, Damodar Swarup Seth, Govind Sahai and Balkrishna Sharma regarding their Resignations from the U.P. Congress Socialist Party, 26 October 1934[1]

The resolution of the All-India Congress Socialist Conference laying down conditions in respect of holding offices and being members of the Congress executive is, we submit, very short-sighted and impracticable and even suicidal. The Socialist Party is still in infancy.

We are passing through a formative period of our existence. By remaining inside the Congress executive and offices in various district Congress organizations, we can use the Congress machinery for the advancement and propagation of socialist ideology. It was because of our influence as Congressmen and office holders in Congress executives, that we were in a position to form effective Socialist party organizations in as many as 30 districts in our province.

Let us not shut our eyes to facts that stare us in face. We have no offices, we have no means to set up our party machinery as separate from the running Congress organizations. Therefore to talk of resignations from Congress offices and executives is anything but in the interest of the Socialist Party.

It is all very well to talk tall but in the cases of some of those at least who were in favour of that fatal resolution it can well be said that the grapes were not quite sweet because they were at a height where these friends could not reach.

We are in possession of a list of those names who tried to come in the Congress executive and failed and who ultimately came out to support the resolution, over which we had to fall out of the party.

As regards the statement of our able and beloved Secretary Mr. Jai Prakash Narain we may assure him and the public in general that we shall be only too glad to see a strong Socialist Party, functioning in our provinces. We ourselves do not want to magnify our family differences nor do we wish to leave an alarmist and misleading impression on the public mind.

Our only fear is that on account of this resolution on the Socialist activities in the country in general and in our province in particular will be greatly handicapped. For instance the treasurer of the Hind Provincial Congress Socialist Party had to tender his resignation on account of difference arising out of such resolutions as the one under discussion. Similarly two secretaries of the party have also resigned. Five other members also have come out with their resignations. This augurs ill. We think Mr. Jai Prakash Narain knows all this. It is no use concealing facts. We appeal to Mr. Jai Prakash Narain to view things in their proper perspective and not to evade issues by calling them alarmist and misleading.

[1] *Bombay Chronicle*, 27 October 1934.

APPENDIX 10

Agreement with the All India Trade Union Congress, 1 November 1934[1]

At a meeting of representatives of the Executive Committee of the All India Congress Socialist Party and the All India Trade Union Congress, the following points of agreement was arrived at:

1. The policy of the All India Congress Socialist Party would be to strengthen the All India Trade Union Congress and attempt to make it the All India Trade Union organization of the working class and the All India Trade Union Congress, while welcoming the formation of the Congress Socialist Party, agrees to strengthen the Congress Socialist Party as an anti-imperialist bloc within the Congress and the policy of the A.I.T.U.C. would be to co-operate with the Congress Socialist Party as an anti-imperialist bloc within the Congress.
2. Unions formed by members of the All India Congress Socialist Party would affiliate to the All India Trade Union Congress.
3. Where only a Trade Union Congress Union or a non-T.U.C. Union exists, the members of the All India Congress Socialist Party will work in it.
4. Where there are two unions in an industry and the non-T.U.C. union is a mass union, the All India Congress Socialist Party will reserve the right to work in the non-T.U.C. union, after consultation with the All India Trade Union Congress Executive.
5. The All India Trade Union Congress Executive will exert its influence in obtaining facilities for members of the All India Congress Socialist Party to work in its Unions, without infringing the autonomy of the unions.
6. The representatives of the All India Congress Socialist Party pointed out the undesirability of there being two parties called Socialist parties and suggested that if possible the All India Socialist Party should merge in the All India Congress Socialist Party, or otherwise its name should be changed to that of the Working Class Party. The representatives of the A.I.T.U.C. promised to give this suggestion a favourable consideration.

Hariharnath Sastri
Sibnath Banerjee
for A.I.T.U.C.
1 November 1934

Jayaprakash Narayan
M.R. Masani
for the A.I.C.S.P.
Bombay
1 November 1934

[1] *Nabakrushna Chaudhuri Papers* (NMML).

APPENDIX 11

Agreement with the All India Trade Union Congress, December 1934[1]

At a joint meeting of the "United Front Committee" of the A.I.C.S.P. and the members of the Executive Committee of the A.I.T.U.C., residing in Bombay, the following agreement was arrived at:

1. There shall be joint action by the A.I.C.S.P. and the A.I.T.U.C. on specific issues, such as the danger of another war, Government repression, the J.P.C. Report, and other issues which may arise from time to time; the nature of joint action being holding of meetings and joint demonstrations, observing of "days" and anniversaries, issuing of statements and literature, etc.
2. There shall be joint action only if the following conditions are fulfilled by both parties:

    (i) There shall be no abuse of each other, nor imputations on the motives or honesty of either party.

    (ii) There shall be no mutual criticism in speeches or by distribution of leaflets, etc., at joint functions.

    (iii) Before every joint action there shall be joint agreement regarding terms of resolutions and slogans, carrying of banners and flags and distribution of literature.

    (iv) There shall be no advocacy of violence or non-violence by either party at joint functions.

    (v) At joint functions there shall be no appeal for support to either party or attempt to enrol members or to draw any other exclusive advantage to either party.

It was also agreed upon that an anti-J.P.C. Report Day should be observed under the joint auspices of the A.I.T.U.C., the A.I.C.S.P. and other organizations, which may agree to joint action, when meetings and demonstrations should be organized all over the country. Both parties agreed to settle the details as soon as possible.

Jayaprakash Narayan
On behalf of the Representatives
of the All India Congress
Socialist Party

D.L. Pathak
On behalf of the Representatives
of the All India Trade
Union Congress

[1] *JP Papers* (NMML).

APPENDIX 12

Subhas Chandra Bose's Views regarding the Formation of the Congress Socialist Party, 15 March 1935[1]

From an objective point of view, the formation of the Congress Socialist Party is a legitimate and natural reaction against the move towards the Right which Congress policy adopted last year. The "Parliamentary policy" of the Congress today as represented by the Parliamentary Board is, in my humble opinion, somewhat different in character from the "Swarajist policy" as represented by the Swaraj Party in 1923-4. The Swaraj Party in those days did represent a dynamic force in the country though there were moderated elements in that party. But the Parliamentary Board does not. In these circumstances, if there had not been a revolt within the Congress against a swing to the Right, then one would have been justified in thinking that the Congress was dying. But because the Congress was neither dead nor dying the revolt did take place and the Congress Socialist Party came into existence. To attempt to suppress the party or brow-beat its members with the threat of disciplinary action, shows a woeful lack of knowledge of the elementary principles of modern politics. This attempt was made in 1923 when the Swaraj Party was born and it only served to strengthen that party and add to its importance. I dare say that history is going to repeat itself now.

While the instinct that has urged the formation of the Congress Socialist Party is correct, I am afraid that there is some lack of clarity in the ideas of the party. In the first place, the choice of the name of the Party has been an unhappy one. "Socialism" today has different complexions and therefore different connotations when used by different people. And there seems to be hardly anything in common between the Socialism of Mr. Ramsay MacDonald and the militant policy and method of the Socialists of Spain. To some people, again, Socialism is synonymous with communism. Why then use a terminology which is used by different people in different senses.

Further, if I am not mistaken, the Congress Socialist Party seems to be under the influence of Fabian Socialism which was the fashion in England 50 years ago. Since then, much water has flown down the Thames and also down the Ganges. So many developments have taken place in different parts of the world since end of the great war and so many socio-economic experiments have been, and are being made—that a modern party cannot afford to hark back to the ideas and shibboleths prevalent in Europe 4 or 5 decades ago.

Let us take one practical example. The Congress Socialist Party seems to think that the constitutional problem in India should be solved by a Constituent Assembly and not by the Joint Parliamentary Committee of England. The historical example of a Constituent Assembly was afforded by France and this was followed by the United States of America. A century and a half have elapsed since the Constituent

[1] *Amrita Bazar Patrika*, 15 March 1935. Letter to the United Press.

Assembly met in Paris in order to draw up a constitution for France. In 1917, when the Bolsheviks seized political powers by force and put Kerensky's Government to flight—the first thing they did was to dissolve the Constituent Assembly, because in that Assembly the Bolsheviks were in a hopeless minority and if the Constituent Assembly had drafted a constitution for Russia, the Bolshevik Government would never come into existence. I have no doubt that if today a Constituent Assembly is convened in India on the basis of adult suffrage—the Congress Socialist Party will be in a minority. The constitution will therefore be drafted by individuals or parties in whom the Congress Socialists have no confidence—the Congress Socialists themselves being consenting party to such an arrangement. Instead of committing political suicide in this way, the Congress Socialist Party, if it has confidence in its own principles, methods and programme and if it does not suffer from an inferiority complex, should claim the exclusive right to draft a constitution for India. The party that is going to fight for freedom is the party that is entitled to draw up the constitution.

What I have just said may shock the democratic and constitutional instincts of many of my countrymen. But I should like to urge most emphatically that democracy as understood today in a large portion of this wide world is different from democracy as understood in the mid-Victorian era. Russia today is ruled by a party—not by a parliament elected on the basis of adult suffrage—but that party claims to act on behalf of the people. Similarly in Italy and also in Germany, a party has usurped all political power, having suppressed all political parties, but this party claims to represent the people. In Spain, on the contrary, when the Socialists were in power they experimented in mid-Victorian democracy. As a magnanimous gesture of good-will, they gave the vote to all adult women, without stopping to think what would be the effect to that measure. The enfranchised women gave their votes to the Catholic and Right wing parties in overwhelming numbers and as a result the Socialists were soon swept out of office. No better example of "political harakiri" can be found in recent history.

Russia is not the only country where mid-Victorian parliamentary methods had to be done away with. The Fascists in Italy and the Nazis in Germany, as we have already noted, also disenfranchised the opposition parties and ultimately suppressed them in order to consolidate their own power. These political experiments have to be taken note of and studied by us, if we are to avoid pitfalls in future.

I am inclined to think that the Congress Socialist Party contains within itself the promise of a great future. It has been able to draw towards itself the radical elements in Indian National Congress—and if it develops along the right lines and adopts the correct ideology, slogans and shibboleths, it will have an irresistable appeal. If, unfortunately, it does not, and if it falls a victim to the same confusion of ideas which has seized the present-day Congress leaders, then the masses will ultimately turn to some other party for their salvation. As the first step towards the clarification of our economic-political ideas, we must give the go-by to the false idea of unity. The experience of the All Parties' Committee and the All Parties' Conference of 1928 should have taught us by now that unity has value only when it represents not only unity in ideas, but also unity in action. A real unity is a source of infinite strength; superficial unity is only a source of weakness. The Indian Liberals chose to cooperate with the Congress only so long as the Government neglected them—as in the case of the Simon Commission. But as soon as seats were offered then at the Round Table Conference they did not stop to consider what the Congress would do but took the earliest boat to England. The Third Round Table Conference was boycotted by even the British Labourites who begged the Indian Liberals to join them in the boycott, but the sacrifice demanded of them was evidently too great.

In the light of these recent experiences, it passes one's comprehension how Congress leaders like Sj. Rajagopalachariar could exhibit such obsequiousness towards Indian Liberals. It is hopeless to expect the Liberals to join hands with the Congress in a common boycott of the new Constitution. If the Liberals do take such a step to begin with they will not hesitate to betray their Congress colleagues at the first official overture that is made towards them. In view of these considerations, I am of opinion that any Party that aspires to win freedom for India should be prepared to draw up the constitution for India and after winning Swaraj should be prepared to put into effect the whole programme of post-war reconstruction. There can be no question of giving up political power after the battle is won, there can be no question of dissolving the Congress after the Congress is victorious. Just as Ghazi Mustafa Kamal Pasha (Kamal Ataturk as he is now called) and his party won freedom for Turkey and thereafter remained in power in order to put Turkey on her feet and put into practice their programme of national reconstruction so also must we do in India. "Dictatorship of the party both before and after Swaraj is won"—that must be our slogan for the future.

I shall conclude by emphasising once again that the Congress Socialist Party, if it really wants to develop into the party of the future, should take stock of post-war economic and political developments in Europe and America and, in the light of that experience, chalk out the lines of India's future development. It should give up once for all the habitual inferiority complex and prepare to accept the full burden of responsibility for India's future. Can the party do that? If it can, then it will be able to rally all the radical elements in the country that are dissatisfied with the present state of things and are groping for light and looking anxiously for a bold lead.

APPENDIX 13

Report of the United Front Committee [before 25 March 1935][1]

In pursuance of the resolution on United Front passed at the Bombay Conference, the Executive Committee of the A.I.C.S.P. appointed the following Committee to negotiate with labour and other radical organizations regarding United Front on specific issues:

Purushottam Tricamdas
S.M. Joshi
Sorab Batliwala
Charles Mascarenhas
M.R. Masani
Jayaprakash Narayan (Secretary).

The Committee met on . . . and arrived at an unanimous decision regarding terms and forms of United Front, except that Com. Batliwala, though present, refused to participate in the discussions and exercise his vote.

The Committee thereafter met the representatives of the A.I.T.U.C. in Bombay, the N.T.U.F. and the Red T.U.C. and the following terms were agreed upon with each of them.

The A.I.T.U.C. Executive which met at Nagpur sometime after was of the opinion that in view of a much wider agreement regarding Trade Union work arrived at much earlier, there was no point in coming to a fresh agreement regarding specific issues. The President of the A.I.T.U.C. wrote to me that his organization was fully in agreement with the terms suggested by our Committee but that it was redundant to come to a fresh agreement in view of the one already made. So the position is that we have the fullest co-operation of the A..I.T.U.C. in our United Front activities.

The Red T.U.C., while its representatives came to a final settlement with the Committee, has not yet conveyed its ratification of the agreement in writing. I hope this will soon be done.

The N.T.U.F. also has not sent its written approval of the agreement, but I trust it is merely due to delay in its office.

All India Congress Socialist Party
Conditions for United Front

1. There shall be joint action by the A.I.C.S.P., the A.I.T.U.C., the N.T.U.F. and the Red T.U.C. on specific issues, such as the danger of another war, government repression, the J.P.C. Report, and other issues which may arise from time to time; the nature of joint action being holding of meetings and demonstrations, observing of "day" and anniversaries, issuing of statements and literature, etc.

[1] *Kamalashanker Pandya Papers* (NMML).

2. There shall be joint action only if the following conditions are fulfilled by the parties to the joint action:

   (i) There shall be no abuse of each other, nor imputations on the motives or honesty of either party.*

   (ii) There shall be no mutual criticism in speeches or by distribution of leaflets, etc., at joint functions.

   (iii) Before every joint action there shall be joint agreement regarding the terms of resolutions and slogans, carrying of banners and flags and distribution of literature.

   (iv) There shall be no advocacy of violence or non-violence by either party at joint functions.

   (v) At joint functions there shall be no appeal for support to either party or to enrol members or to draw any exclusive advantage to either party.

*In the case of the Red T.U.C. the following additional condition, as a sub-clause (i), was agreed upon:

1. Each party to the United Front agreement (i.e. the A.I.C.S.P. on the one hand and the Red T.U.C. on the other) reserves to itself the right of genuine and honest criticism of the political principles and policies of the other from its independent platform.

APPENDIX 14

J.C. Kumarappa's Interview on the Object and Programme of the All India Village Industries Association, 1 April 1935[1]

Questioned whether the All India Village Industries Association contemplated to use merely hand machines or whether they proposed to use power, Mr. Kumarappa said:

> In the first instance, we have to fall back on such equipment as we have got. At present, most villagers have bullocks and as regards human energy that also is limited by lack of nourishment and prevalent disease, like Malaria. So, to start with we cannot advocate expensive motive power and in the nature of things petrol engines and steam power engines tend towards centralized production. But in themselves they are not evils if they come to the aid of the human being and relieve him of drudgery and release his talents to greater purpose. When a man has to do a great deal of routine or drudgery work we do not get the best of his ability. So that a stage comes when we may say the efficiency bar will begin to operate even against human power. Unless a certain amount of leisure, that is, freedom from routine heavy work, is available progress will be long deferred as his whole being is absorbed in mechanical labour and his mind is not released for higher conceptions. In time to come, we hope that we would be able to supply villagers cheap power in the form of electricity if it could be manufactured from natural forces. If each peasant and artisan can have electric-driven machinery for his own production, it will be ideal. We do not shun power for its own sake and we do not hold out the asectic ideals or the primitive ways of life as our goal. Our watchword is progress and improvement of village industries. Whatever makes for this will naturally come under our purview. Of course, we shall have to guard against centralization of production creeping in with the use of power machinery.

Asked if he proposed to decentralize all production and whether this will not lead to individualistic outlook and loss of social sense, Mr. Kumarappa replied:

> Constantly people mistake our Association's purpose and imagine that we advocate primitive life. There are various functions, which can be performed most economically and efficiently only by centralized methods. For instance, it will not be possible for every *chamar* to carry out research work in tanning nor would it be advisable or profitable to do so. Research work in its nature is a centralized function requiring great skill and concentration of mind and material. Similarly, finance, transport and supply of power are naturally centralized functions. Support of village industries does not necessarily run counter to patronage of railways or motor transport. These latter functions, which require

[1] *Searchlight*, 3 April 1935.

centralization, will provide the necessary balance to maintain dependence of one on the other in society.

Further questioned as to what would happen to the cattle when he proposed to supply mechanical power, Mr. Kumarappa said:

In a land like ours where there is a considerable pressure on land no effort should be spared in finding ways and means of relieving this congestion. If the elements could be harnessed to do man's work, there will not be necessary so many animals, horses, bullocks etc. which also have to be provided with sufficient area of land to maintain them. If and when electricity can be obtained from wind and water current, supply of power from a provision of land for fodder will be released for cultivation of food products and raw materials for industries. This will be one method of solving the much-discussed population problem. This will not apply to animals maintained for food purposes, such as milch cows, goats etc. These we shall have to maintain in any case but a large proportion of our cattle can be done away with.

Mr. Kumarappa, questioned as to what was the place of propaganda in his scheme and how long he would depend on it, replied as follows:

Our purpose is not to force crude manufactures against public demand by our propaganda. We shall consider ourselves a failure if in time we do not allow the natural laws to help us to attain our ideals. We do not wish to use the great influence that Gandhiji carries as a force pump. But we want to construct our channels so that the current will flow naturally from the higher level to the lower without any artificial aid in the form of propaganda. Immediately, of course, it will not be possible for the economic contour to accomplish this. We have got to have our surveys made and economic channels constructed to help our peasants and villagers though not to riches at least to a full stomach. At Maganwadi, we are carrying on experiments to find out the reason why gunny-pressed oil and hand-husked rice should not be able to compete in prices with mill-made and adulterated goods. In the same way, our explorations will have to be extended to other fields and pastures. To put in a nutshell, we want that every producer should get the full benefit of the product and that no circumstances should be made to intervene which will deprive him of the benefit of his labour and transfer it to another either by means of machinery or by means of wrongly conceived economic organizations.

Asked further if he did not feel that Socialism, as developed in Russia would help India better, Mr. Kumarappa stated:

There is always a danger of being content with a remedy without curing the ailment. The present lack of alignment in the economic structure under the capitalistic regime is due in a large measure to the fact that all functions irrespective of their merits have been centralized with the result that the profits run like the separated cream into the pockets of the financier, leaving the skimmed milk, if at all, to the producer. By means of artificial dams of idealism, Russia is trying to prevent the evils of capitalism although she is using the very same economic structure, namely, centralized production. Dams are good as long as they hold but there is danger of the dam breaking and flooding the country carrying destruction and devastation with it. The Soviet economic organization is an adaptation of the capitalistic organization but both have as their forbear the predatory, feudal lord who gathered where he did not sow. It is but a step from Soviet economies to the capitalistic organizations. Just as in peace time machinery that produced bycycles can at a moment's notice be converted into producing armaments, so can change of the personnel at the helm of affairs convert Soviet Russia of today into a Rockfeller organization tomorrow. In both organizations the real producer loses his identity and becomes merely tools in the hands of the men at the top. And as long as those who control production are motivated by social ideals every thing goes well and merrily. But human life is mortal and ideals change and, therefore, unless the seed of centralization is taken out of Soviet organization, the danger of reversion to type will always be there. It is with this end in view that our Association is doing all it can to make each individual producer an entity in himself and prevent his being merged into one in a gang of gallery slaves. Whether the gallery is owned by individuals or State makes little difference to the slave himself. Our attempt is to make each individual the owner of his gondola and propel it himself. Apparently, to those who are saturated with admiration for organization and the pulling together of gallery slave, such as individual locomotion as obtained in a canoe or a gondola, appears to have lost its fascination and we are all for largeness forgetting that enormity is not greatness.

Asked further whether there was anything radically wrong in the principles underlying Soviet Communism, Mr. J.C. Kumarappa said:

Both Capitalism and Soviet Communism have as their basis violence. The gallery slaves are driven with a whip for speed and harmony in pulling together. But our Association is the outcome of the philosophy of AHIMSA as propounded by Gandhiji. It is the projection of this philosophy in the economic world and the maxim that underlies it is that no man's loss shall be another man's gain. The moment one individual seeks to profit by the labour of another, violence appears on the scene and if each man is to retain the product of his labour the logical conclusion forces us to adopt decentralization of production as the only way out.

APPENDIX 15

Joint Statement by Narendra Deva and Jayaprakash Narayan on Office Acceptance, 29 August 1935[1]

Asked about Mr. Kidwai's statement that a campaign against acceptance of office by Congressmen is being organized, Acharya Narendradev and Mr. Jayaprakash Narain who had come to Allahabad in connection with their party work said:

> For sometime the feeling has been growing among a large section of Congressmen that the policy of drift which the Congress is following with regard to this question is strengthening the constitutionalist forces and thus weakening the Congress. It has therefore been thought desirable that all elements in the Congress who feel that acceptance of offices will disrupt the national struggle should join hands and give an organized lead to the country so that by the time of the next session of the Congress the ground might have been prepared for the rejection of the suicidal programme of the "Ministerialists".
>
> Accordingly some of us including Babu Siva Prasad Gupta, Babu Sri Prakasa, Dr. Murarilal, Mr. Rafi Ahmad Kidwai, Babu Sampurnanand and Pandit Viswambhar Dayal Tripathi have written to various friends all over the country to join in a campaign against the "Ministerial" programme. Probably an All India Conference will be organized in a month or two in furtherance of this project. It is also proposed to educate the public on this question by publishing pamphlets and other literature.

[1] *Bombay Chronicle*, 31 August 1935.

INDEX